A Theory of General Ethics

A Theory of General Ethics

Human Relationships, Nature, and the Built Environment

Warwick Fox

The MIT Press
Cambridge, Massachusetts
London, England

MIT Press books may be purchased at special quantity discounts for business or sales promotional use. For information, please email special_sales@mitpress.mit .edu or write to Special Sales Department, The MIT Press, 55 Hayward Street, Cambridge, MA 02142.

This book was set in Sabon on 3b2 by Asco Typesetters, Hong Kong, and was printed and bound in the United States of America.

Library of Congress Cataloging-in-Publication Data

Fox, Warwick.
A theory of general ethics : human relationships, nature, and the built environment / Warwick Fox.
    p.   cm.
Includes bibliographical references and index.
ISBN-10: 0-262-06255-0 (hc : alk. paper)—ISBN-10: 0-262-56219-7 (pbk. : alk. paper)
ISBN-13: 978-0-262-06255-8 (hc : alk. paper)—ISBN-13: 978-0-262-56219-5 (pbk. : alk. paper)
1. Ethics. 2. Nature—Moral and ethical aspects. 3. Architecture—Moral and ethical aspects. I. Title.

BJ1012.F69 2006
171'.7—dc22   2006041044

Printed on recycled paper.

10 9 8 7 6 5 4 3 2 1

But what would a "new ethics" involve, and how might it be arrived at?
—John Rodman, "The Liberation of Nature?"

Contents

Preface and Acknowledgments

The ideas in this book have been developing over a considerable period—don't ask! I am sincerely grateful to many colleagues around the world whose thinking and support over the years have aided the development of my own thinking. Even so, contributions from others have generally been diffuse in the case of this book; they have constituted the general background upon which I have drawn in order to develop, and against which I have tested, the ideas presented here. That said, for specific kinds of help at specific times that have enabled me better to advance the ideas developed herein, I would particularly like to thank: Emily Brady, Merlin Donald, Uta Frith, George and Adrienne Green, Simon Hailwood, Daniel Povinelli, Doris Schroeder, Michael Tomasello, Jennifer Vonk, and Terry Williamson. Most of these people were generally unaware of how their particular questions, comments, e-mailed replies, or forwarded papers fed into the overall ideas developed here, and none of them is responsible for what I have made of their help, but they stand out in my mind along the path that has led to this book, and I am grateful to them for their help along the way.

For their thoughtful consideration of a long manuscript I owe a serious debt of thanks, again coupled with absolution from any responsibility for what I have made of their advice, to the following, initially anonymous, reviewers: Roger Gottlieb, Alastair Gunn, Andrew McLaughlin, and Peter Wenz.

In pursuing the path from completed manuscript to publication I am especially grateful to Clay Morgan at MIT Press for his prompt and precise help with all my queries, his editorial guidance in general, and, not least, his title for the book, which is more straightforward and explanatory—and, thus, better—than the title that I had been using.

Most of all by far I want to thank my wife and fellow philosopher, the one and only Isis Brook, Mistress of the Fatal Counterexample, for her philosophical insights, her feedback on the manuscript itself, and her miraculous, wholehearted love and support throughout this project. Finally, if it could understand me, I would offer my heartfelt apologies to my Martin D-28 guitar, which has, indeed, gently wept while I worked on this book.

I

General Ethics—and Its Problems

1

Introduction: The Idea of a General Ethics

We presently lack a *General Ethics*. I capitalize this term to mark it out as the name of a field of inquiry and to distinguish it from coincidental or haphazard references to "general ethics" or "ethics in general," by which an author may well mean something much more limited.

It gets worse: we presently lack even the conception of a General Ethics—there is no such term, or equivalent to what I mean by it, in general usage. Yet we badly need such a conception, not to mention the reasoned content that would fill it out, namely, a truly *general* form of ethics, an ethics that would constitute the ethical equivalent of the physicists' long sought Holy Grail of a "Theory of Everything."

Of course, the physicists' "Theory of Everything" is not literally a theory of *everything*. For starters, such a descriptive theory is never going to answer our normative ethical questions regarding the values we should live by—it might inform our answers, but it cannot, by itself, provide these answers any more than a normative ethical theory can provide a descriptive theory of nature. (A *descriptive* theory is a theory that describes how the world—or some aspect of it—is; what the world is *like*. In contrast, a *normative* theory is one that prescribes the norms or standards that we *ought* to strive to meet in our behavior or way of being.) Scientific theories and ethical theories operate at different levels of concern—one descriptive (and explanatory in that context), the other normative (and explanatory in that context)—and represent intellectual and cultural manifestations of the logical gap that exists between "is" and "ought." What physicists actually mean by a "Theory of Everything" is not a theory of everything, period, but a theory that lies at the basis of all things *physical*: a unified (descriptive) theory that can satisfactorily account for the widest possible range of physical phenomena.

Physicists could therefore, perhaps more humbly, refer to their much-vaunted "Theory of Everything" as a *General Physics*. In a similarly qualified vein, what I mean by the term *General Ethics* can be thought of as a theory that lies at the basis of all things *ethical*: a unified (normative) theory that can satisfactorily account for the widest possible range of ethical concerns.

My aim in this book is to provide a General Ethics.

But first things first: so, in the next two sections of this chapter, I will first provide the background context against which we need to understand the concept of General Ethics and then explain more precisely what I mean by a General Ethics and why we need such an ethics. I will then proceed in the following chapter to provide examples of the formidable range of problems that any General Ethics must be able to address. By the end of these examples, we will see that to ask for a unified ethical approach that can satisfactorily address the full range of problems that any General Ethics must be able to address—even an ethical theory that is capable of (directly) addressing all these questions in the first place, regardless of its success in doing so—is a Big Ask. The rest of this book—from chapter 3 on—is then concerned with attempting to satisfy this Big Ask. It develops an approach to General Ethics that I refer to as the *theory of responsive cohesion*.

The Background to General Ethics

Ethics is concerned, at its core, with the values we should live by. It is not centrally concerned with "values" in some vague, wishy-washy sense, such as whether I prefer my hair long or short or whether I prefer blue to green; rather, it is centrally concerned with the values that I (and you) *should* live by, with those values that we are, for various reasons, rationally obliged to respect. This central concern of ethics is therefore referred to by philosophers as *normative ethics* because it is concerned with the norms, or standards, that we ought to meet, or at least strive to meet, in our conduct.

Since the time of the classical Greek philosophers, Western ethical thinking has essentially been concerned with what I will call *interhuman ethics*. It has focused exclusively, or at least overwhelmingly, upon humans and their relationships with each other—or, in a religious context, also upon their relationship to a God in whose image they supposed themselves to have been made (which rendered God as a kind of Superperson and people as minigods). The guiding idea in the dominant Western secular and religious forms of interhuman ethics has been that the only values that we are rationally obliged to respect (in addition to those that might relate to God Himself [*sic*]) are those of respect for people (and, indeed, depending on the time and place with which we are concerned, not necessarily all people). The reasons given for the special value of (at least certain groups of) people relative to the rest of earthly creation have typically turned on the ideas that humans are uniquely rational or that humans are uniquely endowed with a soul—a special, inner aspect of themselves that could potentially join with God, the ultimate source of all goodness, when they died, and which thereby constituted living testimony to their potential goodness despite their "fallen" state.

Needless to say, the rest of the—nonrational, un-ensouled—world got pretty short shrift on the basis of these ideas. As John Passmore argues in his already classic study *Man's Responsibility for Nature*, the history of ideas reveals that these kinds of anthropocentric views have been employed, in varying forms, again and again to underpin the morally charged conclusion that humans are either exclusively or overwhelmingly valuable relative to all other earthly kinds and that these other earthly kinds are *therefore* ours to do with as we will. Indeed, as Passmore notes, throughout the history of Western philosophical thinking "It is constantly assumed that whatever else exists does so only for the sake of the rational."[1] This sort of thinking has patently obnoxious upshots. To take just one kind of example, Passmore shows that "In so far as cruelty to animals was wrong, this was only because, so it was argued by Aquinas [C13th], by Kant [C18th], and by a multitude of lesser thinkers, it might induce a callousness towards *human* suffering. There was nothing wrong with cruelty to animals *in itself*."[2] It seems almost inconceivable to us today that highly intelligent thinkers of any period could seriously maintain that nonhuman animals either were not capable of suffering (a view to which Descartes, "the father of modern philosophy," was theoretically committed) or else that they could suffer but that this suffering was of no moral consequence in itself. Yet, up until at least Kant's time, the most influential thinkers in the Western tradition thought precisely this.

As incredible as it might seem, Western ethics only really began to explore ethical questions that lay beyond the confines of interhuman ethics—or at least to do this in a concerted, ongoing fashion—as recently as the 1970s. This was when some—a very few—philosophers began to advance serious arguments for the moral status not just of humans but of all sentient beings, that is, entities that have the capacity to feel, entities that it would be *like something* to be, or, in other words, entities that could be described as *beings* as opposed to "merely" (i.e., nonsentient) *living things*. The implications of these arguments were that moral agents had various obligations in respect of all sentient beings (or, in some versions, some more specialized subset of sentient beings, but a subset that nevertheless ran well beyond humans alone). Other philosophers began to go further and develop arguments to the effect that all living things, whether sentient or not, were deserving of at least some degree of moral consideration; there were "in principle" reasons why it was wrong, say, to wantonly destroy living things such as trees. Yet other philosophers began to go further still: not only did they want to overcome what they saw as the highly anthropocentric bias of traditional Western ethics—an aim they shared with both the animal welfare and life-based approaches—but they also wanted to overcome what they saw as a wrongheaded *individualistic* focus in ethics, which applied to both the animal welfare and the standard life-based approaches just as much as it did to interhuman ethics. They wanted, in other words, to develop a *holistic* approach to ethics, specifically, an ethics that proceeded from a primary focus on complex, ecosystemic assemblages of individual living things and that endorsed the overarching value of ecological integrity.

The intellectual explosion that emerged in ethics in the last quarter of the twentieth century marked the end of the roughly two-and-a-half thousand years of essentially purely anthropocentric ethics in the Western philosophical tradition. And, as is often the way with intellectual explosions, once the stranglehold of the reigning orthodoxy had begun to be loosened, new thinkers very quickly rushed out into the "fresh air" to explore and map out the most obvious intellectual possibilities that suddenly seemed to be available—much as organisms can rapidly colonize new ecological niches following recovery from a catastrophic event. Thus, in relatively short order, the ethical landscape was mapped out beyond its familiar anthropocentric borders to include approaches that could be described as *pathocentric* (i.e., centered on the capacity to suffer), *biocentric*, and *ecocentric*—the animal welfare, life-based, and ecological integrity approaches respectively. (Note that I refer to the first of these newer approaches as *pathocentric* rather than *zoocentric*, i.e., animal centered. This is because the leading animal welfare ethicists accept that not all animals can suffer [e.g., sponges and corals], and their approaches focus on those animals than *can* suffer as opposed to focusing on all entities that are formally classified as animals. These approaches are, after all, animal-*welfare*-oriented approaches, not just animal-oriented approaches.) The discovery of this new ethical landscape represented the ethical equivalent of people having believed for thousands of years that they lived at the center of the universe and then in relatively short order finding that their inquiries were necessitating the contemplation of a massively greater range of possibilities: perhaps we just live on a planet in a sun-centered solar system; perhaps our solar system is just one of countless others in a galaxy of stars; ditto our galaxy relative to other galaxies in the universe; and, perhaps, even ditto the universe itself!

Even so, this relative explosion of ethical interest beyond the long-standing traditional confines of human-centered ethical thinking was nevertheless very late in coming, and the stranglehold of the anthropocentric ethical orthodoxy did not make it easy for the pioneers in this area. Indeed, those philosophers who initiated these developments can tell you that many of their mainstream colleagues at the time engaged in the philosophically time-honored put-down of declaring that what they were doing was not "real philosophy" (in which case, God save us from "real philosophy"). Now all that nonsense has largely (but, alas, not completely) passed; these new forms of ethical thinking represent normal and often very popular parts of philosophical conferences; a variety of journals are either devoted to or at least publish papers that explore the issues raised by these new areas; and students vote with their feet to do courses in these areas.

But lest this paints too rosy a picture of the present state of things, it also needs to be said that although the newer forms of ethics have now been granted a legitimate seat at the philosophical table, as it were, it remains the case that the majority of ethicists and ethics courses still ignore these new approaches even if they no longer actively disparage them. It is incredible to me that, in the early twenty-first century, I can pick up brand new books that purport to offer overviews of "ethics" only to find that they often simply omit any reference to, let alone contain detailed discussion of, the newer, nonanthropocentric forms of ethics. For many ethicists and their students, "ethics" still means "interhuman ethics"—and it means "interhuman ethics" so obviously in their view that they don't even call it "interhuman ethics"—or some such term; rather, they just call what they are doing "ethics," period. Thus, if you enroll in an "ethics" course at most institutions (or even if you enroll in a "bioethics" course), you are almost certainly likely to find yourself doing a course that is restricted to interhuman ethics (or, in the case of "bioethics," to interhuman biomedical ethics). In order to do a course that embraces the newer and larger domains of ethics that I have referred to, you generally need to enroll in a course that *sounds* more restricted than the above courses but is not, such as "environmental ethics." It is strange to think that philosophers schooled in the Anglo-American tradition, who generally pride themselves on using language clearly and precisely, still continue to use such outdated, imprecise, and, frankly, misleading titles for their ethics courses.

The Conception of General Ethics and Why We Need Such an Ethics

Sympathetic yet tough-minded philosophers generally consider that the further you want to go along the anthropocentric-pathocentric-biocentric-ecocentric path, the more difficult it is to sustain any kind of rigorous argument for your approach. The suspicion arose early on—and lingers—that some of the "further-out" of these approaches were fueled more by intuition and passion than by rationality and logic. However, the countersuspicion also arose—and lingers—that, as we have only recently begun to explore some of the "further-out" of these approaches, there may exist some arguments for these approaches that are much stronger than those that have been developed so far—and we won't know if we don't try to develop them.

So, does the term *General Ethics* just refer to a form of ethics that embraces the wide range of increasingly accepted concerns that have now been introduced to ethical discussion; that attempts to sort the stronger arguments for these concerns from the weaker ones; and that, where possible, attempts to explore and develop yet stronger arguments across this broad range of concerns? In a (loud) word: *no!* General Ethics embraces considerably more than the concerns that I have mentioned so far in association with the newer, nonanthropocentric forms of ethics. Let me explain. The approaches that I have referred to—animal welfare approaches, life-based approaches, and ecological integrity approaches—are generally collectively referred to as *environmental ethics*. Thus, we have the older forms of interhuman ethics and the newer forms of environmental ethics. But what further forms of ethics could there be? If (for us) a basic way of dividing the world up is between humans and everything else (i.e., "the environment"), then surely interhuman ethics taken together with environmental ethics just about wraps things up in terms of the possible range of ethical concerns, doesn't it? What else is there besides humans on the one hand and everything else on the other hand? What else *could* we give ethical attention to?

The problem lies in the fact that either the term *environmental ethics*, as it has been used to date at least, is a misnomer or else the field of inquiry it describes does not live up to its own name. The reason is this: when we look around the world—our "environment"—we see people, other animals, trees and plants, rain clouds (evidence of ecospherical hydrological cycles) and so on, but we also see buildings, roads, cars, and so on. The world around us—our "environment"—consists not only of a self-organizing, natural environment but also of an intentionally organized, artificial, built, or constructed environment (as well as all manner of combinations of these two kinds of environments). Indeed, many of us in the modern world seem to have even more day-to-day contact with intentionally organized, human-constructed environments than self-organizing, natural environments. And yet, as we have seen from my brief review of the main approaches to environmental ethics, this new field of inquiry has to date been overwhelmingly concerned with the natural environment (or various members or aspects of it)—sentient beings, living things, ecological integrity—and has had next to nothing to say about the intentionally organized, artificial, built, or constructed environment.[3] (I will just refer to the intentionally organized, artificial, built, or constructed environment as the *human-constructed environment* for now—although I will identify this realm in a more formal way and give it a more precise name when we come to the theory of responsive cohesion's *theory of contexts* in chapter 6.)

These two kinds of environments are quite different kinds of environments, and they can prompt quite different kinds of ethical questions. Even if we set aside the profound implications that questions concerning how we construct and live in human-constructed environments have for the natural environment (which is a lot to set aside since the fate of the natural, "green bits" of the planet is now completely bound up with how we construct and live in the human-constructed, "brown bits" of the planet), there remain a multitude of important ethically related questions that we can ask about human-constructed environments themselves. Consider this example: suppose we take two buildings and, for argument's sake, specify the following about them: (i) both have the same overall environmental impact; neither detracts from whatever value we might assign to ecological integrity any more than the other (and we'll also assume here that neither contributes to harming individual sentient beings or living things in general any more than the other); (ii) one of these buildings, to your and my discerning eyes, is "as ugly as sin," "sticks out like a sore thumb," is a "blot upon the landscape," and so on, while the other fits in beautifully with its surrounding landscape—"the line of its roof echoes those hills over there," and so on; and (iii) notwithstanding the previous point, it turns out that people in general "don't mind" the contextually ugly building when their preferences are considered overall—in fact, maybe they even prefer it overall—because, whatever its faults, it is "just so convenient," or offers easier parking, or has stores that offer cheaper prices. Whatever the reasons, suppose that these reasons get all mixed together with whatever preferences people might (or, alas, might not) have in terms of architectural design such that the users of the contextually ugly building come to see it as not even being particularly ugly—or perhaps just come not to *see* it in various ways, such as in terms of any wider contextual understanding.

Surely there are ethically related questions that we can ask about these buildings, and foremost among them is this: Should we build in the contextually ugly way described in (ii) even if it's no worse, ecologically speaking, than building in more landscape-fitting ways, and even if people "don't mind"—or even come to prefer—using the contextually ugly building to the landscape-"fitting" building when their preferences are considered overall? Is doing this consistent with the values we should live by? Or should people prioritize their preferences such that cheaper prices or more parking is simply not a good enough reason to accept contextually ugly buildings—especially since there is no reason in principle why these features cannot also be offered by a contextually fitting building. If we think that building in the contextually ugly way is consistent with the values we should live by, then we would probably feel that we ought to describe any personal preference that we might have for the landscape-fitting building as just that—as "just a personal preference," or as "just an aesthetic preference." But what if we think that we should take our spontaneous expression upon seeing this building that "there ought to be a law against it" seriously? What if we think that there is something wrong *in principle* with building in the contextually ugly way? What if we think that we should not live by the kinds of values that would sanction this kind of building (a building that seems to exemplify a disconnection from, and even a sense of contempt for, its surroundings)? Under these circumstances, we do not consider ourselves to be talking about a merely "personal" or "aesthetic" preference. Rather, we consider ourselves to be talking about an ethically based objection to building in the contextually ugly way—an objection that obtains regardless of points (i) and (iii) in the above example.

But on what grounds can we make such an ethically based objection? The older forms of interhuman ethics can't help us here in any direct way (although some of their theorists might twist and turn in theoretically ungainly ways to try to find an indirect way of addressing this problem—anything but abandon their approach in favor of a more appropriate one). This is because the older forms of interhuman ethics value people and people alone, and we've already seen in the example given that people either don't have much of a preference either way in regard to these buildings or else actually prefer the contextually ill-fitting building overall because of its convenience in various respects. The newer forms of environmental ethics can't help us in any direct way either. As specified in the example, neither of the buildings is any worse than the other in terms of detracting from ecological integrity (and we also assumed here that neither contributes to harming individual sentient beings or living things in general any more than the other). How, then, can these newer approaches hope to get any purchase on the issue—an issue that resides at the intangible and ephemeral level of contextually related design?

This example highlights a profoundly important problem. Quite apart from their ecological implications, there are many serious, ethically based problems—problems relating directly to the values we should live by—that we ought to be able to explore in regard to our (too often thoroughly dispiriting) human-constructed environments. Yet we have no language, no framework, for approaching these problems as *ethical* problems. We spontaneously say "There ought to be a law against it" when we see certain kinds of buildings—which is a pretty strongly formulated, normatively laden reaction—yet we then back down when challenged on our view by describing our reaction as a merely "personal preference" or "aesthetic preference." I think we do this because we don't know how to say in *ethically* weighted terms what we really want to be able to say.

If this is right, then we need an approach to ethics that goes beyond even the newer, natural-environment- (and natural-entities-) oriented approaches that have been developed to date since, like interhuman ethics, these approaches cannot offer us any direct help when we start to consider certain kinds of problems relating to how we should proceed in regard to our intentionally organized, human-constructed environment. If we think of the world as consisting of a biophysical realm (which includes ecosystems and the plants and animals that live in them), a realm of symbolic culture (which is constituted by language-using human moral agents), and a realm of material culture (which includes all the "stuff" that humans make), then we can see that whereas the older forms of interhuman ethics were concerned only with those entities that exist in the second of these realms (i.e., humans), the newer forms of (so-called) "environmental" ethics—the animal welfare, life-based, and ecosystem-integrity approaches—have been concerned with both the first and the second of these realms (since any argument for the value of nonhuman biophysical entities either builds on, or automatically incorporates, an argument for the value of humans). This is an improvement: giving ethical attention to two out of these three realms is better than giving it to just one of them. But a *comprehensive* approach to ethics would provide a unified framework for directly addressing ethical problems in all three realms.

On a personal note, I have been aware of this "third realm" problem for some time. My own search for a General Ethics has been stimulated not only by my study of interhuman and environmental ethics and the many problems that they raise but also by my dawning realization that they both leave out the human-constructed environment and that a new kind of ethical approach is needed to address the issues raised in this area. I realized that the human-constructed environment has represented just as much of a "blind spot" for so-called environmental ethics to date as the nonhuman natural world has been, and remains, for the older, anthropocentric approaches to ethics.[4] Thinking about how to "get a handle" on the problems introduced by this nonhuman, nonsentient, nonliving, and intentionally organized (as opposed to ecosystemically self-organizing) "third realm," in which our lives are now totally enmeshed, has been of the first importance in developing the theory of responsive cohesion to be presented in this book. I thought that if it were possible to figure out a sensible way of coming to grips with problems such as the "two buildings example" offered above, then one might at least have a candidate for an approach that could, with suitable elaboration, be developed into a General Ethics. However, if one did not have an approach that could adequately address this kind of "third realm" example, then one did not even have a candidate for an approach that could be developed into a General Ethics.

All of which brings us to what I mean by General Ethics. General Ethics is concerned with giving ethical attention to all three realms and doing so within an integrated theoretical framework. It is this that enables us to describe General Ethics as being concerned with the development of an ethical "Theory of Everything."

In the light of what I've explained here, we can set out this conception of General Ethics almost as a kind of simple equation:

General Ethics = {interhuman ethics + animal welfare ethics + life-based ethics + ecosystem integrity ethics + ethics of the human-constructed environment}

It should immediately be noted here, however, that I have placed "fancy" brackets around this sum specifically to suggest that General

Ethics is not concerned simply with adding together different "bits" of the ethical approaches that are listed—as if that could be done coherently!—but rather with the development of an *integrated approach* that covers all these areas. Thus, "{ }" does not mean "simply add together what is inside the brackets," but rather "replace what is inside the brackets with a single integrated approach that both covers all the areas referred to inside the brackets *and* irons out the wrinkles between them." Developing an "{ }" approach to any area amounts to theoretical progress in that area. It is good work if you can get it!

With this understanding in mind, we can simplify the above "equation" as follows:

General Ethics = {interhuman ethics + ethics of the natural environment + ethics of the human-constructed environment}

Or even:

General Ethics = {the older forms of ethics + the newer forms of ethics + some even newer form of ethics}

Having now explained what I mean by a General Ethics—by an ethical "Theory of Everything"—it is relatively straightforward to explain why we need such an ethics. First, as we have just seen in regard to the example of the two buildings, we cannot adequately deal with all the ethical problems that we ought to be able to deal with *as* ethical problems if we do not have an ethical framework that can incorporate but also go beyond both interhuman ethical concerns and ethical concerns relating to the natural environment (including natural entities). Second, anyone who works in either the older or newer fields of ethics that I have referred to knows that "they do not add up"; they simply cannot be "glued together" in their present forms in order to produce some seamless "supertheory" of ethics that would constitute, say, two-thirds of a truly General Ethics. Not only are there spectacular conflicts between the claims endorsed by the older, anthropocentric forms of ethics and the newer, nonanthropocentric approaches to ethics, but there are likewise spectacular conflicts between the claims endorsed by the newer forms of ethics themselves—especially between the more individualistic approaches and the more holistic approaches (as we will see when I outline the problems that any General Ethics must confront, which I will do both in the next section and when I return to address these problems toward the end of the book in chapter 10).

In my view, then, we badly need two things. First, we need an ethics that will allow us directly to address ethical problems (i.e., problems regarding the values we should live by) across the broadest possible range of domains of interest (i.e., including all three realms outlined above). Second, we need this ethics in a unified or integrated form; we need an ethics that can account in its own way for all the points that are worthwhile in the various "smaller" ethical approaches that have been developed to date, and yet one that can do this in the context of an overarching theory that offers clear priority rules when different kinds or levels of value come into tension or outright conflict. To have these two things—to have a unified theoretical framework that allows us directly to address ethical problems across the broadest possible range of domains of interest—is to have a General Ethics.

This much is easily said. But can it be done? The range of problems that a General Ethics must be able to address is formidable, as we will see in the next chapter.

2
Problems That Any General Ethics Must Be Able to Address

In this chapter I will outline no less than eighteen problems that confront any attempt to construct a General Ethics. I will outline each of these problems according to the main approaches they relate to—interhuman ethics, animal welfare ethics, life-based ethics, ecosystem integrity ethics, and ethics of the human-constructed environment. I will then return to these problems in chapter 10 and address each of them from the perspective of the theory that I will advance in chapters 3–8 and then summarize in chapter 9.

Central Problems Relating to Interhuman Ethics

Problem 1: The "Why Are Humans Valuable?" Problem

Although we tend to take it for granted that humans are extremely valuable when considered in their own right—as opposed to being merely "human resources" that we can *use*—it is nevertheless important for any ethical theory to be able to give an adequate answer to this question. This is especially so given that the traditional secular and religious answers to this question have come under fire from a number of quarters. For example, the idea that humans are essentially and uniquely rational has been called into question by what we have learned not only from Freud and the panoply of developments in clinical psychiatry and psychology since Freud but also from human cognitive psychology, comparative psychology, and cognitive ethology. These studies suggest, in short, that humans are not as rational as we have traditionally liked to think and that nonhuman animals are not as irrational as we have traditionally liked to think. Similarly, the idea that humans are uniquely endowed with a soul has become entirely contentious. Moreover, insofar as the idea of a soul is linked to human consciousness, neuroscientific evidence clearly points to the conclusion that consciousness is entirely dependent upon neural processes and thus ceases to exist when these neural processes cease.

As if this weren't enough, a number of thinkers—and most notably the animal welfare ethicist Peter Singer—have followed the lead of Jeremy Bentham (1748–1832), the founding father of utilitarianism, and asked what being rational or having a soul has to do with being deserving of moral consideration in the first place. That is, they have suggested that the traditional reasons that have been given for bestowing moral consideration uniquely upon humans are irrelevant! For these thinkers, the reason that we should not, say, torture a six-month-old baby is not because it is rational (or the sort of being that will become rational) and not because it has a soul (if it does) but because it would *suffer*, here and now. Thus, for these thinkers, as for Bentham, the essential moral question is not "Can this being reason (or, for that matter, does it have a soul)?" but "Can it suffer?" However, if that question is accepted as the litmus test of which beings are deserving of moral consideration, then we are into a whole new ethical ball game—one that extends to all sentient beings and not just humans.

We can see, then, that giving a decent answer to the "Why are humans valuable?" question is not a simple matter and much can rest on it in terms of further ethical implications, both within the human sphere (e.g., how should we respond to the issues of abortion and euthanasia?) and beyond the human sphere (e.g., should we stop eating other animals and all be vegetarian?).

Problem 2: The Abortion Problem; and Problem 3: The Euthanasia Problem

In view of what I have just said in regard to problem 1, it ought to be fairly clear that how we answer the "Why are humans valuable?" problem is of the first importance to how we should approach these two problems, which concern the beginnings and ends of human life respectively. For example, if one regards any form of human life as sacred to God and considers that it is therefore a sin against God to take such life—irrespective of the quality of life that a fetus might go on to have or the quality of life that a patient with a terminal illness might now have— then clearly one has a straightforward answer to both of these problems, namely, one of implacable opposition to both abortion and euthanasia. However, given that there are many other views on these issues and that a great many people do in fact want and, where they can, exercise their freedom to make quite different choices in regard to them, it is easy to see why these issues have been sources of considerable conten- tion—especially when considered in the context of the medical means that are now available to us both to support and terminate human life. Clearly, any adequate General Ethics must be able to address these two problems in a sensible and defensible way.

Problem 4: The "What Are Our Obligations to Other People?" Problem
This question is one of the central questions for any form of interhuman ethics. What kinds of obligations do I have to others? Am I obliged sim- ply not to harm others (and if so, why?) or are my obligations more ex- tensive than that? For example, am I also obliged to offer what we might call "saving help" to others even though I might be in no way responsi- ble for the harm or distress that has befallen them? Am I obliged to go even further and offer other people ongoing supportive help rather than just limited forms of saving help? What about completely bonus forms of help? Where do my obligations to other people begin and end? And am I supposed to extend these obligations equally to all other people? That is, do I owe just as much to strangers as I do to my own nearest and dearest? For example, am I just as obliged—or perhaps even more obliged—to relieve suffering by donating to famine relief as I am to fund- ing my children's education, or to taking my family on a holiday? The influential utilitarian philosopher Peter Singer argued in a famous and much reprinted 1972 paper entitled "Famine, Affluence, and Morality" that we are so obliged, for "if it is in our power to prevent something bad from happening, without thereby sacrificing anything of comparable moral importance, we ought, morally to do it."[1] And, in Singer's view, this applies regardless of "proximity or distance": "If we accept any principle of impartiality, universalizability, equality, or whatever, we cannot discriminate against someone merely because he is far away

from us.''[2] Thus, we are, in principle, just as obliged to help strangers as we are to help those to whom we are closest.

Any adequate General Ethics must be able to offer a sensible and defensible approach to all of these kinds of questions regarding our obligations to others. It needn't be anything like Singer's approach to these particular questions, however, and I can assure you now that the approach that I will be developing in this book will not be. Instead, the approach that I will be developing will, I hope to show, be far more defensible than Singer's (because, as we will see, Singer fails to take account of central features that pertain to any moral problem situation) and far more sensitive to the various questions that I have raised above than Singer's one-size-fits-all approach to ethics.

Problem 5: The "What Is the Best Structural Form of Politics?" Problem

It is easy to see from the above discussion that questions regarding our personal obligations to others can easily spread into overtly political questions. For example, to what extent do I *personally* owe saving help to far-away strangers who are experiencing famine or being persecuted in a war (and Singer, as we saw, believes that we owe a great deal at a *personal* level in these contexts) and to what extent might it be more morally reasonable—and not simply a "cop-out"—to say that my *nation-state* has certain obligations in these contexts such that my personal obligations in respect of the above problems actually kick in at the level of my being obliged to support the kind of political system and government that will live up to these obligations (and draw on my taxes to do so)? Clearly, a truly General Ethics must be able to give us some guidance here.

However, the first form of guidance that we want from a General Ethics in regard to politics is guidance with respect to the *structural* form of politics that we ought to support. By this I mean that a General Ethics ought to be broad enough to endorse—and be able to explain why it endorses—one or more kinds of political structure (such as dictatorship, monarchy, aristocracy, plutocracy, oligarchy, democracy, or anarchy) over others. Now, as with the "Why are humans valuable?" question, it is easy for most of us who live in democracies simply to assume the answer here for it seems just as obvious to most of us that democracy is the best structural form of politics as it does that people are extremely valuable. But a General Ethics really needs to provide an explicit answer here, just as it does for the previous questions.

Problem 6: The "What Is the Best 'Flavor' of Politics?" Problem

Essentially the same structural forms of politics can nevertheless take on very different "flavors." For example, a dictatorship (or any system in which power is overwhelmingly concentrated in the hands of a few and from whom that power cannot easily be removed) can, in theory, be brutal, benign, or benevolent; anarchy can, in theory, consist of "mutual aid" or a "war of all against all" that proceeds in the absence of any rule of law whatsoever; democracies can and typically are distinguished in terms of the extent to which they are socially oriented (and so tax accordingly in order to fund socially oriented programs, including all the state administrative apparatus that these programs entail) as opposed to individualistically oriented (and so tax accordingly in order to fund a more minimal state apparatus, including more minimal administrative and social services). Thus, whatever our answer to the "What is the best structural form of politics?" question, we still want to know what "flavor" this structural form of politics ought to have since (political) structure, by itself, does not determine (political) content. Indeed, this is precisely why we vote *within* a democratic *structure*: to determine the "flavor"—or, in other terms, the *content*—we want that democratic structure to have (at least for the next few years!). Ideally, then, we want a truly General Ethics to provide an explicit answer to the question not only of the kind of political structure that we ought to endorse but also of the kind of "flavor" that that political structure ought to have.

The six questions that I have outlined here—the "Why are humans valuable?" question, the abortion question, the euthanasia question, the "What are our obligations to other people?" question, the "What is the best structural form of politics?" question, and the "What is the best 'flavor' of politics?" question—arguably represent the six most central questions in interhuman ethics. A General Ethics needs to be able directly to address them all, to offer sensible and defensible answers to each of them, and also to address a wide range of ethical questions that run far, far beyond these questions, as we will see in what follows.

Central Problems Relating to Animal Welfare Ethics

Problem 7: The "Why Are Sentient Beings Valuable?" Problem

The best-known and most influential answers to this question have been advanced by the utilitarian ethicist Peter Singer and the rights-based ethicist Tom Regan under the names of "animal liberation" and "animal rights" respectively.[3] Both of these approaches turn, in their different ways, on the basic idea that sentient beings in general (which, for Singer, includes anything more complex than mollusks) or some more specialized subset of sentient beings (such as mammals and birds in Regan's more recent expositions) have an experiential welfare that ought to be respected. Singer adopts the utilitarian approach of arguing that we ought to take the interests of other sentient beings into account in our actions by weighing these interests impartially against the interests of other sentient beings (including our own). Regan adopts the rights-based approach of arguing that the possession of an experiential welfare— at least an experiential welfare of a certain order, such that these beings constitute what Regan refers to (quite unclearly in my view) as "subjects-of-a-life"—makes a being sufficiently "inherently valuable" as to possess "rights" to life and liberty. The possession of such "rights" means that the being's interests in continued life and liberty cannot be "traded off" against the interests of others, as in the utilitarian approach. Singer and Regan both argue that it is *speciesist* to recognize only the interests or rights to life and liberty of members of one's own species—and the parallel with the ideas of sexism and racism is quite deliberate here. (The term *speciesism* was coined by Richard Ryder who has himself more recently developed an as yet not very well-known but nevertheless significant partial synthesis of Singer's and Regan's views, which he refers to as *painism*.[4] Basically, Ryder rejects Regan's emphasis on being the subject-of-a-life in favor of Singer's more straightforward emphasis on the moral importance of pain while also rejecting Singer's utilitarian preparedness to aggregate pleasures and pains across different beings in favor of Regan's rights-based opposition to such aggregation.)

In order to refer to the animal liberation and animal rights (and, for that matter, painism) approaches collectively—and without privileging one of these names over the other(s)—a number of commentators, including myself, find it convenient to refer to them as the *animal welfare approach* (or animal welfare approaches, depending upon the degree of specificity intended) since these approaches proceed from some version of the idea that sentient beings are valuable because they have an experiential welfare such that they can fare better or worse. I have used this *animal welfare* terminology earlier in this chapter, as well as in the heading of this section, and will continue to do so as appropriate in what follows.

Although I would want to take issue with the details of Singer's and Regan's (and, by implication, Ryder's) basic arguments for their approaches in a longer discussion, it is sufficient for now to note the following. These approaches assign essentially the same level of moral status to all sentient beings or subjects-of-a-life—including humans. They consider that, other things being equal (such as the level of comfort or distress that a being is experiencing), our obligations in respect of nonhuman sentient beings are just as strong as our obligations in respect of other humans. Considered from the other side, these approaches flatly deny that we have any direct obligations in respect of *nonsentient* living things. Thus, there would be nothing wrong in principle in destroying nonsentient living things such as plants and trees simply because it was our pleasure to do so. As Singer says:

If a being suffers, there can be no moral justification for disregarding that suffering, or for refusing to count it equally with the like suffering of any other being. But the converse of this is also true. If a being is not capable of suffering, or of enjoyment, there is nothing to take into account.[5]

Now any General Ethics obviously needs to address the important question of why sentient beings are valuable—and to what extent they are valuable (e.g., even if we set anthropocentric prejudices aside, is it actually rationally defensible to assign the same general level of moral status to nonhuman sentient beings—or subjects-of-a-life—as to humans?). However, to the extent that we think it is sensible to ask questions about the values we should live by—that is, ethical questions—in respect of a great many things that are not sentient, such as plants, trees, ecosystems, and buildings, and to the extent that we think that the proper answers to these questions cannot simply be reduced to the interests of sentient beings, then a General Ethics will clearly need directly to address a great many more issues than those addressed by the animal welfare approaches. Not only that, but any adequate General Ethics will need to address even the above "Why are sentient beings valuable?"

question within the context of a far more comprehensive theoretical framework than that offered by the animal welfare approaches that I have referred to here. The reasons for this can be seen from considering the problems that I will outline as problems 8 through 13 below.

Problem 8: The Predation Problem

The animal welfare approaches cannot adequately explain why we should, on the one hand, stop the suffering or rights violations of other animals in terms of our (human) predation upon them, but, on the other hand, not attempt to intervene to stop the suffering or rights violations of other animals in terms of their predation upon each other. The problem here, of course, is that from the point of view of the animal being torn apart, it doesn't necessarily make any difference whether it is a human or a nonhuman animal that is causing its suffering or violating its rights. (Indeed, a bullet through the brain might well be "preferable" to being torn apart.) Why, then, stop at opposing human predation alone?

As Mark Sagoff asked in an influential paper, which carried the revealing title "Animal Liberation and Environmental Ethics: Bad Marriage, Quick Divorce": if we accept any of the main versions of the animal welfare argument, then

Where should society concentrate its efforts to provide for the basic welfare—the security and subsistence—of animals? Plainly, where animals most lack this security, when their basic rights, needs, or interests are most thwarted and where their suffering is most intense. Alas, this is in nature.[6]

Arguing that animals typically die violently in nature through predation, starvation, disease, parasitism, and cold; that most do not live to maturity; and that very few die of old age; Sagoff proceeds, with deliberately provocative intent, to suggest that if wild animals could themselves understand the conditions into which they are born, then they "might reasonably prefer to be raised on a farm, where the chances of survival for a year or more would be good, and to escape from the wild, where they are negligible."[7] Thus, "One may modestly propose the conversion of national wilderness areas, especially national parks, into farms in order to replace violent wild areas with more humane and managed environments."[8]

Why not reduce suffering and rights violations by doing this? That way, prey could be killed humanely and fed to predators. Alternatively, we could follow the equally provocatively intended suggestion advanced by the influential ecocentric ethicist J. Baird Callicott in a devastating review of Tom Regan's *The Case for Animal Rights* and simply humanely eliminate all predators. Callicott argues that because Regan makes it clear that all subjects-of-a-life possess equally strong rights, demanding equally strong degrees of respect, it must follow that:

If we ought to protect humans' rights not to be preyed on by both human and animal predators, then we ought to protect animals' rights not to be preyed upon by both human and animal predators. In short, then, Regan's theory of animal rights implies a policy of humane predator extermination, since predators, however innocently, violate the rights of their victims.[9]

Singer and Regan have both attempted to resist these kinds of conclusions by arguing that we should not interfere with nature in these ways because there is a big difference between human predation upon nonhuman animals and nonhuman animals' predation upon each other: specifically, humans are moral agents and so can assess the rights and wrongs of their actions, whereas nonhuman animals are not moral agents and so cannot assess the rights and wrongs of their actions. But it just will not do to dismiss the problem of nonhuman predation by saying that nonhuman animals "don't know any better," therefore cannot be blamed for their actions, and *therefore* should be allowed to carry on with these actions. This is an entirely misplaced argument at best and an egregiously sophistical argument at worst: moral agents (i.e., normal mature humans) can reasonably be held responsible for *allowing* nonmoral agents (such as nonhuman predators) to cause harm or violate the rights of others. As both Steve Sapontzis and J. Baird Callicott have pointed out, respectively, we might not hold a young child who "doesn't know any better" to be morally responsible for tormenting a rabbit, nor might we hold a brain-damaged sadist to be morally responsible for torturing a child, but this does nothing to lessen our responsibility *as* moral agents to stop the young child or the brain-damaged sadist from doing these things.[10] As Sapontzis says:

Young children cannot recognize moral rights and obligations; nonetheless, it is still wrong for them to torment and kill rabbits. Adults who see what the children are doing should step in to protect rabbits from being killed by the children. Similarly, humans can have an obligation to protect rabbits from being killed by foxes, even though the foxes cannot understand moral concepts.[11]

Callicott drives the point home this way:

Imagine the authorities explaining to the parents of a small child tortured and killed by a certifiably brain-damaged sadist that, even though he had a history of this sort of thing, he is not properly a moral agent and so can violate no-one's rights, and therefore has to be allowed to remain at large pursuing a course of action to which he is impelled by drives he cannot control.[12]

Thus, Singer's and Regan's concern with the question of whether or not nonhuman predators are moral agents misses their own morally relevant point: the morally relevant question is not whether these *predators* are *moral agents* but whether their *prey* are *moral patients* (i.e., beings that we, as moral agents, have an obligation to protect from harm). And, according to both Singer's and Regan's versions of the animal welfare approach, there is a broad class of prey animals that fall into this category; thus, it must follow that their views imply that we should intervene where doing so is likely to lessen the overall amount of pain and suffering in the world or, if we adopt a rights-based approach, to stop the violation of the rights of prey (regardless of utilitarian considerations regarding the total amount of pain and pleasure in the world).

If the animal welfarists conceded their shaky ground here and decided to prosecute a worldwide campaign to stop predation in nature generally, then (setting aside the likelihood of ecological meltdown for the sake of the argument!) they would effectively end up domesticating or otherwise taming what remains of wild nature. The animal welfare ethicists *say* that we should not do this, but the problem here is that they are not rationally *entitled* to say this in terms of the theoretical approaches to which they are committed. This means that while accusing human predators of applying a double standard, these ethicists are elsewhere applying a double standard of their own. On the one hand, they charge that human (meat-eating) predators think that we shouldn't cause suffering or violate each other's rights by eating each other (i.e., engaging in cannibalism), but that it's OK to cause suffering or violate the rights of nonhumans by eating them. However, on the other hand, the animal welfarists are themselves saying that humans in general shouldn't cause suffering or violate the rights of any sentient or rights-holding animals, but that it's OK for any other animals to cause suffering or violate the rights of any sentient or rights-holding animals. Thus, Tyler Cowan's damaging, but I think correct, observation: "Through casual conversation I have found that many believers in animal rights reject policing [of other animals with respect to predation] out of hand, though for no firm reasons, other than thinking that it does not sound right."[13]

Suppose, however, that animal welfarists agreed to apply their own arguments consistently, even though that would mean policing nature to the extent of totally domesticating or taming it. This raises the question "What would be wrong with that in any case?," which brings us to the next point.

(Note that from here on I will just refer to sentient animals, but you can substitute subjects-of-a-life/rights-holding animals as you wish, depending upon your preferred version of the animal welfare approach. I will also take it as read—and so won't keep stating explicitly—that any General Ethics needs to be able to offer sensible and defensible responses not only to the predation problem but also to each of the following problems in regard to the animal welfare approach.)

Problem 9: The Wild/Domesticated Problem

Because of their thoroughly individualistic foci, the animal welfare approaches imply that a *wild* sentient animal or a population of wild sentient animals is no more valuable or deserving of moral consideration than a *domesticated* sentient animal or a population of the same number of domesticated sentient animals of the same average level of sentience. (This is because, in both cases, one has just as many sentient animals with just as many total "units of sentience"; or, substituting for the main alternative animal welfare view, just as many rights-holding animals.) This runs against the sense, shared by many reflective people, that—if we set the special case of companion animals (or "pets") to one side—there is, somehow, "something" that is ultimately more valuable about a wild sentient animal or a population of wild sentient animals than a domesticated sentient animal or a population of the same number of domesticated sentient animals of the same average level of sentience. As I have implied, people might well disagree with this statement if it is taken to include the special case of their companion animals, which can come to be seen as members of the household, with many of the status privileges—and even, to some extent, responsibilities—that being a member of the household brings with it. But this potential point of disagreement speaks of the special value of these animals *to us*; it does not speak to the value of these animals in more general, less obviously self-interested terms. If we therefore set the special case of companion animals to one side and consider the issue in terms of those domesticated animals with which we have no special relationship (such as the sheep, cows, pigs, chickens, and so on that we keep for instrumental reasons and that constitute the vast bulk of the domesticated animal population even if they are largely hidden from us), then we can get to the heart of the question being asked here: Are these domesticated-animals-in-general as valuable as wild animals? The animal welfare approaches are theoretically committed to saying that, in principle, they are. This, in turn, implies that a world of totally domesticated animals would, other things being equal, be just as good as a world of wild animals or a world containing a mixture of the two. In that case, then, why not domesticate the planet completely if it suits our purposes to do so?

Not only do the animal welfare approaches invite this question, but there are grounds for thinking that the advocates of these approaches ought to be enthusiastic about realizing such a world. After all, it would help us to sort out the previously discussed problem of nonhuman predation, for we could police nature much more effectively in a totally domesticated world. It would, for example, be much easier to exterminate all predators humanely or, alternatively, kill their prey humanely and then present it to the recalcitrant predators at feeding time. My cat—a skillful wildlife predator when left to her own devices—seems quite happy with this arrangement, especially around 5:30 PM each evening when she gets fed what are, in fact, parts of another dead animal, out of a tin. Why wouldn't every other animal be happy with this arrangement?

Problem 10: The Indigenous/Introduced Problem

Because of their thoroughly individualistic foci, the animal welfare approaches similarly imply that an *indigenous* sentient animal or a population of indigenous sentient animals is no more valuable or deserving of moral consideration than an *introduced* sentient animal or a population of the same number of introduced sentient animals of the same average level of sentience. This runs against the sense, shared by many reflective people (and certainly most nature reserve and wildlife management agencies), that there is, somehow, "something" that is ultimately more valuable about an indigenous sentient animal or a population of indigenous sentient animals than an introduced—especially an *invasive*—sentient animal or a population of the same number of introduced sentient animals of the same average level of sentience. Yet the animal welfare approaches invite the question: Why not populate the world with whatever cute and fluffy, colorful, or otherwise interesting introduced sentient animals we like, even if this leads to a loss of biodiversity overall (which is exactly what it does since a certain percentage of introduced species will turn out to be invasive—although we often don't know which ones in advance—and invasive species represent, after habitat alteration, the second leading cause of loss of global biodiversity[14])? Why should it matter if a sentient animal isn't indigenous to a particular region? After all, who really cares about the standardization of our fauna and flora through the processes of ecological globalization? Home gardeners "mix 'n' match" all the time, using the world's flora as their palette to make pleasing gardens. Why shouldn't we do this to get whatever mix of sentient animals happens to please us?

Problem 11: The Local Diversity/Monoculture Problem

Because of their thoroughly individualistic foci, the animal welfare approaches likewise imply that a *diversity* of sentient animals is no more valuable or deserving of moral consideration than a *monoculture* (or something approaching a monoculture) of the same number of sentient animals of the same average level of sentience. Again, this runs against the sense, shared by many reflective people, that there is, somehow, "something" that is more valuable about a diversity of sentient animals than a monoculture (or something approaching a monoculture) of the same number of sentient animals of the same average level of sentience. Yet the animal welfare approaches invite the question: Why not populate the world with monocultures of sentient animals, especially if it suits our purposes to do so? (It might seem unusual to think of nonhuman animals—rather than plants—in terms of monocultures, but that's effectively what, for example, vast herds of cattle are when the distinction is applied to sentient species.)

This problem can be taken as posing the question of diversity and monoculture on a case by case basis without reference to the overall amount of biodiversity in the world. This follows from the fact that we could at least imagine a world in which there are many, many small monocultures (or near monocultures) but monocultures that are sufficiently different from each other to add up to a world in which the overall diversity is just as great as another world in which there are mixtures of considerable (but not always dissimilar) diversity everywhere (and thus no monocultures at all). This means that the issue of diversity/monoculture at any given local level is conceptually distinct from the issue of biodiversity (or the preservation of a wide range of species) at a global level even if there is a strong relationship between the two at a practical level. With this in mind, we can now turn to consider the conceptually distinct but practically related question of the overall diversity of species globally.

Problem 12: The Species (or Global Biodiversity) Problem

Because of their thoroughly individualistic foci, the animal welfare approaches imply that the last remnants of a population of sentient animals are no more valuable or deserving of moral consideration than the same number of sentient animals of the same average level of sentience drawn at random from a population that exists in plague proportions. This also runs against the sense, shared by many reflective people, that there is, somehow, "something" that is valuable about the preservation of a species as such, even though a species as such can't feel and so has no "experiential welfare" to be concerned about (only the individual flesh-and-blood *members* of a species can feel and thus possess an experiential welfare; a species as such is just an abstract category; it just refers to a *type* of entity not to token instances of that entity). The animal welfare approaches therefore invite the question: Why care about biodiversity at all? Why not populate the world with equal numbers of a relatively small range of those plants and nonhuman animals that are most useful to us or that simply most take our fancy?

Problem 13: The Ecosystem Integrity/Preservation in Zoos and Farms Problem

Because of their thoroughly individualistic foci, the animal welfare approaches imply that free-ranging sentient animals that actively participate in rich networks of ecosystemic processes, including food webs, are no more valuable or deserving of moral consideration than the same number of sentient animals of the same average level of sentience and experiencing the same average level of experiential satisfaction confined in a zoo or on a farm. This similarly runs against the sense, shared by many reflective people, that there is, somehow, "something" that is more valuable about the former animals than the latter—or at least about the former *situation* than the latter. I add this rider because there is perhaps a sense in which we can generally agree that the value of a tiger considered in its own right, which is to say "in isolation" from everything else, is whatever it is regardless of whether it is in the wild or in a zoo. However, the fact is that *nothing exists in isolation*. What we ultimately need to consider, then, is the overall value of the two situations: tiger in the wild and tiger in the zoo.

The problem for the animal welfare approaches, however, is that their thoroughly individualistic foci mean that they cannot "see" contextual issues. All they are concerned about is the value of sentient animals as such (or, as I noted at the end of my discussion of problem 8, above, you can substitute "rights-holding animals" here as you prefer). The very best they can do in accounting for contextual issues is to consider them in a second-order, derivative fashion and argue, for example, that a wild animal would be, say, happier in the wild, and that this would be a reason for preferring this situation to a zoo or a farm. But this argument is quickly countered: we can easily think of examples in which it is plausible to argue that an animal would have a longer and less stressed life living in some reasonable form of captivity than, as it were, taking its ecosystemic chances. (In this connection, recall Mark Sagoff's sober assessment that animals typically die violently in nature through predation, starvation, disease, parasitism, and cold; that most do not live to maturity and that very few die of old age; and that many might "reasonably prefer to be raised on a farm [or, we might add in this context, a good zoo], where the chances of survival for a year or more would be good, and to escape the wild, where they are negligible.")[15] In these cases, animal welfarists should see the zoo or farm scenario as preferable to that of the animal being left to the not-so-tender mercies of nature.

At the very least, the fact that animal welfare approaches are blind to contextual matters in anything other than a second-order, derivative way, means that they have no ultimate grounds for preferring happy or miserable animals in zoos to equally happy or miserable animals in nature. All that these approaches are equipped to "see" are the sentient (or, to repeat, the rights-holding) animals in nature; they cannot "see" or place value upon the more abstract, ecosystemic processes of nature that ultimately connect these animals. It is as if their moral vision allows them to see the individual sentient dots in the picture but not to join them up. Thus, the long and the short of the ecosystem integrity problem for the animal welfare approaches is that their individualistic foci mean that they place no value on ecosystem integrity per se. Its value is purely derivative. Many reflective people think that that is not good enough. The difficult question remains, however, of explaining why it isn't good enough.

Central Problems Relating to Life-based Ethics

Problem 14: The "Why Is Life Valuable?" Problem

The standard argument that has been advanced by the main life-based ethicists—such as Albert Schweitzer, Kenneth Goodpaster, Robin Attfield, Paul Taylor, and Gary Varner—for the value of all living things, whether sentient or not, is that even a nonsentient living thing can be thought of as in some sense embodying a biologically based (but, of course, nonconscious) "will to live" (Schweitzer), "interests" (Goodpaster and Attfield), "needs" (Varner and Attfield), or "good of its own" (Taylor).[16] But, alas, this general form of argument turns out to be seriously flawed in at least two respects. First of all, we simply cannot make proper sense of the argument that nonsentient living things can be said (literally rather than metaphorically) to have *wills, interests, needs,* or *goods of their own*—of any kind. Singer, a staunch defender of the view that the criterion of sentience is "the only defensible boundary of concern for the interests of others,"[17] puts the point succinctly when he argues that the problem with the standard defenses offered by life-based ethicists is that

they use language metaphorically and then argue as if what they had said was literally true. We may often talk about plants "seeking" water or light so that they can survive, and this way of thinking about plants makes it easier to accept talk of their "will to live," or of them "pursuing" their own good. But once we stop to reflect on the fact that plants are not conscious and cannot engage in any intentional behaviour, it is clear that all this language is metaphorical; one might just as well say that a river is pursuing its own good and striving to reach the sea, or that the "good" of a guided missile is to blow itself up along with its target....

[In fact, however,] it is possible to give a purely physical explanation of what is happening; and in the absence of consciousness, there is no good reason why we should have greater respect for the physical processes that govern the growth and decay of living things than we have for those that govern non-living things.[18]

We can easily *attribute* wills, interests, needs, and goods of their own to nonsentient living things, but we are doing so entirely from our own point of view, from our own ways of thinking about things in terms of ascribing intentions to them. We should not kid ourselves, however, that we can seriously—or, as Singer says, literally as opposed to metaphorically—claim that these features exist from the point of view of the nonsentient living thing under consideration, because *a nonsentient living thing doesn't have a point of view*. It is not *like* anything to be a nonsentient living thing; if it were, then, by definition, that thing would be sentient rather than nonsentient. Thus, it is quite misleading of Paul Taylor to suggest, repeatedly, in respect of nonsentient living things that "Things that happen to them can be judged, *from their standpoint*, to be favorable or unfavorable to them" (my emphasis),[19] for we can no more judge benefits or harms "from the standpoint" of a plant or a tree than we can judge these things "from the standpoint" of a rock—and for the same reason. We can easily make these judgments in respect of plants or trees from *our* standpoint or point of view (and note here that *standpoint* literally refers to "a physical or mental position from which things are viewed," i.e., a point of view), but it is not literally possible to make such judgments from *their* standpoint or point of view because they do not have one. The attribution of nonconscious wills, interests, needs, or goods of their own to nonsentient living things is, in the final analysis, incoherent.

The second problem with the rational foundations of the standard argument for the life-based approach—and one that I am not aware of having been raised before—is that it is circular. Consider: it is simply not the case that every desire, interest, need, or good of one's own is automatically valuable; for example, someone might feel that they have an interest in, or a need to, or that it might further their own good to see someone dead, or have sex with someone by force if necessary, or lie badly to someone, and so on. It therefore becomes quite important to specify more precisely which interests, needs, or goods of their own are deemed to be valuable and which are not. For life-based ethicists, the interests, needs, or goods of their own that are deemed to be valuable are clearly those that are directed toward the maintenance of essential life processes, that is, those interests, needs, or goods of their own that make an entity an *autopoietic* system (literally, a *self-making* and, by extension, *self-remaking*, or *self-renewing* system). But in that case we can ask: "Well, why do you think that these essential life processes—autopoietic processes—are valuable?" The answer that we will then get from the life-based ethicists is in terms of living processes being valuable because they embody (nonconscious) interests, needs, or goods of their own! And so the circle continues:

(i) The standard life-based argument: Living things are valuable because they embody (nonconscious) interests, needs, or goods of their own.

(ii) Critical question: But since not all interests, needs, or goods of their own are valuable (e.g., murder, rape, serious lying), what is it that makes these interests, needs, or goods of their own valuable?

(iii) Answer: the fact that they are directed toward the maintenance of living things.

(iv) Question: So what? What is so important about the maintenance of living things?

(v) Answer: Return to (i).

And so it goes. But circular reasoning offers no substantial reasons at all; it just chases its own tail instead of giving a solid answer to a problem.

We can note here that whatever the other strengths and weaknesses of the standard answers to the "Why are humans valuable?" question and the "Why are sentient beings valuable?" question, they are not circular. The standard kinds of answers we will get from the supporters of these approaches are answers like "Because humans are rational," or "Because humans have a soul," and "Because sentient beings are capable of feeling and so can be benefited or harmed from their own point of view." If we then ask, "Well, are these features valuable in themselves?," the supporters of these approaches can easily say "Yes" and proceed to tell us why in a noncircular way. For example, they can tell us that the possession of these features is what makes the possessor's life valuable *to them*—and then expound further why these beings should be respected on that account (just as we wish to be). But suppose we ask the life-based ethicists "Why are even nonsentient living things valuable?" and they say

"Because nonsentient living things embody biologically based (but, of course, nonconscious) wills to live, interests, or goods of their own that are directed toward their own survival." If we then ask, "Well are these things valuable in themselves?," the supporters of this approach cannot give the same kind of answer as those we have just considered; that is, they cannot say "Of course they are—these capacities are the very things that make the lives of nonsentient living things valuable *to them*" because it is not like anything to be a nonsentient living thing; nothing is valuable *to them*. Life-based ethicists must therefore reach for another answer, but, unfortunately for them, that answer is the circular answer outlined above.

In view of these problems, I would suggest that Gary Varner is on safer—albeit extremely vague—ground when he offers a second, non-standard argument for a life-based approach to ethics. In this argument he asks us to imagine two worlds—one that is rich in nonsentient life-forms and one that isn't. Then he asks us which world we think is more valuable. In answering his own question, he drops considerations relating to biologically based needs and so on altogether and simply appeals to our intuitive sense that "the mere existence of nonconscious life adds *something* to the goodness of the world."[20] Many of us would agree with that, as far as it goes, but the problem remains that Varner fails to tell us what this special "something" is—and I am not aware of any other contributors to this approach who have been any more forthcoming; indeed, most don't even mention this second, more intuitively based argument. Even Varner admits to deliberately omitting this argument from an earlier book because he "doubted that it would be persuasive to anyone not already essentially convinced."[21] However, despite this, he nevertheless thinks that "this second argument expresses very clearly the most basic value assumption of the biocentric individualist [i.e., people who believe that all individual living things are valuable in their own right]."[22]

But what Varner fails to see here is that this second argument—which serves to highlight an intuition rather than provide a detailed set of reasons for a conclusion—can be applied just as well to other comparisons. For example, imagine these two worlds: one that is rich in nonsentient life-forms that are arranged in botanical gardens attended by robots and one that is rich in the same number of nonsentient life-forms that exist in

natural, ecosystemic arrangements; or imagine these two worlds: neither
has any life-forms at all, but one consists of nothing more than barren
rock whereas the other is an abandoned world in which all life has died,
but which still retains ruins of buildings and sculptures that would rival
the finest you've ever seen. Could we not equally well argue that the second of the comparisons in each case is the intuitively preferable one, that
"the mere existence of ecosystems in the first example, or the mere existence of such highly organized architectural and sculptural complexity in
the second example, adds *something* to the goodness of the world in
both cases"? Yet if this is reasonable, then Varner's own form of argument undercuts his own biocentric individualist position. Varner does
not wish to say that anything other than individual living things are valuable in their own right, yet his own intuitively based argument can easily be adapted to suggest that *holistic* systems (in this case ecosystems),
rather than what he thinks of as *individual* living things, add something
to the value of the world, and that certain formations of *nonliving* things
can add something to the value of the world as well. Where, then, do
these extensions of his own argument leave his biocentric individualist
view that only *individual living* things can add something to the value
of the world? Thus, it seems that even this second, nonstandard form
of argument cannot be used to sustain a strictly biocentric individualist
position.

As a sweetener (I trust), it is perhaps worth noting here that the
approach that I will be developing in this book to General Ethics tells us
exactly what the mysterious "something" is that is added to the goodness
of the world in each of the "two world" comparisons discussed above—
Varner's and mine. The upshot is that although the approach to be
developed here embraces and explains what is right in Varner's intuitive
demonstration, it is not limited to, and can in no way be summed up as
being, simply a "life-based approach" to ethics.

The Life-based Approach and Problems 8 through 13 Revisited

Beyond these problems with its rational foundations, the individualistically focused life-based approach recapitulates the same range of problems that afflicts the animal welfare approaches on the basis of their
individualistic foci of interest. That is, the life-based approach suffers

from *the wild/domesticated problem* (after all, wild and domesticated plants are just as alive and, therefore, just as valuable as each other); *the indigenous/introduced problem* (similarly, indigenous and introduced plants are just as alive and, therefore, just as valuable as each other); *the local diversity/monoculture problem* (considered at the local level and without reference to overall global biodiversity, we can have just as many living things and, therefore, just as much value whether the living things in question are extremely diverse or all much the same); *the species (or global biodiversity) problem* (the same reasoning applies with respect to overall global biodiversity: we can have just as many living things and, therefore, just as much value whether the living things in question are extremely diverse or all much the same); and *the ecosystem integrity/preservation in zoos and farms problem*, which we can now expand to read: *the ecosystem integrity/preservation in botanical gardens and zoos and farms problem* (e.g., we can put all the plants in an ecosystem into a botanical garden, look after them really well, and have just as much life and, therefore, just as much value in both cases).

The predation problem is a separate kind of problem to those linked to the individualistic foci of the life-based approaches as such, however, it also recapitulates the formulation of this problem for the sentience-based approach—with a vengeance. In this context, the problem is this: Does the recognition of the value of nonsentient living things mean that moral agents should not destroy (and that includes eat) any living things? If so, how are we to live? Moreover, does the recognition of the value of nonsentient living things mean that moral agents should intervene to stop other living things destroying (and that includes eating) any other living things? (We saw that the argument for doing this is much stronger than the argument against it with respect to the animal welfare approaches.) The life-based approach is clearly untenable at a practical level unless it is made compatible with some sensible kind of hierarchy of value that explains why the value of nonsentient living things can be trumped by the value of other living things—and especially other sentient animals—maintaining their own existence. The main life-based ethicists recognize this problem and have generally attempted to develop either a set of priority rules that kick in under different circumstances (e.g., by distinguishing between basic and nonbasic needs) or else explicit hierarchies of value, such that while the idea of something being valuable in its own right kicks in at the level of individual living things (and not before), the value hierarchy goes on to ascribe greater value to more complex kinds of living things, such as sentient beings in general (or certain of their interests) and humans in particular (or certain of their interests).

The fact that the predation question alone more or less forces life-based ethicists to develop priority rules or explicit hierarchies of value in order to give us a workable theory—one that allows us to eat, for a start—might lead some of us to reflect back on the animal welfare approaches and ask: If some sensible hierarchy of value is the only way to make any practical sense out of the life-based approach, then why should the hierarchy of value flatten out at the level of sentient animals? Is there not a sensible hierarchy of value to be found there too? But, if so, what are the implications of this for the best-known animal welfare approaches?

A final point that I will mention in regard to the life-based approach is that it is, obviously enough, a *pro-life* approach, with all that that entails. Any argument for the value of nonsentient individual living things is, therefore, clearly a prima facie argument against both abortion and euthanasia. Life-based ethicists might be quite happy with this—or they might wish to call on their various priority rules or hierarchies of value in order to allow abortion and euthanasia in various circumstances. The problem is, they don't say. Even though their approach is a pro-life approach, we will generally search in vain for any mention, let alone real discussion, of abortion and euthanasia in their arguments. It is as if they haven't made the connection. Clearly, however, any life-based approach needs to address these issues since this kind of approach invites their discussion. And I have already noted earlier in this chapter that any General Ethics—by virtue of being a *general* ethics—must do the same (see my discussion of problems 2 and 3).

Central Problems Relating to Ecosystem Integrity Ethics

This brings us to the ecosystem integrity approaches. These seem to solve a number of the problems that confront the previous, individualistically focused approaches. For example, ecosystem integrity approaches dissolve *the predation problem* created by both the animal welfare approaches and (if adopted sufficiently zealously) the life-based approaches in that predation, in a great many forms at least, is seen as part and parcel *of* the maintenance of ecosystem integrity. Similarly, *the wild/domesticated problem* is cashed out primarily in terms of what contributes to or disrupts ecosystem integrity. I say "primarily" here because ecosystem integrity is not the only kind of value under consideration if we are talking about an inclusive ecosystem integrity approach, that is, one that also recognizes the value of individual living things. However, I also say "primarily" here because I take it that the point of an ecosystem integrity approach is to favor ecosystem integrity over the value of individual living things when and where these values come into conflict. Thus, the right balance with respect to *the wild/domesticated problem* is to be found in terms of humans meeting their own needs for domestication within the context of preserving ecosystem integrity. *The indigenous/introduced problem* is also cashed out in terms of this understanding of what contributes to or disrupts ecosystem integrity. This means favoring indigenous living things (whether wild or not) over introduced living things and especially over invasive living things. The same understanding applies to *the local diversity/monoculture problem*: the right balance here is that which maintains ecosystem integrity and thus the approach that favors characteristic diversity over an increase in diversity for its own sake or a reduction in that diversity. *The species (or global biodiversity) problem* is just the diversity/monoculture problem at the global or ecospheric level as opposed to the local ecosystemic level. Essentially the same answer therefore applies: the right balance is that which maintains ecospheric integrity overall and thus the approach that favors characteristic ecospheric diversity over an increase in diversity for its own sake or a significant reduction in that diversity. Finally, this approach cannot remotely be accused of being blind to *the ecosystem integrity problem* because a concern for ecosystem integrity is its *raison d'être*.

But all is not as rosy as it seems with the ecosystem integrity approach. In particular, this approach adds the following new problems to the list of problems that any General Ethics must be able to address.

Problem 15: The "Why Is Ecosystem Integrity Valuable?" Problem

The prototype of an ecosystem integrity ethics was first advanced by the American forester, wildlife ecologist, and conservationist Aldo Leopold

(1887–1948) in a now famous essay entitled "The Land Ethic," which forms the concluding section of his classic *A Sand County Almanac*, first published in 1949 (a date that is remarkably early relative to the development of environmental ethics as a formal field of inquiry only since the mid-to-late 1970s). Leopold famously asserted that we should expand our traditional notions of ethics to include the "biotic community" by adding the following principle to our existing moral codes: "A thing is right when it tends to preserve the integrity, stability, and beauty of the biotic community. It is wrong when it tends otherwise."[23] Unfortunately, Leopold named this principle the "Land Ethic," which is quite unhelpful given that it can be applied just as much to ecosystemic relationships in riverine, estuarine, marine, and, presumably, atmospheric environments as to terrestrial environments. Alas, the misleading "Land Ethic" label has stuck, but we can think of his proposal as a—even *the*—prototypical form of ecosystem integrity ethics.

Another unfortunate aspect of Leopold's central maxim concerns his use of the term "beauty." Partly because this term can mean different things to different people and partly because Leopold provided no independent elaboration of and defense for his inclusion of this term, later commentators have either ignored this aspect of Leopold's formulation or rendered it in terms of "ecological integrity"—or some roughly equivalent formulation. Thus, for example, James Heffernan says that (i) "The characteristic structure of an ecosystem seems to be what Leopold means by its integrity," and then suggests (ii) that we can equate the idea of the "objective beauty" of an ecosystem with its characteristic structure (which, from (i), also means its integrity).[24] For Heffernan, then, "when Leopold talks of preserving the 'integrity, stability, and beauty of the biotic community' he is referring to preserving the characteristic structure of an ecosystem and its capacity to withstand change or stress."[25] In consequence, Heffernan drops any explicit reference to "beauty" in his own suggested reformulation of Leopold's Land Ethic: "A thing is right when it tends to preserve the characteristic diversity and stability of an ecosystem (or the biosphere). It is wrong when it tends otherwise."[26] J. Baird Callicott likewise drops any reference to "beauty" in his suggested reformulation of Leopold's Land Ethic: "A thing is right when it tends to disturb the biotic community only at normal spatial and temporal scales. It is wrong when it tends otherwise."[27] Thus, Leopold's Land Ethic is generally understood to refer to matters concerning ecological integrity not to what we might ordinarily understand as aesthetic matters as such. In one sense this is just as well because one person's idea of a "beautiful" landscape can be an ecologist's idea of a "disaster area"—a landscape overrun with invasive species and so on; similarly, one person's idea of an ugly or uninteresting landscape—like a "swamp"—can be an ecologist's idea of a precious "wetland." But, of course, the drawback of an ethics that is limited to concerns regarding ecological integrity is that it simply cannot help us with respect to problems such as the "two buildings example" that I gave in the last chapter (since, even though one of these buildings is contextually ugly and the other is contextually fitting, neither disrupts ecological integrity any more than the other).

Leopold's proposal bears a similar relationship to contemporary ecosystem integrity ethics (à la Heffernan and Callicott) as Schweitzer's prototypical "reverence for life" approach does to contemporary life-based ethics. Specifically, neither Leopold nor Schweitzer were professionally trained philosophers, and this shows in the relative looseness of their arguments (as well as Leopold's name for his approach and even his formulation of the Land Ethic), but they did both pioneer ethical directions that later philosophers have been inspired by and have attempted to develop in more detailed and rigorous ways. Thus, notwithstanding the relative fame of Leopold's Land Ethic, the essay in which he advances this ethic, although pregnant with significant ideas, offers little in the way of anything that philosophers would recognize as a rigorously reasoned argument. Even so, we can discern the basic structure of an argument in Leopold's essay if we dig deep enough, and this is what it looks like: Leopold argues that ethics are not a fixed and firm thing but rather a "product of social evolution"; that "All ethics so far evolved rest upon a single premise: that the individual is a member of a community of interdependent parts"; that there are now both theoretical and practical reasons for extending our conception of what our community is—and, thus, what our ethical concerns should cover—from the human level to the ecological level; and that the "mechanism of operation [for this social evolutionary development] is the same for any ethic: social approbation for right actions: social disapproval for wrong actions."[28] What Leopold is suggesting, then, is that the next stage in the social evolution of our ethics needs to be one in which we collectively embrace the wider ecological context of which we are a part as part of our extended community and, thus, as falling within the scope of our moral concerns and sympathies.

J. Baird Callicott has, through a sustained and influential output over many years, done much to draw out the Humean and Darwinian roots of this kind of argument and to develop it further.[29] These Humean and Darwinian roots are essentially as follows. David Hume (1711–1776) argued in his masterpiece *A Treatise of Human Nature* (1739) that ethics is grounded in the sympathies and antipathies that are part and parcel of human nature: "The minds of all men are similar in their feeling and operations" and "sympathy is the chief source of moral distinctions."[30] Thus, rather than our reasoning about ethics driving our feelings (or passions), our reasoning about ethics is, ought, and can only be, as Hume famously said, "the slave of the passions."[31] (Or should that be: "as Hume infamously said"? Given that the general thrust of Western philosophical ethics has been and remains very much concerned with using human reason to channel and curb the acting out of our passions in various ways, we can see why Robert Arrington describes Hume's claim as "one of the most notorious claims in the literature of moral philosophy."[32]) For Hume, then, we express our moral sentiments when we express approval or disapproval for those things and actions that we find useful or agreeable to ourselves and others. Darwinian evolutionary thought, in turn, informs our understanding of human nature and, thus, how our natural sympathies and antipathies got to be the way they are. It also informs our understanding of ecology and, thus, the interdependent relationship we have with the rest of the natural world. Callicott argues that Leopold draws upon and contributes to this line of intellectual and moral development in suggesting that we as a human community should now learn to extend our concerns and sympathies to the wider ecological community of which we are a part.

But where does this get us? If we pursue this line of thinking, then it seems obvious, to me at least, that the natural sympathies we share on the basis of our evolutionary inheritance are such that we do and will continue to feel most strongly for our immediate kin and kith, followed by whatever we take our most immediate wider group to be, and then perhaps outward to our own species and so on, but that the wider "natural world" or "ecological community" will inevitably, when weighed in this kind of balance, remain a relatively distant concern in terms of our evolutionary endowed sympathies, passions, or just plain old gut feelings. It therefore seems "natural" that people will keep clearing land or fishing their seas and lakes not only in order to feed their families in some subsistence sense but even, on grander scales, in order to allow their families to live in luxury—and this even when they are endangering or extirpating the remaining members of a particular species. Thus, Hume's moral sentiments as honed by Darwinian evolution would not appear to provide us with a sufficient degree of motivation to move to Leopold's proposed next stage of social evolution in anything beyond a token sense; that is, we effectively say: "Sure, we are members of a wider ecological community, but the evolutionary distant members or aspects of this community matter much less to me than my immediate kin, kith, and kind."

However, we also know that it doesn't have to be this way, at least not entirely. We know that, contra Hume, we can channel and curb our sentiments—including the natural priorities of these sentiments as they run from kin, kith, and kind to our wider ecological context—if we are given a sufficiently good reason to do so. But what would constitute a sufficiently good reason? Two obvious kinds of reasons suggest themselves. The first is that we should value our ecological contexts much more than we do because doing so is crucial to our own survival and well-being as well as that of our own kin, kith, and kind. This is completely compatible with a Humean and Darwinian account of value, but it pays the price of collapsing Leopold's celebrated Land Ethic into an *instrumental* (or *use*) value approach to the value of ecological integrity. Moreover, this argument is vulnerable to the charge that if our concerns with ecological integrity boil down to its usefulness to us, then these concerns will have to take their place alongside other self-interest-based arguments regarding the possible alternative uses of various natural areas for such things as dams for generating hydro-electricity, housing, farming, logging, mining, and so on. No change there then.

But all this would seem to be a far cry from what it appears that Leopold wanted to say (and is typically taken as saying) because Leopold suggested in his essay that the Land Ethic involved valuing land "in the philosophical sense,"[33] which most philosophers have taken to mean on the basis of its *intrinsic* value, its value in its own right. This, then, brings us to the second kind of reason that might persuade us to override the natural priorities bestowed by our evolutionary endowed sentiments and value our ecological contexts much more than we do: specifically, we might accept that we should regard ecosystem integrity as valuable not only because of its usefulness to us but also because it is valuable in its own right and that "such and such is the reason why." This orientation to the problem leads us away from the kind of subjectivist approach to value that runs through the Hume-Darwin-Leopold line of thinking that Callicott endorses (an approach that locates the basis of our evaluations, as Hume says, "in [ourselves], not in the object [toward which these evaluations are directed]"[34]) and toward an objectively based reason that would explain why ecosystem integrity is valuable in its own right. But what might such a reason be?

The main objectively based reason that has been advanced in regard to the value of ecosystem integrity is that ecosystems are alive and living things are valuable in their own right. Leopold himself toyed with this idea in an essay written much earlier than his famous "Land Ethic" but only published in 1979, and this approach has since been taken up by James Heffernan in his objectivist, distinctly non-Callicottian, interpretation of Leopold.[35] But the problem with this kind of ecosystem integrity argument is that it just reduces to an expanded version of the life-based argument. Indeed, it is an even more controversial version of this argument than those that I have already considered above because, whereas we can at least all agree that, say, individual plants and trees are alive, it is simply not clear that the ecosphere is alive in anything like the same sense (although there is at least a sensible argument to be had here in terms of formal definitions of life and so on). This in turn means that this objectivist approach to the value of ecosystem integrity is just as flawed as the standard argument for the life-based approach because it is just the standard argument for the life-based approach extended to include ecosystems as living things, which just adds another shaky layer to an already incoherent and circular argument.

Perhaps we would do better simply to say, in the style of Varner, that "the mere existence of ecosystem integrity—of longstanding, self-sustaining, complex webs of relationships between individual living things themselves and between them and their physical environments—adds *something* to the goodness of the world." But what *is* that something? As I have already suggested in my discussion of problem 14 (the

"*Why is life valuable?*" *problem*), the approach to General Ethics that I will be developing in this book tells us exactly what that "something" is.

Problem 16: The Subtraction and Addition of Ecologically Benign Species Problem

This might be regarded as more of a worry than a serious problem, but then again ... The worry, or problem, is this: although the ecosystem integrity approach appears to give the right answers with respect to questions about diversity—that is, it supports the maintenance of characteristic diversity over an increase in diversity for its own sake or a significant reduction in that diversity—it is not at all clear that this approach genuinely entitles its advocates to object to *the subtraction and addition of ecologically benign species*. This is because this approach is concerned primarily with the maintenance of the ecological integrity—or self-sustaining capacity—of an ecosystem and "ecologically benign species" refers, by definition, to species whose loss or addition does not significantly disrupt this integrity or self-sustaining capacity. Of course there are two immediate points to be made here both for and against this concern. The pro-point is that it is just not the case that every species is vital to, or even has any great impact upon, the self-sustaining capacity of an ecosystem. Not every species is a *keystone* species—or anything like it. Ecosystems are not like a rug that unravels if a single thread is removed—unless of course it happens to be a "keystone thread" (to thoroughly mix architectural and weaving metaphors). Neither will an ecosystem necessarily unravel if one more species is woven into it. The contra-point, however, is that the relationships in ecosystems are so complex that we often can't know with any certainty what might happen if we do subtract or add a species that we think is ecologically benign. This, then, gives an advocate of the ecosystem integrity approach a *practical* way of responding to *the subtraction and addition of ecologically benign species problem*. They can simply say that we should not attempt to add or subtract species to or from an ecosystem, no matter how ecologically benign we think our actions are, because we can never be sure. We should therefore adopt the maintenance of characteristic diversity, which has been tried and tested through evolutionary processes, as our default position.

But consider, for the sake of the argument, the following rejoinder: "Oh, I see, you think we should adopt the maintenance of characteristic diversity as our default position because you *aren't sure* what would happen to ecosystem integrity if we didn't. Well, have I got news for you! Through a complex procedure known as quantum-relativistic informational time tunneling, I've been able to download a program from an intergalactic civilization far in advance of ours that enables us simply to scan a geographical area (using the well-known Zooly-Mischoff scanning procedure) and then be able to tell *exactly* what will happen if we add or subtract any given species to that area. Now, c'mon, be honest, wouldn't you like to be able to add a bit more ecological diversity around here if it were ecologically benign? It'd make things more interesting, right? And wouldn't you like to be able to remove the odd species—especially those that get in your way one way or the other—if you knew that it wouldn't have any other ill-effects?"

You can say that this response is fanciful, but the point at issue is a serious one: if the ecological integrity approach is concerned primarily with the maintenance of the ecological integrity—or self-sustaining capacity—of an ecosystem, then this approach provides no grounds to object *in principle* to the subtraction or addition of ecologically benign species precisely because, by definition, this subtraction or addition makes no significant difference to the ecological integrity of the ecosystem. This means that advocates of this approach who want to object to the subtraction or addition of ecologically benign species have to fall back on "What *might* happen if . . ." kinds of arguments. Yet many informed judges in this area feel that there ought to be a way of objecting to the subtraction or addition of ecologically benign species in principle. But is there any good argument for this?

Problem 17: The (Catastrophic) Way Evolution Works Problem

A question also arises regarding the relationship of ecosystem integrity to evolutionary processes. Given that we now understand evolutionary processes to include the odd catastrophic cosmic collision between an asteroid and the earth—and that such collisions have constituted a major structuring agent of the biosphere in which we ourselves have evolved; indeed, that they may even be responsible for our existence through seeing off the dinosaurs and allowing the spread and rise of mammals—

then there would seem to be a tension between our normal understanding of ecosystem integrity, on the one hand, and evolutionary processes, broadly understood, on the other hand. How are we to reconcile this tension? If we lean too far in the direction of trying to maintain ecosystem integrity in the absence of evolutionary processes, then we are in danger of deep-freezing ecosystems and regarding any new evolutionary developments as bad. If we lean too far in the direction of embracing any and all evolutionary processes, then our response to the prospect of a catastrophic cosmic collision will be "Bring it on."

J. Baird Callicott has suggested a middle way in his own reformulation of Aldo Leopold's Land Ethic. For Callicott, "A thing is right when it tends to disturb the biotic community only at normal spatial and temporal scales. It is wrong when it tends otherwise."[36] But, even here, the tension remains, for it has in fact been "normal" for cosmic collisions or other equally catastrophic factors to declare "Game Over" for a tremendous number of species every hundred million years or so. This *is* the "normal temporal scale" for catastrophic disturbances of the biotic community, and we owe our existence to it. So any ecological integrity approach that wants to embrace evolutionary processes at "normal spatial and temporal scales" has to accept this normal temporal scale of catastrophe. These considerations therefore raise a significant question: Is there any way in which we can *consistently* embrace the more gradual kinds of evolutionary processes that we usually think in terms of (and, thus, avoid committing ourselves to "deep-freezing" ecological processes) while also rejecting—and acting in whatever ways we can to prevent—catastrophic forms of evolutionary restructuring?

The Central Problem Relating to the Ethics of the Human-Constructed Environment

Problem 18: The Human-Constructed Environment Problem or the Comprehensiveness Problem

If we had some kind of ethics that was *directly* concerned with the human-constructed environment, then it is possible that the discussion of this ethical approach would have generated a range of problems that would enable me to list, say, four or six of the main problems here, much as I have done with respect to the interhuman, animal welfare, life-based, and ecosystem integrity ethical approaches discussed above. However, as I pointed out in chapter 1, we do not at present have such an ethics. Thus, if we think that it is possible to ask sensible *ethical* questions—sensible questions about the values we should live by—in respect of the human-constructed environment itself (and the point of my "two buildings example" in chapter 1 was to show that it is), then it follows that the central problem relating to the ethics of the human-constructed environment is that there presently isn't one!

I explained in chapter 1 that this lack of an ethics in respect of the human-constructed environment represents the lack of an ethics in respect of what we might think of as the third main realm of our existence, that is, the realm of material culture (which includes all the "stuff" that humans make) as opposed to the biophysical realm (which includes ecosystems and the plants and animals that live in them) or the realm of symbolic culture (which is constituted by language-using human moral agents). I also explained that any ethics that cannot directly address problems in this "third realm" is not even a candidate for a General Ethics. Thus, we can think of this last, human-constructed environment problem as a test for the *comprehensiveness* of any approach that is already able to address problems in respect of the biophysical and symbolic cultural realms. For this reason, it is convenient to refer to this problem not only as *the human-constructed environment problem* but also as *the comprehensiveness problem*, which is what I have done in the heading for this section. Moreover, the "two buildings example" that I gave in chapter 1—or some suitable elaboration of it (e.g., I offer a more complex "three buildings example" in chapter 6)—can be taken as the paradigmatic example of the kind of problem that any General Ethics must be able to address in this realm since this kind of example is careful to exclude any attempt to reduce problems in this realm to problems in one of the other realms. As we saw, this kind of example does this by offering a contrast in which, on the one hand, there is nothing to decide between two buildings at the level of concerns such as the maintenance of ecosystem integrity or people's overall preferences, but, on the other hand, there is much to decide between two buildings at the relatively intangible level of concerns regarding their design—specifically, their degree of contextual fit.

What Now?

I trust you will agree that the above eighteen problems represent a formidable range of problems for any single ethical approach to address. You might even think that attempting to come up with an integrated approach that addresses them all would have to be a fool's enterprise—and such late-night thoughts have certainly kept me awake at various times. Yet, if we are to develop a General Ethics—an ethical "Theory of Everything"—then this is the enterprise on which we must embark, in the hope of becoming a little wiser in the process. This quest therefore determines the structure of the rest of the book. Specifically, I will now proceed to develop my approach to General Ethics in chapters 3–8. I will then put all the elements of this approach together in summary form in chapter 9 before proceeding in chapter 10 to apply this approach to each of the eighteen problems that we have now considered in this chapter. Finally, I will offer some concluding thoughts in chapter 11 in regard to future developments in General Ethics.

II

The Foundational Value of Responsive Cohesion

3

Introducing the Idea of Responsive Cohesion

I refer to my own systematic attempt to develop a General Ethics as the *theory of responsive cohesion*. This theory represents a systematic attempt to address the "what," "why," and "how" questions of ethics: What values should we live by? Why should we live by these values? How should we live by these values? However, given the range and magnitude of the problems I have outlined that confront any attempt to develop a General Ethics, the theory that I will be developing here does not attempt to address these questions in a way that bears any particular relationship to the approaches that I have already outlined but rather represents an attempt to rethink ethics from the ground up. Partly for this reason, my exposition of the theory here begins in a way that might at first seem far removed from the range of problems that I have outlined in the previous chapter. However, once the theory has been fully developed, you will see that it ends up grappling precisely with these problems—and does so, I will argue, in a more sensible and defensible way than other approaches to date. With that in mind, let us proceed.

The Idea of the Foundational Value

Consider the initial question: "What value(s) should we live by?" If we were to answer this question in the plural ("These are the values that we ought to live by"), then that would inevitably raise the tantalizing possibility that there might be a still deeper level of analysis that would encompass these "basic" or "fundamental" values in a single, even more fundamental value—much as physicists believe that they will one day be able to theoretically unite the four "fundamental" forces of nature into a single, even more fundamental force from which they will then be able to derive the four forces that were previously thought of as "fundamental" (physicists refer to this Holy Grail of theoretical physics as a *Grand Unified Theory* [GUT] or a *Theory of Everything* [TOE]).[1] Moreover, in the case of ethics, if we accept that there are several "fundamental" values that we ought to live by, then it is difficult to know how we can resolve conflicts of value between them since if they are truly "fundamental," then, by definition, they cannot be reduced to each other or shown to be special instances of each other. This means that genuine conflicts of value between them are likely to be irresolvable because the values themselves are incommensurable, that is, incapable of being discussed in the same kinds of terms and therefore incapable of being compared with each other in a meaningful or nonarbitrary way. Alternatively, if we do have a way of comparing these values in a meaningful way, then that seems to suggest the existence of a deeper, still more fundamental level of analysis, which, in turn, belies the claim that these values are truly "fundamental."

There are, then, both theoretical and practical reasons for thinking, or at least desiring, that any truly fundamental theory of value should resolve to, or be drawn toward, a single ultimate value. If such a value did exist, what should we call it? Rather than calling this single ultimate value *the* fundamental value, I want to mark it out by stipulating that such a value should be referred to—or at least that I will refer to it as—the *foundational* value since it would underpin, or provide the foundations for, other kinds of values that we had hitherto thought of as "basic" or "fundamental." Note also that the term *the foundational value* is always preceded by the definite article "the" since I am defining this value, if it exists, as singular. If it is not, then we might be dealing with *some* fundamental values that cannot be reduced to each other (just as physicists would be dealing with *some* fundamental forces if it should turn out that their fundamental forces cannot be reduced to an even more primitive force), but we would not be dealing with what I am defining as *the foundational value* (or what physicists, for their part, might wish to think of as *the foundational force*).

These kinds of considerations raise two further important points. The first almost goes without saying, but needs to be said just the same. It is this: if a truly foundational value exists, then it stands to reason that we ought to live by this value—at least to the extent that we reasonably can. (This latter proviso is necessary because, as we will see in chapter 5, any moral *ought* has to imply a practical *can* for the straightforward reason that it makes no practical sense to require people to do something that they can't do—indeed, it is arguably *un*ethical to require this.) There would still be much cashing out to do of exactly what it would mean in practical terms to "live by" the foundational value, but it would nevertheless stand to reason that we ought, in some significant sense, to live by such a value to the extent that we reasonably can. The reason that this conclusion "stands to reason" is more or less self-evident: the best answer to the inescapable question "What value(s) should we live by?" is surely "The most fundamental value(s) we can discover" rather than "The second (or third or forty-second) most fundamental value(s) we can discover." (And this question *is* inescapable because we all live our lives by some values, whether by choice or by default, and whether we realize it or not—even the ethical nihilist and even the person who decides to make their choices by the throw of a dice.) It therefore stands to reason that if any form or source of value is to command our serious respect—our own high valuation—then it must surely be whatever form or source of value represents the most basic form or source of value we can discover. (Moreover, to value only the higher-level, or more superficial, manifestations of this value is itself superficial because it fails to value what it is that constitutes the ultimate basis of whatever it is that we are valuing—what it is that actually guarantees the value of what we are valuing.) Thus, if someone accepts that a truly foundational value exists, but proceeds to show by their actions that they have no intention of living by this value, then they are saying, in effect, that they recognize that there is a value that ought to command their serious respect (or high valuation) more than any other, but that they have no intention of respecting it in their actions.

This is clearly a perverse and ethically destructive stance. Although rational, ethically concerned citizens might disagree over questions regarding what is and is not valuable, they do not disagree that it is part and parcel of the notion of ascribing or recognizing value that this ascription is not meaningless but rather implies that we ought to act in ways that are responsive to these ascriptions or recognitions of value (at least insofar as these ascriptions or recognitions of value are held to have some kind of objective basis, that is, to be ultimately anchored in reality and not *only* in idiosyncratic personal preferences). An ascription or recognition of value (of the serious, not merely idiosyncratic personal preference kind) *means* something—and it means something in a normative sense, that is, in terms of what one ought to do, how one ought to behave. Thus, to accept that there is a foundational value, but that this means nothing, or very little, in terms of how one ought to behave is to have *missed the point* of what one has just accepted. Moreover, beyond a certain point, this kind of stance becomes tantamount to a declaration of war upon those who are ethically concerned—assuming that the individual concerned is even of sound mind (and the fact that this arises as an immediate consideration here itself tells us that something is going deeply wrong when a person behaves like this). Ethically cooperating citizens then have no choice but to react to this stance with all the social, economic, legal, and other sanctions that they consider it appropriate to muster.

This response might be intellectually unsatisfying, but we are never going to reach an intellectually satisfying resolution in this kind of situation because the kind of ethical nihilist whom I have just invoked is not interested in self-evident propositions, the reasonableness or otherwise of arguments, and so on. Rationally speaking, they are "not playing with a full deck," just a few cheap jokers. In contrast, rational, ethically concerned citizens ought to accept the self-evident reasonableness of the proposition that "If there is a foundational value, then we ought to live by it"—at least to the extent that we reasonably can. Living by the foundational value, if there is one, is simply the best answer that we will ever find to the question "What value(s) should we live by?"

The second important point I want to make in regard to the possible existence of the foundational value is as follows. If there were a value that is truly foundational, then it is likely to exist at a deep, general, or abstract level of analysis, even if it is essentially simple in the sense of not being reducible to any more primitive kind of fundamental value. But what form might this simple, deep, general, abstract value take? If we are serious about searching for a truly foundational value to live by—the ethical equivalent of a "Theory of Everything" or a Holy Grail of Ethics—then it would seem plausible that there is at least one thing that we should not expect to find. Specifically, we should not expect to find that this foundational value will come packaged in some convenient anthropocentric (or otherwise cosmically parochial) form. Just as physicists have long since given up the expectation that their longed-for "Theory of Everything" will come in this form, so ethicists searching for the foundational value should also give up this expectation. If they did, then it would free them to be more adventurous in their search for a rationally well-grounded, practically workable, and fully comprehensive ethics.

An important step in giving up the expectation that any foundational value is likely to come packaged in some convenient anthropocentric form lies in the following direction. Although we have been used to thinking about notions of value in terms of mental states—with human consciousness as the paradigmatic example—we need to get clear about the distinction between what is required for the registration or *recognition* of value, which *will* be some form of conscious awareness (although not necessarily human), and the *source* of value itself. If a candidate source of value can plausibly be shown to be a source of value for all conscious agents that are cognitively competent to recognize that value (or at least a great many, barring rationally perverse exceptions), then it makes no sense to map the source of the value onto the conscious mental states of the recognizer or valuer. The source of the value in this case is clearly *in the world*, and to mistake the source of the value with the locus of its recognition goes in the direction of saying that the mountains we see on the moon through a telescope are actually in the telescope rather than on the moon—or worse, in the head, since it is our consciousness that recognizes the mountains with the aid of the telescope. Saying that value only inheres in mental states, in other words, is to accept the anthropocentrically fueled idealist fantasy that values do not have their source in the world but are merely projected upon the world by (human) valuers. Reducing values to such a subjective basis, by eliminating any objective anchor in the world for them, can—it doesn't have to, but it can—all too easily fuel in its turn the relativist position that one person's values are just as good as anyone else's. Idealism, subjectivism, relativism—these constitute an ethically deadly slippery slope. After all, what is the point of ethics if one person's values (Hitler's, for example) are just as good as anyone else's?

The way to put an end to this type of nonsense is, to repeat, to insist on the distinction between the recognition of value and the source of value itself. This then enables us to make judgments of the following kinds, which seem eminently defensible to us in everyday life. Specifically, if, say, only one person in the world thinks that something is genuinely valuable—that is, valuable in its own right and not simply because of its usefulness to the valuer or because of some idiosyncratic personal preference on the part of the valuer—then it seems reasonable to say that the source of the value would indeed seem to be more a function of that person projecting a value upon the thing in question than of any independently existing source of value that really is intrinsic to the thing itself, and which everyone else has somehow missed (i.e., it starts to look as if the valuer is expressing some kind of merely personal preference, despite what they themselves think). But if, say, most people—and even extraterrestrials as well, if we can find them—consider that something is genuinely valuable, then it seems more reasonable in this case to say that the source of the value is more a function of the thing itself, which is widely *found* to be valuable, than of the idiosyncratic personal projections of the valuers, which just "happen" to coincide in this case. (Philosophers will often introduce the technical notion of *supervenience* in this context—they will say that certain kinds of value *supervene* upon certain kinds or forms of things—but one hardly needs to resort to this kind of quite slippery technical language in order to make the basic distinction between the recognition of value and its source.) The argument about what is genuinely valuable is therefore not an argument over what kinds of things are capable of consciously recognizing values but rather what kinds of things can plausibly be argued to be sources of value such that any cognitively competent valuer is likely to find them valuable.

In this section on "the idea of the foundational value" I have argued as follows. First, the ultimate ethical theory—the ethical "Theory of Everything," or the Holy Grail of ethics—would be an ethical theory that proceeded from a single, *foundational* value. Second, if the foundational value exists, then it stands to reason that we ought to "live by" this value. Third, if the foundational value exists, then it is likely to exist at such a deep, general, or abstract level of analysis that we should not expect it to come packaged in some convenient anthropocentric (or otherwise cosmically parochial) form, such as consisting in human mental states and human mental states alone. I then noted that an important step in giving up the expectation that any foundational value is likely to come packaged in some convenient anthropocentric form lies in the direction of getting clear about the distinction between the recognition of value, which will consist in some form of conscious awareness (although not necessarily human), and the source of value itself.

The Theory of Responsive Cohesion I: Preliminary Considerations

The argument that I will be advancing over the next two chapters makes the claim that the source of the most fundamental value there is in the world—the foundational value—consists in a basic *relational quality* or *form of organization* that can be described as one of *responsive cohesion*. I will explain what I mean by the term *responsive cohesion* in the next section, but, for now, it is more immediately important to make the following terminological notes. The terms *relational quality* and *form of organization* can often be used interchangeably, and I will do so as appropriate. On the whole, however, I will tend to use the term *relational quality* as that term seems to make it more obvious that its usage is intended to be applicable to physical as well as nonphysical things, such as, for example, meanings (e.g., the meanings of visual signs, or of words and sentences). In contrast, the term *form of organization* can tend to sound as if it is referring to physically instantiated things, even though its usage need not be restricted in this way.

As we will see in what follows, the theory of responsive cohesion advances a tripartite categorization of relational qualities or forms of organization, which I will refer to as *fixed cohesion, responsive cohesion,* and *discohesion,* and advances the claim that one of these relational qualities—responsive cohesion—is more valuable than the other two and ought to be respected as such. Thus, the theory of responsive cohesion is a *normative* theory of relational qualities; it tells us what relational qualities *ought* to be respected.

This peek at what is to come raises five preliminary points that we need to bear in mind when I come to elaborating the theory itself. First, as we will see, the theory of responsive cohesion is pitched at the broadest or most comprehensive possible level of discussion in that it proceeds in terms of arguing for the value or otherwise of certain basic relational qualities or forms of organization that "things" can have, and *everything* can be classified as having certain relational qualities or being organized in one way or another—even if that means saying that the thing in question lacks *relational* qualities, that it is *not* organized, that it is *disorganized*. This point can be reinforced by noting that the usefully nonspecific term "things" in the above context is intended to refer to anything at all: people's minds, people's relationships, arrangements of physical stuff, arrangements of units of meaning, arrangements of shapes and colors—whatever.

Second, in outlining the theory, I will be speaking in terms of the way in which the relational qualities that different things have can be "characterized" rather than in terms of the way they "are." There is an obvious reason for this: the relationships that exist between things don't exist in the same way that, say, a cup or a book does. We can pick up a cup or a book, but we can't (physically) pick up the relationship that exists *between* things (or between the component elements of things), even though it is clear that such relationships exist. It is therefore obvious, in the case of relationships at least, that the nature of the relationship that exists between any set of things must be *inferred*, that it is subject to *interpretation*, and that the case for that interpretation must be made out and defended against rival interpretations if it is to be considered to be a defensible interpretation. Having said this, however, it is important to point out that the situation is actually no different even when it comes to obviously physical things like cups and books. It just seems that the characterization of relational qualities is a more interpretive affair than the characterization of cups and books *as* cups and books because relational qualities are intangible whereas cups and books are tangible. Yet we are in fact interpreting the world every moment of the day, whether we are talking about relational qualities or the identification of cups and books *as* cups and books. Indeed, if there is a single basic message that comes out of the cognitive sciences in general, it is this: we don't see the world "as it is" (whatever that might mean); rather, we interpret it. This obviously applies to the ways in which we characterize relational qualities or forms of organization, but then it applies to everything else as well.

Third, the interpretations we offer of the relational qualities that exist between any set of things will always be to greater or lesser extent metaphorical. But this just comes with the territory of interpretation. Our interpretations are *always* metaphorically loaded. As Jeremy Campbell notes in a well regarded overview of artificial intelligence and cognitive science, our interpreting device—the mind—is

> a great deal less literal-minded than we might suppose, in all its various and sundry dealings with the world.... As far as psychology is concerned, there is no clear distinction between the two kinds of language [i.e., literal and metaphorical language], and an artificial device that is unable to deal with metaphor is likely to be too weak to cope with the plainest prose. The mind seems to be metaphorical to its foundations.[2]

This means that the relational qualities that pertain to things that seem to exist in fundamentally different kinds of ways—such as cups and books on the one hand and thoughts and emotions on the other hand—can often quite easily be described using the same kind of language: it is just that in some cases we might interpret this language as applying "literally" whereas in other cases we might interpret it as applying "metaphorically."

What I'm driving at here is that, in referring to the relational *qualities* that different things have, I want to make it clear at the outset that I am not just talking about *physical* things that can be (as we say) *literally* organized into certain *physically* instantiated patterns. Rather, the theory of responsive cohesion can be applied to any frame of reference or domain of interest at all. We have no trouble, day-to-day, speaking of the relational qualities that are possessed by things that are obviously physical and things that are not obviously physical. For example, we can equally well say that someone's desk is "chaotic" or "all over the place," that someone's verbal presentation is "chaotic" or "all over the place," or that someone's mental state is "chaotic" or "all over the place." The desk example refers to a relational quality that is instantiated in an obviously physical way. However, the second two examples are not instantiated in anything like the same obviously physical way—we can't show someone a jumble of meanings or a jumble of thoughts and emotions in the same way in which we can show them a jumble of books, files, and papers. We are therefore often tempted to say that we are speaking *metaphorically* in the second two instances rather than *literally*. Even so, we have no trouble, day-to-day, understanding that a similar general relational *quality* (or form of organization) is being said to apply in each case, regardless of whether or not what we are saying might formally be *characterized* as applying literally or metaphorically.

For the sake of ease of exposition in what follows, I am simply going to outline the theory of responsive cohesion in the most straightforward terms I can and so (at least to a great extent) omit references to the allegedly literal or metaphorical senses in which my central organizing categories of fixed cohesion, responsive cohesion, and discohesion will be employed. This might run the risk of allowing my discussion to sound in places as if I am only talking about the relational qualities of tangible, physically instantiated things, but the point of advancing these preliminary remarks *as* preliminary remarks has been precisely to kill off any such interpretation.

The fourth point that needs to be made here is this: specifying something as deep, general, and abstract as a relational quality (or form of organization) as the foundational value that lies at the basis of a complete ethics is clearly an example of specifying a foundational value that does not come packaged in some convenient anthropocentric (or otherwise cosmically parochial) form. That is, this foundational value is not specifying, say, pleasurable (or, at least, preferred) *human* mental states or respect for *persons* as ends-in-themselves (and, hence, respect for their *autonomy*, or freedom to be self-determining) as anything like the foundational value of ethics—even though these two values are undoubtedly important (especially to us!) and can roughly be thought of as lying at the basis of the great ethical systems of classical utilitarianism and Kantian ethics respectively. (Although utilitarianism has always been theoretically committed to the incorporation of concerns regarding the interests of all sentient beings, it was really not until Peter Singer's intervention that this theoretical commitment was taken seriously. Prior to that utilitarianism had generally been discussed in a purely anthropocentric context, notwithstanding its obvious theoretical commitments.) The point I want to drive home here, then, is this: if it can indeed be shown that something as deep, general, and abstract as a *relational quality* lies at the foundation of a comprehensive approach to ethics, such that other significant values like pleasurable human mental states and a recognition of the value of persons as ends-in-themselves can be *incorporated into* this broader and deeper ethical framework, then these previously thought of "fundamentals" will start to look theoretically rather shallow and parochial in comparison. (Hmmm, now there's a title to conjure with: *The Unbearable "Liteness" of Traditional Forms of Ethics*.)

The fifth and final point I want to make here requires some exposition, but ends up delivering an even more serious charge against the classical modern approaches to normative ethics of Kantian ethics and utilitarianism than the charge of being *theoretically* shallow and parochial. This new charge is that these dominant modern approaches have in fact aided and abetted what amount to acts of vandalism on a planetary scale. Let us consider this serious charge.

The theory of responsive cohesion is concerned with identifying the deepest, most general source of value that exists. Now, if we draw upon the distinction made earlier between sources of value and the conscious registration or recognition of value, then we can say that the classical modern approaches to normative ethics of Kantian ethics and utilitarianism effectively collapse this distinction such that the only things that are considered to be genuine, independent, or intrinsic sources of value— sources of value in their own right—are the recognizers of value themselves. Moreover, the class of recognizers of value in these approaches has typically been limited to the class of human beings. Consider: the general thrust of Kantian ethics is one in which only human beings are recognized as being "ends in themselves"; nothing else is considered to be valuable in its own right (i.e., intrinsically valuable). And prior to Peter Singer's intervention, the only form of intrinsic value that utilitarian ethicists really took seriously was the pleasurable or (in later, arguably more advanced, versions) preferentially satisfied mental states of human beings. Thus, in both Kantian ethics and the dominant, traditional versions of utilitarianism (which are far from dead), the only things or beings in the world that are considered to be valuable in their own right are the recognizers of value themselves, or their mental states, where, to repeat, the recognizers of value are construed narrowly as corresponding to the class of human beings.

The problem with these approaches is that if our ethical focus is entirely upon the recognizers of value (because they are the only things or beings in the world that are intrinsically valuable), then this essentially permits these recognizers of value to value whatever they wish to, in whatever ways they wish to, subject to respect for other recognizers of value to do the same. The upshot of this view is that the dominant mainstream approaches to ethics, whether wittingly or unwittingly, have sanctioned the development of a world in which it makes sense to pave paradises with parking lots—to borrow a memorable image from Joni Mitchell's song "Big Yellow Taxi." After all, if humans are the only intrinsically valuable things or beings in the world, and if turning a wetland into a shopping complex—complete with parking lot—is my way of exercising my autonomy in order to make lots of money so as to live a life of continual preference satisfaction, and if, in doing this, I am not unduly interfering with your freedom to do much the same, then what the hell, hey? Put like this, we can see the sense in which the anthropocentric mainstream approaches to ethics can be charged with having aided and abetted what amount to acts of vandalism on a planetary scale. And put like this, it is obvious what these anthropocentric mainstream approaches to ethics leave out, namely, a detailed consideration of exactly what general sources of value we should attempt to preserve and create—out there, in the world—in order to have *sources of value that are worth recognizing.*

Some of the classical mainstream ethicists have been aware of this problem at some level. For example, J. S. Mill famously tried to refine Bentham's classical formulation of utilitarianism by distinguishing between "higher" (or more refined) and "lower" (or more base or coarse) pleasures. At first blush, this move does indeed seem to go in the direction of suggesting that some sources of value are inherently better than others and so ultimately serve to guide and inspire the development of an inherently better world. However, Mill still justified his argument in favor of higher pleasures in terms of the richness of pleasure that these higher pleasures would ultimately bestow upon the experiencers of pleasure. Thus, the emphasis was still ultimately fixed upon the conscious mental states of the recognizers of value rather than venturing deeply into the question of what potential sources of value really are valuable, or are the most valuable examples of their kind, irrespective of how much pleasure or preference satisfaction they might or might not bestow upon the recognizer of value. (Indeed, this question is not even thinkable within a classical utilitarian framework since the greatest or "sovereign" good is defined *in terms of* the pleasurable or preferentially satisfied mental states of human beings.) The upshot is that Mill left himself wide open to attack from those who would say, in true self-determining, democratic spirit, "Who are you to tell me that the pleasure I get from watching my favorite sport on TV or making a bet on the horses is a lower, or in some sense less significant, pleasure than the pleasure that some others might get from watching opera or playing chess?"

The widely accepted force of this criticism returns us to the inescapable fact that if our ethical focus is upon the recognizers of value, then this essentially permits these recognizers of value to value whatever they wish to, in whatever ways they wish to, subject to respect for other recognizers of value to do the same. And this returns us to our previous point regarding paving paradises with parking lots and the general criticism that the anthropocentric mainstream approaches to ethics have aided and abetted what amount to acts of vandalism on a planetary scale. Thus, to the charge that the fundamental values of the dominant mainstream approaches to ethics would look pretty "lite" if it turned out that something as deep, general, and abstract as a *relational quality* lies at the foundations of a comprehensive approach ethics, we can also add this one: in focusing ethical attention exclusively or overwhelmingly upon the *recognizers* of value, the dominant mainstream approaches to ethics must be viewed as implicated in having made much of the world an uglier and drearier place than it might have been.

In contrast to these approaches, we will see that the theory of responsive cohesion advocates a fundamentally different kind of approach. More specifically, we will see that the relational quality of responsive cohesion picks out a feature of the world that is so deep and general that it includes many, many more kinds of things as being intrinsically valuable than just the class of recognizers of value, although it does of course include them as well. But so what? Why is this important? Well, if it is the case that the relational quality of responsive cohesion can be shown to represent the foundational value that lies at the basis of a comprehensive approach to ethics, then it follows that self-conscious recognizers of value (moral agents) should respect the relational quality of responsive cohesion in the world *generally*.

This has been quite a list of preliminary considerations to keep in mind, so here is a summary. I began by indicating that I will be arguing that the foundational value does indeed exist and that it corresponds to a relational quality or form of organization that can be characterized as *responsive cohesion*. Several further setting-the-scene considerations followed from this. First, the theory of responsive cohesion is intended to apply as broadly as possible (that is, to apply to any item of interest at all). Second, this theory should be explicitly understood as being concerned with the *characterization* of relational qualities, which are, of course, a matter of interpretation. Third, the central organizing categories of the theory of responsive cohesion (namely, *fixed cohesion*, *responsive cohesion*, and *discohesion*) should be explicitly understood as cutting across the literal/metaphorical distinction. (The fact that the central categories of the theory are intended to apply to both tangible and intangible items of interest—which is covered by the first point here—and the fact that we tend to associate literal and metaphorical usages of terms with their application to tangible and intangible things respectively means that this third point follows as a matter of course.) Fourth, if it is the case that my claim about the foundational nature of the relational quality of responsive cohesion can be made out, then the kinds of anthropocentrically focused values that have been thought of as constituting the fundamental values of some of the great ethical systems that have dominated the modern period will start to look theoretically shallow and parochial—quite "lite"—in comparison. Fifth, these dominant ethical approaches will also be revealed as having aided and abetted what amounts to acts of vandalism on a planetary scale. This is because these approaches have identified the *recognizers* of value as the only genuine or intrinsic *sources* of value in the world and this, in turn, has meant that the recognizers of value have been viewed as being at liberty to value whatever they wish to, in whatever ways they wish to, subject to respect for other (likewise intrinsically valuable) recognizers of value to do the same. In contrast, the theory of responsive cohesion is concerned with (i) identifying the deepest, most general source of value that exists; (ii) showing that this source of value includes but extends well beyond the class of human beings, or well beyond the class of recognizers of value in general; and (iii) arguing that we should respect this foundational source of value in each and every context of interest.

With these scene-setting, preliminary considerations out of the way, we can now proceed to introduce properly the main organizing categories in the theory of responsive cohesion.

The Theory of Responsive Cohesion II: Introducing the Central Organizing Categories

Anything of interest to us can be characterized in terms of its relational qualities (or form, kind, or pattern of organization). We can characterize relational qualities in many, many different ways. For example, we might say that two people have a *good* or a *bad* relationship, or a *contented* or a *stormy* relationship; that two subatomic particles interact *strongly* or *weakly*—or have *no relationship with each other at all*; that two propositions *contradict* each other, are (merely) *consistent* with each other, or mutually *support* each other; that two colors *contrast sharply* with each other or *blend in well together*. You get the idea.

Now the most fundamental distinction that we can make between things in terms of their relational qualities (or form of organization) is, naturally enough, between things that can be characterized *as* relating to each other in some way (or *as* organized in some way) and things that cannot. Things that can be characterized as relating to each other (or as organized) in one way or another can be said to "hold together," "hang together," or *cohere* in some way. (Dictionary definitions of "hold together" and "hang together" render their meanings precisely in terms of the concept of cohesion: "to cohere or remain or cause to cohere or remain in one piece" and "to be cohesive or united" respectively.[3]) Things that cannot be characterized as relating to each other (or as organized) in one way or another cannot be said to "hold together," "hang together," or cohere. Instead, we typically characterize such instances as being chaotic, anarchic, "all over the place," in disarray, a mess, as having "no logic to them," and so on.

This gives us a basic distinction between the relational quality of *cohesion* and the relational quality of (what I will refer to as) *discohesion*. These terms are fundamental to the theory of responsive cohesion, so it is important to be as explicit as possible about their meanings. The term "cohere"—surely one of the most significant and beautiful words in the language—literally means to cling, hold, stick, or adhere together (from Latin *cohaerēre*, from *co-* together + *haerēre* to cling, adhere). In contrast, I am using the obvious neologism *discohesion* (on the analogy of, say, *order* and *disorder*) to indicate a lack or absence of cohesion (the prefix *dis-* being used, as standard, to indicate reversal, negation, lack, deprivation, removal, or release; thus, the elements *dis- + co- + haerēre* add up, etymologically, to the meaning "lack of clinging or adhering together"). It would, of course, be tempting simply to use the common terms "chaos" or "anarchy" instead of the term *discohesion* here, but the former terms nowadays carry such a burden of more specialized associations—mathematical-scientific in the case of "chaos" and political in the case of "anarchy"—that I hesitate to use them as my formal way of labeling the basic, essentially simple notion of lack or absence of cohesion. Thus, my formal term for the lack or absence of cohesion is *discohesion*, which, by virtue of being a neologism, does not carry a preexisting burden of uninvited associations. I will still use the terms "chaos" and "anarchy" in the nonspecialized, everyday senses of "complete disorder" or being "all over the place" in order to characterize instances *of* discohesion, but I hope that, by using the term *discohesion* as my formal term for this category of relational quality, I will avoid any uninvited semantic interference effects. In any case, the neologism *discohesion* is, syntactically speaking, such an obvious contrast with the term "cohesion" that it is hard to believe that the word does not already exist.

Two important points must immediately follow upon the identification of the cohesion/discohesion distinction. The first is that instances of cohesion and discohesion can obviously be brought about in all manner of ways. Thus, the category of discohesion, for example, will come into play not only in those cases where there presently is and always has existed a lack of relationship between certain things but also where one is speaking about things whose typical or ideal relationship to each other has, say, simply decayed or "fallen apart" on the one hand or been forcibly destroyed or "blown apart" on the other hand. There are, in short, many, many ways in which things can simply fail to cohere or come to fail to cohere; likewise, there are many, many ways in which things can cohere or come to cohere.

The second point is that there is obviously a *continuum* between clear examples of cohesion and discohesion; we are not talking in terms of black-and-white categories here. That said, however, this distinction does, and ought to, play a powerful and fundamental role in our existence, for even to identify something—anything at all—*as* such-and-such a thing is to identify a set of *elements* or *features* as *constituent elements* or *salient features* of that thing. That is, it is to identify a set of elements or features as belonging together, "hanging together," or cohering in such a way as to constitute such-and-such a thing—such as a cat, a conversation, or a car—and not something else.

I will be using the general phrase "the elements or salient features" (of whatever we wish to consider) quite a lot in what follows so let me elaborate on this phrase a little more so that its meaning is quite clear. By "the elements or salient features" of something—anything at all, not necessarily a tangible object—I mean the elements or salient features that constitute it *as* the thing in question, that is, under the description that has been applied to it, for example, "a painting." Thus, the precise natures of the molecules that constitute the canvas of a painting are of marginal relevance to our consideration of the painting as a *painting* whereas the brush strokes of paint are "the elements or salient features" that constitute the painting *as* a painting. Identifiable formations of paint—the main compositional aspects of the painting—in turn constitute higher-level "elements or salient features" that constitute the painting *as* a painting. There can of course be considerable debate about precisely what the elements or salient features of something *as* that something really are, but this should not obscure the fact that we also experience a tremendous amount of day-to-day agreement about these kinds of things. For example, we all agree that assemblages of certain elements or salient features are, unquestionably, "cats," "conversations," "cars," or whatever. We experience such a wide degree of unchallenged agreement about things of this kind that we generally don't need to think twice about most of the identifications that we make in our day-to-day lives.

Having now distinguished between cohesion and discohesion, I need to make an equally crucial distinction in regard to the kinds of ways in which things can be said to cohere. We can refer to these two basic forms of cohesion as *fixed cohesion* and *responsive cohesion*. Fixed cohesion can be characterized as the kind of cohesion that exists:

(i) When things hold together with a minimal or relatively insignificant degree of mutually modifying interaction between the elements or salient features that define them. Example: the collection of molecules that collectively constitute a rock or a brick as a rock or a brick. This can apply at a less tangible, metaphorical level as well, such as between the elements or salient features of a painting, where these features are, as it were, stuck together, but there is "nothing happening between them."

(ii) When things are forced and fixed into place because of some fixed (immovable, nonnegotiable, intransigent, dictatorial) master feature that exists within the thing that interests us. Example: a dictator whom people are forced to obey in the case of a certain society.

(iii) When things are effectively forced and fixed into place by some externally imposed blueprint, master plan, or formula. Example: a hackneyed, stereotypical TV script that is "as predictable as clockwork."

(iv) When things hold together—perhaps even in a (literally or metaphorically) interactive way that seems neither unduly forced from within nor unduly forced from without (and, thus, they hold together in a way that stands in contrast to each of the first three points respectively)—but do so at the expense of screening out a whole range of the salient features of the situation under consideration. An example of this more complicated variety of fixed cohesion would be the all-the-fun-of-the-fair, higgledy-piggledy, seafront development of a strip of gaudy amusement arcades, thrill rides, hamburger joints, and so on that betray not even a hint in their "design" of taking into account the highly salient fact that they represent a transition between a bustling town behind them and a seashore in front of them. (We could imagine that this seafront development had just been parachuted in and happened to land between this particular town and this particular seafront.)

In this case, it is as if the people who developed the seafront have been tuned to a very narrow waveband of the broad range of salient features that apply in that situation. The upshot is a seafront development that, despite whatever cohesive qualities it might have in its own (blatantly tacky) fashion, represents the social and architectural equivalent of a fixed idea: In this case, "We're bright and shiny; what more do you need to have fun? Hand over your money!" The answer to the rhetorical question here is that we ought to want a lot more. As it happens, the powers-that-be behind the actual situation I have in mind here realize that they need to change *something*; however, it turns out that their idea of improving their tacky and tactless seafront is one of building glitzier versions of the same thing. But this is just like turning up the volume on the same narrow bandwidth that is presently being received and broadcasted. It does nothing to address the full range of salient features that apply in this situation, such as the fact that this area represents a transition between a bustling town and its seashore.

Another example of this fourth, more complicated variety of fixed cohesion would be someone whose conversation holds together extremely well and who may even be able to vary the way in which they say things every time you talk with them (come up with new angles, and so on) but who always talks about the same thing (perhaps themselves!). They, too, are in the grip of an *idée fixe*; they, too, are tuned to a very narrow bandwidth within the full range of salient features that are relevant to the situation, in this case, social interaction.

Examples like this do represent complex cases because, up to a point, they can be viewed as representing instances of (what I will outline below as) responsive cohesion, but *only* up to a point. This is because any thoughtful inspection reveals them to be low-level (or, in the case of "tacky" building developments, it might be more appropriate to say "low-rent") examples of responsive cohesion, for they are so severely constrained in terms of the range of salient features to which they are responsive that they are more appropriately thought of as being an *apparent* form of responsive cohesion that is actually *stuck*, or *fixed*, within an inappropriately limited range of responsive options. We could therefore refer to this kind of relational quality as *paradoxical fixed cohesion* since the term "paradox" can be used to denote "a person or thing exhibiting apparently contradictory characteristics," and here we are meaning to refer to a relational quality that can superficially appear to be an example of responsive cohesion but whose deeper features are actually better understood in terms of being stuck or fixed within an inappropriately limited range of responsive options (thus, one could also refer to this kind of relational quality as *narrow bandwidth fixed cohesion*).

In summary, then, instances of fixed cohesion occur when something can be said to hold together, or cohere, in one way or another but to do so on the basis of little or no significantly mutually modifying interaction between its elements or salient features (the rock/brick example); disproportionately one-way direction of elements or salient features from within (the dictator example); disproportionately one-way direction of elements or salient features from without (the formulaic script example); or an obvious failure to appreciate the full range of salient features that apply to the situation under discussion (the seafront development and tedious conversationalist examples). We could, for convenience, label these varieties of fixed cohesion, respectively, as *inert fixed cohesion*, *internally imposed fixed cohesion*, *externally imposed fixed cohesion*, and *paradoxical fixed cohesion* (or *narrow bandwidth fixed cohesion*). There may be other varieties too, but I hope not. There's more than enough fixed cohesion—and varieties thereof—in the world as it is!

In contrast, the relational quality of responsive cohesion may be said to exist *whenever the elements or salient features of things can be characterized in terms of interacting (either literally or metaphorically) with each other in mutually modifying ways such that these mutually modifying interactions serve (at least functionally if not intentionally) to generate or maintain an overall cohesive order—an order that "hangs together" in one way or another*. Let me clarify the parenthetical additions to this complex sentence in order to make things as clear as possible. To begin with, I have spoken in terms of things interacting either *literally* or *metaphorically* with each other in order to make it clear that we are not just talking about things that can be characterized as interacting with each other in literal, physical ways, such as the ways in which, say, the components of a living system or the biosphere in general can be said to interact. Rather, we are also talking about things that can be characterized as interacting with each other in less obviously physical ways, but as interacting nonetheless, such as the ways in which, say, the meanings of the various sentences of a novel or the forms and colors in a painting can be said to play off each other so as to mutually modify the ways in which these elements or salient features are understood or perceived. Moreover, I have also spoken in terms of these mutually modifying interactions serving *functionally if not intentionally* to generate or maintain an overall cohesive order in order to make it clear that instances of responsive cohesion can be brought about not only as a result of deliberate intention (as in the examples I've just used of novels and paintings) but also as a result of the kinds of purely nonintentional, spontaneous self-organizing processes that are common in nature and which constitute the stock-in-trade of evolutionary theorists and complexity theorists in general. In the case of these kinds of self-organizing processes, we can say that the mutually modifying interactions that are of interest to us serve *functionally* to generate or maintain an overall cohesive order (i.e., they can be characterized as fulfilling that *function* in the overall economy of the system, such as an ecosystem) without in any way committing ourselves to the view that there is anything *intentional* about these processes. Thus, just as we have already seen in the case of discohesion and fixed cohesion, instances of responsive cohesion can be brought about in many ways, including some fundamentally different *kinds* of ways.

With these clarifications in mind, allow me, if you will, to repeat the admittedly complex opening sentence of the previous paragraph to which these clarifications obtain and then proceed with my exposition of responsive cohesion: the relational quality of responsive cohesion may be said to exist whenever the elements or salient features of things can be characterized in terms of interacting (either literally or metaphorically) with each other in mutually modifying ways such that these mutually modifying interactions serve (at least functionally if not intentionally) to generate or maintain an overall cohesive order—an order that "hangs together" in one way or another. Now the fact that these (literal or metaphorical) interactions are *mutually modifying* means that they can be characterized as being (functionally or intentionally) *responsive* to each other. Thus, *responsive cohesion is cohesion that arises through the mutual responsiveness of the elements or salient features of the matter under consideration* (regardless of whether that responsiveness can best be characterized as intentional or merely functional, literal or metaphorical).

It is also extremely useful in these cases to speak of the elements or salient features of the thing in question as (literally or metaphorically) *answering* to each other in some sense—and not necessarily in an entirely agreeable way either, but at least answering to each other with a sufficient overall (or system-wide) degree of agreement as not to fall into a state of discohesion. Thinking in terms of the ways in which things can be characterized as answering to each other is an instructive and illuminating way of approaching the judgment of whether something can or cannot fairly be characterized as exhibiting the relational quality of responsive cohesion. This extremely useful *responsiveness = answering to* formulation follows quite naturally from the root meanings of these terms for the word "response," from which the adjectival term "responsive" is derived, derives from the Latin *rēsponsum*, which itself means "answer."

Yet even here we really want to say more: specifically, we really want to say that true responsiveness occurs when things can be characterized as answering to each other in a deep, significant, meaningful, or genuine sense as opposed to a superficial, insignificant, "going-through-the-motions," or inauthentic sense. For example, consider the paradigmatic example of responsiveness: a conversation. Some conversations take the form of more or less unvarying, routine exchanges, perhaps because they are conducted in a highly regimented or bureaucratic context, perhaps because the two people involved have simply become "stuck in a rut" such that their exchanges now have a "going-through-the-motions" quality about them, and so on—we all know these conversations! Other conversations take the form of people more or less "talking past each other," each being a slave to their own agenda or ego such that neither of them really "hears" the other person. Yet other conversations take the form of people genuinely responding to each other such that the conversation develops in a wholly coherent, yet fluid, nonroutine way. (Interestingly, these conversations are the only ones that are true to the hopes embodied in the word "conversation" itself for "converse" comes from the Latin *conversārī*, "to keep company with," and this word comes in turn from *conversāre*, "to turn constantly," from *verter*, "to turn"; thus, the beautiful promise embodied in the word "conversation" itself of "keeping company with each other through constant turnings.") Now people can be said to be "answering" to each other in the first and third of these examples, but hardly in the second if they are really "talking past each other." However, the kind of "answering" that is involved in the first and third examples is dramatically different: it is a superficial, insignificant, "going-through-the-motions," inauthentic form of answering in the first example—a kind of pseudo-answering—whereas it is a deep, significant, meaningful, or genuine form of answering in the third example.

These examples clearly represent examples of fixed cohesion in the first case because the conversation "holds together" but in a predictable, thoroughly routine, or fixed way; discohesion in the second case because the parties to the conversation "talk past each other" such that their conversation "doesn't add up" to any sort of cohesive whole; and responsive cohesion in the third case precisely because the participants do indeed "keep company with each other through constant turnings." Moreover, it should be clear that the kind of answering that we are talking about in the case of responsive cohesion is one in which there is a deep, significant, meaningful, or genuine form of answering between the elements or salient features that make up the conversation. Thus, when we look at the ways in which the elements or salient features of something can be said to "answer to each other" in order to decide whether the thing in question is an instance of responsive cohesion or not, we need to bear in mind that we are talking about answering in the deep, significant, meaningful, or genuine sense. Alas, we cannot give a simple definition of this "deep" sense, even though we can point to all kinds of good examples of it. But as the adjective "deep" itself suggests, this sense is something one gets a better and better "feel" for and understanding of in particular areas as one *deepens* one's study of these areas. Even so, you don't need to be a genius to know when a conversation with someone is "stuck in a rut" or "going around in circles" (and, hence, an example of fixed cohesion in the domain of conversation), or when the two of you are "not connecting at all" or "talking past each other" (and, hence, an example of discohesion in the domain of conversation), or when it is just "flowing" (and, hence, an example of responsive cohesion in the domain of conversation). However, even here, it can of course still help to have studied the finer points of conversational communication.

Having now briefly distinguished between fixed cohesion and responsive cohesion it is important to echo the same two points that I made after introducing the cohesion/discohesion distinction: first, as already indicated, instances of fixed cohesion and responsive cohesion can be brought about in a great many ways, including, within each category, some fundamentally different kinds of ways; and, second, there is obviously a continuum between clear examples of fixed cohesion and responsive cohesion; we are not talking in terms of black-or-white categories here either (my category of paradoxical fixed cohesion speaks to this point especially).

I now want to elaborate further upon the distinction between fixed cohesion and responsive cohesion because it is important that we get as clear as possible about what is and is not meant by this distinction. In particular, it is important to point out that although the term *fixed cohesion* might sound as if it refers only to some completely static order, this need not be the case. As has already been suggested by the conversation example, things can be *dynamically* "fixed in place" in the sense that they follow in some predictable, fixed, and determined sequence. (Moreover, this sequence might be endlessly repetitive *or it might not be*; e.g., consider the phenomenon of what chaos and complexity theorists refer to as "deterministic chaos." Superficially, this appears to be an example of discohesion, but at a deeper level of analysis, it is revealed as an example of fixed cohesion, albeit an example of nonrepetitive fixed cohesion!) It is this general sense of the term *fixed*, as opposed to the more simplistic *fixed = static* understanding, that I have in mind when I refer to examples of fixed cohesion. We are talking, in other words, about things that hold together in a way that exhibits a rigid or frozen order (and hence a metaphorically static order), regardless of whether or not this order is literally static or dynamic.

In contrast, things that exhibit responsive cohesion hold together in a way that exhibits a more flexible or fluid order (and hence a metaphorically dynamic order), regardless of whether this order is literally static or dynamic. For example, the marks of paint on a canvas do not literally move, they are not literally dynamic; and yet we have no problem in understanding what it means to say that one (literally static) painting is (metaphorically speaking) more *fluid* than another, or that its salient features are more *responsive* to each other than those in another painting.

It follows that the terms *fixed cohesion* and *responsive cohesion* cannot be neatly mapped on to the distinction between (literally) static order and (literally) dynamic order. Things that are literally or physically *dynamic* (i.e., that change) can nevertheless exhibit the relational quality of *fixed* cohesion. Conversely, things that are literally or physically *static* can nevertheless exhibit the relational quality of *responsive* cohesion. For example, the meanings embodied in the physically fixed word order of a novel or a play, or the colors and forms of a physically fixed canvas of dried paint, can feed into and play off each other in such a way as to exhibit a greater or lesser degree of the relational quality of modifying each other, or answering to each other, in such a way as to create an overall quality of *responsive* cohesion.

The most obvious example of the distinction that we implicitly make in everyday life between (what I am referring to as) responsive cohesion and fixed cohesion occurs when we distinguish between living things and nonliving things respectively. Healthy, thriving living organisms are obvious embodiments of the relational quality of responsive cohesion whereas rocks and bricks are obvious physical instantiations of the relational quality of fixed cohesion. Yet, here too, the terms *responsive cohesion* and *fixed cohesion* cannot be neatly mapped on to the distinction between (literally) living things and (literally) nonliving things. This is because the distinction between living and nonliving things immediately lends itself to metaphorical uses as well, and the *responsive cohesion/ fixed cohesion* distinction is much more true to these extended meanings of *living* and *nonliving* than it is to their narrower, literal meanings. Thus, for example, some nonliving things, like a painting, a play, the sound of a musical instrument, a building, or even just an arrangement of rocks, can nevertheless still seem more "alive" than others of the same kind. And the converse can apply to living things: for example, I might be just as alive today as I was yesterday in some literal, technical sense of the term, yet I might both feel and appear to be "half dead"—or much less "alive"—today than I was yesterday in a more metaphorical sense of the term. Indeed, we are often much more preoccupied, day-to-day, with feeling "alive" in this latter sense than we are with the question of whether or not we are technically alive, which, most (but clearly not all) of the time, we tend to take for granted. As Christopher Alexander eloquently expressed this point in *The Timeless Way of Building*, his classic book on building and being:

The search which we make for this quality [of being "alive"], in our own lives, is the central search of any person, and the crux of any individual's story. It is the search for those moments and situations when we are most alive.[4]

When we do feel most "alive" there are simultaneously two kinds of ways of being that we do not feel: we feel neither that we are "stuck in a rut" or merely "going through the motions" nor that we are "falling apart" or are "all over the place." Instead, we feel that all our forces are responsive to each other and are working in concert; that we are "together," such that there is a flowing or fluid quality to our experience. These kinds of expressions clearly map on to the categories of fixed cohesion, discohesion, and responsive cohesion, respectively, at the level of our sense of personal well-being. Thus, even in the case of living systems, such as ourselves (which, as *living* systems, represent examples of responsive cohesion in the domain of biophysical systems), it is perfectly possible to speak in terms of higher-order, more metaphorical senses of being "alive" that enable us to distinguish, in relative terms, between examples of fixed cohesion, discohesion, and responsive cohesion *within* the same responsively cohesive, living system.

The Theory of Responsive Cohesion III: Various Ways of Referring to or Invoking the Central Organizing Categories

Different kinds of approaches to any problem are typically so closely bound up with certain forms of expression that the mere use of these expressions can be taken as a good indication of the approach that is being adopted, even if that approach is only being adopted implicitly. For example, if an approach to ethics is couched largely in terms of virtues, vices, or good and bad qualities of character, then we know that we are dealing with a *virtue ethics* approach; if it is couched in terms of rights, duties, obligations, or principles, then we know that we are dealing with a *deontological* (i.e., duty-based) or, as I would prefer to say, *principle ethics* approach; if it is couched in terms of valued goals, outcomes, or consequences—especially goals, outcomes, or consequences that are to be maximized—then we know that we are dealing with a *consequentialist* approach to ethics. Now, although the categories of fixed cohesion, discohesion, and responsive cohesion do not represent an approach to ethics in themselves (we are still preparing the groundwork for that at this stage), they do represent approaches to the problem of how to categorize certain kinds of relational qualities. Thus, it should be becoming obvious by now—from my discussion of the examples that I have been employing in the previous section—that these categories of relational qualities are themselves so closely bound up with certain forms of expression that the mere usage of these expressions can be taken as a good indication of the category of relational quality that is applicable in each instance. With this in mind, then, let us try to pick out, in a concentrated way, the kinds of expressions that are associated with each category of relational quality.

The elements or salient features that constitute examples of fixed cohesion can only be characterized as responding or answering to each other—if at all—in a superficial, insignificant, "going-through-the-motions" kind of way. To the extent that these elements or salient features do affect each other, they do so in a way that can variously be characterized as *routine, rigid, frozen, formulaic,* or *mechanical.* Examples of fixed cohesion therefore seem *tired* or *dead* rather than *alive* and so can be characterized, albeit bluntly, as constituting *dead patterns* (the fact that we are dealing with an example of cohesion means that we are dealing with a pattern of some kind, it is just that the nature of the pattern can variously be characterized as routine, rigid, frozen, formulaic, mechanical, tired, or dead).

At the other extreme and just as with examples of fixed cohesion, the elements or salient features that constitute examples of discohesion cannot be characterized as responding or answering to each other—if at all—in any deep, significant, or meaningful way either. However, whereas examples of fixed cohesion can at least be characterized as holding together in some way, as constituting some kind of pattern, even if it is a "dead pattern," examples of discohesion cannot be characterized in this way; rather, they are simply *nonpatterns* (bearing in mind that the term "pattern" refers to "an arrangement of repeated or corresponding parts"). Thus, examples of discohesion can be characterized as being *chaotic, anarchic, "all over the place," in disarray, a mess;* as having *"no logic to them,"* and so on. And this is really about all we can say about discohesion. Tor Norretranders puts the matter crisply (albeit within the context of a thought-provoking discussion of the nature of consciousness) when he says: "Total disorder is uninteresting. A mess. Not worth talking about, because we cannot describe it in any explanatory way. There is no more to be said about disorder than it says about itself."[5]

Responsive cohesion is impressively different from both fixed cohesion and discohesion. In contrast to examples of discohesion, examples of responsive cohesion *can* be characterized as holding together. And in contrast to examples of fixed cohesion, examples of responsive cohesion can be said to hold together in the more complex sense that the elements or salient features that constitute them can be characterized as responding or answering to each other in deep, significant, or meaningful ways. The

Table 3.1
Various Ways of Referring to or Invoking the Categories of Fixed Cohesion, Responsive Cohesion, and Discohesion

Fixed Cohesion	Responsive Cohesion	Discohesion
A fixed structure or process	An internally and contextually responsive structure or process	A chaotic, anarchic, or random "structure" or process
Rigid, regimented, stuck	Flexible	"All over the place"
Frozen	Fluid, flowing	Turbulent *or* decayed, thermodynamically exhausted (depending on whether the discohesion is expressed in a high- or low-energy form)
Forced, strictly regimented, tightly bound or coupled, severely constrained	Free within bounds, loosely coupled, moderately constrained (via the mutual accommodation of constituent elements)	"All over the place," "out of control," uncoupled, unconstrained
Conveys the sense that the order is imposed (whether from within or without); regimented	Conveys the sense of an immanent, self-organizing, organic, or collectively arising order	Conveys no sense of order
Fixed structure, no flexibility	Flexible structure	No structure
"Stuck in a rut," "going through the motions," formulaic, stereotypical	Adaptive, creative	"All over the place," random, arbitrary, illogical
The *elements or salient features* (ESFs) "keep company with each other through either no turnings or highly routine, predictable turnings"	The ESFs "keep company with each other through constant turnings, no matter how surprising or unpredictable"	The ESFs simply *don't* "keep company with each other"; the ESFs demonstrate nothing other than so many unrelated, or independent, "turnings"

Table 3.1
(continued)

Fixed Cohesion	Responsive Cohesion	Discohesion
Highly or totally predictable order (once you grasp the key to it); unchanging or repetitive pattern, no surprises; therefore, boring	Semipredictable order; mixes predictability and surprise; changing patterns; therefore, continually interesting	Highly or totally unpredictable; no pattern at all; therefore, any initial interest quickly gives way to either boredom (since *predictably* unpredictable) or anxiety (if the discohesion takes the dynamical form of a never-ending barrage of incomprehensible change)
Essentially simple	Genuinely complex	Merely complicated
Mechanical	Organic	Chaotic, anarchic
"Tired" or "dead" patterns	"Alive" patterns	Nonpatterns

elements or salient features of a responsively cohesive arrangement can reasonably be described (in either literal or metaphorical terms) as playing into each other and playing off each other, as exciting and inhibiting each other, or as mutually modifying each other *in ways that generate or maintain an overall cohesive order*. This kind of cohesion has the qualities of being *fluid* rather than fixed, frozen, or rigid; *free-within-bounds* as opposed to fixed, forced, or "stuck in a rut"; *responsive, adaptive*, or *creative* as opposed to fixed, formulaic, routine, stereotypical, or "going through the motions"; *organic* as opposed to mechanical. Things of this kind have an "alive" quality about them rather than a "tired" or "dead" quality; it is *as if* they are parts of a voluntary association, *as if* they "want to be there," *as if* their "hearts are in it," *as if* they "belong" there, *as if* "the part (they play) was made for them." Examples of responsive cohesion can therefore be characterized, again rather bluntly, as constituting *living patterns* (or, perhaps, *organic patterns*).

A number of forms of expression that usefully capture the distinctions between the relational qualities of fixed cohesion, responsive cohesion, and discohesion are summarized in table 3.1. I will draw heavily on these (and similar) forms of expression in the next chapter in which I will be exploring the application of these categories and assessing their relative merits across a wide range of domains of interest.

Another point worth bearing in mind in getting a feeling for these central organizing categories of the theory of responsive cohesion is this: rather than picturing these categories as lying along a linear continuum, with fixed cohesion at the left-hand end, responsive cohesion in the middle, and discohesion at the right-hand end (and, thus, as far away from fixed cohesion as possible), I think it is more helpful to picture these three categories as arranged in a circular fashion. But this circle has a particular characteristic: it is a circle in which the categories of fixed cohesion and discohesion can be thought of as shading into the category of responsive cohesion (and vice versa), but in which there is a sharp disjunction between the categories of fixed cohesion and discohesion.

Let me explain. Instances of fixed cohesion can become freed up and more responsive in various ways and so move in the direction of responsive cohesion. Conversely, instances of responsive cohesion can become increasingly frozen or fall into a rut in various ways and so move in the direction of fixed cohesion. Equally, instances of discohesion can become more responsive in various ways and so move in the direction of responsive cohesion, just as instances of responsive cohesion can become increasingly chaotic in various ways and so move in the direction of discohesion. It is perfectly possible to think of these categories as blending into one another, such that various things can be thought of as exhibiting hybrid qualities rather than being pure examples of a single category. Moreover, all of this can be captured by a linear continuum picture of the three categories. But what cannot be captured by this kind of picture is the fact that fixed forms of cohesion can also shatter or collapse into their apparent opposite, that is, discohesion. We see this in the domain of politics, for example, every time a dictatorship is overcome by a revolutionary movement that initiates a period of chaos and lawlessness. In fact we see it when any rigid structure is overwhelmed by internal or externally imposed forces and shatters into pieces. Thus, rather than representing any kind of "move in the direction of" discohesion, this kind of change from fixed cohesion to discohesion is typically abrupt—and rarely pretty to witness; someone generally has to sweep up the pieces afterwards. Equally, order can forcefully be imposed upon a chaotic situation, as, say, when a new dictatorial regime emerges from civil chaos and imposes a strict order overnight—closing down whatever media they wish to, imposing curfews, and so on. But, again, it typically takes such a degree of brute force to impose a fixed form of cohesion upon a highly discohesive situation that the transition—if it really is powerful enough to quell these discohesive forces—tends to be fairly abrupt in this direction too.

The upshot of these considerations is that there are situations in which it is useful to think of the categories of fixed cohesion and discohesion as lying next to each other, despite their apparent differences, but as separated by an abrupt border rather than as shading into each other. Hence, the usefulness of thinking of all three categories as lying in a circular arrangement—albeit with an abrupt border between the categories of fixed cohesion and discohesion—rather than on a linear continuum in which the categories of fixed cohesion and discohesion lie far apart.

Another reason for thinking of the apparently wildly different categories of fixed cohesion and discohesion as lying in some ways surprisingly close to one another is that there are some situations in which it is effectively a matter of choice—or of one's level of analysis—as to whether or not a certain arrangement is classified as belonging to one of these categories or the other. For example, instances of *deterministic chaos*—the kind of chaos that is referred to in "chaos theory"—play out in ways that are absolutely fixed by the initial conditions that generated them (thus rendering them instances of fixed cohesion), yet the fact that we can never measure these initial conditions to an infinite degree of precision means that the fixed (but nonrepetitive) playing out of these initial conditions can, for all practical purposes, be treated as random (and, thus, as instances of discohesion). Or consider the heat death of the universe. If, as predicted, everything eventually falls apart and the temperature of the universe winds down to absolute zero (-273 degrees centigrade, or -460 degrees Fahrenheit), then the resulting "arrangement" could be viewed as the ultimate instance of discohesion since everything that can possibly fall apart has done so to the maximum extent, *or* as the ultimate instance of fixed cohesion since nothing is going to change—ever again. These examples, then, just go to show that for all their apparent differences, the relational qualities of fixed cohesion and discohesion can, in certain circumstances, be thought of as sharing a paradoxically close relationship. Even so, the fact that thermodynamic exhaustion implies a completely decayed, structureless state of affairs means that I prefer to refer to it (as can be seen from table 3.1) as an instance of discohesion and to reserve the concept of fixed cohesion to refer to forms that are fixed or frozen in a structured way as opposed to an unstructured or random way.

Having considered a range of ways of invoking the central categories of the theory of responsive cohesion as well as how we might visualize their relationship to each other, we are now in a position to explore their application, and assess their relative merits. I will do this in the next two chapters (chapters 4 and 5). Beyond that I will then develop these ideas in much more detail—in chapter 6 and beyond—by distinguishing between *internal* and *contextual* forms of responsive cohesion, which, as we will see, itself generates a need for a *theory of contexts*, which I will also develop in chapter 6. This theory of contexts will then introduce us to an extremely important distinction between *mindsharers* and *isoexperients*. I will explore this distinction in some detail by drawing on sources of evidence ranging from philosophical and linguistics-based arguments regarding the nature of language to studies of wild (or feral) children, studies of prelingually deaf and deaf-blind people who have been denied access to sign language, and cutting-edge research on the cognitive worlds of chimpanzees, our closest evolutionary relatives. This will then enable me to generate a *differentiated* (as opposed to a one-size-fits-all) *model of our obligations in respect of all beings*, which, as we will see, has itself to be understood within the context of the theory of contexts that I have already mentioned. All this lies ahead of us, but it all proceeds from the understandings that have been developed here in regard to the central organizing categories of the theory of responsive cohesion. Our immediate task over the next two chapters is, then, as I have said, to explore the application of these categories and assess their relative merits.

4

The Best Approach to Everything

For anything we like to think of—and we will consider an extremely wide range of examples in this chapter—we can think of examples of that thing that exemplify, to a greater or lesser extent, the relational qualities of fixed cohesion, responsive cohesion, or discohesion. The sweeping general claim at the center of the theory of responsive cohesion is this: *In any genuinely open consideration of the matter, it is always the example that exemplifies the relational quality of responsive cohesion—or that most exemplifies this relational quality—that is typically judged to be the best example of its kind by informed judges, or that, in any case, ought to be judged to be the best example of its kind.*

Three qualifications are immediately necessary here in order to guard against misdirected criticisms. The first is this: by "any genuinely open consideration of the matter," I obviously mean a form of consideration in which the view that I am arguing for is not ruled out by definition. For example, if someone asks you to judge which example of something best exemplifies a fixed, rigid order, or which example of something best exemplifies a completely chaotic, anarchic order, then, by definition, you are being asked to judge which example does *not* exemplify a responsive form of cohesion. The above claim is therefore intended to apply, as stated, to "any genuinely open consideration of the matter," that is, to situations in which all three kinds of relational qualities can be contrasted and compared.

The second qualification is this: by "informed judges," I do not mean "people (or other rational agents) who happen to agree with me," but rather people (or other rational agents) who have invested time and energy in becoming familiar with a problem situation; who are therefore able to make finer distinctions between the various aspects of a problem situation, and do so in a reliable way, than others who are not as familiar with that problem situation; who are concerned to reach the conclusions they do reach on the basis of reasons and evidence; and who are concerned to test these conclusions by presenting them and the reasons and evidence for them to the scrutiny of other informed judges and to modify their conclusions in the face of telling criticisms by these judges (just as these other informed judges should also do if the reasons and evidence presented to them tell against their own views).

The third qualification here has to do with the two-part claim that it is always the example that most exemplifies the relational quality of responsive cohesion that is "typically judged to be the best example of its kind by informed judges, or that, in any case, *ought* to be judged to be the best example of its kind." The reason for this two-part claim is as follows. First, as we will see, I believe we can show that, within widely varying domains of interest, informed judges typically judge examples of things that most exemplify the relational quality of responsive cohesion to be the best examples of their kind. And since informed (as opposed to uninformed) judgments about value are the best guides to value that we have, it follows that *the relational quality of responsive cohesion lies at the heart of the best guides to value that we have.* However, when there is a variance between the judgments of informed judges and the verdict of the theory of response cohesion, I believe we can show that this is because even the most informed judges, or at least a significant number of them, have failed to take certain demonstrably salient features of a problem situation into account. When this happens, it will often be because these apparently informed judges have ignored salient *contextual* features of the problem situation; because, in other words, their focus of interest has been too narrow. Thus, I am claiming that mismatches between the judgments of informed judges and the theory of responsive cohesion can be explained in terms of the fact that the former judgments are not as informed as they ought to be precisely because they have failed to take salient features of the problem situation into account. If this is so, then it follows on the basis of informed judges' own standard of judgment, namely, *informed* judgment, that the judgments reached through the theory of responsive cohesion are better judgments than other "informed" judgments precisely because, by taking salient features of the problem situation into account that were previously over-looked, they are *more informed* judgments.

This is why I am claiming that it is always the example that most exemplifies the relational quality of responsive cohesion that is typically judged to be the best example of its kind by informed judges, or that, in any case, *ought* to be judged to be the best example of its kind. I am not "having it both ways" here, just the one way. I am arguing that the more informed a judgment is, the more it will correspond to the verdict of the theory of responsive cohesion. We should therefore not be sur-prised that a great many "informed judgments" already do this. But, by the same token (rather than a different, "having it both ways" token), this claim also suggests that mismatches between allegedly informed judg-ments and the verdict of the theory of responsive cohesion speak to the fact that these informed judgments will be found, upon closer inspection, not to be as "informed" as they have been taken to be precisely because they can be shown to have overlooked demonstrably salient features of the problem situation.

With these qualifications in mind, let us turn to the substance of this central claim of the theory of responsive cohesion.

The Best Approach to Informed Judgment

The first substantive thing to note about the central claim of the theory of responsive cohesion is that it is not just a claim about what we find *when* we bring informed judgment to bear upon a problem situation, as if the notion of informed judgment were a tool that floats free of the theory of responsive cohesion itself. Rather, this claim is intended to apply *even to our most informed judgments about what constitutes an informed judgment*. Let me illustrate this. Even if a view holds together internally (i.e., is internally cohesive), we do not think that it represents an informed judgment if it is a fixed and dogmatic view (i.e., if it is *un-responsive* to or does not *cohere* with relevant reasons and evidence). Rather, such a view represents an example of *fixed cohesion* in the domain of ideas or judgments. On the other hand, we do not think that a view that is internally inconsistent, that "doesn't hold together," or "doesn't add up" (i.e., a view that is discohesive) represents an informed judgment either. Rather, such a view represents an example of *discohesion* in the domain of ideas or judgments. Instead, our most informed judgments *about* what constitutes an informed judgment suggest that an informed judgment is a view that is based on and remains open to reasons and evidence (i.e., a view that *answers to* or is *responsive to* relevant reasons and evidence) while also "holding together" internally. And a view of this kind is clearly an example of *responsive cohesion* in the domain of ideas or judgments.

To see which example in a particular domain of interest—or, equally, which possible solution to a particular problem situation—is best, we are directed by the theory of responsive cohesion to ask three questions:

(i) What is the domain of interest or problem situation? (That is, how can this domain of interest or problem situation best be characterized?)

(ii) What are the salient features of this domain of interest or problem situation?

(iii) Which example in this domain of interest, or which possible solution to the problem situation, can best be characterized in terms of these salient features answering to (i.e., being responsive to) each other in the service of generating and maintaining cohesion overall?

We can refer to this three-part approach as describing the *method of responsive cohesion*. The claim at the heart of the theory of responsive cohesion is that the answer delivered by this method will be the answer that is typically judged to be the best example of its kind by informed judges, or that, in any case, *ought* to be judged to be the best example of its kind (for the reasons just explained in the previous section, i.e., because the answer delivered by this method can be shown to have taken salient features of the problem situation into account that have been overlooked by rival approaches).

(I am aware that my reference to the *method of responsive cohesion* might put some readers in mind of John Rawls's *method of reflective equilibrium*, which Rawls advanced, albeit quite briefly, in his highly influential book *A Theory of Justice*.[1] Although this method was hardly original with Rawls—as he himself points out in a note—his terminology for this method is now fairly well known in philosophical circles. Moreover, my characterization of the concept of responsive cohesion in the previous chapter might have already sparked off associations in some people's minds with other concepts, such as those of *organic unity* or *complex nonlinear dynamical systems*—as opposed to both linear and chaotic dynamical systems. I therefore discuss these associations—and *mis-associations*—in the appendix at the end of this chapter.)

But the theory of responsive cohesion does not just advance the thesis that the relational quality of responsive cohesion lies at the basis of our most informed judgments about what constitutes an informed judgment. Rather, to repeat, the theory of responsive cohesion advances the thesis that it is always the example that most exemplifies the relational quality of responsive cohesion that is typically judged to be the best example of its kind by informed judges, or that, in any case, ought to be judged to be the best example of its kind. In order to illustrate this, I will consider examples across an extremely wide range of domains of interest in this chapter, including epistemology in general and science in particular; ethics (as conventionally understood, i.e., as interhuman ethics); individual psychology; personal relationships; politics, economics, and organizational management generally; skills (including sports) and the arts; the natural environment; and the human-constructed environment.

The Best Approach to Epistemology in General and Science in Particular

Throughout history people have claimed—and continue to claim—to know things on many different bases. These include (i) authority: "Because the King/Big Man says so"; (ii) tradition: "Because my forefathers said so, and their forefathers, and so on, back into the mists of time"; (iii) revelation: "And then the Archangel appeared to me and said: 'You have been chosen for this great task'"; (iv) intuition, which can be thought of in terms of revelation from within: "It just popped into my head"; "I just have this *feeling*"; (v) reason, the elaboration of which gives rise to rationalism; and (vi) the evidence of the senses, the elaboration of which gives rise to empiricism. Informed judges generally consider that the best way of coming to know what the world is like involves a responsive interplay between theory (reason) and observations (the evidence of the senses) in the service of reaching an account of the world in which theory and observations best fit together, or cohere with each other. This means that informed judges generally consider rational-empirical methods—which we ordinarily refer to as scientific methods—

to constitute the best answer to the epistemological problem of coming to know what the world is like.

The interplay that I have just described between theory (reason) and observations (the evidence of the senses) clearly exemplifies the relational quality of responsive cohesion in the domain of epistemology. Consider: on the one hand, a theory must be answerable to relevant observations and, on the other hand, what counts as a relevant observation is answerable to—a function of—the theory that one is testing. Moreover, the interpretations of observations are, as philosophers of science like to say, *theory laden*. But, that said, good theories are not magicked out of thin air either: they are themselves *observation laden*, and at least some of these observations can be made at such a basic level—for example, the reaction did/did not occur; the dial reads "7"—that the degree to which they are theory laden can itself be pretty minimal. What is always true, however, is the former point that what counts as an observation is heavily constrained by theory: data about the behavior of ducks do not constitute relevant observations—are not a salient feature of the problem situation—if you're testing a theory in quantum cosmology, but they might constitute highly relevant observations if you're studying the ecology of a wetland. Thus, there is an ongoing mutually modifying chicken-and-egg interplay—or responsive cohesion—between theories and observations.

This responsive cohesion approach to knowing the world stands in stark contrast to the objectionable alternatives that lie, as it were, on either side. On the one hand, there is the alternative of rigid adherence to a theory in spite of substantial contrary evidence. This alternative exemplifies "stuckness" or rigidity in the domain of scientific theory; a theory in this condition has gone into theoretical rigor mortis. It represents an example of fixed cohesion in the domain of scientific theory. On the other hand, there is the alternative of rejecting the organizing role of rigorously tested theory altogether. In this case, one either lives in "a wilderness of single instances" (observational chaos) or extrapolates from experience left, right, and center ("wild speculation," theoretical chaos). This alternative represents an example of discohesion in the domain of scientific theory.

More generally, it is a fairly straightforward matter to show that the alternative epistemological bases to rational-empirical methods that we considered above (i.e., authority, tradition, intuition, and revelation) typically succumb to one or the other of the objectionable alternatives of fixed cohesion or discohesion in the domain of epistemology. In doing so, these alternative epistemological approaches have often actively misled us about what the world is like or been sufficiently vacuous as to tell us virtually nothing of any real consequence about what the world is like. Thus, informed judges generally consider the best approaches to epistemology in general and science in particular to be those that most exemplify the relational quality of responsive cohesion between theory and observations.

The Best Approach to Ethics

This is, of course, the Big One, the Holy Grail question of ethics, but I need to impose a significant caveat before addressing it at this stage of the argument. Specifically, I am still very much in the process of arguing that the relational quality of responsive cohesion is the foundational value, and that it therefore ought to constitute the basis of a General Ethics. When that conclusion is established, I will then be in a position to outline what the best approach to a truly General Ethics would look like. Until then, what I want to do for present purposes is to address this question about the content of the best approach to ethics in terms of our traditional, conventional understanding of ethics, that is, in terms of "ethics" as referring to interhuman ethics.

Interhuman ethics is essentially concerned with the question: How should people act in respect of each other? And since it is flesh-and-blood *individuals* who act, we can express this question more fully as: How should *each* of us act in respect of other people—and how should *each* of them act in respect of us? Moreover, since ethics is ultimately a practical enterprise, to ask this question in a practical context—in the context of real flesh-and-blood people who have their own individual range of cares and concerns—as opposed to asking it in a thoroughly idealized, God's-eye-view kind of context is ultimately to ask: What are the nature and limits of the kinds of behaviors that it is reasonable for us to *expect* from others and reasonable for each of these others to *expect* from us?

Not only does this question regarding the *reasonable expectations* that people can have of each other's behavior define the essence of the interhuman ethics problem situation, but the very nature of the question suggests that the nature of the answer will be one that exemplifies the relational quality of responsive cohesion. This is because any form of interhuman "ethics" that relies upon the fulfillment of *unreasonable expectations* would necessarily be one that, if taken seriously, would either have to rely upon forceful imposition for its maintenance (and, thus, represent an example of fixed cohesion) or else collapse into discord and enmity (and, thus, represent an example of discohesion). In contrast, any form of ethics that relies upon the fulfillment of reasonable expectations will, by definition, be one that reasonable people can agree to as a sensible and defensible way of mutually accommodating each other's reasonable expectations in respect of the kinds of behaviors that they expect from others and that others can expect from them. This kind of mutually accommodating solution to the interhuman ethics problem situation would clearly represent an example of responsive cohesion in the domain of interhuman interaction.

I will explore the theory of responsive cohesion's solution to the interhuman ethics problem situation in considerable detail in the next chapter, but it is enough for the purposes of this present survey for us simply to note that any reasonable solution to the interhuman ethics problem situation will necessarily have to take the form of a responsively cohesive solution.

The Best Approach to Individual Psychology

Informed judges generally consider that a person is in the best psychological state—in "good (psychological) shape"—when there is a responsive cohesion between their various internal psychological forces (in which case their thoughts, emotions, and desires—or cognition, affect, and volition—are judged as being well integrated) and between the person as a whole and their external surroundings, including their social environment (in which case their responses are judged as being appropriate to their context). These two aspects of psychological well-being represent examples of *internal* responsive cohesion and *contextual* (or external) responsive cohesion, respectively, in the domain of individual psychology.

In contrast, we consider a person to be in "bad (psychological) shape" when they exemplify the alternatives that lie on either side of the above.

One alternative occurs when there is a rigid or fixed quality to a person's inner psychological organization and ways of dealing with the world (psychological and behavioral rigidity/inflexibility). In this case, we might colloquially describe the person (depending upon the nature of the case) as "stuck," "in a rut," "in the grip of an idée fixe," "acting like a zombie," "obsessive-compulsive," and so on. This alternative clearly represents an example of fixed cohesion in the domain of individual psychology. The other alternative occurs when there is a lack of integration (or cohesion) in a person's internal psychological organization and ways of dealing with the world (psychological chaos and/or they cause havoc through their behavior). In this case, we might colloquially describe the person (depending upon the nature of the case) as "falling apart," "all over the place," "a mess," "not together," "crazy," "psychotic," and so on. This alternative clearly represents an example of discohesion in the domain of individual psychology.

The Best Approach to Personal Relationships

Conversation—talking with each other—is central to our personal relationships as a language-using species. You will recall that I have already highlighted the example of conversation in the previous chapter, in which I introduced the three basic categories of fixed cohesion, responsive cohesion, and discohesion. Although my purpose in that chapter was primarily to show how different kinds of conversations can be used to illustrate the difference in depth between different kinds of answering or responsiveness, it should also have been obvious from that discussion that the best kinds of conversations are clearly those that represent an example of responsive cohesion in the domain of conversation; those that fulfill the promise inherent in the very word "conversation" of "keeping company with each other through constant turnings." As I noted at the time, you don't need to be a genius to know when a conversation with someone is "stuck in a rut" or "going around in circles" (and, hence, an example of fixed cohesion in the domain of conversation), or when the two of you are "not connecting at all" or "talking past each other" (and, hence, an example of discohesion in the domain of conversation), or when it is just "flowing" (and, hence, an example of responsive cohesion in the domain of conversation). The not-so-implicit point here, of course, was that you do not need to be a genius, or even an expert, to judge that the latter kind of conversation—the kind of conversation in which people do indeed "keep company with each other through constant turnings"—represents the best kind of conversation.

What goes for the domain of personal interaction through conversation can be extended to apply to the domain of personal relationships in general. The best kinds of personal relationships are typically judged to be those in which the parties concerned are genuinely responsive to each other in a way that keeps the relationship "alive" rather than those in which the parties concerned are "stuck in a rut" or "going through the motions" with each other on the one hand (fixed cohesion), or "really out of touch" or, worse, "at war" with each other on the other hand (discohesion). And yes, this judgment can be applied in quite obvious ways to the domain of personal relationships that includes sex and lovemaking too. It is easy enough to imagine the fixed cohesion ("We're stuck in a rut") and discohesion ("It was a complete disaster!") correlates of sex and lovemaking; it's also easy enough to imagine the responsive cohesion correlate ("We really turn each other on!"; "We're both really responsive to each other's needs"). I will leave the more detailed "fleshing out" of these imaginings to readers, but the essential point here, of course, is that when it comes to sex and lovemaking, you definitely want to go for the responsive cohesion variety, not the fixed cohesion or discohesion varieties: the best examples of sex and lovemaking are clearly those that most exemplify the relational quality of responsive cohesion.

The Best Approach to Politics, Economics, and Organizational Management Generally

Informed judges generally consider that the best forms of politics are those in which there is a responsive cohesion between a government and the population it governs, that is, where there are mechanisms in place to ensure that the government answers to the people (e.g., through democratic elections, an independent judicial system, and a free press) and that people answer to the government (e.g., through the rule of law, and enforcement of the law by police and the judicial system). This responsive cohesion approach to politics stands in stark contrast to the objectionable alternatives on either side. On the one hand, there is the contrast of rigid, dictatorial, totalitarian forms of "government" in which the people must be responsive to the "government" but in which there are no mechanisms to ensure that the "government" must be responsive to the people. This typically results in a rigidly imposed form of political cohesion rather than a form of political cohesion that arises by virtue of the mutual responsiveness of people and government to each other, and its grip is often only broken through a rebellion that flips the society (at least temporarily) from a situation of rigidly imposed control to one of social anarchy and chaos in which people (or at least some people) become "a law unto themselves." This flip side of a dictatorial approach then exemplifies the other contrast to a responsive cohesion approach to politics. It is a contrast in which the legitimacy and organizing role of government is rejected altogether, with the inevitable result: lawlessness reigns, and those least able to defend themselves typically end up paying a tragic price. Clearly, these objectionable dictatorial and anarchic alternatives represent examples of fixed cohesion and discohesion, respectively, in the domain of political organization.

These observations concerning politics—and, thus, in part, the organizational management of a country—can easily be extended into other realms involving various forms of management, from economics to organizational management in the more everyday sense of, say, the organizational management of a business, school, or hospital. Mapping the categories of fixed cohesion, responsive cohesion, and discohesion onto the domain of economics provides us, respectively, with a contrast between hierarchical, top-down, state-controlled "command" or "planned" economies, which are infamous for being unresponsive to the actual needs and desires of ordinary citizens; market-based economies, in which people are free within politically agreed-upon—and therefore, *ideally*, collectively agreed-upon—bounds to produce, sell, and buy in response to their needs and desires; and completely chaotic economies, which are also infamous for being unresponsive to the actual needs and desires of ordinary citizens, and in which, for example, money can become "not worth the paper it is printed on." Mapping the categories of fixed cohesion, responsive cohesion, and discohesion onto the domain of organizational management provides us, respectively, with a contrast between organizations that operate in fixed, rigid, or inflexible ways;

organizations whose various aspects remain open and responsive to each other in flexible ways that serve to generate and reinforce the overall cohesion of the organization; and "organizations" that are patently *disorganized* in various ways. It remains only to add the obvious: informed judges agree—and many people know from bitter personal experience—that the responsive cohesion option is a far, far better one than either of the other alternatives when it comes to the domains of both economics and organizational management.

The only caveat that I would wish to add here is that although informed judges—as well as thoughtful ordinary people who may nevertheless *say* that they "don't really understand economics"—generally agree that market economies are far better (in a variety of ways) than either command economies or complete economic chaos, they will often disagree vigorously over which *kind* of market economy is best. Should it be a completely unregulated market or should it be regulated to some extent? If the latter, then how and to what extent should it be regulated? This is a more detailed issue than that of deciding between the three quite different kinds of economic arrangements outlined above since, from the perspective of the theory of responsive cohesion, it involves deciding which *particular* variety of market-based (and, therefore, broadly responsively cohesive) economic arrangement exemplifies the highest degree of responsive cohesion. When fully developed, the theory of responsive cohesion can offer a quite detailed answer to this more detailed question. However, I cannot offer this answer in any detail at this stage because it relies on an understanding of aspects of the theory that I will develop later in the book. These include the theory of responsive cohesion's *theory of contexts* (which I will develop in chapter 6) as well as the theory of responsive cohesion's *differentiated model of our obligations in respect of other people* (which I will develop in chapter 5) together with the implications of these views for the *"What is the best 'flavor' of politics?"* problem (first outlined as problem 6 in chapter 2 and addressed in terms of the fully developed theory of responsive cohesion in chapter 10). In short, however, the answer to the "degree and kind of market regulation" question that emerges from the full development of the theory of responsive cohesion is one that supports the operation of a market economy within the context of (i) *serious* deference to issues concerning the preservation and regeneration of responsive cohesion in the biophysical realm (i.e., ecological considerations), and (ii) progressive taxation in support of social welfare. I argue that these forms of regulation characterize the most responsively cohesive kind of market economy overall, and, therefore, the kind of market economy that ought to be judged to be the best, precisely because it exemplifies responsive cohesion between all of the most salient features of the economic problem situation rather than, in contrast to its rivals, failing to take any or sufficient account of some of these salient features (e.g., ecological considerations, or the kind and extent of our obligations toward people who may be nothing more than others-in-general to us at a personal level but who nevertheless live in our nation-state, and so, relative to people who live in other nation-states, nevertheless represent our significant others at the political level; on this second issue, see my discussion of problem 6 in chapter 10).

The Best Approach to Skills (Including Sports) and the Arts

Informed judges generally consider that the best examples of skills (including sports) and the arts (whether we are talking about high diving, tennis, furniture making, dancing, music, drama, novel writing, or painting) exhibit an internal responsive cohesion in that they are judged to "hang together" well (or be cohesive) in virtue of the various ways in which each aspect of the whole is seen to answer to (or be responsive to) the others. As ever, this favored responsive cohesion approach to the domain under consideration stands in stark contrast to the objectionable alternatives on either side. In this case, we have, on the one hand, the contrast of a skill or art that coheres in a way that is judged to be rigid, forced, imposed, or "wooden" (i.e., where the elements of the skill or art are judged as being unresponsive to each other, all of which bespeaks a rigidity of imaginative or technical capacity). This alternative represents an example of fixed cohesion in the domain of skills and the arts. On the other hand, we have the contrast of a skill or art that is judged as being "all over the place," as "not hanging together," or, like a high dive that goes wrong or a bad move in chess, as coming "unstuck." This alternative represents an example of discohesion in the domain of skills and the arts.

Skills and arts can also be judged in terms of their responsive cohesion in respect of a salient context of understanding, or a tradition, that informs them. Informed judges generally consider that the best examples of skills and arts are those that not only make sense within, and so *cohere* with, a recognizable tradition but also *respond to* that tradition and so add to its development. Again, this favored alternative stands in stark contrast to the objectionable alternatives on either side. On the one hand, if an example of a skill or art blindly repeats a tradition (as, say, a straightforward forgery does in an extreme way), then it is only cohesive with that tradition in a fixed, rigid, unresponsive way (even if the resulting product displays considerable *internal* responsive cohesion considered in its own right). It then pays the price of being judged as "clichéd," "stereotypical," "hackneyed," "formulaic," "plodding," "unimaginative," "derivative," "unoriginal," even "plagiaristic," and so on, in its design or execution. This alternative represents a contextual example of fixed cohesion in the domain of skills and the arts. On the other hand, if an example of a skill or art bears no obvious connection with the tradition in which it can most reasonably be judged as partaking, then it doesn't make any sense in terms of that tradition and is judged as a bad example of its kind. It is variously dismissed as "novelty for the sake of novelty," "pretentious," having "more flash than substance," "confused," "all over the place," and much worse! This alternative represents a contextual example of discohesion in the domain of skills and the arts.

The Best Approach to the Natural Environment

Every tangible environment is part of Nature if we understand the term *Nature* (with a capital "N") in the broadest sense, that is, as referring to everything that exists in the universe; as everything that is not "supernatural." However, we generally refer to the *natural environment* when we want to distinguish between, or at least highlight the role of, spontaneously self-organizing ecological systems and subsystems in contrast to intentionally organized, human-constructed environments. Understood in this commonly intended sense, it automatically follows that informed judges consider the best examples of natural environments to be those that most exemplify the relational quality of responsive cohesion. This is because any self-organizing system, not just an ecosystemic form of self-organization, must exemplify the relational quality of responsive cohesion in order to qualify *as* a self-organizing system. It is simply of the essence of *self*-organizing systems that they maintain their integrity—their cohesion—through the mutual responsiveness of their constituent features; if they do not do this, then they are not *self*-organizing systems. Thus, the best examples of natural environments—understood as spontaneously self-organizing ecological systems and subsystems—are necessarily those that best exemplify the relational quality of responsive cohesion since they are natural, spontaneously self-organizing ecological systems only by virtue of this feature.

We can say the same thing in somewhat less abstract terms here—and we typically do. For example, we could say that informed judges generally consider that the best examples of natural environments are those in which the processes of mutual accommodation that characterize the relationships between the various living and nonliving things that constitute these natural environments have been allowed to unfold in their own spontaneously self-organizing ways. In these cases, the overall system typically exemplifies the quality of *ecological homeorhesis* (from Greek *homoio-*, from *homos* same, and Greek *rheos* stream, anything flowing, from *rhein* to flow), that is, it maintains itself as an identifiable (or the "same") dynamical, collectively evolving ecological flow. (Aldo Leopold memorably described ecosystems—or biotic communities—as fountains of energy.[2]) But talking about processes of mutual accommodation that collectively bind entities to each other in various ways such that they can be thought of as existing as parts of a dynamical, collectively evolving ecological flow is itself just another way of talking about the relational quality of responsive cohesion.

The kinds of spontaneously self-organizing, responsively cohesive, natural environments that I have just described stand in stark contrast to the objectionable alternatives that lie on either side. On the one hand, there is the contrast of a natural environment being "managed" by being kept just as it is such that normal evolutionary processes are effectively frozen in their tracks. This "deep-freezing" approach attempts to rigidly maintain the existing cohesion of natural processes, but does so in such a tightly constrained or fixed way that it robs them of their genuinely responsive, long-range dynamical, and, thus, evolutionary nature. This corresponds to a strictly enforced form of *ecological homeostasis*, that is, the maintenance of the same ecological *state*, as opposed to ecological homeorhesis, and represents an example of fixed cohesion in the domain of the natural environment. On the other hand, there is the contrast of an "anything goes" policy in which we effectively say "Who cares about another exotic, invasive species?" This approach rapidly accelerates the dynamical nature of ecological processes, but does so in ways that are chaotic and even catastrophic with respect to the long-standing forms of ecological cohesion that had characterized them. In particular, this approach accelerates extinction and the loss of biodiversity overall since the same "weedy" species come to outcompete many more diverse, specialized species in place after place. This "anything goes" approach represents an example of discohesion in the domain of the natural environment.

Where the "deep-freezing" approach seeks to maintain ecological cohesion at the cost of discarding deep, evolutionary forms of ecological responsiveness, the "anything goes" approach discards any concern with deep, long-standing forms of ecological cohesion and allows an ecological free-for-all in which species respond as they will. Informed judges would generally agree that it would be a Big Mistake to live in either kind of world—although we are, as it happens, moving rapidly in the "anything goes" direction. Thus, if ever one wanted to draw on the importance of respecting the relational quality of responsive cohesion, it is surely in regard to the natural environment, which, for all earthly purposes, represents "the context of contexts"—"the Mother of all contexts," if you like.

This "Mother of all contexts" will come to play a powerful role in the full development of the theory of responsive cohesion. This is for at least two reasons. The first is that if we trace any concern with *contextual* forms of responsive cohesion far enough, we must eventually end up addressing that concern in the widest context available for all earthly purposes, namely, the ecosphere. The second is that if, as I will argue, responsive cohesion is the foundational value, then we must, for all earthly purposes, consider the earth to be the most valuable thing around because it exemplifies the foundational value in the ultimate context within which we live our lives. We will come to the details of all these matters later, but, for now, it is worth clearly noting the importance that the natural environment will come to play in the full development of the theory of responsive cohesion.

The Best Approach to the Human-Constructed Environment, with Special Reference to the Built Environment

I take the built environment to represent the paradigmatic example of the human-constructed environment. It is the form of the human-constructed environment that most structures our lives; that is most "in our faces" (whether it be beautiful and enlivening or ugly and dispiriting); and, yet, that we often have the least say in affecting (we can choose whether or not to buy this kind of kettle, but we typically have little choice about the buildings and roads that come to dominate and structure our lives). The built environment is also the form of the human-constructed environment that has the most effect upon the rest of the planet: the fate of the "green bits" of the world is now intimately tied up with the future of the "brown bits," that is, with how we build and live our lives in built environments. I will therefore discuss the question of the best approach to the human-constructed environment in terms of the best approach to the built environment, but it is a simple matter to expand these remarks out to refer to other aspects of the human-constructed environment as well (like kettles).

Informed judges generally consider the best examples of the built environment to be represented by buildings whose salient features feed into and play off each other—in other words, whose salient features answer to or are responsive to each other—in such a way as to form a cohesive whole overall. This kind of whole is often referred to as an "organic unity" since it is a form of cohesion that seems to embody its own internal logic, almost as if it might have grown of its accord in a self-organizing way rather than an intentionally organized way; each element seems to "belong" exactly where it is. Buildings that display the relational quality of responsive cohesion stand in stark contrast to the objectionable alternatives that lie on either side. On the one hand, there is the alternative of buildings that represent an unimaginative or formulaic solution to narrowly imposed objectives, such as the maximum enclosed space for the minimum cost, or to have the "showiest" house in the neighborhood. A building of this kind might well "hold together" (be cohesive) literally, in terms of its physical structure, and even metaphorically, in terms of its own "minimum cost" or "showiest house" agenda. However, each aspect of the building will nevertheless seem to answer far more to a narrowly imposed master factor—such as "minimum cost" or "showiest house"—than to either the other aspects of the building itself or the full range of salient features that actually bear on the problem situation—such as what it's actually like to work or live in these buildings! On the other hand, there is the alternative of buildings whose basic elements are so "all over the place" with respect to each other that they simply fail to "hold together" literally, in terms of their physical structure, or metaphorically, in terms of how the overall design "works." Needless to say, the two objectionable alternatives that I have just outlined represent examples of fixed cohesion and discohesion, respectively, in the domain of the built environment (and, by extension, the human-constructed realm generally).

We can judge buildings (and artifacts generally) not only in terms of their degree and type of *internal* cohesion (as above) but also in terms of their degree and type of *contextual* cohesion. This raises interesting questions for us all since it is a matter of common experience that many buildings represent either dull, unimaginative responses to their contexts or responses that seem to be so thoughtless of their contexts that they "stick out like sore thumbs." As I noted in chapter 1, we have probably all experienced the kind of immediate gut level response to the inappropriateness of some buildings with respect to their context that we have been spontaneously led to exclaim to ourselves if not to others as well: "Ugh, there ought to be a law against it!" (and, indeed, there are laws in some places to prevent some kinds of violations of context). It is no surprise, then, that informed judges—which, given the generally public nature of the built environment includes those members of that public who reflect seriously upon these issues—generally consider that, contextually speaking, the best kinds of buildings are those that are neither dull, unimaginative responses to their context nor violations of context but rather those that are "alive to" and "answer to" their context. It remains to add that whereas the two objectionable alternatives that I have just outlined represent contextually based examples of fixed cohesion and discohesion, respectively, in the domain of the human-constructed environment, the third alternative—the one that is typically endorsed by informed judges—represents a contextually based example of responsive cohesion in the domain of the human-constructed environment.

The two objectionable alternatives that I have just outlined in the preceding paragraph are exactly the alternatives that the architectural theorist Christian Norberg-Schulz identifies in his book *Genius Loci* as "general monotony" on the one hand and "arbitrary fancies" on the other hand when he says: "The modern environment in fact offers very little of the surprises and discoveries which make the experience of old towns so fascinating. When attempts to break the general monotony are made, they mostly appear as arbitrary fancies."[3] In contrast, the term *responsive cohesion* seems to be a very good way of describing (in formal language) what it is that makes "the experience of [some] old towns so fascinating"; of describing what it is that can imbue the built environment with the sense that it exemplifies a "timeless way of building," to borrow Christopher Alexander's evocative phrase from his book of the same name.[4]

Responsive Cohesion, Brains, Consciousness, and the Very Possibility of Valuing

We have now seen that the relational quality of responsive cohesion underpins our most informed evaluative judgments in an extremely broad variety of domains of interest. But what about the actual act of valuing? What about the very possibility of valuing? The icing on the cake here is this: not only do our most informed judgments suggest that we do most value those things that most exemplify the relational quality of responsive cohesion, but this relational quality even underpins our very capacity *to* value. If we go back to the distinction that I introduced in chapter 3 between sources of value and the recognizers of value, then we can put this point this way: not only does the relational quality of responsive cohesion lie at the heart of all those things that our most informed judgments of value indicate are genuine sources of value, but it also underpins the recognition *of* these sources of value since it underpins the very possibility of valuing.

The argument for this runs along the following lines. First, we need to begin by noting the extremely important distinction that we can and routinely need to make in the world between those kinds of things that are capable of conscious experience of some kind and those that aren't. This distinction necessarily takes us into standard philosophy of mind territory. Philosophers of mind are fond of saying that those kinds of entities that are capable of conscious experience possess *subjectivity*, *intentionality* (in the technical sense that their mental states are always *of* or *about* something), and a *perspective* of some sort on the world; that it is, in short, *like* something to be these entities, even if we don't or can't know exactly *what* it is like. In contrast, it is not *like* anything to "be" something that is not capable of any kind of conscious experience, something that completely lacks subjectivity, intentionality, and a perspective of some sort on the world.

Second, it follows that the capacity for conscious experience is a prerequisite for being able to engage in the process of valuing anything at all. This is because valuing is clearly (what philosophers of mind refer to as) an *intentional* state (i.e., it is a conscious state that in some way *refers to* a value or to something as being valuable), and the only kinds of things that have intentional states—states that are intrinsically *about* things, or that intrinsically *refer to* things—are things that are capable of conscious experience. It's not *like* anything to be a rock; a rock doesn't have "inner," subjective states that are *about* anything. Accordingly, a rock is incapable of valuing anything. In short, where there's no consciousness, there's no valuing.

Third, the only entities that we presently know of that are capable of generating conscious experience and therefore of valuing are brains of a sufficient degree of complexity.

Fourth, the interacting networks of mutually modifying neuronal processes that constitute brains represent exquisitely complex examples of responsive cohesion. Moreover, we now seek to explain not only conscious experience itself but also its unified, seamless, or cohesive quality through an increased understanding of these interacting networks of mutually modifying neuronal processes. (Nonpathological forms of human consciousness have an undeniably unified, seamless, or cohesive quality, no matter how "scattered" our thoughts themselves might be.) Any state-of-the-art analysis of how brains work to produce conscious experience speaks to these points. Thus, for example, the Nobel laureate Gerald Edelman and his collaborator Guilo Tononi write in their book *Consciousness: How Matter Becomes Imagination*:

Our analysis leads to several conclusions. First, conscious experience appears to be associated with neural activity that is distributed simultaneously across neuronal groups in many different regions of the brain. Consciousness is therefore not the prerogative of any one brain area.... Second, to support conscious experience, a large number of groups of neurons must interact rapidly and reciprocally through the process called reentry. If these reentrant interactions are blocked, entire sectors of consciousness disappear, and consciousness itself may shrink or split. [Note that this latter point suggests that we must seek to understand not only conscious experience itself but also its unified, seamless, or cohesive quality in terms of interacting networks of mutually modifying neuronal processes.][5]

Reentry is elsewhere defined by these authors as "a process of signaling back and forth along reciprocal connections that ... offers the key to resolving the problem of integrating the various functionally segregated properties of brain areas despite the lack of a central coordinative area."[6] The process of reentry is therefore these authors' way of saying that the overall cohesion of conscious experience is constituted out of the responsive interplay between large numbers of groups of neurons across the brain, notwithstanding the lack of any overall control center for consciousness. Everything they say about the brain speaks to the responsively cohesive nature of its processes: "These millions of neuronal groups are linked by a huge set of ... reciprocally organized connections that make them all hang together in a single, tight meshwork while they still maintain their local functional specificity."[7] This kind of language— "reciprocally organized" (i.e., mutually modifying or mutually responsive) connections that enable millions of neuronal groups to "hang together" (i.e., operate in a cohesive way)—is the language of responsive cohesion. No matter how detailed our exploration of the formidably complex operations of the brain, the overall picture that emerges is one of responsive cohesion. As the neuroscience writer John McCrone says at the beginning of his own detailed account of recent work in neuroscience: "The brain is above all an organ that is lively, responsive, and acts as a whole."[8]

Fifth, it seems inconceivable that something that did not embody the relational quality of responsive cohesion would be capable of generating conscious experience and therefore of valuing. Another way of putting this is to say that if any artificial or extraterrestrial entity were to be capable of generating conscious experience, then its form of organization would also have to represent an example of responsive cohesion.

I see this fifth point as the only vaguely speculative move in this argument, but, even so, I don't think that it is particularly speculative. I take it that these days the first four points in this argument are safely established, that is, (i) that some things are capable of conscious experience (and that some things aren't); (ii) that an entity has to be capable of at least some form of conscious experience to be able to value anything; (iii) that the biological wetware of (at least certain kinds of) brains is the only kind of stuff that we are presently aware of that is capable of generating conscious experience (and therefore of supporting the process of valuing); and (iv) that this biological wetware represents a paradigmatic example of the relational quality or form of organization of responsive cohesion. These points are enough to secure the conclusion that the relational quality of responsive cohesion underpins the only kind of stuff that we are presently aware of that is capable of generating conscious experience (and therefore of supporting the process of valuing). But what about this fifth point? What about the claim that this relational quality *must* underpin the capacity for valuing, that is, that responsive cohesion is a necessary condition for valuing, that it underpins the very possibility of valuing?

Let us grant that we are still a long way from understanding precisely how conscious experience is generated, and that even though we are undoubtedly making progress on this question—the famous "mind–body problem"—it has for a long time verged on seeming to be impossibly difficult. And let us grant that it is therefore impossible at this stage to be certain about claims in this area, such as my fifth point above. Granted all that, we are these days nevertheless in a position to make some very educated guesses, and I suggest that the fifth point above is one of them for the following reasons. It now seems as obvious as anything can be obvious that anything sophisticated or complex enough to generate conscious experience would have to be a highly *adaptive* system, both in terms of its internal operations and in terms of its operations with respect to its environment. I don't think that any informed thinker who seriously considers the prospect of artificial or extraterrestrial forms of conscious experience would therefore doubt that such an entity would have to fall into the category of being what complexity theorists refer to as a *complex adaptive system* (CAS). Yet all complex adaptive systems exhibit the relational quality of responsive cohesion:

the elements or salient features that constitute them modify each other's operations in awesomely complex (because highly nonlinear) ways that enable the overall system to function in a sufficiently unified—or cohesive—way as to adapt to changing external and internal influences. Now, if anything sophisticated or complex enough to generate conscious experience would have to be a complex adaptive system, and if all complex adaptive systems exhibit the relational quality of responsive cohesion, then it follows that anything sophisticated or complex enough to generate conscious experience would have to embody the relational quality of responsive cohesion, which is precisely the fifth point I made above.[9]

We can conclude from the above five points that the relational quality of responsive cohesion not only underpins all known cases of conscious experience but must also underpin all possible cases of conscious experience. It follows from this that although the relational quality of responsive cohesion is not a sufficient condition for conscious experience (since many things can represent examples of this relational quality without being conscious), it is undoubtedly a necessary condition for conscious experience (since there will be no conscious experience without it). The relational quality of responsive cohesion therefore necessarily lies at the basis of conscious experience and, thus, as claimed, underpins the very possibility of valuing. QED.

The Relational Quality of Responsive Cohesions as the Foundational Value

I have argued to this point that our most informed judgments suggest that the relational quality of responsive cohesion lies at the basis of the best approaches to an extremely wide range of domains of interest: epistemology in general and science in particular; conventional, interhuman ethics; individual psychology; personal relationships; politics, economics, and organizational management generally; skills (including sports) and the arts; the natural environment; and the human-constructed environment. Given the extremely wide range of domains of interest that I have considered, the clear implication of my argument is that our most informed judgments will show that the relational quality of responsive cohesion lies at the basis of the best examples of, or approach to, whatever general domain of interest one cares to nominate. Moreover, we have seen that the relational quality of responsive cohesion even lies at the basis of our most informed judgments about what constitutes an informed judgment as well as at the basis of the very possibility of valuing. If we accept all this, then we are inexorably driven to the conclusion that the relational quality of responsive cohesion constitutes the foundational value. All manner of things constitute the best examples of their kind when they most exemplify this relational quality.

In my view there is no one set reason that will explain why examples of the relational quality of responsive cohesion are repeatedly judged to represent the best examples of their kind across all manner of domains of interest. Rather, different kinds of reasons will be given to explain what makes something a good—or the best—example of its kind in different domains. Thus, for example, conversations and personal and sexual relationships might be judged to be among the best examples of their kind because of the way they *flow* or provide *mutual pleasure* to the participants; the best approach to epistemology in general and science in particular might be judged to be so because it represents our best way of approximating to or modeling *the truth about what the world is like*; the best approach to conventional, interhuman ethics because of the way in which it issues in a *workable as well as fair and reasonable* guide in our daily conduct with others; the best type of individual psychology because it *feels best* (especially when considered over the longer term) both to the person themselves and to those with whom they deal; the best type of politics because it *feels best*, seems *fair and reasonable*, provides appropriate *channels for the expression of grievances*, and so on to those who participate in it or are subject to it; the best examples of all manner of skills (including sports) and the arts for all manner of reasons—because they illustrate *dramatic flair*, because they *blend together harmoniously*, because they are *superbly executed*, because they are *fascinating*, because they *make us feel more alive*, because they "*work*," and so on; the best examples of the natural environment because they are well *preserved* (i.e., precisely because they are, in a common use of the word, "natural"); and the best examples of the human-constructed environment for any number of the reasons that have already been given for the other domains as well as others that could be added (e.g., anything from their *user-friendliness* to their *energy efficiency* to their *enhancement of the cityscape*).

The reasons I have given here with respect to each domain of interest are merely illustrative; other kinds of reasons might be given by different judges with respect to these various domains of interest, especially when considering specific examples within these domains. But this just amplifies my point that different judges will formulate their reasons differently for judging something to be a good—or the best—example of its kind in different domains; that there is no one reason—or even one single set of reasons—that will apply in each and every case. That said, the overall point of my argument is that however differently formulated these judgments of "good" and "best" might be by different judges in different domains, informed judgments in these areas tend to "boil down to," "pick up on," or in some way ultimately rely on the fact that those things that are judged to be the best examples of their kind typically exhibit the relational quality of responsive cohesion. Another way to put this is to say that when we ask informed judges to explain more precisely why it is that certain things exemplify the evaluative reasons that these judges have given—that is, what it is about these things that means that they can be judged to "flow," "provide mutual pleasure," "approximate or model the truth about the way the world really is," "provide a workable as well as fair and reasonable guide in our daily conduct with others," "feel best," "provide channels for the expression of grievances," "offer dramatic flair," "blend together harmoniously," be "superbly executed," be "fascinating," "make us feel more alive," "work," be "well preserved," be "user-friendly," be "energy efficient," or "enhance the cityscape" (just to take the sample formulations given above)—then they will start to explain these reasons in terms of the way in which the salient features that apply in each case are *responsive* to each other in such a way that they *work together* (and, thus, *cohere* in some way) so as to achieve the overall higher-level effect that these judges value.

In other words, the relational quality of responsive cohesion—as very distinct from fixed cohesion or discohesion—will be found to underpin each of the other evaluative notions that I have listed. The general idea of responsive cohesion will be drawn on—in effect if not in name—in order to explain what it is that is "good" or "best" about things that are "fair and reasonable," "feel best," "blend together harmoniously," "make us feel more alive," "work," are "energy efficient," and so on. However, the reverse does not apply; these higher-level evaluative notions cannot be drawn on to explain what is "good" or "best" about responsive cohesion: the idea that something is "fair and reasonable," "feels best," "blends together harmoniously," "makes us feel more alive," "works," or is "energy efficient," and so on cannot be used to explain something as basic as the relational quality of responsive cohesion itself, let alone what is good about it. Thus, the relational quality of responsive cohesion is the most primitive—or nonreducible—of these evaluative notions; it underpins them, but they do not underpin it.

Moreover, the relational quality of responsive cohesion is not reducible to some even more primitive notion than itself: speaking in terms of something as basic, deep, and abstract as a relational quality is as primitive as we can get (and still be able to speak of anything). The fact that we cannot reduce the idea of responsive cohesion to anything else necessarily means that insofar as there is something that is good or best about this relational quality, we cannot explain this goodness or "bestness" in terms of anything more basic. Thus, if you ask me, "What is it that makes this abstract quality of responsive cohesion so good?" all I can do is point back to where we have come from—to all the evidence that points to this conclusion. I cannot take you "further down the track" (in which case you could, in any case, just ask a new version of the same question) because there is no "further down the track." Our examination of the issue across an extremely wide range of domains of interest suggests that, notwithstanding the extremely wide range of reasons given for judging one thing to be a better example of its kind than another in different domains of interest, it just seems to be the case that there is something that is intrinsically better about those forms of things that can be characterized as holding together by virtue of mutual responsiveness between the elements or salient features that constitute them than there is about those forms of things whose elements or salient features can be characterized as holding together in a fixed or unresponsive way on the one hand or not holding together on the other hand.

The upshot of these considerations is this: the claim that the relational quality of responsive cohesion is the foundational value is and can only be a conclusion. As with any ultimate or foundational conclusion, this conclusion can be reached only at the end of a long and wide range of considerations, such as those that I have given above in regard to the nature of those things that represent the best examples of their kind across an extremely wide range of domains of interest. All the evaluative evidence from across the widest range of domains of interest, together with the fact that we cannot reduce something as basic, deep, and abstract as a relational quality to anything else, points to the fact that the relational quality of responsive cohesion is the foundational value. That's it.

I take this conclusion to be a positive result in philosophy. Moreover, it is a puzzle to me how one would go about refuting it. For example, if you wanted to argue that, actually, fixed cohesion (or some particular form of it) or just plain old, formless discohesion is better or more fundamental for evaluative purposes than responsive cohesion, then how would you go about doing it? To the extent that your argument is judged to be any good and, thus, worth taking seriously, it would need to do the following. First, not only would it need to avoid obvious internal contradictions but its various elements would also need to "tie together" or "add up" in a more positive sense; a sense that goes well beyond merely avoiding internal contradictions. For example, the statements "All men are mortal," "The moon is made of blue cheese," and "My Martin D-28 guitar needs retuning" do not obviously contradict each other (they are, in this sense, perfectly consistent with each other), but neither do they "tie together" or "add up" to anything. As the elements of an "argument," they appear, as they stand, to be "all over the place." In contrast, the statements "My guitar is badly out of tune," "It's very important that I tune my guitar properly before I play in front of people" (tuned instruments offering yet another example of the value of responsive cohesion), and "I'm playing a big concert tonight" clearly "add up" or point toward the conclusion that I'd better tune my guitar before tonight's concert. Thus, you can see that the first thing that your argument would need to do to be taken seriously would be not merely to avoid obvious internal contradictions but also to actually "tie together" in some way or "add up" to something. This means that your argument must not exemplify the relational quality of discohesion.

The second thing that your argument would need to do is show that you had considered—or at least had some awareness of—counterviews (just as I am considering counterviews to my own argument right here), that you had sound responses to these counterviews, and that your argument is at least potentially responsive to further criticism. If, in contrast, you were just to assert a view, plain and simple, with no account taken of the fact that powerful and well-known counterviews had been developed elsewhere, and with clear indications that you really had no interest in fairly and squarely addressing these existing counterviews or any future counterviews (that is, that your argument was not even potentially open to criticism), then, no matter how internally cohesive your argument is, informed judges will rightly dismiss it just as quickly as if it were "all over the place." This means that your argument must not exemplify the relational quality of fixed cohesion.

Taken together, these considerations mean that, in order to be taken seriously, your argument against responsive cohesion must embody the very relational quality that you are arguing against since it must both hold together (be cohesive) and be actually and potentially responsive to existing and future counterviews. Yet, if the success of your anti-responsive-cohesion argument must trade on the very relational quality that you are arguing against, then the very form of your (responsively cohesive) "counterargument" will serve to undermine its own allegedly anti-responsive-cohesion content. You will, in other words, be engaging in a performative contradiction; your deeds (the form of your argument) will belie your words (the content of your argument); your means will undermine your ends.

To be consistent with the content of your pro-fixed-cohesion or pro-discohesion argument, you would need to trade on those relational qualities in the form of your argument, but if you do the former, then informed judges will consider that you are not worth arguing with because you cannot be argued with (your views are fixed, and that's that) whereas if you do the latter then informed judges will not listen to you because your argument won't make any sense in the first place—it will be "all over the place." Either way, your anti-responsive-cohesion argument will be stillborn.

The only way that I can see out of this would be to concede that the relational quality of responsive cohesion is indeed the best kind of relational quality when it comes to rational argumentation, and then trade on that concession to provide a responsively cohesive argument to the effect that the relational qualities of fixed cohesion or discohesion are superior in (at least some) other domains of interest. However, this move raises a host of major problems. First, you have automatically conceded the fact that the other relational quality or qualities that you are arguing for (i.e., in addition to responsive cohesion) are not foundational since, at a minimum, they don't apply to the best form of rational argumentation (for which you've conceded that responsive cohesion is supreme). Second, you have made a move that looks arbitrary and desperate: arbitrary because there would appear to be no obvious reason why the realm of rational argumentation should be so different from other domains of interest as to require one kind of fundamental (as opposed to foundational) value with respect to rational argumentation and another with respect to (at least some) other domains; and desperate because this looks exactly like the kind of ad hoc maneuver that one would expect from someone who would do almost anything to save a fixed idea (which would tag you as an advocate of the fixed cohesion variety) or, alternatively, someone who is just not interested in playing by any rules at all (which would tag you as an advocate of the discohesion variety). Finally, even if you were to make this nonfoundational, arbitrary, and desperate move, then where's the evidence? I mean, why would you bother?

In view of these considerations, it is difficult to see why anyone would want to argue in favor of fixed cohesion or discohesion as opposed to responsive cohesion as the foundational value, but if someone did want to do this, then we ought to say, in sporting spirit: "Good luck—oh, and do remember to use responsively cohesive arguments against the theory of responsive cohesion if you want to be taken seriously by informed judges."

Appendix to Chapter 4: A Note on the Concepts of *Responsive Cohesion, Reflective Equilibrium, Organic Unity, Complex Systems,* and So On

Tediousness warning: the following is potentially rather tedious and should be skipped, with a clean conscience, by anyone who finds it so. It's really for those who already have an interest in the notions of reflective equilibrium, organic unity, complex systems, or other "high-level" concepts that they think might have something in common with the ideas that I am in the process of developing here.

The *method of responsive cohesion* that I describe in chapter 4 might seem to some readers to be rather like John Rawls's well-known *method of reflective equilibrium* (advanced, albeit quite briefly, in his influential book *A Theory of Justice*[1]), but such resemblances as there are begin and end in the domain of methodology, for the concept of responsive cohesion is at once a broader, deeper, and more specifically defined concept than that of reflective equilibrium. I will explain these points in turn. Responsive cohesion is a broader concept than that of reflective equilibrium because Rawls uses the latter only in relation to the question of methodological procedure in the domain of theoretical reasoning; specifically, to refer to the process of mutual adjustment between the principles of a theory and our considered judgments in regard to those principles. (And note that, even at the level of methodology, this is, in any case, emphatically not the same as the method of responsive cohesion as I outlined it in chapter 4.) In contrast, responsive cohesion does not refer only to a methodological procedure in the domain of theoretical reasoning, but rather, as I have been at pains to point out throughout, to a relational quality (or form of organization) that can apply to anything. And because this relational quality can apply to anything, it should come as no surprise that examples of this relational quality can be found in the domain of theoretical reasoning. Thus, some methodological procedures in the domain of theoretical reasoning—such as Rawls's method of reflective equilibrium—will exemplify the relational quality of responsive cohesion while others will not, but the range of application of the concept of responsive cohesion extends well beyond the domain of methodological procedure in the domain of theoretical reasoning itself. Thus, the concept of responsive cohesion is a much broader one than that of reflective equilibrium. Moreover, the concept of responsive cohesion is employed in the service of generating a much broader approach to ethics than is the concept of reflective equilibrium. This is because Rawls employs his method of reflective equilibrium in the service of generating a "theory of justice" that is wholly confined to the realm of conventional, interhuman ethics, whereas I employ the concept of responsive cohesion to underpin the development of an entire General Ethics, that is, an ethical "Theory of Everything" (see chapter 1 of this book for my outline of the difference between conventional, interhuman ethics and General Ethics).

Responsive cohesion might be a much broader concept—and one that is put to much broader use—than that of reflective equilibrium, but in what sense is it also a deeper concept than that of reflective equilibrium? Again, the answer stems from the fact that reflective equilibrium refers to a rational procedure in the domain of theoretical reasoning, whereas responsive cohesion refers to a relational quality that can exist in any and all domains of interest. As a rational procedure in the domain of theoretical reasoning, the method of reflective equilibrium refers ultimately to the *mental states* of rational agents. As Simon Blackburn puts it in the first sentence of his characterization of "reflective equilibrium" in *The Oxford Dictionary of Philosophy*, reflective equilibrium is "A state in which all one's *thoughts* about a topic fit together; in which there are no loose ends or recalcitrant elements that do not cohere with an overall position" (my emphasis).[2] But what is it that ought to guide or drive one's thoughts toward the mental state indicative of reflective equilibrium? If one is engaging in this rational procedure in a genuine way, then, as Rawls would agree, what ought to guide or drive one's thoughts toward reflective equilibrium is not the imposition of one's own preferences or principles upon the outcome (which is undoubtedly one way of achieving a kind of mental equilibrium), but rather the extent to which considered judgments (or data in the case of a scientific rather than a normative theory) and general principles can genuinely be said to answer to each other. But this is just another way of saying that the achievement of the mental state of reflective equilibrium ought to be driven by the degree of responsive cohesion that actually exists between the salient features of the problem situation under consideration. Of course, making judgments about the degree of responsive cohesion that actually exists between the salient features of the problem situation under consideration is itself a function of interpretation, which, seemingly, brings us back to the mental state of reflective equilibrium. However, if we are realists, we should not kid ourselves that our interpretation decides the degree of responsive cohesion that actually exists in any given situation; rather, our interpretation ought to be responsive to the degree of responsive cohesion that actually exists in that situation. In other words, my mental state of reflective equilibrium ought to be a function of the extent to which the salient features of a problem situation actually do answer to each other. Thus, responsive cohesion is a deeper concept than that of reflective equilibrium in the sense that the former specifies the actual relational quality (between the salient features of a problem situation) that ought to drive the achievement of the latter mental state.

Finally, in what sense is responsive cohesion a more specifically defined concept than that of reflective equilibrium? The answer to this question is quite straightforward. The concept of reflective equilibrium tends only to be discussed in terms of an implied contrast, which, presumably, we must take to be something like "the kind of lack of 'equilibrium' that exists between theoretical principles and considered judgments when an insufficient degree of reflection has been brought to bear on them." Yet in order to be able to say when an instance of reflective equilibrium has been achieved, partly achieved, or is some way off yet, and so on, one necessarily needs to have a pretty clear idea of what is meant by a *lack* of "reflective equilibrium." Alas, this contrasting catchall category tends to lurk in the literature on reflective equilibrium only in a shadowy, implicit way.

In contrast, the concept of responsive cohesion is explicitly defined from the outset in terms of its contrast with not one, but rather two other kinds of relational qualities—those of fixed cohesion on the one hand and discohesion on the other hand. Moreover, I do not just define responsive cohesion in terms of these contrasting categories at the *outset*; rather, in every example in every general area I consider in chapter 4, I explicitly discuss the three categories of fixed cohesion, responsive cohesion, and discohesion and make the case for the superiority of the relational quality of responsive cohesion *in that context*. Doing this not only makes my task easier but also aids general understanding. This is precisely because the categories of fixed cohesion and discohesion can be thought of as lying "on either side" of the category of responsive cohesion: if an instance of responsive cohesion "fossilizes," gets "stuck in a rut," and so on, then it deteriorates into an instance of fixed cohesion; if, on the other hand, it "spins out," blows up, breaks down, comes apart, or whatever, then it deteriorates into an instance of discohesion. And to the extent that something can reasonably be characterized as an instance of either fixed cohesion or discohesion, then, to that extent, and precisely to that extent, it cannot be characterized as an instance of responsive cohesion (at that level of discussion at least), and vice versa. All in all then, the concept of responsive cohesion is not only a broader and deeper concept than that of reflective equilibrium but also a more specifically defined one.

Whereas I have argued that any similarities that might exist between the concept of responsive cohesion and Rawls's well-known concept of reflective equilibrium are fairly limited, there are probably deeper similarities to be found between the ideas that I am advancing here and some much less well-known—and rather densely formulated—ethical ideas advanced by Robert Nozick in his book *Philosophical Explanations*.[3] (Nozick is much better known for his work in political philosophy, especially his defense of libertarianism entitled *Anarchy, State, and Utopia*, which, as it happens, effectively established him as John Rawls's primary opponent in the domain of political philosophy.[4]) Nozick's ethical ideas in *Philosophical Explanations* were focused on the idea that "the basic dimension of value" is that of *organic unity*, which is an idea that itself taps into a diffuse but longer standing tradition of thought. Given the breadth and depth of this claim, Nozick could probably argue, as I have in regard to the concept of responsive cohesion, that Rawls's concept of reflective equilibrium can be understood as an *example* of organic unity in regard to methodological procedure in the domain of theoretical reasoning.

However, in this case too, there are substantial differences between Nozick's ideas and the ideas that I am introducing here. A full elaboration of these differences would, for example, need to cover at least the following points. First, there are some significant conceptual differences between Nozick's core concept and mine. Specifically, Nozick thinks of organic unity in quasi-quantifiable terms such that item A is viewed as having more organic unity (and therefore as being more valuable) than item B if A contains more diversity than B while also being just as unified as B. That is, the more diversity that one can pack into the same degree of overall unity, the greater the degree of organic unity. But this suggests that, for example, a very complicated painting or symphony (a painting or symphony consisting of *lots* of elements) that nevertheless has the same degree of overall unity as a simple Zen garden (consisting of relatively few elements) must be judged to have "more" organic unity than the Zen garden. In contrast, my approach to this would be to say that the complicated painting or symphony and the simple Zen garden can both be thought of as equally good examples of responsive cohesion in their own domains of reference. In my view, the differences that do exist between these examples can better be captured as follows: different kinds of equally good examples of responsive cohesion can convey quite different kinds of experiential qualities depending upon their more precise constitution. Thus, highly responsively cohesive paintings or symphonies that are complicated in the sense of being very "busy" might convey an exhilarating sense of excitement whereas a highly responsively cohesive Zen garden might convey a sense of calmness and serenity. Equally good, but quite different kinds of, examples of responsive cohesion are just that—equally good but different. One kind of responsive cohesion is not necessarily any better than another just because it packs more diversity into the same degree of unity.

Second, even if we set these conceptual differences to one side, the term *organic unity* is not as illuminating as the term *responsive cohesion* since the latter can be taken to explain how it comes to be the case that something gives us the sense of possessing this mysterious quality of "organic unity."

Third, as already noted in my discussion of Rawls's work, I explicitly present my central concept of responsive cohesion from the outset in terms of its contrast with not one, but rather two other kinds of relational qualities—those of fixed cohesion and discohesion—and explicitly argue for the superiority of responsive cohesion over both of these other kinds of relational qualities in one domain of interest after another. In contrast, Nozick, like Rawls in his discussion of reflective equilibrium, does not explicitly define his central concept of organic unity in contrast to other categories from the outset, nor does he proceed by explicitly arguing its superiority over contrasting categories as a matter of course. His concept of organic unity is therefore a much less specifically defined one—or, more bluntly, a considerably vaguer one—than that of responsive cohesion. Indeed, commentators on this aspect of Nozick's work have criticized his concept of organic unity primarily on the grounds of its vagueness.[5]

Fourth, I develop and elaborate the ideas associated with the idea of responsive cohesion in quite different directions to those pursued by Nozick and in considerably more specific detail in regard to our actual ethical obligations. For example, you will see by the end of this book that I explicitly distinguish between *internal* and *contextual* forms of responsive cohesion; develop the implications of this distinction into a detailed, ethically significant *theory of contexts*; and, in conjunction with the development of a *differentiated model of our obligations in respect of other people*, proceed to develop a distinction inherent in this theory of contexts—namely, a distinction between beings that are *mind-sharers* and beings that are *iso-experients*—into a detailed *differentiated model of our obligations in respect of all beings*. This is getting well ahead of the argument that I have presented at this stage of the book, but the point of noting what is to come in this context is simply to say that these developments are quite different from, and more specifically detailed in regard to our actual ethical obligations than, anything that Nozick presents in developing his central concept. (Needless to say, all these differences in argumentative direction—and more—also apply in regard to the contrast between the argument that I develop in this book and Rawls's argument.)

Fifth, I have developed the ideas associated with the concept of responsive cohesion specifically in response to the challenges posed by the range of problems that any General Ethics must be able to address. This has necessitated developing and introducing for the first time the concept of

General Ethics in chapter 1, outlining a detailed list of the kinds of problems that any General Ethics must be able to address in chapter 2, and addressing each of these problems from the perspective of the fully developed theory of responsive cohesion in chapter 10. None of these kinds of features figures in Nozick's proposal that we consider "organic unity" to be "the basic dimension of value."

It might also be worth adding two further contextualizing points in regard to Nozick's ideas on organic unity and mine on responsive cohesion. First, any general, preliminary kinds of similarity that there might be between Nozick's ideas and mine are, as it happens, coincidental because I was simply not aware of this aspect of Nozick's work at the time that I developed the main ideas herein. Moreover, I have not found it profitable, in terms of advancing my own ideas, to draw upon Nozick's work once I learned of it (from, and with my thanks to, Simon Hailwood, who is one of the few philosophers to have written on this aspect of Nozick's work).[6] Second, it might also be of interest to note that Nozick did not pursue his ideas on organic unity in any detail in his later work; thus, they are completely absent from *Invariances*, his last book, despite the fact that he devotes a sixty-five-page concluding chapter to ethics, including a section specifically devoted to what he calls the core principle of ethics.[7]

Yet another set of ideas that some people might associate with the ideas developed here are those that have been emerging in the (note: distinctly nonnormative) context of the study of *complex systems* since these systems (which also get referred to under a variety of other descriptions such as *nonlinear dynamical systems*—at least certain kinds of them, *self-organizing systems*, *complex adaptive systems*, and so on) are typically characterized in terms of lying between the domains of strict order on the one hand and chaos on the other.[8] There are similarities—as well as major differences—to be mined in regard to the relationship between these two sets of ideas, but while I have for some time had a reasonable degree of familiarity with the ideas that have been emerging in regard to the study of complex systems (in contrast to my previously expressed ignorance in regard to Nozick's work on organic unity), I have again not found it profitable, in terms of advancing my own ideas, to draw upon this work.

There are, again, significant reasons for this. For starters, the ideas that I am advancing in this book have been developed within a wholly normative framework of reference, whereas the ideas associated with the study of complex systems have been developed within a wholly descriptive framework of reference. For seconds, while all "self-organizing systems" or "complex adaptive systems" will exemplify the relational quality of responsive cohesion, the reverse does not apply: a painting or a novel can exemplify the relational quality of responsive cohesion, but a painting or a novel is neither a *self*-organizing system (instead, it is a highly *intentionally* organized piece of work) nor a complex adaptive system (since it clearly does not adapt to changes either internally or in terms of its outward behavior). Thus, the concept of responsive cohesion includes but goes well beyond referring only to the kinds of systems that are of primary interest to complexity theorists. These two reasons alone, then, should be enough to suggest why I have not found it profitable to draw upon work in complexity theory in advancing the theory of responsive cohesion; to do so would serve on the whole to confuse things more than clarify them, especially in an initial exposition of the theory.

I have gone out of my way here to point out some of the differences between the concept of responsive cohesion and other ideas with which it might—or, in some of my work-in-progress presentations, already has—been associated. I have done this because I have found from experience that people—including, and perhaps especially, philosophically literate people—will often proceed immediately to map any relatively new idea on to some idea that they have previously heard, even when this mapping may obscure things more than illuminate them. Indeed, I think that many philosophers can think of a colleague or two, somewhere along the way, who, upon the presentation of any relatively new idea, can be counted on to inform them that, apparently, Plato, for example, said "much the same thing" around 2,400 years ago (a comparison that I would find particularly tiresome since I personally consider Plato to have got it pretty much comprehensively wrong in regard to the main ideas that he is taken—albeit through his dialogic form of exposition—as having advanced). The upshot of this kind of practice is that people too often simply introduce unwanted mental "interference effects" in approaching a relatively new set of ideas. I shall therefore leave the mining of such similarities and differences as may exist between the ideas that I am developing herein and the ideas of others—including Plato no doubt!—to stronger minds than my own and settle for a plea that the ideas that I am advancing herein first be considered in their own terms of reference and not someone else's.

5

The Best Approach to Conventional, Interhuman Ethics

In the previous chapter I presented a general survey across an extremely wide range of domains of interest in order to work toward the conclusion that the relational quality of responsive cohesion is the foundational value. This is the basic claim of the theory of responsive cohesion. However, although the theory of responsive cohesion proceeds from this basic claim, its full elaboration extends well beyond this basic claim alone, as we will see in this and the following chapters.

Whereas I was concerned in the previous chapter with pursuing a considerable breadth of analysis in order to establish the claim that the relational quality of responsive cohesion is the foundational value, I want in this chapter to pursue a particular domain of interest—or problem situation—in considerable depth. Specifically, I want to show how we can use the kind of thinking that is inspired by the theory of responsive cohesion to take us further in our understanding of what constitutes the best example of its kind in a particular domain of interest. The domain of interest that I want to focus on here is that of conventional, interhuman ethics, and I want to focus on this domain of interest for five reasons. First, this is the domain of interest that has traditionally been associated with the sum total of what "ethics" is about. It is therefore important to show in a more detailed way than I was able to go into in the last chapter how the theory of responsive cohesion approaches this domain of interest. Second, the analysis that I will present here in regard to interhuman ethics can be taken as an illustration or model of the way in which the kind of thinking that is inspired by the theory of responsive cohesion can be employed in considering other domains of interest in greater depth. Third, pursuing the theory of responsive cohesion's approach to interhuman ethics will enable me to introduce a range of important ideas—including a *harm–help spectrum*, a *multiple perspective account of moral agency*, and a *differentiated model of our obligations in respect of other people*—that I will expand upon in chapter 8 when I consider our obligations in respect of *all* beings.

Fourth, I hope to show that the theory of responsive cohesion's approach to interhuman ethics is better than that of the other dominant approaches on offer, and that this is precisely because it manifestly takes into account salient features of the interhuman ethics problem situation that the other dominant approaches overlook. Fifth, showing this will help to make good my claim that it is always the example that most exemplifies the relational quality of responsive cohesion that is "typically judged to be the best example of its kind by informed judges, or that, in any case, ought to be judged to be the best example of its kind." If you agree that the approach that I develop here is better than that of the other dominant approaches on offer and that this is because it manifestly takes into account salient features of the interhuman ethics problem situation that these other approaches overlook, then you will be agreeing that, notwithstanding the support that these other approaches have enjoyed from informed judges, it is the approach developed here— or something very like it—that ought now to be accepted as the best approach to interhuman ethics.

There are two further points to note in this introductory section. First, the general term *interhuman ethics* can in principle refer to the study of ethical concerns that arise at all levels of human interaction. This can include interaction between not only individuals but also collectivities of individuals. We could therefore refer to ethical concerns that arise in the context of interaction between individual people on the one hand and collectivities of people on the other hand as *interpersonal ethics* and *sociopolitical ethics* respectively. Although interhuman ethics technically embraces both of these kinds of ethics, the fact of the matter is that conventional discussions of interhuman ethics tend to be couched in terms of questions relating to interpersonal ethics; questions concerning how a particular, individual moral agent (i.e., a person who is capable of understanding the ethically related issues that are at stake in a situation) should act in regard to other individual people (whether or not these others are themselves moral agents). Thus, in order to keep the present discussion manageable as much as anything else, I will proceed to discuss interhuman ethics in this chapter as if it refers simply to the conventional, *interpersonal ethics* understanding of *interhuman ethics*. However, I will turn this discussion to sociopolitical account when I address problem 6: the *"What is the best 'flavor' of politics?" problem* in chapter 10 (this is the chapter in which I will address each of the eighteen problems that I outlined in chapter 2 from the perspective of the, by then, fully developed theory of responsive cohesion).

The second further introductory point is the following. The representative branch of interhuman ethics that I am referring to as *interpersonal ethics* can itself be subdivided in various ways. Perhaps the most obvious way is this: following a fundamental division that now exists in many of our own lives, we often distinguish between interpersonal ethics in our everyday lives and interpersonal ethics in our professional lives. Obviously a range of constraining factors kicks in when we talk about interpersonal ethics in our professional lives, such as the fact that the profession we belong to might simply require adherence to a particular code of conduct whether we, as individuals, agree with all of this code of conduct or not. Professional interpersonal ethics will also generally require us to hold everyone (even our own family and friends) at, as it were, roughly the same personal distance from us; indeed, it might even require that we hold our family and friends at a greater distance from us than people we don't know at all. For example, it might require us not to treat them ourselves if we are a doctor or to exclude ourselves from a selection committee that is going to interview them for a job or promotion. For this reason, then, I am also going to discuss interhuman ethics in the commonly understood sense of interpersonal ethics as it applies in our everyday, nonprofessional lives; interpersonal ethics construed as concerning how we should act in respect of other people as other *human beings* rather than simply as the occupiers of certain professional or social *roles*, such as those of, say, accountant and client, doctor and patient, teacher and student. I will therefore be discussing what we could refer to as *everyday interpersonal ethics* in contrast to *professional interpersonal ethics*.

Taken together, these remarks add up to the fact that I am going to discuss interhuman ethics in its purest, simplest, and most open (or least constrained) form. That is, I am going to discuss interhuman ethics as concerned with how we, as individual human beings, should act in respect of other individual human beings—pure and simple. This means that I am, for now at least, explicitly setting to one side political considerations regarding, say, "what the government should do" (rather than us) as well as professional considerations regarding how we should act as occupiers of a professional role rather than as individual human beings as such. If we wish to bring political and professional considerations to bear on the question of interhuman ethics, then we will be introducing new kinds of salient features into the "pure and simple" version of the interhuman ethics problem situation that I will be discussing in this chapter. However, the kind of analysis that I will present in this chapter provides a model for how to proceed in the light of adding further, or other, salient features to the interhuman ethics problem situation—such as considerations concerning the nature of, and the responsibilities that come with, the assumption of professional roles.

Let us now proceed to consider how the kind of thinking that is inspired by the theory of responsive cohesion can be applied to the domain of interhuman ethics, where interhuman ethics is understood in its purest, simplest, and most open form; where it is understood, in short, as what I have referred to as *everyday interpersonal ethics*. To begin with, it will be necessary to revise a little of what I have said in the previous chapter in regard to the method of responsive cohesion and the theory's approach to interhuman ethics; however, the ideas to be developed here will end up going far beyond the little that I had to say about interhuman ethics in the previous chapter.

The Method of Responsive Cohesion

Any domain of interest can also be thought of as presenting us with, or being defined by, a particular kind of problem situation. In order to see which example in a particular domain of interest—or, equally, which possible solution to a particular problem situation—is best, the theory of responsive cohesion directs us, as I have already noted in the previous chapter, to ask three questions:

(i) What is the domain of interest or problem situation? (That is, how can this domain of interest or problem situation best be characterized?)
(ii) What are the salient features of this domain of interest or problem situation?

(iii) Which example in this domain of interest, or which possible solution to the problem situation, can best be characterized in terms of these salient features answering to (i.e., being responsive to) each other in the service of generating and maintaining cohesion overall?

As also previously noted, we can refer to this three-part approach as describing the *method of responsive cohesion*. The claim at the heart of the theory of responsive cohesion is that the answer delivered by this method will be the answer that is typically judged to be the best example of its kind by informed judges, or that, in any case, ought to be judged to be the best example of its kind (for reasons that I explained at the beginning of the last chapter and referred to again briefly at the beginning of this chapter, i.e., because the answer delivered by this method can be shown to have taken into account salient features of the problem situation that have been overlooked by rival approaches).

If we take the first of these questions and direct it toward the interhuman ethics problem situation, then it becomes: What is the interhuman ethics problem situation? The "pure and simple" version of the interhuman ethics problem situation can be characterized as one in which individual, flesh-and-blood people, each of whom has their own range of cares and concerns, interact with other individual, flesh-and-blood people, each of whom has their own range of cares and concerns, and both affect and are affected by each other in different ways, some of which they like and some of which they dislike. Now, whereas some ethicists might want to attach various bells and whistles to their definition of this problem situation—perhaps even smuggling their own preferred answer to this problem situation into the way in which they characterize it in the first place—this represents a common or garden variety, straight-down-the-line characterization of the "pure and simple" version of the interhuman ethics problem. As Hugh LaFollette says in the opening sections of his widely adopted textbook *Ethics in Practice*: "Morality, traditionally understood, involves primarily, and perhaps exclusively, *behavior that affects others*"; and "Choices that clearly *affect others* are moral choices" (my emphases).[1] This is the context in which people try to establish an answer to the question: What are the nature and limits of the kinds of behaviors that it is reasonable for us to expect from others and reasonable for each of these others to expect from us?

The method of responsive cohesion next directs us to consider the salient features of this problem situation. If the general territory of conventional, interhuman ethics can be described as outlined above, then the central salient features of this problem situation can be found in the answers to these questions:

(i) What are the basic ways in which people *can* affect others?
(ii) What are the basic ways in which moral agents *wish* to affect others?
(iii) What are the basic ways in which people *wish to be affected* by others?

Once we have drawn out the salient features associated with these questions, the method of responsive cohesion finally directs us to consider how we can best get these features to answer to (i.e., be responsive to) each other in the service of generating and maintaining cohesion overall. According to the theory of responsive cohesion, the solution that is produced by this method will represent the best approach to interhuman ethics; it will represent the approach that informed judges either do consider to be the best kind of approach to the interhuman ethics problem situation or ought to consider to be the best approach (because the answer delivered by this method can be shown to have taken into account salient features of the problem situation that have been overlooked by rival approaches).

I will therefore proceed by considering in the following sections, first, the three questions that I have just outlined in order to draw out their salient features and, second, how we can get the salient features associated with these questions to answer to each other in the most responsively cohesive way. We can then see if we think that this answer represents the best overall approach to the interhuman ethics problem situation.

What Are the Basic Ways in Which People Can Affect Others? The Harm–Help Spectrum

Harming

Consider the basic ways in which people can affect others. The most salient basic distinction here is surely that between *harming* and *helping*. Moreover, some simple reflection on this basic distinction suggests that it makes sense to distinguish two basic subcategories of harming and three basic subcategories of helping. We can think of these categories as constituting a spectrum of possibilities that range from harming to helping. I will therefore refer to this spectrum as the *harm–help spectrum* and will consider each of these possibilities in turn—although, as we will see, I will need to devote rather more discussion to the harming end of the spectrum than the helping end because understanding the basic forms of harm (especially one of the two main subcategories that I will come to) is a considerably more complex matter than understanding the basic forms of help. I also hasten to add here that I am using the convenient term "spectrum" in a very loose way here, simply to indicate "a range of possibilities"; it should not be taken to mean that the forms of harming and helping that I will outline can all be arrayed along a particular kind of continuous dimension.

The most significant subcategories of harming are *causing unnecessary pain and suffering* on the one hand and *causing unwanted death* on the other. However, several points of clarification are necessary. First, causing unnecessary pain and suffering and causing unwanted death fall into separate subcategories because it is possible to cause death in a relatively or even completely painless way (e.g., not just sedation until death—like having a general anesthetic but never reemerging—but any death that follows on from instant loss of consciousness such that the person "didn't know what hit them"). Conversely, it is entirely possible to cause pain and suffering without causing death. Not only do these harms represent empirically separable kinds of harm, but even understanding exactly why they *are* harms needs to be understood in different terms, which I will come to shortly. Indeed, even understanding exactly *what kind of death* we are talking about when we take causing unwanted death to be a form of harm requires considerable thought. I will consider this question shortly as well.

Second, I have phrased these two subcategories of harming in terms of causing *unnecessary* pain and suffering and causing *unwanted* death to allow for the fact that people will give their consent to other people causing them pain and suffering when they themselves deem such pain and suffering to be sufficiently necessary (e.g., in the course of medical and dental care) and will also seek to end their own lives or request that their lives be ended or allowed to end as soon as possible in the face of irresolvable, and possibly worsening, pain and suffering caused by a terminal illness (these three situations refer to *suicide, active euthanasia,* and *passive euthanasia* respectively; etymologically, "euthanasia" means a "good," "pleasant," or "easy" death). Actively terminating someone's life or allowing them to die in these kinds of circumstances does not harm them from their point of view, but rather both *stops further harm* occurring to them (by ceasing their pain and suffering) and *helps* them here and now by responding positively to what is now their dying desire. For these reasons, we need to distinguish those kinds of caused pains and sufferings and those kinds of caused deaths that give people what they genuinely want (whether it be dental treatment or euthanasia) from those kinds of caused pains and sufferings and those kinds of caused deaths that do not. The former constitute forms of *help*; the latter constitute forms of *harm*. (That said, we generally consider that if it is reasonable to help a person to die, then—barring authorized forms of capital punishment, which in fact amount to authorized forms of harm rather than help—it is only reasonable to do so in the context of the person having an underlying and worsening organic disease whose prognosis provides us with a strong reason for believing that their request would not be reversed if they were, as it were, "made," "forced," or "condemned" to endure their disease for longer.)

Third, I have referred to pain *and* suffering in regard to the first of the two basic forms of harm that I have distinguished because people will sometimes want to distinguish between *pain*, in the sense of an essentially bodily based sensation, and *suffering*, in the sense of mental anguish, that is, as a more cognitively based phenomenon. Even so, pain and suffering clearly lie on the same kind of (affective) scale—they both *feel bad*—and, whatever nuances people might sometimes want to read into these words, they are actually defined in terms of each other in standard dictionary definitions (e.g., my dictionary not only defines "suffering" in terms of "a state or an instance of enduring *pain*" but it also gives one of the meanings of "pain" as "*emotional suffering or mental distress*" [my emphases]).[2] Thus, while nothing much hangs on the nuances that people might wish to read into these words, I nevertheless use them both to imply that I am intending to refer to the whole range of negative affects, from physical pain to mental distress. For convenience, I will also at times refer to harm of the "pain and suffering" kind in more formal terms as *affective harm* (i.e., harm in respect of our sensations, feelings, and emotions).

With these qualifications in mind, I now want to consider this question: What is it about unnecessary pain and suffering (or affective harm) and unwanted death that makes them forms of *harm*? This is easy to answer in regard to unnecessary pain and suffering. It is effectively true by definition that people do not like to experience pain and suffering, pure and simple. (I add this "pure and simple" here to take account of cases of masochism: the masochist's experience of pain and suffering is never pain and suffering, pure and simple; it is mixed in with a peculiar form of pleasure. So peculiar, in fact, that genuine cases of masochism, in which a person takes pleasure, especially sexual pleasure, in experiences that would normally be thought of as genuine—and often humiliating— forms of pain and suffering are regarded in psychology and psychiatry as an aberrant, and at times even life-threatening, condition.) Now, although people do not like to experience pain and suffering, they will nevertheless voluntarily submit to these experiences if they consider them to be necessary (e.g., in the course of medical and dental treatment) since these forms of pain and suffering are viewed as part and parcel of being helped rather than harmed. However, it also follows that people will strongly object to, and will actively fight against or flee from, being caused unnecessary pain and suffering for the obvious reason that they do not like these experiences and so do not wish to submit to them unnecessarily. Thus, the simple fact of the matter is that people universally experience unnecessary forms of pain and suffering as harmful. (Note again that masochists do not experience certain forms of pain and suffering that would ordinarily be regarded as harmful *as* harmful precisely because they feel a compelling *need* to undergo these experiences and so regard them as in some sense *necessary* to them, as, in a peculiar sense, helpful to them.)

It is much easier to answer the question regarding what it is about unnecessary pain and suffering (or affective harm) that makes it a form of harm than it is to answer the question regarding what it is about unwanted death *as such*—that is, shorn of considerations regarding pain and suffering—that makes it a form of harm. This is because if my death is unanticipated (so that I have not experienced any mental distress beforehand in regard to it), painless, and, in any case, instant, then I can at no stage *experience* it as a harm to me: I do not experience it before-hand as a harm that is about to be done to me; I do not experience it at the time as a harm that is being done to me; and (obviously) I do not ex-perience it afterward as a harm that has been done to me. Clearly, then, unwanted death—shorn of any form of pain and suffering—constitutes a different kind of harm to that of unnecessary pain and suffering since death need not be experienced (in which case it cannot be experienced as a harm), whereas the harms of pain and suffering are the harms they are in virtue of what a person does experience. If painless death is not *experienced* as harmful, then in what sense can we say that it *is* harmful? The answer lies in our understanding of what it is to be a *person*.

Persons do not simply experience things in terms of some kind of raw, primary form of awareness but fail to be aware, in a secondary way, *of* their awareness; rather, they are conscious *of* their awareness, they can reflect on the fact *that* they are aware. Moreover, persons are conscious of their awareness not only here and now but also as an ongoing, con-nected inner process. This ongoing, connected inner process is consti-tuted by an awareness of the past (the salient points of which can be reviewed in the present), a present form of experience, and plans, hopes, and dreams for the future (which can also be rehearsed and further developed in the present). Taken in combination, the two features of *self-consciousness* and *temporally structured awareness* give rise to *auto-biographically structured awareness*: self-conscious, temporally struc-tured awareness *is* autobiographically structured awareness. It is the combination of these two features that gives each person the sense of being an ongoing, inner, psychological identity—a *self*—that is con-scious of being the subject of an unfolding life-story. And the very fact that persons exist as self-conscious, temporally structured forms of self-awareness—the very fact that their experience is autobiographically structured—also means that they can contemplate the end of their own autobiography, the end of their own sense of themselves and their own sense of time. They can, in other words, consciously contemplate their own death. In doing this, persons always have regard to their life-story: they want to live rich and full lives in general, and, at any given moment, they have future-oriented plans, hopes, and dreams that they want to see realized. This understanding provides us with the key to understanding why even painless unwanted death represents such a grave harm to persons.

The harm that we do in killing someone painlessly and without warning when they do not wish to die (even if this wish is, as philosophers say, *dispositional* rather than consciously *occurrent* at any particular moment) is clearly not a harm of the "pain and suffering" kind—that is, an affective harm—since, by definition, no pain and suffering is involved in their death. But how should we characterize this kind of harm and what should we call it? It is tempting simply to say that killing someone against their wishes in this way is a harm because it violates their wishes in the most fundamental way possible, namely, it terminates their capacity *to* wish for anything at all, and to suggest that this kind of harm be referred to as, say, *mortal harm*, since this term is already understood by people and seems, on the face of it, to straightforwardly label what is being referred to, namely, the death of a human being. But this is to move too fast. The precise nature of the harm that is done here can be described in more precise terms as follows: unwanted painless killing terminates a form of temporally structured self-conscious existence (against the wishes of the person concerned, obviously). This means that it terminates the life of a personal self—of an "I"—that has autobiographical memory claims upon its own past and anticipatory plans, hopes, and dreams in regard to the future. It obliterates the person's sense of self and severs for all time their consciousness of any connection with their past and future.

If a person does not want these things to happen then causing them to happen is clearly to harm them (in their own terms of reference) in the deepest sense imaginable. This is because a person's sense of self is not merely some external thing that they can "just happen to value"; rather, it is the locus of the realization *of* all that they—as an individual "I"— value. Similarly, a person's sense of connection with their past and future is not an "added extra" that they can "just happen to value"; rather, it is *constitutive of* their personal identity and therefore of who they are when they value anything. Thus, to describe the harm that is caused by the loss of either self-conscious awareness or temporally structured awareness as a "loss" that can be thought of in the same way as other "losses," like the loss of one's sight or the loss of a loved one, is to misunderstand the nature of what is lost. Whereas *we* can lose things like our sight or a loved one, *we* cannot lose either our self-conscious awareness or the temporally structured dimension of our experience and still *be us*. Rather, to lose either of these things is to lose our personal identity; it is to lose who we *are*; it is the death of our *selves*.

Consider: "You" and "I" are painlessly sedated into a deep, permanent coma and then kept alive for another thirty years before dying of "natural causes." We are thereby effectively killed: each of us "dies," in the only sense that can really matter to us personally, at the moment that we lose consciousness for all time. There is no more "inside story" of our lives from that point on; nothing else *can* matter to us. But events do not even have to take such a fundamentally consciousness-deadening turn for us to "die" in the only sense that can really matter to us. For example, suppose I were to remain conscious but lose any sense of higher-order consciousness *of* my consciousness; that is, suppose that I remain conscious but lose any form of *self-consciousness* and thus any sense of self. In this case, things would happen in my experience from moment to moment, but there would be no "I" to which these events would attach. The form of consciousness that existed would simply experience *this* now, and *this* in the next moment, and so on, but there would be no overarching awareness *of* this awareness—no "I" to whom things happen—because "I" would not exist. To reduce me from being self-conscious to being merely conscious is to obliterate "me": by definition, "I" would no longer exist.

Alternatively, suppose that I remain self-conscious but that any sense of living a temporally structured life is stripped from my consciousness by immersion in a temporal awareness zapper. I might then know *that* I exist in some sense, but I wouldn't be able to put "my" life together in any coherent order. I would simply live in a kind of eternal but changing present in which I would not experience myself as deeply informed by and connected to my "past" or as living in any way for my "future," because the very notions of "past" and "future"—and even "present"— would not exist for me. (If this seems bizarre, then it will seem less so when I come to consider what is involved in temporal awareness in chapter 8, where we will see that temporal awareness—let alone awareness of death itself—represents a very high form of cognitive achievement, one that the available evidence suggests is possible only for language users.)

So, if I remain self-conscious but have all sense of living a temporally structured life stripped from my consciousness, then I would no longer have a sense of being an ongoing, inner, psychological identity that is conscious of being the subject of an unfolding life-story. Yet, as I said earlier, persons are, if nothing else, the subjects of a life-story; their experience is not constituted by temporally isolated and thus temporally disconnected point forms of awareness but rather by a "joined up" *temporally structured form of self-awareness*. In short, a person's sense of self takes the form of an *autobiographically structured* form of awareness.

The upshot of these considerations is that if I were stripped of my temporally structured form of self-consciousness, then "I" would no longer exist in any form that is recognizable to me now. As far as "I" am concerned, the "I" that is *me* would have died since there would be no conscious linkage between the "temporalized me" that I have been for as long as I can remember and the "detemporalized me" that remains after my immersion in a temporal awareness zapper. Not only that, but this unrecognizable "detemporalized me" would not be able to contemplate "its" own death because, having no sense of time in the first place, "it" could not have any sense of "its" own personal time ending. It follows that if this "detemporalized me" were to be painlessly killed, it is difficult to see how any actual harm would be done: painlessly killing this "detemporalized me" would not violate any desire on my part not to be killed, because the fact that I have no conception of the future means that I have no genuinely future-oriented desires and hence no dispositional or occurrent desires not to die; the very idea of not wanting to die (or even wanting to die) is unthinkable to a "detemporalized me." The fact of the matter is that the only "I" that really matters to me—that is, my autobiographical self, the temporally structured life of this particular self-conscious being—would have died at the time that my temporal awareness was stripped away from me.

It seems, then, that I can "die," in the only sense that can really matter to me, in a variety of ways—by being made permanently comatose, stripped of my self-consciousness, or stripped of my temporally structured awareness—without actually dying biologically. Thus, if the term *mortal harm* is taken to mean *causing biological death*, then it is far too general a way of describing the nature of the harm that we are really concerned about when we contemplate the painless killing of someone against their wishes. For it turns out that we are really concerned about not the *biological death* of a person's body, but rather their *autobiographical death*, that is, the death of the *person*, the termination of their temporally structured self-conscious existence. This means that we don't *just* think that it is harmful to cause pain and suffering on the one hand and unwanted *biological death* on the other hand, for if we did think that, then we would not be in a position to object to painlessly sedating people into a permanent coma (while otherwise keeping them alive until they died of "natural causes"), or painlessly stripping them of self-consciousness (with a self-consciousness-zapping device, which leaves basic, non-self-conscious forms of awareness intact), or painlessly stripping them of any form of "temporalized" awareness (with a temporal awareness zapper), since none of these actions causes pain and suffering or biological death. Instead, we think that these things should not be done because they cause *autobiographical death*; they kill the *person* even if they do not cause the biological death of their body. Thus, the best way to describe the kind of harm that is really at issue when we are discussing unwanted painless killing is in terms of the termination of a person's basic *autobiographical capacities*, which includes both *self-conscious awareness* and *temporally structured awareness*. To destroy either of these, let alone both, means that the person "dies to themselves"; they lose any sense of their own identity; they no longer exist from their own first-person point of view.

We clearly need to reach for a more precise term than *mortal harm* in order to capture these points. I therefore propose to refer to this kind of harm—the harm that is done in terminating a form of temporally structured self-conscious existence—as *autobiographical harm*. However, it should be absolutely clear from this discussion that by *autobiographical harm* I do not mean anything like calling people names or saying scandalous things about them. These actions can cause lots of pain and suffering and so are readily captured by the idea of *affective harm*. Yet these are pretty superficial forms of autobiographical harm in the context that I am referring to, since by *autobiographical harm* here I clearly mean autobiographical harm in the deep sense of harm to the basic structural features of a person that enable them to *have* a sense of themselves as an ongoing, inner, psychological identity that is conscious of being the subject of an unfolding life-story. I mean, in other words, the kind of harm that is done by terminating self-conscious awareness, or temporally structured awareness, or both. We could therefore refer to this form of harm as *deep autobiographical harm* in order to distinguish it from *superficial autobiographical harm* (i.e., harm of the "she said nasty things about me" kind), since the former refers to harm to a being's basic autobiographical capacities whereas the latter causes the pain and suffering that it does precisely because it leaves these capacities intact—a fact that, in itself, demonstrates the world of difference that exists between superficial and deep forms of autobiographical harm. However, given that superficial autobiographical harm is just one of the many varieties of affective harm that we can experience, I will for the sake of convenience simply distinguish here and later (in chapter 8) between *affective harm* and *autobiographical harm* rather than always using the longer term *deep autobiographical harm*, or always spelling out the fact that by this term I actually mean *harm to a person's (or any being's) fundamental autobiographical capacities*. Finally, it is perhaps worth noting here that if a person has been the victim of deep autobiographical harm—that is, if they are already "autobiographically dead"—then they can in any case no longer experience any affectively disturbing, superficial forms of autobiographical harm, since they will no longer have the capacity to make the connection between what has been said and themselves.

Helping

In contrast to the two basic forms of harm, the most significant subcategories of helping would seem to be those that I will refer to as *saving help*, *ongoing supportive help*, and *bonus help*. These are rather more straightforward to explain than were the two main forms of harm. *Saving help* is any form of help that relieves or prevents an actual or potentially negative or problematic situation for someone. It can vary from help in the sense of intervening to prevent or relieve a genuine crisis situation for someone to simply helping someone out when they're "in a fix"—perhaps they just urgently need a babysitter for the evening ("Thanks so much, you really saved our night"). This form of help typically involves a strictly limited form of intervention. In contrast, *ongoing supportive help* represents a more embracing form of help than saving help: it is the kind of help that not only relieves or prevents crises or "fixes" but that is extended in a regular, positively supportive way, irrespective of crises or "fixes." This is the kind of help that members of a well-functioning family or intimate relationship generally offer each other on a day-to-day basis and in a variety of ways ranging from ongoing forms of physical help to ongoing forms of emotional and financial support.

Whereas we can think of ongoing supportive help as including but going well beyond saving help, *bonus help* does not build on these other two forms of help in any way, but rather exists as a "world unto itself." (Recall my earlier comment that in outlining the harm–help range of possibilities and referring to them, purely for convenience, as constituting a spectrum of possibilities, I have not meant to suggest that these possibilities can all be arrayed along a particular kind of continuous dimension.) We can think of *bonus help* as help that is given in the spirit of a "No good reason; just because I felt like it" contribution to a situation that is already positive—or at least already pretty reasonable—for those experiencing it. (If the situation is not already pretty good for the recipient, then this form of help is likely to be experienced as a form of saving help, although possibly a misdirected one, because it may not bear an appropriate relationship to the kind of help that is actually needed.) Bonus help effectively takes the form of an unexpected gift when life is going well enough anyway—perhaps an ice cream, an unexpected compliment, or a free holiday courtesy of your rich uncle. It is precisely the whimsical nature of this kind of help—the fact that it is so much within the "gift" of the giver as to whether it is given or not—that explains why it says nothing about whether the person who gives this kind of help would also be prepared to help you out in a crisis (especially in the ways in which you needed to be helped out) or whether they would be prepared to offer you ongoing supportive help. Moreover, whereas there are circumstances in which all of us feel that it would be reasonable to expect others—or at least certain others—to offer us saving help or ongoing supportive help, there are no circumstances under which it is reasonable to expect others to offer us genuinely bonus help. This is simply true by definition: a bonus is "something given, paid, or received above what is due or expected." This means that it is purely within the giver's gift to bestow such help as and when they see fit, since, by definition, the receiver has no legitimate claim to expect to receive such help. If we genuinely think that someone ought to give us bonus help, then we have misunderstood the nature of bonus help.

This, then, completes my analysis of the harm–help spectrum. Having now identified the basic ways in which people can affect others, it is time to turn to the next question.

What Are the Basic Ways in Which Moral Agents Wish to Affect Others?

The Multiple Perspective Account of Moral Agency

The most obvious salient feature of moral agents is a capacity for rational thought (and, thus, the capacity to understand things like: it makes no sense to require or expect people to act in ways in which they genuinely cannot act). This is an uncontested necessary condition for any form of moral agency, since we all accept that people (or any other beings) who are incapable of reasoned thought—and thus are incapable of understanding what they do or the implications of what they are do— cannot be held morally responsible for their actions; it simply makes no sense to hold people, or any other beings, morally responsible for respecting principles that they cannot understand in the first place. However, if we move beyond this uncontroversial salient feature of moral agents, then the most salient feature of actual flesh-and-blood (as opposed to ridiculously idealized) individual moral agents is surely the fact that every moral agent brings—and cannot avoid bringing— multiple perspectives to bear on every moral problem situation. The upshot of these multiple perspectives, which I will outline in this section, is that there is no one-size-fits-all answer to the question "What are the basic ways in which moral agents wish to affect others?" Rather, moral agents wish to affect "others" in different ways depending upon who these "others" are.

I will therefore proceed in this section to offer an account of the basic forms that moral agents' multiple perspectives assume. This will enable us to see more clearly which "others" moral agents are not only most inclined to act on behalf of but also in the best position to act on behalf of (precisely because each moral agent is better informed about the desires of some "others" than other "others"). I will refer to this account as, naturally enough, the *multiple perspective account of moral agency*. However, I want to point out the following at the outset. First, this account represents a straightforward working out of the three-part method of responsive cohesion, which, as we have seen, directs us to define the problem situation and then to identify the salient features of that problem situation (which I am now in the process of doing) before moving on to seeing how we can best get these features to answer to (i.e., be responsive to) each other in the service of generating and maintaining cohesion overall. Second, even though you would think that leading ethical theories would take the highly salient features of the moral problem situation that I am about to outline—that is, those associated with a multiple perspective account of moral agency—into account, the fact is that *they don't*. Third, it follows from the first two points that the multiple perspective account of moral agency that I am about to develop is a distinctive feature of the theory of responsive cohesion. This is because this account is a direct outgrowth of the method of responsive cohesion and plays a major part in the fully developed theory of responsive cohesion, yet it plays no part at all in the other leading approaches to ethics. Fourth, the theory of responsive cohesion's multiple perspective account of moral agency assumes a considerable significance in the context of the overall theory because it represents a fundamental contribution to what I will later outline as the theory of responsive cohesion's *differentiated model of our obligations in respect of all beings*. As I have already noted, I will be outlining a version of this model in regard to our obligations in respect of other *people* later in this chapter. However, once we have explored the theory of responsive cohesion's theory of contexts (in chapter 6) and its implications in regard to our understanding of other beings in general (in chapters 7 and 8), I will then expand this differentiated model so as to embrace questions regarding the nature and extent of our obligations in respect of *all* beings.

Let us now identify the basic forms of the multiple perspectives that any moral agent brings—and cannot avoid bringing—to bear on any moral problem situation. First, the fact that we are self-conscious agents, that is, conscious *of* ourselves, means that we can adopt the stance of objectifying ourselves, of turning ourselves into objects of our own consideration. In this sense, we can consider ourselves *as if* we were just one conscious experiencer among others; *as if* we were seeing ourselves from an external, third-person, objective, "God's-eye-view," or, as ethicists say, *agent-neutral* perspective. When we do this, we can see that there are good reasons for believing that there are a great many other people besides ourselves who want to preserve their capacities to have conscious experiences, and thus to value and pursue certain kinds of conscious experiences, and thus to pursue certain sources of value. (Of course we can extend this reasoning to nonhuman animals as well, but, as I have already said, I am for now—but only for now—restricting this discussion to the domain of conventional, interhuman ethics. This will enable me to introduce a range of theoretical features here that I will extend in chapter 8 into a full-blown model of our obligations toward all other beings, both human and nonhuman.) Furthermore, we can see that from this external, third-person, objective, "God's-eye-view," or agent-neutral perspective, we have no principled reason to favor our own *desires, pursuits, and projects* over those of others (note: see my comments in the next paragraph in regard to the expression "desires, pursuits, and projects"). After all, from this perspective we are just one "other" among others. Utilitarianism famously adopts this agent-neutral stance whereby each person (or sentient being, when utilitarianism is taken seriously) is held to count for one and no more than one.

(On the useful expression "desires, pursuits, and projects": Please note that from here on I will, for the sake of simplicity, just speak in terms of "desires" rather than the more precisely nuanced but also more long-winded expression "desires, pursuits, and projects." I want to make this point explicit because the term "desire" can often suggest something along the lines of an immediate and possibly fleeting mental state, whereas a pursuit tends to suggest a more sustained kind of desire, and a project—especially as in a major *life project*—an even longer-term, more deep-seated kind of desire still. In simplifying things by speaking in terms of "desires" alone then, I am certainly not meaning to imply anything along the lines of immediate and possibly fleeting mental states only but rather am intending to encompass all of the above understandings. Consider "desires" to refer to any and all motivations, however fleeting or sustained.)

This is where the plot thickens. When we also take into account our moment-to-moment, internal, first-person, subjective, personal (as opposed to "God's-eye-view") or *agent-relative* perspective—which we cannot avoid doing since it is we flesh-and-blood *individuals* who are the ones that must act, not some *impersonal* force—then there are at least two outstanding asymmetries between our experience of ourselves and our experience of others. We can refer to these in formal terms as the *epistemological asymmetry* and the *motivational asymmetry*.

The epistemological asymmetry concerns the fact that, in general, each of us is better placed to know our own desires than those of others. It is just a fact that we are epistemologically hooked up to our own desires in a way in which we are not epistemologically hooked up to the desires of others. If this were not the case—if, say, each individual body were epistemologically hooked up to a group or composite mind—then we would know the composite desires of the group as intimately as we presently know our own individual desires. As it happens, however, things are not like that; the universe is just not organized that way.

The motivational asymmetry concerns the fact that, in general, each of us is more motivated, more pushed and pulled, on a moment-to-moment basis, by our own desires than those of others. Thus, not only do I generally know my own desires better than those of others, but I am also generally more motivated to act on behalf of my desires than those of others—and this generally applies even in those cases in which I do happen to know the desires of others as well as I know my own, perhaps even better than I know my own. Although it is true that we often desire to meet the desires of others in certain ways, we simply cannot deny the immediate pushes and pulls that our own desires exert upon us on a moment-to-moment basis in spite of that, whether it's to eat, make love, pursue our favorite hobby, continue to work on our masterpiece, or whatever. It is simply the case that we are motivationally hooked up to our own desires in a way in which we are not motivationally hooked up to the desires of others. If this were not the case—if, say, each individual body were motivationally hooked up to a group or composite form of desire—then we would feel the composite desire of the group as intimately as we presently feel our own individual desires. But, again, things are not like that; the universe is not organized this way either.

The upshot of these considerations is that every moral agent experiences a tension between at least two perspectives. On the one hand, considerations from a purely third-person, agent-neutral perspective tell us that the desires and pursuits of others may be as important to them as our own are to us and that, to the extent that we are capable of viewing ourselves as just one "other" among others, there is therefore no principled reason why the desires and pursuits of *this* particular "other," who just happens to be *me*, should be favored over the desires and pursuits of any other individual. A third-person, agent-neutral perspective views equal interests equally or, we could say, symmetrically. On the other hand, we also have to live with the insistent, inescapable, first-person, agent-relative fact that each of us is on the experiential receiving end of powerful epistemological and motivational asymmetries with respect to our relationships with others. Once we recognize this tension, however, we can then jump back to the third-person, agent-neutral perspective and see that the epistemological and motivational asymmetries that we experience as individuals are also experienced by all other self-conscious moral agents—we're all in the same asymmetrical boat, it's just that it leans a different way for each of us, depending on where we're sitting.

It gets worse too—or at least more complex. This is because what goes for first-person asymmetries also goes—often, but not always, to a lesser extent—for second-person asymmetries. Each of us has a variety of special, second-person relationships. These are relationships in which we think of the individuals concerned as not just any old "others" but rather those for whom we have developed varying degrees of affection and who have therefore assumed varying degrees of personal significance in our lives on that basis. These people are decidedly not those whom we would think of from a third-person, agent-neutral perspective as *them*—or whom we would be happy to think of in this way even if we do happen to know them since they do not really mean anything to us personally— but rather those whom we think of from a *second-person* (and still completely agent-relative) perspective in terms of an affectionate form of *you*. But even within this category of people who have assumed a special degree of personal significance in our affections, there will typically be a very few who are, as it were, "supersignificant" to us. It is therefore useful—indeed, it is more or less necessary—to distinguish between what I will refer to as *significant others* and *supersignificant others*.

We can think of the categories of *significant others* and *supersignificant others* as follows. *Supersignificant others* includes the fuzzy and frequently overlapping subcategories of (psychological) *intimates*, such as one's partner, and *dependents*, such as children (these subcategories are fuzzy and frequently overlap because their members can in some cases and senses belong to either or both categories at any given time). These are typically the people that one lives with (or has lived with and brought up in the case of grown children) and does so because one wants to. The category of *significant others* includes one's friends, that is, it does not necessarily include people like, say, your teacher or boss unless you are also personally close to them; if you are not, then, in terms of any kind of genuine personal closeness, these people remain at a distance for you; they are effectively interchangeable for you; they still belong to the general category of others-in-general for you even though you need to interact with them for a part of your life.

Precisely because of my psychological closeness to these significant and supersignificant others, I have, in general, a better knowledge of their desires than I have of the desires of others-in-general. These significant and supersignificant others also typically mean much more to me than others-in-general, which means, frankly, that I care more about their desires than I do about those of others-in-general—indeed, I can't help doing this—and am, accordingly, more immediately motivated to act on their behalf than I am on behalf of others-in-general. Taken together, these considerations mean that I have both a better knowledge of and a stronger motivation to act on behalf of the desires of those people to whom I feel personally closest than I do in regard to the desires of others-in-general.

It turns out, then, that just as our own first-person perspective reveals powerful epistemological and motivational asymmetries in regard to our relationships with others-in-general, so too do the second-person perspectives we adopt. And we cannot help experiencing these second-person asymmetries any more than we can help experiencing these asymmetries from a first-person perspective. Just as it is a fact that I am epistemologically and motivationally "hooked up to myself"—if I can put it in that somewhat peculiar, schizophrenic ("split mind") way—so it is just as much a fact that the desire for emotional and empathic closeness to a number of *individual* others is hard-wired into us, *and that* life plays out in such a way that this individual is *my* mother, this individual is *my* father, this fantastic person is *my* wife or husband, and so on. Second-person epistemological and motivational asymmetries are therefore just as inescapable as first-person epistemological and motivational asymmetries: we cannot escape our desire for emotional closeness and we cannot escape having particular kinds of relationships with particular individuals. The upshot is that we cannot escape knowing and caring more about the desires of significant and, especially, supersignificant others than we do about the desires of others-in-general.

Even so, the fact that we are physiologically and psychologically more hooked up to ourselves than we are even to those significant others with whom we are most intimate means that we still have a more immediate knowledge of and motivation to act on behalf of our own desires on a moment-to-moment basis than we do in regard to the desires of significant and supersignificant others. That said, it is important to point out that there may be many specific exceptions to this generalization. For example, in this particular instance, I might be rather confused about what I want, whereas you might know me well enough to see (accurately) that there's something I'm really not wanting to see, that what I really want is such-and-such, and that I just haven't admitted it to myself yet. (All of which will provide you with a grand opportunity to say "I told you so" when the truth finally dawns on me.) In this case, your second-person knowledge of my desires trumps my own first-person knowledge of my desires. Second-person motivation can trump first-person motivation too: we can sometimes be more motivated to act on behalf of a loved one's desires than they are themselves—or than we are to act on behalf of our own otherwise equally strong desires, which we might willingly set to one side in favor of our loved one's desires.

Yet for every example that we could give in which second-person knowledge and motivation might trump first-person knowledge and motivation (and similar reversals with respect to third-person knowledge and motivation, such as caring more for a stranger than for yourself or for a friend), we can also give other examples in which, epistemologically speaking, significant others and even supersignificant others are, or have become, a "mystery to us" ("I just don't understand her these days"; "Our son just drops in for meals, but he's like a stranger these days"), or where, motivationally speaking, we are so angry with some significant other that we feel that we just "can't be bothered making the effort any more." Thus, specific exceptions notwithstanding, the general rule is that our first-person knowledge and motivation trump our second-person knowledge and motivation, which, in turn, trump our third-person knowledge and motivation.

Once we've sorted all this out, we can again jump back to the third-person, agent-neutral perspective and see that both the first-person *and* second-person epistemological and motivational asymmetries that we experience as individuals are also experienced by all other self-conscious moral agents. So, again, we're all in the same asymmetrical boat, but it's one that leans a different way for each of us in an even more complex way than we observed earlier. Specifically, it leans a different way for each of us depending not only on where we are sitting (our first-person perspective), but also on where *our* significant and supersignificant others are sitting (our second-person perspective). Welcome to the cruise!

Any *practical* ethics—which is to say, any form of ethics that is worthy of the name—must take these first- and second-person, agent-relative asymmetries very seriously indeed; especially the first-person asymmetries. This is because, when all is said and done, it is the first-person perspective that frames any other perspective we take on. That is, even when we adopt an external, third-person, objective, "God's-eye-view," or agent-neutral perspective, we are still adopting that perspective from an inescapably first-person point of view. And when I adopt a second-person perspective and empathize deeply with how you are feeling and tell you that "I know exactly how you feel," I am still feeling what you are feeling from *my* inescapable first-person point of view rather than from *your* inescapable first-person point of view. In contrast, I cannot choose to adopt or not adopt my own first-person point of view because I cannot be said to adopt it in the first place; rather, this point of view simply comes with the territory of being *me*; it's just how things are. Moreover, I cannot view this first-person point of view through some more intimate point of view (as when I view second- and third-person points of view through my own first-person point of view) because it *is* my intimate point of view.

These considerations mean that second- and third-person perspectives have in common the fact that they are both mediated perspectives, since they are both perspectives in regard to others (significant others and others-in-general, respectively) that are mediated through the perspective of a first-person point of view. In contrast, a first-person perspective is not mediated *through* a first-person point of view, rather it *is* that first-person point of view; it is, in this sense at least, immediately experienced as opposed to being a (first-person) mediated experience. This sets a first-person perspective apart from both second- and third-person perspectives. However, the fact that second-person perspectives occupy a middle ground between first- and third-person perspectives means that there is another sense in which first- and second-person perspectives can be grouped together in contrast to a third-person perspective. Specifically, first- and second-person perspectives share the fact that they are agent-relative perspectives, whereas a third-person perspective is an agent-neutral perspective. That is, exactly whom I am referring to as "I" and "you" or "my friend" can only be determined relative to me—when *you* refer to "I" and "you" or "my friend," then you are referring to different individuals than those that I am referring to by these terms—whereas "him," "her," or "them" can be the same "him," "her," or "them" to anyone. (The former terms are, as philosophers say, *indexical*—that is, what they refer to is dependent upon the context of an utterance, upon exactly who says what, where, and when—in a way in which what the latter terms refer to need not be.) Thus, whereas the mediated/unmediated distinction outlined above sets first-person perspectives apart from second- and third-person perspectives, the agent-relative/agent-neutral distinction sets first- and second-person perspectives apart from third-person perspectives. This analysis of the ambiguous nature of the second-person perspective, which is revealed as being more like the first-person perspective than the third-person perspective or vice versa depending upon the criterion of categorization that is being employed, demonstrates in a rather formal way how and why second-person perspectives can be said to occupy a middle ground between first- and third-person perspectives.

Because we cannot escape from our respective agent-relative, first-person and second-person points of view, we therefore have no choice but to act at least in part from these points of view, however much we might see the good sense in adopting an agent-neutral, third-person point of view as well (we can see the "good sense" in this because we can also see that others are relevantly like us in having desires, pursuits, and projects of their own). Yet, despite this highly salient feature of the interhuman ethics problem situation, other ethical approaches typically emphasize just one of these three perspectives. For example, advocates of the theoretical position known as "ethical egoism"—if there really are any—are committed to emphasizing the primacy of the first-person perspective and ignoring or negating the relevance of second- and third-person perspectives in their "moral" deliberations. Some recent feminist ethicists who argue for an "ethics of care" explicitly disparage the kinds of impartial, impersonal, detached, and abstract principles that they see as typical of masculinist ethical thinking and instead emphasize first- and, especially, second-person perspectives at the expense of these impartial, third-person perspectives.[3] And both the dominant utilitarian and Kantian styles of ethical theorizing (both of which, as duly charged by recent feminist ethicists, have been masculine initiated and, in terms of further contributions and developments, largely masculine driven) emphasize the primacy of third-person perspectives—and thus impartial, impersonal, detached, abstract principles—and do this explicitly at the expense of first- and second-person perspectives.

That said, the influential consequentialist theory of utilitarianism is the worst offender here since it is committed to a third-person, agent-neutral perspective in principle, whereas it would seem to be possible in principle to tweak Kantian-style ethics (i.e., duty-based—or, as I would prefer to say, principle-based—approaches to ethics) in ways that might allow it to take account of all three perspectives. In insisting that each individual is to count for one and no more than one, utilitarianism requires us to adopt the external, third-person, objective, "God's-eye-view," or agent-neutral perspective *only, all the time*, which we cannot do, and to ignore our own desires—and those of our supersignificant and significant others—beyond giving them the weight of a mere one x-billionth part in our calculations (depending on how many people—or, when taken seriously, how many sentient beings—there are altogether, the strengths of their preferences, and so on), which we equally cannot do. And since it simply makes no sense to tell moral agents that they ought to do what they cannot do (hence the sense in the dictum that "ought implies can"), it follows that people ought not to be asked to do what utilitarianism asks them to do because they cannot do it. Utilitarianism does not just set up impossibly high standards of behavior; it sets up impossible standards of perspective taking.

One can, of course, see the appeal of utilitarianism to politicians and other people who sit above "the masses" in various ways and so are (supposedly) able to adopt something like a "God's-eye-view" when it comes to, say, matters of resource allocation. But to prescribe utilitarianism as a basis for, say, Sarah and Bill's day-to-day moral choices is to oblige Sarah and Bill to do things that they cannot do. And since we ought not to tell people that they ought to do what they cannot do—unless we want to drive them mad—it follows that utilitarianism ought not to be advocated to individuals. (It shouldn't be advocated to politicians either, but the reasons are different in this different case. The prime reason is that utilitarianism rationally allows for the sacrifice of innocent individuals in the name of the greater good, which can render it a rationalization for exactly the kind of "political expediency" that can lead us to call into question the integrity of some of our political leaders.)

The thrust of this section has been to introduce the theory of responsive cohesion's multiple perspective account of moral agency, which shows us that moral agents bring—and cannot avoid bringing—multiple (first-, second-, and third-person) perspectives to bear on any interhuman ethics problem situation, and that this leads them to group "others" into different categories, which, for convenience, I have referred to as supersignificant others, significant others, and others-in-general. It follows from these considerations that any form of interhuman ethics that fails to take into account all three perspectives that each moral agent brings—and cannot avoid bringing—to the interhuman ethics problem situation fails to take into account highly salient features of the problem situation that it is attempting to address. If we accept the thrust of this argument, then, other things being equal, we ought to judge a form of interhuman ethics that takes appropriate account of all these highly salient features of the interhuman ethics problem situation (such as the approach that I will go on to develop in this chapter) as better than any rival ethical theory that does not take account of all these features (such as ethical egoism, the "ethics of care" approaches that have largely been advocated by feminist ethicists, and the dominant approaches associated with Kantian-style forms of duty-based ethics on the one hand and, especially, utilitarianism on the other).

Still, we have a few more salient features of the interhuman ethics problem situation to consider.

The Onerousness Factor

In this section I will continue to consider the interhuman ethics problem situation from the perspective of the moral agent who affects others; we will come to the perspective of those who are affected in the next section. What we have seen in the previous section is that moral agents inescapably experience different degrees of motivation in regard to acting on behalf of others as well as different degrees of knowledge in regard to how best to act on their behalf, depending on their personal closeness to these others. However, another highly salient feature of the interhuman ethics problem situation that must be considered in regard to the general question of the ways in which moral agents wish to affect others is the question of how personally burdensome, laborious, or onerous it would be for moral agents to fulfill the desires of others in respect of their not being harmed and positively being helped.

The best way to divorce this question—which I will refer to as the *onerousness factor*—from questions of motivation and knowledge based on personal closeness is to imagine how easy or otherwise it would be for moral agents to honor each form of not harming and positively helping in respect of all people, impartially (i.e., we are being asked, for the sake of the argument, to do the impossible and set aside all questions concerning our motivations to act on behalf of supersignificant others, significant others, and others-in-general as such). Here we can see that, in general, it would become increasingly onerous to apply each form of not harming and positively helping as we move from the not-harming end of the harm–help spectrum toward the helping end (and note that, for the sake of laying out the argument, I am talking here about the most straightforward examples of harming and helping—that is, examples of intentionally causing harm and intentionally helping; moreover, as noted at the beginning of this chapter, I am discussing these issues in the context of everyday interpersonal ethics as opposed to sociopolitical ethics, although I will address sociopolitical issues when I turn to problem 6: the *"What is the best 'flavor' of politics?" problem* in chapter 10).

Let us now consider the claim that, in general, it would become increasingly onerous to apply each form of not harming and positively helping as we move from the not-harming end of the harm–help spectrum toward the helping end. In general, it is pretty easy for us not to cause pain and suffering or not to cause unwanted autobiographical death. Indeed, it is, generally speaking, far more onerous to cause pain and suffering or to cause the unwanted autobiographical death of a person than not to cause these things—and the onerousness of doing these things is exacerbated by the fact that we are likely to meet considerable resistance (indeed, possibly fierce and even life-threatening resistance) if we try to do them. And because we can, in theory, *not do something* (in this case, not cause harm) in respect of everyone with relative ease (whereas to try to harm everyone would be unbelievably onerous and would no doubt lead to a very short life), it is relatively easy for us to apply the principle of not harming people to everyone. Much the same reasoning applies in respect of taking basic precautions in any given situation to ensure that we do not cause harm indirectly through our own recklessness or negligence. Although this can involve doing something, what we need to do in this respect is generally pretty easy when considered in the overall context of the task at hand. Thus, for example, simply not doing something if you are not qualified to do it is pretty easy; and if you are qualified to do it, then taking the basic precautions that you have been trained to take is generally pretty easy when considered in the context of the overall demands of that task. Finally, there is no obvious onerousness factor difference in regard to not causing pain and suffering on the one hand and not causing autobiographical death on the other hand since both involve simply not doing something or, in both cases, taking certain basic precautions that are generally fairly easy to take when considered in the overall context of the task at hand. Thus, in terms of the onerousness factor, there is no need to distinguish between these two basic forms of harm. Instead, we can simply refer to the category of harm in general when discussing this factor.

In contrast to the situation with not harming, positively helping is a far more onerous affair: we generally have to go out of our way to help; simply considered in terms of the effort involved, it is generally much easier not to help. Thus, offering saving help is, in general, far more onerous than simply not causing harm (whether directly or indirectly) since the person doing the saving has to drop whatever they want to do themselves and go out of their way (perhaps even at considerable cost and personal risk) to respond to whatever the emergency is. Even so, offering saving help typically represents a short, sharp episode in one's own life. However, if we were obliged to offer saving help to all people on an impartial basis, then we would quickly find that our personal resources were drastically limited. Whereas it is relatively easy not to cause direct or indirect harm to everyone, offering saving help on an impartial basis would be extremely onerous. Moreover, it would rob us of any ordinary conception of what it is to have a "life of one's own"; we would effectively have to ignore our own first-and second-person desires as we rushed from crisis to crisis. It is not surprising that people can "burn out" or come to feel that they don't have a life of their own when they try to or are required to distribute their saving help in too many directions at once. Their personal resources—physical, emotional, financial—are simply overwhelmed.

If offering saving help on an impartial basis is onerous, then attempting to offer ongoing supportive help on an impartial basis is onerous to the point of being ludicrous. It makes a mockery of the very idea that impartial obligations can—let alone should—be extended to this level of helping. If we were seriously obliged to offer ongoing forms of physical, emotional, and financial help to everyone on an impartial basis, then we would burn out within the hour. Anything resembling a life of our own would be over.

As for bonus help, I noted before that this falls into a special, "world unto itself" category. It is easy to give bonus help—even to everyone, in a sense—because the giver of bonus help only gives it if they feel like it, and not if they don't. Thus, it makes no sense to ask "But what if you had to give bonus help to everyone on an impartial basis?" because the essence of bonus help is that it is whimsical and therefore entirely partial; if it becomes something that can reasonably be required or expected to be given to anyone—let alone everyone—then it is no longer bonus help.

In sum, then, the onerousness of giving everyone what they want (i.e., not to be harmed and to be helped) increases dramatically as one moves along the harm–help spectrum up to the special, nononerous case of bonus help, which, in the nature of the case, it is simply impossible to require or expect of anyone. That is, the onerousness factor increases as we move from not harming, to offering saving help, to offering ongoing supportive help.

What Are the Basic Ways in Which People Wish to Be Affected by Others? The Beneficiaries' Desires Factor

What are the basic ways in which people wish to be affected by others? What do those who stand to be harmed or benefited by the actions of others desire? We can refer to this as the *beneficiaries' desires factor*. The initial answer is easy: in general, people desire not to be harmed and to be helped. In terms of the harm–help spectrum of possibilities, this means that, in general, people desire not to be caused unnecessary pain and suffering, not to be caused to die when they do not wish to die, to be offered saving help, to be offered ongoing supportive help, and to be offered bonus help. But it is also a fact of human experience, underwritten by our biologically based drives for survival, that people do not desire each of these forms of not being harmed and being helped in equal measure. Our primary desire is not to be harmed in any way, shape, or form. This means that, as we also saw when discussing the onerousness factor, we do not need to distinguish here between pain and suffering on the one hand and unwanted autobiographical death on the other hand. It is simply the case that we have extremely strong desires not to be harmed in either way, and there is no principled way of prioritizing these two forms of harm. If forced to "choose," then there are some circumstances in which we would choose one of these forms of harm over the other and other circumstances in which we would "choose" the other way around. Basically, we just don't want to be harmed—period.

Beyond not wanting to be harmed in the first place, our next strongest desire is to be helped if it should turn out that we are being harmed—or are likely to be harmed—in some way. That is, our next strongest desire is to be offered saving help in order to relieve or prevent any harmful situations that do arise. Beyond that, it would also be good to receive ongoing supportive help from others, but the general strength of this desire is nowhere near as strong as our fundamental desire not to be harmed in the first place or our next strongest desire to be offered saving help if we are in a negative or problematic situation. As for bonus help, well, that just comes if it does and is like icing on the cake if it does. This means that although people would like never to be harmed and always to be helped, their priority ordering of these wishes, from strongest to weakest, generally runs: not to be harmed, to be offered saving help as necessary, to be offered ongoing supportive help, and to be offered bonus help.

Although people will intuitively prioritize their desires in respect of how they wish to be affected by others in this way—thereby reflecting their biologically based drives for survival—they also have additional reasons for agreeing on the reasonableness of this priority ordering if they are themselves moral agents. This is because if they are themselves moral agents, then they will know that meeting these desires in the case of every person becomes increasingly onerous, to the point of impossibility, for any moral agent as one proceeds across the harm–help spectrum (setting aside the special case of bonus help). Moreover, the fact that these people have their own first- and second-person desires means that they themselves know that they desire a certain amount of personal freedom in order to have a "life of their own," which can, of course, include giving special attention to their own loved ones and friends. And because, as rational beings, these potential beneficiaries realize that others are like them in this respect—that is, that others have their own first- and second-person desires, which lead them to desire a certain amount of personal freedom in order to have a "life of their own"—they are forced to accept that it is unreasonable for them, as potential beneficiaries, to expect all others to be responsive to all of their desires given that they are themselves unwilling and unable to be responsive to all the desires of all others.

The Responsive Cohesive Solution to the Interhuman Ethics Problem Situation

We have now considered the central salient features of the interhuman ethics problem situation as outlined toward the beginning of this chapter, namely:

(i) What are the basic ways in which people *can* affect others?
(ii) What are the basic ways in which moral agents *wish* to affect others?

(iii) What are the basic ways in which people *wish to be affected* by others?

What we have found is that essentially three factors are at work:

(i) The multiple perspective factor: The theory of responsive cohesion's multiple perspective account of moral agency provides an explanation of why it is that moral agents are epistemologically best suited and motivationally most predisposed to act on behalf of themselves, super-significant others, significant others, and others-in-general in that general order of preference.

(ii) The onerousness factor: Considering the theory of responsive cohesion's harm–help spectrum from a flesh-and-blood moral agent's point of view enabled us to see that the onerousness of giving everyone what they want (i.e., not being harmed and being helped) increases dramatically as we move along the harm–help spectrum from not harming to helping (up to the special case of bonus help, which, in the nature of the case, cannot be onerous because it cannot be required or reasonably expected). Specifically, the onerousness factor increases as we move from not harming, to offering saving help, to offering ongoing supportive help.

(iii) The beneficiaries' desires factor: People would in general like never to be harmed and always to be helped, but if they have to prioritize these desires, then their priority ordering generally runs: not to be harmed, to be offered saving help as necessary, to be offered ongoing supportive help, and to be offered bonus help. Moreover, if these potential beneficiaries are themselves moral agents, then they can also see that accepting this priority ordering is the most reasonable option for moral agents.

Happily, the priority orderings given by the onerousness factor in (ii) and the beneficiaries' desires factor in (iii) coincide (setting aside, as always, the special case of bonus help). This immediately suggests that the most reasonable way to get the onerousness factor to answer to the beneficiaries' desires factor is to wind down the expectation that moral agents will or should act on behalf of potential beneficiaries as we move along the harm–help spectrum. This is basically because, although the personal demands that are made on the moral agent become progressively more onerous as we move along the harm–help spectrum, the potential beneficiary's level of desire to have these demands met in any case decreases. Thus, it is relatively easy for moral agents to respect what beneficiaries most strongly desire (i.e., not to be harmed) and is increasingly more onerous for moral agents to respect what beneficiaries desire with progressively less strength in any case (i.e., to be offered saving help and to be offered ongoing supportive help, respectively).

That said, it is also a fact of common experience that the onerousness of doing something is counterbalanced by one's knowledge of what is needed and one's motivation to respond to that need. This means that I am generally more prepared to do something that requires a lot of me if I know what I need to do and am motivated to do it than I am to do something that requires very little of me yet constitutes a situation in which I do not have a good idea of what needs to be done and have no motivation to do it in any case. In this respect we have already seen from the multiple perspective account of moral agency (summarized as point (i) above) that moral agents are epistemologically best suited and motivationally most predisposed to act on behalf of themselves, supersignificant others, significant others, and others-in-general in that general order of preference. This means that we need also to take the moral agent's multiple epistemological and motivational perspectives into account when it comes to the question of winding down the expectation that a moral agent will or should act on behalf of a potential beneficiary as we move along the harm–help spectrum. This, in turn, means that we are now juggling three factors: (i) the moral agent's multiple epistemological and motivational perspectives; (ii) the level of onerousness involved in acting on behalf of a potential beneficiary; and (iii) the potential beneficiary's level of concern to have their desires met.

When this first, multiple perspective factor is also taken into account, we can see that the most responsively cohesive solution to the problem situation is not to wind down the expectation that a moral agent will or should act on behalf of a potential beneficiary as we move along the harm–help spectrum such that these expectations just stop at some point for all potential beneficiaries, but rather to wind this expectation down in a progressive way as we move from the category of others that the moral agent is least epistemologically informed and motivationally concerned about (i.e., others-in-general) to the category that they are most informed and concerned about (i.e., supersignificant others). That is, we should distribute our "winding down" expectations across categories of others, with those who are least close to us being the first to be eliminated and those who are closest to us being the last. Another way to put this is to say that it is wholly reasonable to expect that moral agents will limit their help to those to whom they are increasingly personally close as (a) the onerousness of helping everyone in a particular way increases and (b) the desires of potential beneficiaries to be helped in this way in any case decreases.

This approach represents the best way—the most responsively cohesive way—of getting the central salient features of the interhuman ethics problem situation to answer to each other. In doing this, it provides us with a structured set of what we can think of as the *reasonable expectations* that humans can have of each other in regard to their interpersonal interaction. It is the very reasonableness of these expectations that leads us to believe that they constitute standards of behavior that ought to be met. If we formalize these reasonable expectations, then we can—and do—refer to them as obligations. Table 5.1 summarizes this set of reasonable expectations, which I have expressed formally in the table as obligations. Reflecting the conclusion reached in the previous paragraph, this table shows that these obligations are differentiated in terms of the categories of people in respect of whom they are held to apply. I have

Table 5.1
The Theory of Responsive Cohesion's Differentiated Model of Our Obligations in Respect of Other People
This matrix addresses our obligations in respect of other people. The cells are responses to the question: *Are you obliged to respect injunctions 1–5 in regard to the categories of people listed across the top of the table?*

Obligations	A: Super-significant others	B: Significant others	C: Others-in-general
1. Don't cause unnecessary pain and suffering	✓	✓	✓
2. Don't cause unwanted autobiographical death	✓	✓	✓
3. Offer saving help	✓	✓	✗
4. Offer ongoing supportive help	✓	✗	✗
5. Offer bonus help	✗	✗	✗

Table 5.2
The Theory of Responsive Cohesion's Differentiated Model of Our Obligations in Respect of Other People (Condensed Version)

Obligations \ Other People	A: Super-significant others	B: Significant others	C: Others-in-general
1. Don't harm	✓	✓	✓
2. Offer saving help	✓	✓	✗
3. Offer ongoing supportive help	✓	✗	✗
4. Offer bonus help	✗	✗	✗

therefore referred to this table as the *theory of responsive cohesion's differentiated model of our obligations in respect of other people.*

Now, given that causing unnecessary pain and suffering and causing unwanted autobiographical death constitute the two main forms of harm and given that there is no difference between the reasonable expectations—or, more formally, the obligations—that moral agents can be held to have in respect of all people in regard to these forms of harm, we can, if we like, simply collapse these two forms of harm into a single, more inclusive category of harm in order to produce a slightly simpler, and in some ways (given the neat stepwise picture that results) "prettier picture" of our obligations in respect of other people. This "picture" is shown in table 5.2.

Notwithstanding the arguably "prettier picture" shown in table 5.2, the initial, more detailed "picture" shown in table 5.1 will nevertheless come into its own in chapter 8. This is because we will see at that point, when we come to consider the broader question of our obligations in respect of *all* beings, that there are circumstances under which it becomes very important to respect the distinction between causing pain and suffering (i.e., affective harm) and causing unwanted autobiographical death (i.e., autobiographical harm).

Before concluding this chapter, it is important to emphasize that the obligations outlined here represent prima facie obligations of the "other things being equal" variety. It is of the nature of the theory of responsive cohesion that these general obligations allow for reasonable exceptions based on any new salient features that enter into any particular situation.

Consider two examples. First, the argument here, as summarized in the above tables, suggests that as a general rule we can reasonably be expected—or, more formally, we have an obligation—not to cause unwanted autobiographical death (i.e., deaths other than those that represent genuine cases of euthanasia, which is to say, genuine cases of wanted autobiographical death, justified by reasons that are sufficiently compelling as to suggest that the person making the request would never wish to reverse it if they were forced to live longer, e.g., a dismal prognosis in the late stages of a terminal disease). However, moral agents generally accept that extreme circumstances can arise under which it may be reasonable to cause an unwanted autobiographical death. These include cases of genuine self-defense and, in the view of some collectivities of moral agents, legally sanctioned forms of capital punishment for horrific crimes. Physical attacks upon oneself or another person obviously introduce new, highly salient features to this particular, extreme version of the interhuman ethics problem situation and so can issue in solutions to that particular, extreme version of the problem situation that violate the prima facie, "other things being equal" obligation not to cause unwanted autobiographical death. But then the method of responsive cohesion is geared precisely to the incorporation of new salient features into the interhuman ethics problem situation.

Second, the argument here, as summarized in the above tables, suggests that as a general rule we cannot reasonably be expected—or, more formally, we do not have an obligation—to offer saving help to all other people (i.e., others-in-general). However, if a stranger—an other-in-general—is about to step off a traffic island into the path of an unseen car, then of course you have a strong obligation to help them there and then because it is so trivially easy (i.e., not onerous) in that *particular* case for you to give the stranger the saving help that you instinctively judge them to require and that they so desperately need at the very instant that you just happen to be present. But, even here, we can still note that the level of obligation we are talking about is in some ways not particularly strong. This is because a relatively trivial excuse like "I just froze in fear" would be enough to absolve you from any real blame for the person's possible death. In contrast, you would be viewed as far more responsible for a death of this kind if it was one of your own children (or even your own adult partner), because the fact that they are supersignificant others to you means, among other things, that you can be reasonably expected to keep much more of a lookout for them than for the safety of others-in-general. Thus, even in this kind of situation, it still seems reasonable to divide up our degrees of responsibility in terms of a multiple perspective account of moral agency.

The final point I want to make about the responsive cohesive solution to the interhuman ethics problem situation is this. This solution does not proceed from some claimed moral high ground, such as a grand-sounding principle like "Jesus says: 'Love your neighbor'" or "Treat people as ends-in-themselves and never only as a means" or "Treat everyone with an equal degree of consideration," and then roll forward like a theoretically weighty steamroller that crushes more mundane concerns in its way. Rather, the responsive cohesion approach begins with the mundane concerns. It asks how people can affect each other, how we wish to affect other people, and how these others wish to be affected by us, in order to work toward an answer to the central question of the interhuman ethics problem situation: What are the nature and limits of the kinds of behaviors that it is reasonable for us to expect from others and reasonable for each of these others to expect from us? The responsive cohesion approach shows us that the most reasonable answer to this big question is the one that is generated by getting the answers to the three previous, smaller questions to be responsive to each other in the most cohesive way possible. It is the very reasonableness of the differentiated set of behavioral expectations that are generated in this way (as shown in tables 5.1 and 5.2) that leads us to believe that we have every right to expect others to behave in accordance with this differentiated set of behavioral expectations and believe that others have the same right to expect this of us. The very reasonableness of these mutual expectations and the corresponding sense of violation that is involved when they are broken leads us to refer to these expectations in formal terms as obligations.

If we take people in general who care about their interactions with others in the world to represent informed judges in regard to these matters, then the approach that I have now outlined in a formal way as the theory of responsive cohesion's approach to interhuman ethics is much more in line with the judgments of such people than are the dominant formal ethical approaches that currently exist. This is because these other approaches have manifestly failed to take into account salient features of the interhuman ethics problem situation that the theory of responsive cohesion's approach does take into account. It is for this reason that these other approaches, if taken seriously, can be seen to issue in the kinds of obligations that people in general who care about their interactions with others in the world rightly judge to represent unreasonable expectations of our behavior in respect of others, and vice versa.

The fact that people in general who care about their interactions with others in the world can be taken to represent relatively informed judges in the sphere of interhuman ethics—which is something that we all do think about to varying degrees—does not mean that people in general are necessarily the most informed judges in all domains of interest. In particular, one of the things that all of us have trouble doing is thinking in sufficiently contextually based terms: thinking in terms of how what we do "fits in" in terms of larger contexts and how those larger contexts "fit in" in terms of still larger contexts and so on. I will turn to this question, which is central to the overall theory of responsive cohesion in the next chapter. However, when I have explored this question, I will return (in chapter 8) to many of the ideas introduced in this chapter—albeit in a way that will build on some of the central ideas that I will introduce in the next two chapters (chapters 6 and 7)—in order to develop an informed approach to the question of our obligations not just in respect of other people (as here), but rather *all* beings.

III

Contexts, Mindsharers, and Iso-Experients

6

The Theory of Responsive Cohesion's Theory of Contexts

The thrust of the three chapters in part II has been to argue that:

(i) There are three basic kinds of relational qualities, which can be characterized as fixed cohesion, responsive cohesion, and discohesion (chapter 3).

(ii) The relational quality of responsive cohesion characterizes the best examples to be found in every domain of interest (chapters 4 and 5)— and even the very possibility of valuing (see my discussion regarding the responsively cohesive form of organization of the brain in chapter 4). The particular range of reasons given for judging one thing better than another may vary from domain to domain and from case to case, but the fact that the relational quality of responsive cohesion underpins the object of each of these judgments remains invariant; thus, the relational quality of responsive cohesion is a deep feature, often perhaps not even explicitly recognized, of the object of informed evaluative judgments. Putting the matter bluntly, we can say that responsive cohesion trumps both fixed cohesion and discohesion in informed evaluative judgments.

(iii) The evaluative evidence from across the widest range of domains of interest, together with the fact that we cannot reduce something as basic, deep, and abstract as a relational quality to anything else, points to the fact that the relational quality of responsive cohesion is the foundational value (chapter 4).

The purpose of this chapter is to develop the theory of responsive cohesion further by distinguishing between different kinds *of* responsive cohesion and arguing that some kinds of responsive cohesion are ultimately more important than others.

Distinguishing between and Evaluating the Claims of Internal and Contextual Responsive Cohesion

In addition to the distinctions that I have made between fixed cohesion, responsive cohesion, and discohesion, there is another distinction that also plays a fundamental role in the full development of the theory of responsive cohesion. This distinction has been implicit in the discussion that has run through the last few chapters (especially chapters 3 and 4), but it is now crucial to make it explicit. I am referring to the distinction between *internal* and *external* or, as I would prefer to say, *contextual* forms of responsive cohesion. This distinction can be expressed very simply: *internal* responsive cohesion refers to the degree of responsive cohesion that any item of interest can be said to have within whatever the boundaries are that define that item of interest as an item of interest, whereas *contextual* responsive cohesion refers to the degree of responsive cohesion that an item of interest has with respect to its immediate and wider contexts. For example, suppose that a table or a chair is your item of interest. It is perfectly possible that you might think that this object has a high degree of internal responsive cohesion, that is, that the various elements or salient features that constitute it *as* a table or a chair answer to each other very well; that it "fits together beautifully." However, you might also think that, much as you like the object in itself, it simply wouldn't "work" in your carefully designed kitchen or study, that it would clash badly (i.e., be discohesive) with what is already there. Perhaps it's worse than that; perhaps you find that, much as you like the object in itself, it's simply the wrong height or shape for your body. This simple, mundane example illustrates the fact that an item of interest might have a high degree of internal responsive cohesion but be lacking in all sorts of ways when it comes to the question of contextual responsive cohesion. Alternatively, you might find a table or a chair that would be "just perfect" for the room you have in mind but then find, to your considerable disappointment, that it is not very well made, that, for example, the parts that make it up don't join together very well. In this case you have a situation in which the item of interest seems to have a lot of contextual responsive cohesion (in terms of where you'd like to put it) but is lacking in internal responsive cohesion.

We make these kinds of judgments concerning internal versus contextual responsive cohesion all the time. Indeed, I'm doing this as I write these words: I want my words, sentences, paragraphs, chapters, and overall argument to answer to each other, thereby giving the book a high degree of internal responsive cohesion, but I also want the book itself to answer to a wider conversation on ethics in general as well as to the general interests of a wider public who are interested in the fundamental question of the values we should live by, thereby giving the book a high degree of contextual responsive cohesion in the wider realm of intelligent discussion regarding important issues. That said, this example also shows that the question of what constitutes internal and contextual responsive cohesion is purely a matter of focus, purely a matter of what we take our primary item of interest to be. If my primary focus of interest (for the purposes of making the previous kind of point) is this book as a whole, then my previous division of what constitutes internal and contextual responsive cohesion applies. However, if I had taken this chapter as my primary focus of interest in the above example, then I would have discussed internal responsive cohesion in terms of the quality of the internal connections within this chapter and contextual responsive cohesion in terms of the quality of the connections that this chapter makes with the other chapters in the book as a whole as well as the even wider context that I included in my previous example, in which the whole book was taken to be the primary item of interest. The dividing line between what counts as an example of internal responsive cohesion and what counts as an example of contextual responsive cohesion is therefore purely a function of whatever happens to constitute the primary focus of our interest in any given context.

Now, up to this point in my presentation of the theory of responsive cohesion, I have generally been introducing the ideas associated with the relational quality of responsive cohesion as if responsive cohesion were pretty much just an internal affair, something that an item of interest can be judged to possess or not possess considered more or less on its own, which is to say in isolation. But of course nothing exists in isolation. This means that the idea of responsive cohesion is always "pushing outwards" as it were. This is because, in line with my chapter/book comments above, we can always take the original item of interest *plus* its immediate context as our new item of interest and ask about *its* degree of contextual responsive cohesion, and so on, pressing further and further outward. The upshot of this line of thinking is that a thoroughgoing example of responsive cohesion is only achieved in the case of an item of interest that possesses not only the highest possible degree of internal responsive cohesion but also the highest possible degree of responsive cohesion with its immediate context, which in turn possess the highest possible degree of responsive cohesion with its immediate context, and so on, outward and outward. The notion of responsive cohesion is, therefore, a *context saturated* one.

However, although our thinking has to work in an inward to outward direction in order to understand the concept of contextual responsive cohesion, we can also see that, in practice, we actually have to work from the outside—which is to say, from the largest possible context—inward in order to achieve a paradigmatic example of responsive cohesion. (And here we can generally take it that, for all earthly purposes, which means for virtually all of us virtually all of the time, the largest relevant context is indeed the earth—or ecosphere—taken as a whole.) This is because if an item (call it A) has a high degree of internal responsive cohesion and is also responsively cohesive with its context (which itself must have a high degree of responsive cohesion if we are looking for a paradigmatic example of responsive cohesion), then that item will be consistent with, or might even be said to add to, the overall responsive cohesion in the world. In contrast, if an item (call it B) has a high degree of internal responsive cohesion but is not responsively cohesive with its (highly responsively cohesive) context, then that item will be discohesive with its context and so will definitely subtract from the overall responsive cohesion in the world. Why? Couldn't we just say here that item B "adds nothing" (as opposed to "subtracts from") the overall responsive cohesion of the world, since it possesses internal responsive cohesion on the one hand but detracts from contextual responsive cohesion on the other hand, thereby leaving a more or less even balance sheet? The answer is no and is tied up with the fact that the division between what counts as internal and contextual responsive cohesion is, as I noted before, an arbitrary function of our focus of interest. If we take the whole context in the examples just given as our *item* of interest in each case, then we can now say that A is either consistent with (because it "fits in" with) or perhaps even adds to the degree of (what we have now redefined as the) *internal* responsive cohesion of that whole context. In contrast, we would have to say that B subtracts from the degree of (what we have now redefined as the) *internal* responsive cohesion of that whole context since the overall degree of internal responsive cohesion of the context itself, which was "high," has now been lessened by this inclusion of a distinctly discohesive item—like a badly jarring note added to an otherwise harmonious chorus. It follows that if we remove B, then we restore the degree of responsive cohesion that was internal to the context. (Of course B, which considered in isolation has, as we've said, a high degree of internal responsive cohesion, might well contribute to the overall responsive cohesion of the world if placed in a more appropriate—or "fitting"—context.)

These considerations mean that whether we regard a new item as *lacking contextual responsive cohesion* or *subtracting from the degree of internal responsive cohesion* in the world is purely a function of how we construe the primary item of interest under discussion: *to lack contextual responsive cohesion is to subtract from the overall degree of internal responsive cohesion in the world at a more inclusive level of discussion.*

There is of course an alternative way of repairing the discohesion that is introduced to a situation when something that exhibits a high degree of internal responsive cohesion is added to a context that also exhibits a high degree of responsive cohesion, but where the new item and the context are not themselves responsively cohesive. Rather than focusing (primarily) on modifying the new feature to fit the overall context—or even getting rid of the new feature altogether—we could instead demand that the context itself be fundamentally reconstructed so as to answer to the item that has just been introduced. However, to do this is to destroy vastly more responsive cohesion than we have introduced—a context's worth as opposed to an item's worth. It is like adding a few bars of music that fit together very well internally to a beautiful symphony, finding that these new notes don't "work," fit, or cohere in the overall context of the symphony and then proceeding to fundamentally reconstruct the already existing responsive cohesion of the symphony in order to wholly recreate the work around the ill-fitting notes. Although the addition of some new notes to a symphony will often have ripple effects that will lead the composer to modify some other aspect(s) of the symphony, it is nevertheless clear that responsive cohesion is best preserved overall when the preexisting responsively cohesive context (in this case the symphony) has the major share of the influence relative to the new feature. Speaking about exactly this kind of problem in the context of the built environment, the architect Christopher Day captures the general thrust of this point quite simply when he says that "To be harmonious, the new needs to be an organic development of what is already there, not an imposed alien."[1]

We can see, then, that the conclusion that contextual responsive cohesion must be given priority over internal responsive cohesion in those situations in which there is a tension or clash between the two follows directly from the idea that responsive cohesion is the foundational value. Not to accept this priority rule is to work against this foundational value. For example, to operate on the reverse principle (or even on something like a 50:50 basis) would amount to a state of permanent revolution on the largest contextual scale, for one would always be tearing apart and reconstructing the whole so as to be responsively cohesive with any newly introduced ill-fitting part—and then doing the same for any even newer ill-fitting part, and so on. But a state of revolution interrupted only by revolutions with fundamentally different bases, which are, in turn, interrupted by further revolutions with yet other fundamentally different bases, and so on is functionally equivalent to an ongoing state of *discohesion*. Consider: having builders in to do work on your house can be chaotic enough, but just imagine if these "builders" happily ignored Christopher Day's advice and decided to rebuild the whole house in order to make it responsively cohesive with the "wrong" bit of wood they got for a certain job, and so on, again and again, each time some minor thing didn't fit with their latest brilliant idea! If these builders fail to understand the appropriate "direction of fit" (to borrow a term that John Searle has used in another context[2]) between contexts and introduced elements, if they "come at things from the wrong end," then they will actually end up promoting one of the two kinds of relational quality to which the theory of responsive cohesion is explicitly opposed, namely, discohesion.

Equally, however, it is sensible to add here that if we are overzealous or fetishistic about preserving the contextual responsive cohesion that already exists in a certain situation, then we will end up "deep-freezing" that contextual responsive cohesion and so condemn it—ironically enough—to become just a sophisticated form of fixed cohesion. Metaphorically speaking, we will have succeeded in "smothering it with good intentions" or "loving it to death." The trick, as always, is to seek a genuinely responsive cohesion between the introduced element and its overarching context such that the "claims" of both are weighted in ways that seem appropriate to each other and such that both are made to "answer" to each other in the context of these appropriately weighted "claims." The theory of responsive cohesion tells us that responsively cohesive contexts make altogether weightier "claims" in any problem situation than responsively cohesive introduced items, but that the latter should not be considered to be without their own influence. Their relative relationship in "mental decision space" can thus perhaps be envisaged in terms of a somewhat strained yet nevertheless (at least gravitationally!) attractive metaphor: the earth and moon mutually modify each other's orbits, yet the earth has the weightier say in this transaction (thus, the moon revolves around the earth rather than vice versa), although the moon is not without its own influence (such as the tides). This provides us with a mental picture of the dance of mutual accommodation that is endorsed by the theory of responsive cohesion. Even so, if there really is a flat-out contradiction between the kind of responsive cohesion that is exemplified by an overarching context and the kind that is exemplified by an introduced item—if push really does come to shove in this situation—then it is also clear that concerns regarding contextual responsive cohesion should trump concerns regarding internal responsive cohesion. To get this "direction of fit" wrong—or, in the extreme no-mutual-accommodation-possible case, to get the decision as to what trumps what wrong—is to pursue the functional equivalent of discohesion.

Contextualizing Contexts: Introduction to a Theory of Contexts

We have now seen that acceptance of the foundational value of responsive cohesion guarantees the priority of contextual responsive cohesion over internal responsive cohesion. However, an extremely important question now arises. Consider the following. For any particular kind of thing, it is quite possible that different evaluators might reach quite different kinds of judgments about how contextually responsive that thing is, depending upon which particular context they have in mind. For example, suppose we consider three physical structures of the kind that we refer to as "buildings." And suppose, for the sake of the argument, that informed judges all agree that these buildings are just as well designed as each other considered purely from the point of view of their internal responsive cohesion; that the various elements or salient features that constitute these physical structures as "buildings" feed into and play off each other beautifully, thereby making them good examples of buildings (of whatever kind). Let's take all that for granted. But suppose that one of these buildings blends into the (let's say, relatively responsively cohesive) preexisting built environment in which it has been constructed much better than the other two, which, for all their internal responsive cohesion, nevertheless clash badly with their preexisting (responsively cohesive) built environments. And suppose that another of these buildings caters to the society—or aspect of society—that it is intended to serve much better than the other two, which, for all their internal responsive cohesion as the kinds of physical structures we call buildings, are simply not in the same class when it comes to these kinds of criteria. The kinds of things we are talking about here might include not only the extent to which the building enables or hinders the carrying out of the primary business for which it is used—which might range from displaying art or showing films to processing applications for immigration or social security—but also such things as closeness to public transport, car-parking facilities, ease of entry to the building for all potential users, relaxed and convenient places to meet, eat, rest, wait, and so on. Finally, suppose that the third of these buildings is much better than the other two when it comes to criteria of ecological sustainability in both its construction and its energy use in day-to-day operation; indeed, suppose that the other two buildings, for all their internal responsive cohesion, verge on being the building equivalent of gas guzzlers.

Here we have a situation in which, for the sake of the argument, there is nothing to decide between the three buildings in regard to their degree of internal responsive cohesion but in which it is nevertheless possible for three thoughtful people to argue that each one of the three buildings has a greater degree of contextual responsive cohesion than the other two, depending on whether the context that each person has in mind is the preexisting built environment, the human social environment, or the natural, biophysical environment. A vital question therefore arises: Is it possible to decide between these conflicting judgments and, if so, how? Should satisfying some kinds of contexts have a higher priority than satisfying other kinds of contexts?

The answer given by the theory of responsive cohesion is a definite "Yes." If some of these contexts can be shown to be subsumed by others and thus to be internal to them, then the relationship of the larger context to the subcontext is equivalent to what I described in the previous section as the relationship between a context and an internal item. And it follows straightforwardly from the "direction of fit" rule established in the previous section—namely, that the foundational value of responsive cohesion guarantees the priority of contextual responsive cohesion over internal responsive cohesion—that responsiveness to the largest responsively cohesive context should have priority over responsiveness to its responsively cohesive subcontexts.

For the sake of clarification here, it is important to insert the following rather densely formulated paragraph, but the "take-home message" is summarized more simply in the paragraph after this. Here we go. Where overarching contexts approximate forms of fixed cohesion or discohesion, then, of course, any form of internal responsive cohesion trumps them since, according to the theory of responsive cohesion, any form of responsive cohesion trumps any form of fixed cohesion or discohesion. The idea that internal—or subcontextual—forms of responsive cohesion should bend themselves to "fit in" with overarching contextual forms of fixed cohesion or discohesion therefore represents about as fundamental a misunderstanding of the essence of the theory of responsive cohesion as it is possible to make. Because the theory of responsive cohesion renders the judgments so clear cut in respect of mismatches between examples of *internal forms of responsive cohesion* and *contextual forms of fixed cohesion and discohesion* on the one hand (in which case, so much the worse for both of the latter) and mismatches between examples of *internal forms of fixed cohesion and discohesion* and *contextual forms of responsive cohesion* on the other hand (in which case, so much the worse for both of the former), I am only concerning myself here with the far

more interesting and instructive case of mismatches between *responsively
cohesive items (or subcontexts) and their responsively cohesive overarching contexts.*

All we really need to remember is this: if we are comparing any form
of responsive cohesion with any form of fixed cohesion or discohesion,
then we can throw any considerations about what constitutes the context
of what out the window: responsive cohesion always wins. The internal/
contextual or subcontext/overarching context distinction becomes relevant only when we are comparing different kinds *of* responsive cohesion,
in which case the theory of responsive cohesion guarantees the priority
of contextual responsive cohesion over internal or subcontextual responsive cohesion.

The question we must now confront is this: is it possible to develop a
theory of contexts—a model that provides an informed account of precisely what-constitutes-the-context-of-what? If this can be done, then
the direction of fit priority rule will enable us to say in more specific
terms which particular forms of contextual responsive cohesion are ultimately the most important and, therefore, which should be given the
greatest weight in our decisions and judgments (e.g., the preexisting built
environment, the human social environment, or the natural biophysical
environment—hint: reverse the order!).

Mercifully, a particular theory of contexts is already implicit in the
context-saturated idea of responsive cohesion from the outset: far from
having to tack a theory of contexts onto the theory of responsive cohesion in an ad hoc fashion, the theory of responsive cohesion itself *generates* a way of contextualizing contexts. This follows because the question
"What constitutes the context of what?" is actually a version of the
question "What is the world like?," for in order to be able to say what-
constitutes-the-context-of-what, we first need an informed, general account of what the world is like. This puts us in familiar territory since,
as we have already seen in chapter 4, informed judges generally consider
that the best way of coming to know what the world is like involves
a responsive interplay between theory (reason) and observations (the
evidence of the senses) in the service of reaching an account of the world
in which theory and observations best fit together, or cohere with
each other. This means that informed judges generally consider rational-
empirical methods—which we ordinarily refer to as scientific methods—

to constitute the best answer to the epistemological problem of coming to know what the world is like.

What the World Is Like

How, then, do rational-empirical methods reveal the world to be at the most general level? A by-now familiar yet rather rough answer runs along the following lines: the natural, biophysical world gives rise to conscious beings, some of which then develop complex, symbolically mediated cultures; these cultures, in turn, provide the context for the development of culturally mediated artifacts. Another way to put this is to say that the self-organizing realm of nature gives rise to a realm of symbolic culture, which gives rise to a realm of (intentionally organized as opposed to self-organizing) material culture. I want to express this general picture in more precise terms by saying that the *biophysical realm* constitutes the basic context for the development and continuance of what (following Merlin Donald)[3] I will refer to as the *mindsharing realm* and that the mindsharing realm constitutes the basic context for the development and continuance of what I will refer to as the *compound material realm*. However, since the "*nature* gives rise to *symbolic culture*, which gives rise to *material culture*" sequence provides a reasonable first approximation of what we are talking about here, I will explain my reasons for using the more unusual yet ultimately more precise and helpful terms *biophysical realm*, *mindsharing realm*, and *compound material realm*, respectively, when we come to the discussion of each of these realms.

Before proceeding to discuss these three realms in greater detail, it is important to point out that they should not be thought of as discrete realms situated along some linear scale so much as concentric circles nested within each other. Thus, if I say that certain beings belong to the mindsharing realm—or are *mindsharers*—then it should be taken as read that I am simultaneously saying that these beings are nested within the biophysical realm, which is to say that they have been generated out of and are reliant for their continued existence upon the wider biophysical realm. Similarly, if I refer to something as an example of the compound material realm, then it should be taken as read that it is nested within the mindsharing realm and, thus, that it is nested, in turn, within the biophysical realm. Moreover, to say that an example of the compound material realm is nested within the mindsharing realm is likewise to say that it has been generated out of and is reliant upon the wider mindsharing realm for its continued existence *as* the artifact it is—after all, a bath is not a *bath* unless it is recognized as having the *function* of being a bath; if not, it is just "stuff" that has a certain mass and shape.[4]

It should also be understood that these concentric circles themselves include all sorts of gradations, or further nested circles, within them. For example, references to the biophysical realm embrace the evolutionary sequence that runs from the origins of the universe to the evolution of complex life forms. Or, in more detail, from the Big Bang through to the formation of the elementary particles, atoms, molecules, and collections of molecules that gave us the galaxies, stars, and planets that now exist, and, ultimately, on to the emergence and evolution of life on our particular planet (and presumably others). The last part of this story in turn runs from the very first kinds of self-organizing and self-replicating collections of molecules that we might refer to as minimally living things to the complexity of life that we see around us today. (This outline also suggests that if we paid strict attention to the order of development within the biophysical realm, then it would be more accurate, assuming we sought to capture this order in our name for this realm, to refer to it as the *physico-biological realm* since the nonliving physical realm of nature preceded the—nonetheless physical—living realm of nature. However, as long as we understand this, it is more convenient to use the more common and more readily pronounceable term "biophysical," which is the adjectival form of the already accepted term "biophysics.")

Although our most informed views nowadays support the view that the three realms to which I am referring shade into each other, this was not always the case. Most people used to think—and many people still do think—that there is some kind of complete separation between the material realm (i.e., the biophysical realm) and the mental realm. Thus, earlier thinkers thought that the appropriate place to "carve nature at its joints" was at the disjuncture between the material realm (to which all nonhuman animals were generally thought to belong) and the mental realm (to which all human beings were thought to belong). However, this is very far from our most informed views these days. The Big-Bang-to-emergence-of-living-things story that I have just sketched continues along the lines that some of the more complex of these life forms came to exhibit a degree and kind of inner sensitivity that constituted the first, primitive forms of awareness, sentience, or consciousness. (Language is notoriously slippery when it comes to trying to capture the qualitative nature of subjective experience. Thus, the complex and variously used terms "awareness," "sentience," and "consciousness" are just so many ways of attempting to label the fact that, as Thomas Nagel has taught us to say, it is *like* something to be these kinds of living things.[5] This applies even if the form of awareness, sentience, or conscious experience that we are referring to is of a rudimentary and completely unreflective kind—that is, very far indeed from anything like *self-consciousness*). Thus, our most informed views today completely reject any kind of ("substance") dualistic view of matter and mind. Minds—or *mental states* as philosophers of mind generally prefer to say, in order to escape from the dualistic idea that "the mind" is something that is separable from the internal states of certain kinds of biophysical entities—have a thoroughly biophysical basis. Accordingly, John Searle, one of our leading philosophers of mind, can justifiably *begin* his important book *The Rediscovery of the Mind* with the statement:

The famous mind–body problem, the source of so much controversy over the past two millennia, has a simple solution. This solution has been available to any educated person since serious work began on the brain nearly a century ago, and, in a sense, we all know it to be true. Here it is: Mental phenomena are caused by neurophysiological processes in the brain and are themselves features of the brain.... Mental events and processes are as much part of our biological natural history as digestion, mitosis, meiosis, or enzyme secretion.[6]

Accepting the weight of evidence in favor of this informed judgment (and it is the acceptance of this weight of evidence that constitutes it *as* an informed judgment) means that there is a quite straightforward sense in which we can say that awareness, sentience, or consciousness is an emergent feature *within the biophysical realm*. There is nothing "unnatural" or "supernatural" about mental states; they are simply a feature of certain kinds of complex, responsively cohesive, biophysical forms of organization, just as digestion is. We therefore do not need to think, and should not think, that we have somehow jumped to a new realm of nature (or reality) that lies beyond the biophysical realm just because we have reached the part of the story of the universe at which some form of experiential capacity begins to emerge. Rather, we are still very much in the realm of what Searle rightly refers to as *biological naturalism*.

Cognitive Transcendence of the Biophysical Realm

If matter, life, and mind are just so many facets of a naturalistically understood biophysical universe, then is there any point in the story of the universe at which it does make some sense to talk in terms of a realm of existence that exists over and above the biophysical realm? I want to spend some time examining this question and its implications in both this section and the next, because it is only through a careful examination of these matters that we can appropriately identify and name the second of the three realms that make up the theory of responsive cohesion's theory of contexts, namely, what I will refer to (borrowing Merlin Donald's term *mindsharing*) as the *mindsharing realm*. This exploration will begin by considering the nature, role, and significance of language, but it will ultimately issue (in chapter 8 in particular) in significant ethical implications.

Is there any point, then, at which it makes sense to talk in terms of a realm of existence that exists over and above the biophysical realm? Whatever we might wish for in this regard, the best evidence we have suggests that the answers to this question are, respectively, "No," if we are talking about some kind of *metaphysical* transcendence of the biophysical realm, that is, some kind of other-worldly realm that exists independently of the natural order, and "Yes," if we are talking "simply" about some kind of *cognitive* transcendence of the biophysical realm. By *cognitive* transcendence of the biophysical realm I mean a form of awareness that can take the operations *of* the biophysical realm (including mental states themselves) as its object of thought—even though this form of awareness, like all forms of awareness, is ultimately constituted by and dependent upon the biophysical realm for its existence (i.e., in our case, human brains). Beings that have this form of awareness are no longer enmeshed in unreflective or first-order mental representations of the world but rather are *aware of* their representations of the world (and can perhaps then become aware of *these* representations, and so on).

Thus, what I am referring to here as *cognitive transcendence*—largely in order to capture the contrast with some kind of metaphysical or "other worldly" transcendence—is more often referred to in philosophy of mind discussions as higher-order (mental) representation or metarepresentation. Whereas a metaphysically (or more strictly, ontologically) grounded form of transcendence of the biophysical realm suggests a nonreducible two-level (i.e., "dualistic") picture of the ultimate nature of things, the thoroughly naturalistic picture that I have given of cognitive transcendence suggests a concentric-circle picture of the ultimate nature of things: cognitive transcendence lies within the biophysical realm in an ultimate sense, yet it also constitutes a vantage point (of awareness) upon the surrounding landscape of the biophysical realm, like a mountain that arises out of a landscape: everything in the landscape is ultimately part of the same natural order, but we can see vastly more of the various formations of that natural order from the top of the mountain.

But cognitive transcendence of the biophysical realm is no simple matter. The biophysical realm exerts a tremendous pull upon the sensory, perceptual, and attending capacities of any sentient being for at least two strong reasons. First, attending to what is happening in the biophysical realm in the here-and-now is fundamental to any being's survival. And second, even setting that powerful first reason to one side, it just is the case that the biophysical realm has a raw, in-one's-face, here-and-now immediacy; it floods one's senses from moment to moment. How can internally imagined forms of representation compete against that? Just as a rocket requires a tremendously powerful source of thrust in order to escape capture by the Earth's gravitational pull, so a being requires tremendously powerful cognitive resources in order to escape complete "experiential capture" by the biophysical world, that is, to escape complete experiential immersion in the biophysical realm such that one lives in a cognitive world that consists of nothing but unreflective, first-order mental representations.

But exactly what kinds of resources are necessary in order to escape from complete experiential immersion in the biophysical realm? The answer, in short, is the acquisition of a *detached, highly integrated representational system* (although, as we will see, especially in the next chapter, even these resources will only work for certain kinds of beings; they will just be squandered on others). Let me unpack what I mean by a *detached, highly integrated representational system*. To transcend the biophysical realm in a cognitive sense, it is not enough simply to consciously represent it to ourselves (and thus become aware *of* it) in any old fashion; rather, we need to be able to represent it in ways that are spatially, temporally, and formally (in the sense of a thing's form) *detached* from what we are representing. This can be explained as follows. If our forms of representation are routinely tightly coupled to what they represent in space, time, or form, then they amount to a fixed code that is completely beholden to the appearance of what is being "represented" (and "appearance" can be understood here in either the "here and now" sense or the "what it looks like" sense). Examples here include illustrating the form that something takes by engaging in an imitative action, which conveys information about the appearance that something takes in terms of its *form*, or making a particular kind of sound each and every time a particular kind of predator appears, which conveys information about the *here-and-now appearance* of a particular thing, albeit in a limited one sound–one meaning kind of way. Linguists and philosophers of language refer to the first kind of example as an *iconic* form of signaling because it relies on a physical correspondence between the signal and the item of interest and the second kind of example as an *indexical* form of signaling because it effectively represents a form of (vocalized) pointing at something ("index" derives from the Latin for "pointer," hence our use of the term "index finger").[7]

The "waggle-dance" of honey bees and the alarm calls of vervet monkeys illustrate celebrated examples of these two forms of signaling. The waggle-dance of honey bees is both indexical and iconic: these bees perform it in the hive directly after, and only after, they have found nectar (which is the indexical part: "nectar now"), and their dance physically corresponds to the form of the nectar's location: the angle of the dance to the vertical corresponds to the angle of flight relative to the sun, and hence the direction of the nectar, and the intensity of the "waggle" reflects the distance to the nectar (all of which is the iconic part: "nectar's location corresponds to this physical form"). The alarm calls of vervet monkeys are indexical; they represent a fixed, one sound–one meaning form of response to the here-and-now appearance of each main kind of predator.

But these forms of representation are so tightly coupled to the biophysical contexts in which they are produced ("lion, here, now"; "nectar, there now"), or so *stimulus bound* or *context bound* as some linguists say, that they hardly allow for any degree of cognitive *transcendence* of the biophysical realm. Cognitive transcendence of the biophysical realm requires a far more powerful form of representation than that provided by icons and indices. After all, if your communicative possibilities remain strictly bound to the here-and-now biophysical context, then clearly these tools will not do the job of cognitively *transcending* it. Instead, what is required in order to cognitively transcend the biophysical realm are forms of representation that are not tied to the physical form and/or here-and-now appearance of the items they betoken, forms of representation that are, in principle, *detached* from these forms of tight coupling to the biophysical realm. Now the way to achieve a form of representation that is genuinely detached from what it refers to is to ensure that it bears an *arbitrary* relationship to its reference. This is because to be genuinely detached a form of reference must neither resemble what it refers to, which would mean that it was merely iconic, nor be limited in its use to the actual appearance of what it refers to, which would mean that it was merely indexical. This in turn means that the meaning of detached forms of reference must and can only be a function of *social agreement*. It is easy to see why this must be so: if a form of reference is genuinely detached from the actual physical form of what it refers to, as well as anything to do with the actual here-and-now appearance of what it refers to, then there is no way of knowing what the form of reference is supposed to mean other than that of what we collectively agree that it is supposed to mean—no other clues are available.

Detached, arbitrary forms of representation have a special name: *symbols*. In contrast, nondetached (iconic and indexical) forms of representation are often referred to as *signals*. Now, although it might at first seem counterintuitive, the power and the glory of symbols derives precisely from the fact that, in themselves, they don't mean anything! The word "horse" does not resemble a horse in any way (so it is not iconic), and the fact that I have drawn your attention to it does not necessarily mean that there are any horses around (so it is not indexical). And as for the word "unicorn" ... The words "horse" and "unicorn" do not, in themselves, resemble or point to anything. They are completely arbitrary relative to what they refer to; we could just as easily replace them with "sohre" and "orcinun," or "pffltz" and "pffltx." The words "horse" and "unicorn" mean what they mean because we buy into a collective agreement that that's what they mean. Herein lies the beauty of words: their *intrinsic meaninglessness* means that they can be *used to refer to anything*, providing we first learn the connection between an arbitrary sound and its referent(s) (so that the word makes sense to us in the first place) and agree to abide by the socially agreed conventions that govern these arbitrary associations (so that the word continues to make sense). And make no mistake: the socially agreed conventions that govern these arbitrary associations constitute *rules* of language use just as much as our social conventions about which side of the road to drive on constitute the rules of the road. Thus, for example, I cannot use the word "horse" to refer to a "unicorn" because we've agreed that a unicorn is a different kind of creature than a horse (and this notwithstanding the fact that unicorns don't exist!), but you would readily understand what I meant if I said that a unicorn is in some ways *similar* to a horse. (We also have rules about the spelling of symbols and, as we will come to, their grammatical combination. Indeed, computer-based word-processing programs have a nasty habit of telling you every time you break one of these rules, which means that many of us are these days rather painfully aware of how often and easily we ... um ... "bend" these rules.)

But while symbols might give us the *basis* out of which to construct a form of cognitive transcendence of the biophysical realm, they don't get us very far considered as isolated entities. For example, if I say the word "fish"—and no more than that, just "fish"—then what on earth does that mean? Am I referring to all fish (fish in general), some fish, a fish, *those* fish, *that* fish? Does it mean that I just saw a fish, that I'm only thinking about fish, or that I'm not even really thinking about fish but just like the sound of the word as it rolls off my tongue (say it with me now: "fish")? Does it mean that I like fish, would like to eat a fish, or that I would like *to* fish? Does it mean ... well, we could fill the rest of this book with "fish questions." We could "fish" for an answer forever (mmm ... did I initially mean "guess"?) and be none the wiser. It follows that if all we have is a number of isolated symbols—symbols that link only "vertically" to the referents that we place them "on" (like horses, unicorns, and fish) and not also "horizontally" to other symbols—then we will just be living in a wilderness of single symbolic instances. The consequence is that—as in the case of "fish"—these isolated symbolic utterances will not make much sense. And they will not make any more sense even if they are said one after the other, so long as we continue to assume, as we presently are for the sake of the argument, that these symbols are genuinely isolated symbols; that there is no form of "horizontal" linkage between them.

Clearly, what is required to unleash the full power of symbolic—or detached—representations is, as politicians might say, a "joined up" or "integrated" policy of symbolic usage. And just as we need socially agreed conventions—rules—to establish the linkage between an arbitrary sound and a particular referent(s) in the first place, so we also need socially agreed conventions—other rules—to establish the ways in which these symbols can be connected with each other in order to make intelligible combinations. These latter rules are referred to as *grammar* or, more precisely, what Noam Chomsky has referred to as *generative grammar*.[8] A generative grammar consists of a finite set of rules that allows its users to employ the symbols at their disposal and new symbols that they create to generate a virtual infinity of comprehensible phrases and sentences—a virtual infinity of meanings, much as the quite limited rules of chess allow for the generation of an endless variety of games consisting of legal, or rule-bound, and thus comprehensible, moves.

These considerations add up to the following. Symbols (as opposed to signals) give us a *detached* form of *representation*: *detached* because, unlike icons and indices, the nature of the form of reference that is used bears no necessary relationship to its referent; and *representation* because the symbol "stands for" something other than itself—it is a socially agreed way of *re-presenting* or *referring to* something else. However, we clearly need a generative grammar to have anything like a *highly integrated* representational system, that is, a set of discrete parts (in this case, symbols) that can be combined with each other in complex ways to form a coherent collective entity (from a sentence to a novel). (An example of a detached representational system with a low degree of integration would be the essentially grammatically structureless expressions that the influential linguist Derek Bickerton refers to as *protolanguage* and which he sees as characterizing the verbal behavior of four classes of beings: "trained apes, children under two, adults who have been deprived of language in their early years, and speakers of pidgin."[9] These kinds of expressions consist of what Stephen Pinker, referring to pidgin in particular, describes as nothing more than "choppy strings of words"[10]—and often little more than essentially two-word "strings" at that.) Without a generative grammar, we have very little. As Piero Scaruffi puts it in his veritable compendium of worthwhile ideas about the nature of the mind: "The individual symbol is meaningless: what has meaning is the symbol within the vast and ever changing semantic space of all other symbols."[11] We need a generative grammar to get the symbolic parts moving, as it were—and, like cars, they only really "work" when they move. Thus, *symbols combined with generative grammar* give us a *detached, highly integrated representational system*. This kind of representational system is tremendously powerful and comes packed with all kinds of "special features." Let us consider some them.

First, this kind of representational system is an infinite or *open-ended* (as opposed to finite or closed) representational system. This is because the rules of grammar allow for an endless variety of intelligible symbolic combinations. Consider: chess has only six kinds of pieces and not many more basic rules in regard to how they can be moved (these rules constitute the generative grammar of chess, if you will), yet nobody imagines that we will ever reach a point when every game will necessarily be a repetition of some previous game because every possible game has already been played. Well, the situation with respect to language in terms of both kinds of pieces (i.e., symbolic forms of reference) and combination rules (i.e., grammatical rules) is unbelievably more complex to start with, so the range of possible linguistic meanings is completely open ended. Moreover, we have, can, and will continue collectively to admit more symbols and combination rules to this already open-ended representational system. Thus, symbols in the service of generative grammar give us a linguistic world without end. In contrast, the number of meanings that a grammarless being that operates purely on a one sound–one meaning basis can hope to relay is necessarily limited by the number of individual sounds that it can make—and, as William Calvin notes, humans, like chimpanzees, only have "about three dozen units of vocalization, called phonemes."[12]

Second, the employment of symbols in the service of a generative grammar provides us not only with an open-ended representational system but one that is *multidimensional* on an unimaginable scale. Not only can we array our meanings on any number of dimensions in what we might call (infinite or open-ended) "semantic space"—for example: past-present-future, near-far, me-you-them, mine-yours-theirs, male-female, want-don't want, happy-sad, relaxed-agitated, like-dislike, good-bad, right-wrong, and on and on, without end—but the specific words we use to array our meanings along various dimensions in semantic space also modify each other in complex ways; they warp the semantic space around them, as it were, and so push, pull, bend, and twist the dimensions along which the words with which they are associated are arrayed, just as these other words do to them. This gives us a (seriously complex) *multidimensional* representational system. And this picture also makes it clear that any coherent statement will exhibit the relational quality of responsive cohesion in semantic space—even more so when we make an interesting coherent statement since the interest will flow from the way in which the words serve to modify (i.e., are responsive to each other) in semantic space.

It follows from these considerations that employing symbols in the service of a generative grammar will give us a *detached, highly integrated, open-ended, multidimensional representational system*, and that nothing else will do the trick. We need symbols to have the *detached representations* part (well, symbols are *defined* as detached representations), and we need a generative grammar of some kind to obtain the *highly integrated, open-ended, multidimensional system* part—a way of systematically relating symbols to each other so as to offer an infinity of potential meanings and shades of meaning. Once we have all this, we have a representational system of real depth and texture. Indeed, we have a representational system that is so rich in its own right that the mind it constitutes can even become "lost in (its own) thought" to the extent that it hardly even notices the otherwise powerful pull of the raw, in-one's-face, here-and-now immediacy of the biophysical world as it floods our senses from moment to moment.

By the same token, the richness of this kind of "world-unto-itself" representational system is such that it can allow us to draw back from complete experiential immersion in the biophysical realm to a limited, even quite carefully calibrated, extent. Thus, rather than getting so lost in our own thoughts that we largely block the biophysical realm out of our awareness, we can simply draw back to the extent of taking the biophysical realm—or any aspect of it—as the object *of* our thoughts and so reflect *on* it. This is *cognitive* (but only cognitive) transcendence of the biophysical realm, and it enables us to move from a world of *percepts*—that is, perceptions and, perhaps, generalizations based on perceptions (which we might think of as nonverbal kinds of concepts)—to a world that also includes *abstract concepts* (i.e., concepts that are not necessarily based on perceptions or not based on perceptions alone). Crucially, the category of abstract concepts includes things that are putatively real yet nevertheless unobservable directly by the senses, such as *physical causes* and the *mental states of others*, both of which "stand behind" the phenomena we observe directly by our senses. Abstract thinking enables us to "fill in the gaps"—the missing links or hidden variables—that we believe it is necessary to account for in order to explain both the behavior of things in the physical world and the behavior of others.

Putting all this together, we can express the main points as follows: to obtain cognitive transcendence of the biophysical realm we need to have a *detached, highly integrated representational system*, and to have a detached, highly integrated representational system we need to employ *symbols in the service of a generative grammar*. Now, it turns out that the use of symbols in the service of a generative grammar is what we are implicitly referring to, and what linguists are explicitly referring to, when we or they speak of *language*; this is, at base, what language is. Thus, only language, understood in the formal sense of symbols in the service of a generative grammar, can provide the kind of representational system that enables a being to experience full-blown cognitive transcendence of the biophysical realm.

Language and the Mindsharing Realm

The next point I want to emphasize is that language is never acquired (or invented) in complete linguistic isolation. This is supported by both careful reasoning and, more importantly, evidence. I will first consider the reasoning. In one of the great developments of twentieth-century philosophy, Ludwig Wittgenstein advanced some "in principle" reasons against the possibility of a purely private language (philosophers now refer to this collection of tersely expressed remarks as the "private language argument").[13] Wittgenstein's argument can be glossed by saying that if, as I have already argued above, the use of rules regarding symbols and their meaningful combination is a function of social agreement, then we are clearly open to subtle and not-so-subtle *correction by others* each and every time we employ these rules. However, if I were privately to invent my own linguistic rules—my very own symbols and grammar—then how would I be able to tell the difference between those occasions when I thought I was employing these rules correctly, and was, and those occasions when I also thought I was employing them correctly, but wasn't? From an internal point of view, which is all I would have if there was no one else who shared my "language," my usages would seem equally right to me on both occasions. But if there is no way that I can actually tell if I'm wrong with respect to my employment of a rule, then the very notion of a "rule" loses its meaning; it is rendered incoherent. (Consider further: even if I think that I have made a mistake, how can I tell from a purely internal point of view that I have? Maybe I just think I've made a mistake in terms of my own rules but haven't really.) In the absence of the external checks afforded by other language users, the private "rules" by which I regulate my private language would drift, and I would end up in a situation in which any term or linguistic construction could end up "meaning" anything. But if a term or expression can end up meaning anything, then it actually means nothing—any sense of stable "meanings" would be lost. I would end up talking my own form of gibberish to myself. Thus, for Wittgenstein, the very idea that someone could invent a purely "private language" is incoherent.

The available evidence not only supports this general view, but, for reasons we will come to, it supports it with a vengeance. Unfortunately, we have quite a number of cases of humans who have been deprived of immersion in linguistically mediated culture from a very young age, before anything like the proper acquisition of language—or at least before any acquisition that has taken place has developed to the point where it will not atrophy more or less entirely in the absence of human company. These cases are of two general kinds. First, there are those who have been physically deprived of human company. These include (i) "wild," or "feral," children who have grown up with animals, like the famous cases of Victor, "the wild boy of Aveyron," discovered at about the age of twelve in 1800 in France, or the wolf-girl sisters Amala and Kamala, discovered living with wolves at about the ages of three and five in 1920 in India, and (ii) others who have been kept in solitary confinement, locked away in a room and not spoken to, and so have not even enjoyed the company of animals, like the famous cases of Kaspar Hauser, kept in a dungeon without human contact from early childhood until about the age of sixteen, when he was discovered abandoned in a street in Nuremberg in 1828, or "Genie," kept physically constrained and isolated in a room in a house in Los Angeles by her psychotic father from infancy until the age of thirteen, when her largely blind mother fled the house with her in 1970.[14]

The second kinds of cases are those who have been, at least in part, physiologically deprived of the means for language acquisition. These include deaf and deaf-blind children who, for one reason or another, have not been introduced to one of the various sign languages. Sign languages are languages in the full and proper sense of that term: they employ detached (i.e., symbolic) representations in the service of a generative grammar to produce a cognitive world that is as rich—as open ended and multidimensional—as spoken languages. Thus, being deaf does not in itself deprive a child of language acquisition, but this physiological impairment can radically limit a young child's access to language input for at least two reasons. First, the parents of these children are very likely not proficient in a sign language. Second, these children can and have been variously ignored and misdiagnosed as retarded and so not sent off in the right direction to learning language in the first place. If these children then come to learning sign language relatively late in their childhood developmental processes—or perhaps not even until they are adults— then considerable damage has already been done because the brain becomes increasingly less "plastic" as we mature (i.e., less capable of making new neuronal connections and of "rewiring" those that have been made). Learning the fundamentals of language between the ages of two and four is "child's play"; learning it as an adult is hard work.

Examples of late sign language acquisition in deaf or deaf-blind people include the contemporary cases of Joseph, the eleven-year-old boy discussed by the clinical neurologist Oliver Sacks in his important study of deafness entitled *Seeing Voices*, and Ildefonso, the twenty-seven year-old deaf Mexican discussed by Susan Schaller in *A Man Without Words*, an engaging account of her struggle to introduce Ildefonso to the rudiments of sign language.[15] But surely the most significant account that we have of someone who came to language late is the remarkable case of Helen Keller (1880–1968), who, through illness (possibly scarlet fever), went both deaf and blind at the age of nineteen months, but who, through her dedicated teacher Annie Sullivan, was able to begin to acquire language from shortly before the age of her seventh birthday and, ultimately, to be able to write her own account of what it was like to be without language.[16] Keller provides us with the single most articulate account in existence of what it was like to be a nonlinguistic but emotionally supported child raised in normal human company, which means that we cannot dismiss her prelinguistic view of the world as a function of emotional deprivation or lack of human company. Moreover, we may well only have this account due to the rare combination of Keller's own inherent intelligence and drive to express herself and the freak nature of her illness. This illness robbed her of her sight and hearing at nineteen months, which was early enough for her subsequently to have no conscious understanding of symbols, but late enough—given her exposure to language up to the time of the illness—to have laid down or stimulated some neural foundations that could later be reinvigorated and built on by her teacher, thus enabling Keller to cross the linguistic Rubicon so successfully.

Studies of wild, or feral, children and of prelingually deaf and deaf-blind people (i.e., those who are born or become deaf or deaf-blind prior to acquiring any significant language skills) show us two profoundly important things. The first is that, as Wittgenstein's argument against the possibility of a purely private language already suggests, language does indeed come "from the outside." The second is a chilling insight into what it is like to be without language. I will consider this intriguing, second issue in the next chapter (chapter 7) because it links directly to important ethical considerations that I will then move on to discuss in the chapter after that (chapter 8). Here, however, I want to focus on the first point, that is, the way in which studies of the above kinds of people show how language comes to us "from the outside" and is never generated from within, as a purely private affair. I particularly want to maintain this focus of interest here because it will provide us with further insight into how we should understand and label the realm of existence that is characterized by linguistically mediated cognitive transcendence of the biophysical realm.

Although at least some people who come to language late learn to use some indexical and iconic signs in their prelinguistic state (like pointing and performing imitative actions to indicate, say, their mother or father), none of these people shows any development of a private language. Indeed, it's worse than that: as I said earlier, it turns out that Wittgenstein's views are confirmed "with a vengeance." Let me explain. Wittgenstein's argument trades on the possibility that a mentally isolated being might at least vaguely conceive of the idea of developing a private language and might want to develop such a language, even if such an attempt is, as Wittgenstein argued, doomed to failure. What we find, however, is that people who have been cut off from immersion in linguistically mediated culture—such as the kinds of people that I have referred to above—never even conceive of the possibility of using symbols to stand for things. When people who came to language late are introduced to symbolic forms of reference, they give their teachers—who attempt in all manner of ways to get them to connect symbols such as "w-a-t-e-r" to the substance water, or "c-a-t" to a cat—the clear sense that they have no idea what their teachers are trying to do. Thus, Oliver Sacks accurately sums up the plight of these people in general when, in his foreword to Susan Schaller's book, he says of Ildefonso that he "not only lacked any language but lacked any *idea* of language: he had no conception, at first, of what Susan Schaller was trying to do, or of what other people, so mysteriously, 'did,' between themselves."[17] And in those extremely rare cases in which these people are able to break through into language to such a degree that they can reflect back on what it was like to be without language (such as the case of Helen Keller, whom I will discuss below), they will themselves report that in their prelinguistic state they had no idea about symbols or what people were doing when they used them.

Thus, it appears that the idea of symbolic usage is inconceivable in the first place for those who are isolated from immersion in linguistically mediated culture from a young age. This means that the project of attempting to develop a private language never even gets off the ground in order *to* fail. And if you think about it yourself for a moment, why should it? On the face of it, it surely seems stupid to use a sound or gesture that has *nothing to do with what you're referring to* (i.e., a genuinely detached representation or, in other words, a symbol) to refer to it. It just seems dumb—completely counterintuitive. Surely the natural thing to do is to refer to something by either directly pointing to it or else invoking it through some kind of imitative action (i.e., by using indexical and iconic signals rather than genuine symbols). But if this is all that it ever occurs to you to do, then you will never even begin to head off in a genuinely linguistic direction. These considerations therefore suggest that Wittgenstein was right about the impossibility of developing a purely private language, but right in a deeper way than even he realized. Such a project will be impossible, not simply because it is impossible to follow private rules as such, but, more fundamentally, because the idea of developing any such rules in regard to detached—or symbolic—forms of reference will not occur to you in the first place.

So how do people who come to language late manage to break through and get some idea of what a symbolic form of reference is? This is a good question, yet our present understanding is not much better than "and then a miracle happens," albeit thanks, in every case, to the persistence of dedicated teachers. Whatever the actual neurological underpinnings of this breakthrough process might be, it manifests itself experientially as a classic "aha!" moment; indeed, it is *the* "aha!" moment—the "Big Aha!"—in these people's lives. The personal experience of late language learners who achieve this breakthrough is one in which, having been confronted by teaching session after teaching session in which they don't have a clue as to what is really going on, they suddenly "get" a particular symbol and, with it, the *point* of symbols. This is invariably reported—either by the eyewitness of their teachers or, later, by the students themselves—as a transporting moment of awakening, as a revelation, a kind of miracle, and as a release from a kind of solitary confinement in a prelinguistic prison. This breakthrough moment is then immediately followed by an explosion of interest in the names (i.e., the symbols) for things. Sure, there is a tremendous amount still to learn about language, but once this barrier is broken, the rest is, in a sense, details. And this exuberant phase is then just as often followed by a sense of great sorrow as these people begin to glimpse what they have missed out on for so long.

Helen Keller's reporting of her own experience can be taken as emblematic of these cases. Her teacher, Annie Sullivan, would spell words into her hand; Keller says she was "interested in this finger play and tried to imitate it."[18] But she was, by her own account, completely uncomprehending of what she was doing; it was just "monkey-like imitation." Then, one day, after some weeks, she and her teacher happened to go for a short walk along a path to a well-house; her teacher placed her hand under the water spout and spelt the word for water into her hand, "first slowly, then rapidly." Keller describes what happened in this famous passage in her early autobiography entitled *The Story of My Life* (1902):

I stood still, my whole attention fixed upon the motions of her fingers. Suddenly I felt a misty consciousness as of something forgotten—a thrill of returning thought; and somehow the mystery of language was revealed to me. I knew then that "w-a-t-e-r" meant the wonderful cool something that was flowing over my hand. That living word awakened my soul, gave it light, hope, joy, set it free! There were barriers still, it is true, but barriers that could in time be swept away.

I left the well-house eager to learn. Everything had a name, and each name gave birth to a new thought. As we returned to the house every object which I touched seemed to quiver with life. That was because I saw everything with the strange, new sight that had come to me. On entering the door I remembered the doll I had broken. I felt my way to the hearth and picked up the pieces. I tried vainly to put them together. Then my eyes filled with tears; for I realized what I had done, and for the first time I felt repentance and sorrow.

This was *the* moment of realization for Keller; the rest was, in a sense, details; as Keller herself notes: "There were barriers still, it is true, but barriers that could in time be swept away."

Susan Schaller's account of Ildefonso's breakthrough moment is structurally identical to that of Keller's experience. Just like Annie Sullivan, Schaller tried variation after variation after exhaustive variation in order to get Ildefonso to make a connection—any connection—between a word and the thing in the world to which the word referred. Schaller's efforts all seemed to be to no avail. Like Keller, Ildefonso would just uncomprehendingly imitate what Schaller did. Then, suddenly, with Schaller willing herself on in a "one more time" fashion, there came a *moment* in which Ildefonso broke through and "got it." Just like Keller, Ildefonso became stock still in this moment: Keller (above) says that she "stood still, my whole attention fixed upon the motions of [my teacher's] fingers"; Schaller says of Ildefonso: "Suddenly he sat up, straight and rigid, his head back and his chin pointing forward. The whites of his eyes expanded as if in terror."[19] Once having experienced this moment of insight into the *point* of symbols, Ildefonso, like Keller, then hungrily demanded to know the names of everything around him. Following that, and again like Keller, Ildefonso, having had this first glimpse of the "prison where he had existed alone, shut out of the human race for twenty-seven years," just as quickly collapsed in tears.[20]

Oliver Sacks describes several of the rare cases of people who have crossed over the language divide late in their development, such as those of Jean Massieu and his teacher Sicard in France in the eighteenth century, Kasper Hauser in Germany in the nineteenth century, and, of course, Ildefonso and his teacher Susan Schaller in California in the 1980s.[21] The details of these stories vary, but their overall structure remains essentially the same: there is a moment of realization in which the learner "gets" the symbolic nature of the stimulus, followed by a comparative intellectual explosion in which they glimpse the possibilities that have thereby been unlocked, and which were formerly beyond their conception. Thus, Sacks writes in regard to Kasper Hauser: "This sudden, exuberant explosion of language and intelligence is essentially similar to what occurred with Massieu [and, as we have seen here, with Keller and Ildefonso]—it is what happens with the mind and soul if they have been imprisoned (without being completely destroyed) from early life, and the doors of the prison are suddenly thrown open."[22]

Thus, in such documented cases as we have, it seems that *if* these late language learners "get" the fact that a visual or tactile stimulus is a *symbol*, *if* they realize that it is not just a meaningless gesture or touch *but stands for something else*, then the experience that their teachers or, later, they describe is one of an inspirational *moment* of realization, of an awakening, an escape from a prison, and so on, that initiates an intellectual explosion, forever marking a "before" and an "after." (In view of these reports, I am tempted to note that it is perhaps instructive to contrast these rare accounts with accounts given of similarly rare states of "mystical realization." In the case of states of mystical realization, the world is typically held to be seen anew when the realizer transcends the labeling, distinguishing, discursive mind, the prison house of language and concepts, and so on, which allegedly keeps us from the direct, unmediated experience of a primordial unity or reality. In the case of late "language realization," the world is seen anew precisely because the discursive mind gets kick started and allows these people to escape from the prison house of what Keller describes as a "death-in-life existence."[23]

Now, which seems more worthwhile to you? Or, if you want both, which would you want first—or most?)

Reflecting on the development of language in the prelingually deaf, Oliver Sacks writes:

One is born with one's senses; these are "natural." One can develop motor skills, naturally, by oneself. But one cannot acquire language by oneself: *this* skill comes in a unique category. It is impossible to acquire language without some essential innate ability, but this ability is only activated by another person who already possesses linguistic power and competence. It is only through transaction (or, as Vygotsky would say, "negotiation") with another that the language is achieved.[24]

The psychologist Merlin Donald likewise observes with respect to the development of language: "The direction of flow is clear: from culture to individual; from outside to inside."[25] Although this can be seen quite clearly in the case of late language learners, it was not until the earlier part of the twentieth century that developmental psychologists realized that language development proceeds on the basis of this "Outside-Inside principle" for children of normal hearing as well. Instead, it used to be assumed that language was such a quintessentially human attribute that it would just unfold from within, even in an isolated human. The prime mover behind the establishment of the Outside-Inside principle of language development was the brilliant Russian psychologist Lev Vygotsky (1896–1934). (In this sense, Vygotsky was, if you like, psychology's version of Wittgenstein.) Vygotsky's studies suggested that higher mental functions appear first on the interpersonal, social, or "intermental" level —in the context of parent-child interactions—and only later become internalized so as to operate on the intrapersonal, private, individual, or "intramental" level. Thus, Vygotsky viewed the fact that young children talk to themselves as they play or try to solve problems as indicative not of a kind of egoism (as the influential developmental psychologist Jean Piaget thought) but rather of the fact that the initially audible or essentially public performance of speech "plays an essential role in the transition from social speech to inner speech on the intramental plane."[26]

It seems, then, that language is quintessentially a *mindsharing* activity —not only in the everyday sense that we need it if we are truly to share experience, knowledge, and understandings with each others, but also, and even more fundamentally, in the sense that we simply never develop this mindsharing capacity in the first place if we do not have any contact with other language users. It is for these reasons that I want to apply Merlin Donald's highly evocative term *mindsharing* to the realm that I have been outlining here, that is, the realm that is characterized by beings that are capable of cognitive transcendence of the biophysical realm, beings that are capable, in other words, of using language. I will therefore refer to the linguistically mediated realm of cognitive transcendence of the biophysical realm as the *mindsharing* realm and to those who occupy it directly or, like newborn humans, are on their way to doing so as *mindsharers*. (I say "occupy it directly" here because, for reasons we will come to in chapter 8, some nonmindsharers can become deeply *incorporated* into the mindsharing *realm* even though they are not themselves mindsharers.) Mindsharers are mindsharers because they have successfully acquired language, and mindsharers give birth to new mindsharers when they give them language, when they touch them with what Sacks tellingly refers to (in the previous quotation from him) as "linguistic power and competence." Once we are touched in this way, then both we and other mindsharers can engage in the culturally immersed process of what Merlin Donald incisively describes as *mindbuilding*.[27]

If you are a mindsharer, then you live not only in the biophysical realm but also in the mindsharing realm, the realm of linguistically mediated cognitive transcendence of the biophysical realm. However, if an entity is a *being* (that is, if it is like something to be that entity) but not a mindsharing being, then it exists only in the biophysical realm. This raises an obvious question: What are the differences between "biophysical realm only" beings and mindsharers? As we will see in the next two chapters, the evidence overwhelmingly supports the view that the inner, cognitive worlds of "biophysical realm only" beings are very much worlds of the here-and-now, conditioned by what each solitary individual has experienced in its own right, as opposed to the cumulative amassing of experience, knowledge, and understandings between and across generations that characterize mindsharers. I will therefore refer to "biophysical realm only" beings, or nonmindsharing beings, as *isoexperients*, to capture the fact that they are essentially "islands of awareness and experience." Since they have no way of explicitly sharing with each other the experience, knowledge, and understandings that they acquire, these all die with them. They could in a loose way be said to suffer from a cognitive (as opposed to a behavioral) version of "locked-in syndrome."

I will turn to the differences between what it is like to be a non-language-using iso-experient as opposed to a language-using mindsharer —including the ethical implications of these differences—in the next two chapters. But, first, I need to outline the third and final realm in the theory of responsive cohesion's theory of contexts.

The Compound Material Realm (or the Human-Constructed Realm)

It is at least theoretically conceivable that the biophysical beings we refer to as humans—us—might have become extremely adept at exploring the linguistically mediated mindsharing realm of meanings, knowledge, and experience, but might have hardly developed any artifacts at all. To employ the anthropological distinction between symbolic and material forms of culture: we might have developed a sophisticated form of *symbolic culture*—in other words, a fairly rich form of sociocultural life— but might have had very little to show for ourselves in terms of *material culture*, by which I mean biophysical material that we had intentionally fashioned for our own purposes (and the unintended products of this too, which gives us another sense of the term "artifact"). We might have used the environmental *affordances*[28] that we came across, but might have done so in a passive way, such as sheltering in caves that already existed, and otherwise spending our time telling stories, making up explanations, gossiping, grooming each other, and so on. However, this is not the way that things have turned out, and the overwhelming evidence of the fact that things have not turned out this way means that we must also recognize another realm of nature to that of the biophysical and mindsharing realms as such.

I will refer to this third realm of nature as the *compound material realm* for two reasons. The first is that this third realm represents a combination—or *compound* mixture—of both the biophysical realm and the mindsharing realm. It includes all the material (and, hence, tangible, biophysically instantiated) products that are produced as a result of the ideas that emerge from the linguistically mediated knitting together of minds that constitute the mental bases of a culture. The compound material realm can be viewed as a direct outcome of the combination of the biophysical realm and the mindsharing realm, almost like a loosely formulated equation:

The biophysical realm (BP) multiplied, amplified, or intensified by the linguistically mediated mindsharing realm (MS) equals, gives, or produces the compound material realm (CM).
In short: BP × MS = CM.

The book you are reading is an example of this "equation": it is made of stuff that derives ultimately from the biophysical realm (even if this stuff has itself been modified by processes that are themselves the outcomes of ideas developed in the mindsharing realm), and it contains meanings that were developed, and could only have been developed, in a mindsharing context. These meanings, which could be physically recorded in any number of ways, languages, and so on, have been realized in the particular physical form that you now have in front of you, which constitutes an example of the compound material realm.

The second reason for referring to this third realm of nature as the *compound material realm* is that ideas in the mindsharing realm can be retained and improved upon, which means, in turn, that the means of manufacturing the material products that issue from any compound of the biophysical and mindsharing realms can also be retained and improved upon. Moreover, these compound material products can themselves immensely accelerate the development of ideas in the mindsharing realm itself and so can accelerate the grounds of their own development in a self-catalyzing kind of process (e.g., the manufacture of new kinds of scientific instruments can accelerate the development of new scientific theories, which, in turn, can accelerate the development of still newer kinds of scientific instruments, and so on; or consider the advent of personal computers). Thus, the processes at work in the interplay between the mindsharing and compound material realms are such that they can have a *compounding* effect, much like compound interest, where the interest accrued on an initial sum of money is added to that amount and so feeds the accrual of further interest. This process of intensification provides us with our second reason for referring to this realm as the compound material realm: whereas the first reason is simply that the compound material realm consists of material things that represent a compound mixture of the biophysical and mindsharing realms, the second reason is that the interplay between the mindsharing and compound material realms is such that they feed off each other and so compound each other's effects.

Identifying this third realm in this way allows us to see that when animals that are iso-experients fashion the world around them in various ways, they are still operating *within* the biophysical realm. Their material products might be the product of instinctual programs, of individual forms of trial-and-error learning, or of what is known as *emulation learning* as opposed to *imitative learning*, but they are not a function of genuine mindsharing. It is important to be clear about this last point. Emulation learning refers to a form of social learning in which a being learns something about an object, such as the fact that it contains food, by watching a conspecific manipulate it, and then basically devises its own behavioral strategy in order to get at that food itself. In contrast, imitative learning refers to a form of social learning in which an observer deliberately "attempts to copy the goal-directed behavioral strategies of others."[29] Although the point is still controversial, the available evidence suggests that genuine forms of imitative learning are actually rare or nonexistent among nonhumans—even among nonhuman primates, our closest evolutionary relatives—and may be uniquely human.[30] Moreover, the claim that even nonhuman apes do not, as it happens, ape (in the sense of genuinely imitate) is further supported by considerable evidence that suggests that in the wild, nonhuman apes do not deliberately show things to each other and, thus, do not engage in intentional teaching of each other.[31] (I will discuss these matters further in the next chapter.)

Now, if nonhuman primates did engage in genuinely imitative learning, then this would amount to an *implicit* (because nonlinguistic) form of mindsharing. This form of mindsharing would be nowhere near as powerful as explicit, linguistically mediated forms of mindsharing, but it would still be a form of mindsharing. However, emulation learning is nothing of the sort. In emulation learning, an animal's attention is drawn to an object because of the activities of another animal (a process that is referred to as "stimulus enhancement"), it may then learn something about that object (such as the fact that it contains food), and it may then "have a go" at getting the food itself. There is nothing in this process that suggests even an implicit form of mindsharing. An animal that learns about its world only in this way remains an iso-experient: it is wholly dependent upon what it can glean about the world through its own efforts and is not aided in this process by any understanding of the communicative intentions of others, if, indeed, they have any such intentions.

The fact that iso-experients' instinctual and emulative ways of fashioning the world around them are not a function of implicit or explicit forms of mindsharing means that these ways of fashioning the world do not possess a compounding quality; instead, these beings keep playing out the same instinctual programs or, as it were, reinventing the branchless twig and the nut-cracking stone. In contrast, mindsharers exhibit historically cumulative and collectively intensified processes of linguistically mediated social learning that issue in a compounding of their knowledge, skills, and compound material products. The respected primate researcher and developmental psychologist Michael Tomasello usefully refers to this process as "the ratchet effect" and notes that

In general, then, human cultural traditions may be most readily distinguished from chimpanzee cultural traditions—as well as the few other instances of culture observed in other primate species—precisely by the fact that they accumulate modifications over time, that is to say, they have cultural "histories." ... These cultural learning processes are especially powerful because they are supported by the uniquely human cognitive adaptation for understanding others as intentional beings like the self—which creates forms of social learning that act as a ratchet by faithfully preserving newly innovated strategies in the social group until there is another innovation to replace them.... Developing children are thus growing up in the midst of the very best tools and symbols their forebears have invented for negotiating the rigors of their physical and social worlds.[32]

Only mindsharers produce compound material products in the sense in which I have characterized these products here. The term *compound material realm* is therefore an informative way of distinguishing the artifacts that nonmindsharing animals produce from the artifacts that mindsharers produce, of distinguishing ant nests, beehives, and chimpanzees' nut-cracking stones and ant-collecting twigs from books, computers, and cities. However, although the term *compound material realm* is an informative way of identifying this realm in a formal way and of doing so without prejudice to the question of exactly what beings are mindsharers, we will nevertheless see in the next chapter that the evidence suggests that (on this planet at least) only humans are mindsharers. This means that for all practical, earthly purposes, we can, if we wish, refer to the compound material realm less formally as the *human-constructed realm* since it includes, essentially, all the compound material products that humans and only humans create.

The Theory of Responsive Cohesion's Theory of Contexts

I have now distinguished the biophysical, mindsharing, and compound material (or human-constructed) realms, and have done so in their general evolutionary order. However, lest this sound too much like a linear, unidirectional story, it is important to stress that these realms also act back on each other (a point that I have already stressed in discussing the relationship between the mindsharing and compound material realms and that is central to understanding both the nature of the compound material realm and the reason for the name that I have given it). For example, not only does the *biophysical realm* deeply inform the development of the shared and shareable meanings, knowledge, and experiences that constitute the *mindsharing realm* (for starters, brains are made of biophysical stuff, and, for seconds, the biophysical realm—which ultimately means the biophysical universe!—surrounds and sustains us), but the meanings, knowledge, and experiences that constitute the *mindsharing realm* also determine the ways in which we conceive of and value the biophysical world and so, in turn, have an enormous impact on the *biophysical realm* itself in terms of the way we view it and act in regard to it.

Similarly, and as already noted, not only does the *mindsharing realm* deeply inform the development of the *compound material realm* (e.g., in regard to what we decide to make or build and where and how we decide to make or build it), but the *compound material realm* also has an enormous impact on the meanings, knowledge, and experiences that constitute the *mindsharing realm* (e.g., just think of the impact that living in cities—not to mention highly technologically developed cities—has on the overall stock and quality of any society's shared and shareable collection of meanings, knowledge, and experiences). Finally, not only does the *biophysical realm* also deeply inform, via the mindsharing realm, the development of the *compound material realm* (e.g., in terms of what kinds of biophysical materials are available, what kinds of natural forms exist and, thus, what kinds of natural forms might inspire and provide models for artifacts, and even major cosmological constraints like the strength of gravity), but the *compound material realm* also has an enormous impact on the *biophysical realm* (e.g., just think of the effects that the caterpillar tractor or greenhouse gas emissions produced by our modern forms of compound material culture are having and will have on the biophysical realm generally). The collective interrelationships between these three realms are, therefore, complex, to say the least.

But even though these realms interact with each other in complex ways, there can be no doubt as to which realm constitutes the primary context of which. Rational-empirical methods clearly suggest that the best theory of contexts is one in which we understand that *the biophysical realm constitutes the basic context for the development and continuance of the mindsharing realm, and the mindsharing realm constitutes the basic context for the development and continuance of the compound material realm.* Whatever qualifications we might want to make about the degree of interaction between these realms, we now all know that, when all is said and done, if there were no biophysical realm, then there would be no mindsharing realm, and if there were no mindsharing realm, then there would be no compound material realm. Another way to put this is to imagine what would happen if these existing realms were stripped away from us in reverse order, one by one. If the compound material realm were stripped away, then we would still have a mindsharing realm. It would be an impoverished one to be sure (there goes my guitar, computer, tennis racquet, eating utensils, and toiletries!), but we could still huddle together in caves and tell stories, make up explanations, and gossip. If the mindsharing realm were also stripped away, then there would still be a biophysical realm of rocks, plants, trees, and nonlinguistic animals, but any sentient animals of this kind would, under these circumstances, necessarily be iso-experients—"islands of awareness"—rather than mindsharers.

This general point regarding which realm constitutes the primary context of which can be driven home even further by pointing out the following. When I say that the biophysical realm constitutes the basic context for the development and continuance of the mindsharing realm and that the mindsharing realm constitutes the basic context for the development and continuance of the compound material realm, it is important to understand that the preexisting contexts of each subsequent realm did not just happen to be "hanging around" prior to the emergence of these subsequent realms. Rather, the antecedent realms constitute the contexts out of which the subsequent realms have been *generated*: the mindsharing realm did not just emerge *in* but rather emerged *from* the biophysical realm; the compound material realm did not just emerge *in* but rather emerged *from* the mindsharing realm. Thus, the biophysical realm constitutes not just the *preexisting context* of the mindsharing realm but rather what we could refer to as the *formative context* of the mindsharing realm, and the mindsharing realm constitutes not just the *preexisting context* of the compound material realm but, again, the *formative context* of the compound material realm.

If we now sum up this general survey of the nature of things, it comes to this: *the biophysical realm constitutes the overarching (indeed, the formative and sustaining) context of the mindsharing realm, and the mindsharing realm constitutes the overarching (indeed, the formative and sustaining) context of the compound material realm.* The first of these realms is often just referred to as "nature" (employing an important, but limited, sense of that term), and the second and third realms are often just referred to as symbolic and material forms of "culture." In fact, all three realms are part of Nature (in the largest sense, hence the capital "N"), since there is nothing supernatural about any of them; they simply constitute three realms of a single unfolding reality, about which we can tell a single, coherent, rationally-empirically informed story. And this story provides us with our best, our most informed *theory of contexts*—our best model of precisely what-constitutes-the-context-of-what.

Now, you will recall that I argued at some length earlier in this chapter that acceptance of the foundational value of responsive cohesion guarantees the priority of contextual responsive cohesion over internal responsive cohesion. However, we also saw that this conclusion raised a crucial problem: for any particular kind of thing, it is quite possible that different evaluators might reach quite different kinds of judgments about how contextually responsive that thing is depending upon which particular context they have in mind (and here I gave the example of three buildings, each of which exemplified a high degree of contextual responsive cohesion with respect to one of the following three contexts: the natural environment, the human social environment, and its own built environment). It therefore became important to understand, at a fundamental level, which context(s)—such as the natural environment, the human social environment, and the human-constructed environment—constituted the overarching context(s) of which. This led to the need to develop the theory of responsive cohesion's theory of contexts. If we now combine this (descriptive) theory of contexts with the (normative) priority ordering that the theory of responsive cohesion gives to contextual responsive cohesion over internal (or subcontextual forms of) responsive cohesion, then we can see that *priority should be given to contextual responsive cohesion with the biophysical realm, the mindsharing realm, and the compound material realm—or the natural environment, the human social environment, and the human-constructed environment—in that order of preference.* Another way to express this is to say that the biophysical realm, the mindsharing realm, and the compound material realm should constitute the primary, secondary, and tertiary contexts of consideration, respectively, in any assessment of the degree to which an item of interest exhibits contextual responsive cohesion.

This conclusion provides us with a *direct* answer to the question that I used to open up the issue of the need for a theory of contexts, namely, the question regarding which of three buildings that exhibit equal degrees of internal responsive cohesion but different kinds of contextual responsive cohesion is better than the others overall. The answer is that if a forced choice must be made here, then the building that exhibits a high degree of responsive cohesion with its biophysical (or primary) context is better than the other two, and the building that exhibits a high degree of responsive cohesion with its mindsharing (or secondary) context is better than the last one, which only exhibits a high degree of responsive cohesion with its human-constructed, built environment (or tertiary) context. However, the immediate follow-up comment to this forced-choice answer is as follows: all three buildings are so much less than they could be from the perspective of the theory of responsive cohesion since they all exhibit what turn out to be variously limited forms of contextual responsive cohesion. Indeed, the fact that each of these buildings is severely limited in this way means that it is possibly more enlightening to think of the rank ordering that I have just given for them in terms of which of the buildings is *less bad* than the others, rather than which of them is, in some straightforwardly positive sense, *better* than the others. For there is simply no need for a building to be responsive only or overwhelmingly to one kind of context alone, and, indeed, it is a stupid form of design that does this (not that this seems to stop people from designing in this way). From the perspective of the theory of responsive cohesion, what we need in place of buildings that exhibit limited forms of contextual responsive cohesion are buildings that are responsive to their biophysical, mindsharing, *and* compound material (or human-constructed) contexts, albeit in that order of priority. Thus, the real point of the forced-choice example above is only to show which context should have the primary say relative to which, not which should have the only say. Within the constraints that are imposed by the primary-secondary-tertiary-context way of proceeding that I have outlined, there are all manner of creative options open to planners, architects, designers, and builders to realize forms of contextual responsive cohesion in each of these contexts.

This hopeful-observation-*cum*-plea concludes my exposition of the theory of responsive cohesion's theory of contexts, although I will have more to say about the application of all the ideas associated with this theory of contexts in chapter 10.

I now want to turn to explore in considerable detail an important distinction that has emerged from the theory of responsive cohesion's theory of contexts, namely, the distinction between mindsharers and iso-experients. I will explore the cognitive worlds of these two kinds of beings in the next chapter (chapter 7) and then draw out the important ethical implications that flow from these considerations in the chapter after that (chapter 8). Once I have done this, I will then be in a position to put the various aspects of the theory together in summary form (chapter 9) before proceeding (in chapter 10) to apply this theory to all of the eighteen problems that I introduced in chapter 2.

7

Exploring the Cognitive Worlds of Mindsharers and Iso-Experients

As we have now seen in the previous chapter, some simple reflection on the nature of the relational quality of responsive cohesion suggested that it was necessary to draw a distinction between internal and contextual forms of responsive cohesion. This distinction in turn necessitated an informed account of precisely what-constitutes-the-context-of-what, that is, a theory of contexts. And this theory of contexts in turn necessitated distinguishing, among other things, between those kinds of beings that live purely in the biophysical realm—iso-experients—and those that live also in the mindsharing realm—mindsharers. However, the fact that my primary concern in the previous chapter lay with outlining the theory of responsive cohesion's theory of contexts meant that, so far as the distinction between iso-experients and mindsharers is concerned, I was primarily concerned with explaining how the contrast between iso-experients and mindsharers arises (i.e., through the latter's acquisition of language—in, as we will see, the normal case) and why the existence of mindsharers is important in terms of an adequate theory of contexts (because mindsharers can cognitively transcend the here-and-now perceptual immediacy of the biophysical realm).

What I have not yet done is explore the cognitive worlds of iso-experients and mindsharers in any degree of detail. This is what I want to turn to now. Doing this will provide us with a considerable degree of insight into significant questions concerning which kinds of beings are mindsharers and which are iso-experients, what it is actually *like* to be a mindsharer (which is already intuitively known to you if you are reading this) or an iso-experient (which, as we will see, is virtually unimaginably different from the experience of what it is like to be a mindsharer), *and what the ethical implications of this might be.* I will pursue these questions in both this chapter and the next one. The reason for this is simple: once we have answered these questions, we will be able to see how the theory of responsive cohesion furnishes us with a complete, rationally defensible, workable framework in which to understand our obligations in respect not only of mindsharers but of all beings (i.e., including iso-experients). When this framework is then put together (in chapter 9) with the other central features of the theory of responsive cohesion—namely, the idea that responsive cohesion is the foundational value and the theory of contexts that flows from this central idea— we will have before us the complete theory of responsive cohesion. And when we have this, we will, I believe, have a General Ethics that is worthy of that name.

What Is Involved in Being a Mindsharer?

Analytically at least, we can distinguish several gradations on the path to becoming a fully fledged mindsharer. Here I want to introduce (and then explain) a useful schema consisting of three progressive stages: *implicit mindreading* (by which I mean pre- or nonlinguistic forms of *mindreading*), *implicit mindsharing* (by which I mean pre- or nonlinguistic forms of *mindsharing*), and *fully developed mindreading and mindsharing* or *explicit mindreading and mindsharing* (by which I mean fully linguistically developed forms of *mindreading and mindsharing*). I will just refer to this last stage in what follows as *explicit mindsharing* since, as we will see, we can take it as read that explicit mindsharing skills will always include *explicit mindreading* skills. Let us now consider each of these stages.

Highly intelligent social beings might understand other beings of the same species (i.e., their conspecifics) not just as animated, externally observable bodies that are capable of spontaneous, and not always easily predictable, movement but rather as beings with minds like their own and, therefore, as *intentional agents*. If sentient beings do understand this, even at some implicit, pre- or nonlinguistic level, then they can be thought of as engaging in what is variously described in the literature as implicit *mindreading* as opposed to suffering from what Simon Baron-Cohen, a leading researcher and theorist on autism, evocatively refers to as *mindblindness*; as having an (implicit) *theory of mind* (often abbreviated as ToM) as opposed to lacking a theory of mind; as implicitly adopting what Daniel Dennett refers to as an *intentional stance* toward other beings as opposed to what Baron-Cohen refers to as a *contingency stance*; as being implicit *mentalizers* as opposed, obviously, to *nonmentalizers*; or as acting like *intuitive psychologists* as opposed to *intuitive behaviorists*.[1]

To be a *mindreader* (in this cognitive research as opposed to "spooky action at a distance" or show business sense of the term) is to understand others, at least implicitly, not just as outwardly observable animate bodies but as the possessors of (strictly unobservable and, thus, hidden) mental states of their own, such as beliefs and desires. To understand others properly in this way is to understand (at least implicitly) that the mental states of these others might differ in significant ways from your own, that this understanding can help you to predict and account for what they do, and that, given all this, it might even be to your advantage on some occasions to try to manipulate what others believe and desire, since these others will act on the basis of what *they* believe to be true (or most desirable) rather than on the basis of what *you* know to be true (or most desirable). This outwitting game can be played by more than one player of course, and its potential advantages to the most successful player are sometimes viewed as having set in motion a kind of cognitive arms race that has selected for progressively better mindreading skills. This form of socially savvy intelligence is therefore sometimes also referred to as *Machiavellian intelligence*. If I can outwit you by getting you to believe that all the bananas are gone when I in fact know that one has been dropped behind that rock, then I can go back to the rock later and get the extra banana. Equally, if I can get you to believe that I'm on my own behind the rock and not with your favorite sexual partner, then that's good for me here and now and perhaps, in another sense, for my genetic heritage. It's easy to tell a story of this kind that might explain how mindreading ability might have been selected for among highly social, large-brained animals.

To understand your conspecifics in mentalistic terms is to believe that there is "someone at home" when you look into their eyes; that you are, as it were, doing business with another conscious being, not just an animate "skin bag." It follows that if you were a highly social but non-linguistic being *and* a mindreader, then you would presumably be highly motivated, *and* it would also make sense in terms of your own basic understanding of others, to attempt to communicate with your fellow beings in whatever nonlinguistic ways you could. You might therefore direct another being's attention to items of interest by pointing, by taking that being to an item of interest or bringing the item to that being, by deliberately showing that being how to do things, and so on. If you did these things, then you would be demonstrating not only *implicit mindreading* skills, since you would be relating to these others as the possessors of mental states of their own, but also *implicit mindsharing* skills, since all of these activities involve nonlinguistic ways of recruiting the attention of others in order to engage in episodes of *shared* or *joint attention*. These are the kinds of ways in which you would attempt to reach out to and connect with the minds of others if you were an intelligent, highly social, but nonlinguistic being that implicitly understood others as having *mental* states that you could affect and in some sense connect with.

But *implicit* forms of mindsharing such as these would still represent extremely clumsy and inefficient forms of communication compared with fully developed, explicit, linguistically mediated forms of mindsharing, which is the kind of mindsharing that I was referring to in the last chapter. This is because interpreting what, precisely, someone *had in mind* by simply *showing* you something would still be a matter of immense guesswork; and trying to figure out what they were trying to communicate on those occasions when what they wanted to refer to was not physically present and so could *not be shown* would, in the absence of language, verge on trying to interpret charades in a totally nonlinguistic context. Thus, if the quintessentially mindsharing activity of language is added to an implicit mindsharing (and, of course, implicit mindreading) context, then it is clear that this *explicit* form of mindsharing (and, of course, mindreading) would take massive precedence. Indeed, the very context of any continued use of implicit forms of mindreading and mindsharing would be completely changed since they would now be thoroughly embedded within a linguistically saturated social context (as when *language users* play charades).

For convenience of reference in the discussion that follows, I summarize the notions of implicit mindreading, implicit mindsharing, and explicit mindsharing in box 7.1. It turns out that there is considerable

Box 7.1

Brief Summaries of Implicit Mindreading, Implicit Mindsharing, and Explicit Mindsharing

Implicit mindreading	A purely pre- or nonlinguistically framed awareness that at least some other beings possess their own internal mental states, together with some degree of awareness as to the likely contents of the mental states of these other beings in various situations. More simply: a pre- or nonverbal awareness that it is *"like something"* to be another being, together with some degree of awareness as to *what* it might be like, or what might be "going through the mind" of that other being in a particular situation. (Note that implicit mindreading could conceivably be a purely private affair, with no attempt made to reach out and engage in implicit *mindsharing* with others.)
Implicit mindsharing	The purely pre- or nonlinguistically framed means by which implicit mindreaders might build on their implicit mindreading abilities in order to share various contents of their inner mental states with each other, for example, by pointing, by taking another being to see an object or by bringing the object to that being, by miming, by engaging in deliberate (but purely nonlinguistically framed) forms of teaching, and so on.
Explicit mindsharing	Linguistically framed forms of sharing the contents of one's mental states with others, and vice versa. (Note that explicit mindsharing abilities automatically include explicit mindreading abilities.)

empirical support for the *implicit mindreading–implicit mindsharing–explicit mindsharing* developmental progression that I have outlined here. As we will see, this is the normal progression that human infants move through in acquiring fully fledged linguistically mediated mindsharing skills. But, of course, things can go wrong, and the obvious example here is the tragic neurodevelopmental disorder of *autism* (literally, "self"-ism), which manifests as a spectrum disorder (i.e., a disorder that ranges from mild to severe) and is a lifelong condition for which there is no known medical treatment.[2] Autism is initially perplexing in this context because, on the one hand, considerable research suggests that autistic people suffer especially from what Baron-Cohen refers to as *mindblindness*, that is, they suffer from significant deficits in the normal mindreading and mindsharing capacities that the rest of us take for granted; yet, on the other hand, some autistic people can be linguistically highly competent.[3] So doesn't this suggest that the progression that I have outlined is incorrect, because a consideration of autistics suggests that it is possible not to be a mindreader and yet still develop linguistic capabilities, which are associated with explicit mindsharing?

Well, no, the picture is more complex than this question suggests. For a start, the cognitive developmental and comparative psychologist Michael Tomasello notes that: "Despite the popular image, which mainly focuses on high-functioning children with autism, about half of all these children learn no language at all—presumably because they do not understand the communicative intentions of others in the species-typical manner."[4] Second, the autism expert Peter Hobson notes that those high-functioning autistic children who do acquire language are nevertheless generally more impaired in regard to their language development than they are in regard to "other areas of intellectual functioning ... [such as] solving jigsaw-type tasks that suggest their own solution."[5] Third, the autism and Asperger's syndrome expert Lorna Wing notes that those autistics who become (relatively) linguistically proficient also perform relatively better on theory of mind tests than those who don't.[6] This is entirely consistent with the developmental progression that I have outlined in regard to becoming an explicit mindsharer, which suggests that it is those autistics who most lack mindreading skills that will be most lacking in linguistic proficiency. Finally, those autistics who do become linguistically proficient nevertheless do not use their linguistic competence in anything like the normal mindsharing ways, which is exactly what one would expect if language abilities develop in the context of damaged mindreading and mindsharing abilities. In particular, these individuals are characterized by a failure to understand communicative *intentions*; they will, for example, "understand" a metaphor, joke, or sarcastic comment literally rather than in terms of the intentions of the speaker.[7]

With these considerations in mind, I can now refine my characterization of mindsharers in the previous chapter as follows. First, my characterization of mindsharers was always in reference to what I have now referred to as explicit (i.e., language-using) mindsharers rather than implicit mindsharers (i.e., pre- or nonlinguistic sharers of attention). Second, I characterized language users as mindsharers on the implicit understanding that they had acquired language in a developmentally normal context, and, thus, that their language skills were built on the preexisting implicit mindreading and implicit mindsharing (or shared attention) skills that characterize the normal development of language-using beings. Bearing these distinctions in mind, I can now characterize what I originally meant by *mindsharers* more precisely as follows: *Mindsharers (in the sense of fully fledged or explicit mindsharers) are beings that have acquired language in the presence of developmentally normal implicit mindreading and implicit mindsharing (i.e., shared attention) skills.* Studies of late language learners prior to their encounter with language show us that without any exposure to other normal, language-using mindsharers a person has no chance of becoming an explicit mindsharer (because they do not develop language by themselves). And studies of normal human infants, on the one hand, and autistic children, on the other hand, suggest that with early exposure to language, you will automatically become an explicit mindsharer to the extent that your explicit mindsharing skills are underpinned by the presence of implicit mindreading and implicit mindsharing (shared attention) skills.

These considerations regarding the range of cognitive capacities that are built into the idea of fully fledged mindsharing are extremely important when it comes to the (as I will later argue, ethically significant) question of what kinds of beings are mindsharers. This is because they allow us to see that there is more to being a mindsharer than possessing language skills alone. If you lack the prerequisite cognitive capacities of implicit mindreading and implicit mindsharing—which, to repeat, are present in the normal course of (human) language acquisition, and thus whose presence I was taking for granted in my discussion of mindsharers in the previous chapter—then you will fail to become anything like a fully fledged mindsharer.

We can gain considerable insight into these points regarding what is involved in being a true mindsharer, as well as what kinds of beings are true mindsharers, by looking at recent research into the cognitive abilities of our closest evolutionary relatives and comparing these cognitive abilities with those of human infants.

Are Our Closest Evolutionary Relatives Implicit Mindreaders?

Our closest surviving evolutionary relatives are chimpanzees and their rarer evolutionary cousins, bonobos, or pygmy chimpanzees. Most research in this area is conducted with chimpanzees, in part, no doubt, precisely because of the relative rarity of bonobos. Where, then, do chimpanzees fit into the implicit mindreading–implicit mindsharing–explicit mindsharing developmental progression that I have outlined above? Are they implicit mindreaders, implicit mindsharers, or explicit, fully fledged mindsharers? Many people would be surprised to learn that recent research suggests that chimpanzees are *none* of the above, not even implicit mindreaders, that is, they do not even have an implicit sense of each other as intentional agents; they do not, in other words, possess even an implicit theory of mind. Instead, they seem to adopt a contingency stance rather than an intentional stance in respect of each other. That is, they understand their conspecifics as animated, externally observable bodies that are capable of spontaneous movement rather than as beings with minds like their own and, therefore, as intentional agents; they behave, in other words, like intelligent behaviorists rather than natural psychologists.

The researcher who has done more than anyone to show us this, through a quite brilliant series of well-controlled experiments, is Daniel Povinelli—and Povinelli himself says that his group was "not prepared" for the "astonishing" results they found.[8] What Povinelli and his research group did can be briefly explained as follows. Humans routinely interpret each other's eye orientation behavior in terms of the inner, experiential state of *seeing*: if someone turns their eyes toward something and we follow their gaze, we can generally make a good guess as to what they are *seeing* and, thus, what they *know* on the basis of this. (By the same token, we can assume that if, say, a young child's mother doesn't orient her eyes in the direction of her child when the child's hand is, against her instructions, in the cookie jar, then the child's mother hasn't *seen* the child steal the cookie and so doesn't *know*—at least on this basis—that the child has been naughty.) What this means is that we don't just form a mental link between eye-orientation *behavior* and another human's next move (i.e., their next piece of overt *behavior*);

rather we automatically insert a hidden, mental-state-connecting-link between the two behaviors. For example, we infer that if a person's head and eyes turn in the direction of a friend of theirs on the other side of the street and they then cross the street to their friend (a behavior–behavior link), then they have crossed the street because they have just *seen* someone that they *know* is their friend. That is, we attribute a particular mental state to the person on the basis of their head and eye orientation and then explain the person's subsequent behavior on the basis of this mental state attribution. We therefore understand others not on the basis of *behavioral contingencies*, in which we simply link one behavior with another (end of story), but in terms of *mental state attributions*, in which we link behaviors together in terms of underlying mental states, and, thus, at least implicitly, in terms of what a situation is like as experienced by that other person. In this sense, we engage in *mindreading*—modeling what another is *seeing, thinking, feeling,* or *wanting*—all the time.

Povinelli and his colleagues therefore asked this question: Do chimpanzees understand seeing in much the same way as we do? That is, do chimpanzees act as if they make (at least implicit) attributions of mental states to others or do they act on the basis of purely behavioral generalizations in which they learn simply to link one kind of behavior of their conspecifics with another, without realizing that these conspecifics are experiencing mental states of their own under the surface, as it were, of their externally observable behaviors? In terms of the cognitive research lingo, this question can be cast in a variety of other forms: Are chimpanzees mindreaders or are they mind blind? Do they have an implicit theory of mind or not? Do they adopt an intentional stance or a contingency stance toward others? Are they mentalizers or nonmentalizers? Do they behave like clever, albeit intuitive, psychologists or clever, albeit intuitive, behaviorists? We can refer to these alternative models of understanding as the *mental state attribution model* and the *behavioral generalization model*.

Povinelli and his colleagues have pitted these models against each other in a variety of experimental contexts that have focused on one of the most common communicative gestures shown by their chimpanzees: begging for food. This research can briefly be summarized as follows:

(1) Chimpanzees were made accustomed to begging for food from a single experimenter who was just out of reach. When they did this, they were given food.

(2) They were then given a choice of begging from two familiar experimenters, one of whom held food and one of whom held a block of wood. After a quick glance at both, the chimpanzees immediately knew who to gesture to for food.

(3) With this familiarization training behind them, the chimpanzees then entered the experimental phase, in which the mental state attribution and behavioral generalization models of chimpanzee understanding were tested against each other. Here, the chimpanzees were again confronted by two experimenters from whom they could beg, but, this time, one had a blindfold over her eyes while the other wore one over her mouth. In another series of tests, one experimenter had a bucket over her head and one didn't; in yet another series of tests, one experimenter covered her eyes and one didn't. (The chimpanzees were familiar with these situations from their own everyday play: "They frequently covered their heads with blankets, toy buckets or even their palms and then frolicked around their compound until they bumped into something—or someone.")[9] In each case, then, both experimenters were physically oriented toward the chimpanzee, but only one of the experimenters had their eyes uncovered—only one of the experimenters could *see*, and so *knew*, whether or not they were being asked for food. Now, if the chimpanzees were operating on the basis of a simple behavioral generalization like "Gesture to the person who is facing me," then they would be expected to gesture indifferently to either experimenter in each experiment since both experimenters were always facing them in these experiments. If, on the other hand, the chimpanzees were operating on the basis of more complex mental state attributions—if, in other words, they were behaving much as we would in these situations—then clearly they would be expected to gesture only to the person who could actually see them.

Povinelli reports that the results of these initial tests were "astonishing":

[T]he apes entered the lab and paused but then were just as likely to gesture to the person who could not see them as to the person who could. In several cases, the apes gestured to the person who could not see them and then, when nothing happened, gestured again, as if puzzled by the fact that the experimenter did not respond.[10]

The chimpanzees acted in accord with the behavioral generalization model as opposed to the mental state attribution model.

(4) In another series of tests, Povinelli found that, unlike in the above situations, the chimpanzees had no difficulty gesturing specifically to the experimenter who could see them when the contrast between the two experimenters consisted in one experimenter facing them while the other could not see them because she had her back to them. However, Povinelli realized that this discrimination was actually perfectly consistent with the kind of simple behavioral generalization given above: "Maybe they were just doing what we had taught them to do in the first part of the study—gesture to the front of someone who was facing them."[11] If this was the case, then the chimpanzees were succeeding on the one-person-facing-them-and-one-person-facing-away task not because they understood that only one of the experimenters could *see* them, but simply because only one of the experimenters was actually facing them. To test this, Povinelli had both experimenters face away, but one turn her head around so that she alone could see the chimpanzee. (Chimpanzees look over their own shoulders at one another, so this is not an unfamiliar sight to them.) If the chimpanzees were operating on something like the behavioral generalization "Gesture to the person who is facing me," then they would be expected to gesture indifferently to either experimenter (even though one is looking completely in the other direction) since neither is facing them. In contrast, the mental state attribution model clearly predicts that the chimpanzees would be expected to gesture to the experimenter who is turning their head around to see them. Again, the results were consistent with the behavioral generalization model rather than the mental state attribution model: the chimpanzees were just as likely to gesture to the experimenter who could not see them at all as the one who could.

(5) To test their interpretation of the data further, Povinelli and his colleagues then enabled their chimpanzees to learn, through trial-and-error training, the behavioral generalization that there was no point in begging to someone whose face was obscured by a cardboard disk because they would not receive any food if they did. If the chimpanzees were operating on the basis of the behavioral generalization model, then

this training ought to shift them from working on the basis of the implicit behavioral rule "Gesture to the person who is facing me (i.e., whether or not their face is actually visible)" to "Gesture to the person whose face is visible (i.e., whether or not they are actually facing me)." Now, if the chimpanzees were operating on the basis of behavioral generalizations and did indeed tighten up their implicit behavioral rule in this way, then they ought to succeed when retested in the bucket-over-the head and hands-over-the-eyes situations (as opposed, in both cases, to an experimenter who can see them) because, in both cases, one person's face is fully visible while the other person's face is not. However, they ought still to fail in the blindfold-over-the-eyes as opposed to blindfold-over-the-mouth situation because, in both cases, the experimenters' faces are obscured to the same degree, even though only one person can *see* them and so *know* that they are begging. This constitutes an increasingly stiff test for the behavioral generalization model, yet the results were again consistent with this model rather than the mental state attribution model: "Just as the low-level [i.e., behavioral generalization] model predicted, the chimpanzees were more likely to gesture to the experimenter who could see them in all the tests except one—the blindfold test."[12]

(6) When Povinelli's team retested their chimpanzees on several of the original seeing/not-seeing tests one year later, they found "much to our surprise" that they initially responded randomly on these tasks. Yet these were tasks that they had previously learned, even if they had done so through the behavioral contingency method of trial-and-error learning as opposed to developing a generalized understanding based on what others could *see*. Thus, it turns out that the chimpanzees did not even remember the behavioral generalizations they had worked out for these specific situations, and, even in this retest situation, their "performance improved only gradually, after considerable trial and error."[13] Additional tests another year later provided even further evidence for the behavioral generalization model. The upshot was that, some four years after the chimpanzees were able to demonstrate that they could recognize themselves in a mirror, Povinelli's team "had no evidence that they genuinely understood one of the most basic empathic aspects of human intelligence: the understanding that others *see*."[14]

Povinelli and his team have experimentally pursued these questions much further, but the above should be enough to give the flavor of their work and findings. Povinelli's overall conclusion from this work is that "models which posit that chimpanzees reason about the behavioral propensities of others, not their mental states, have consistently done a better job of predicting how chimpanzees will behave in crucial experimental situations."[15]

If these results surprise us, then this is no doubt because *we* are such compulsive mentalizers: it seems only natural to us to regard other intelligent beings as intentional agents and to assume that they regard others in this way too. But Povinelli and Jennifer Vonk argue that this says more about our habitual ways of thinking than it does about the minds of chimpanzees: we have too readily recreated the chimpanzee mind in our own image rather than attempting to understand it in its own terms.[16] Neither should we be fooled into thinking that these kinds of results can't be right because, for example, "we share so much of our DNA with chimpanzees that they *must* be more cognitively similar to us than these results allow." As Jonathan Marks notes in his deconstruction of "what it means to be 98% chimpanzee," we share perhaps a third of our DNA sequences with daffodils (indeed, because DNA is made up of exactly four subunits, we will on average share 25 percent of our DNA sequences with even a random sequence of DNA), yet "There are hardly any comparisons you can make to a daffodil in which humans are 33% similar."[17] The fact is that the human and chimpanzee evolutionary lineages parted company some five to six million years ago, and, as Povinelli and Vonk argue:

Of the two lineages, the human one has undergone dramatic evolution since its divergence from the common ancestor. From head to toe, the human body is stamped with the legacy of those changes—changes that dwarf modifications that occurred in the chimpanzee lineage. Humans have re-sculpted the pelvis for bipedalism, evolved unique muscles in the hands for precision gripping, lost an opposable toe, tripled the size of the brain, and evolved the most complex system of communication the planet has ever seen—natural language. Would it be any wonder, then, to discover that our minds also changed?[18]

In the face of these kinds of considerations and, above all, the experimental evidence, Povinelli and Vonk argue that those observations that we have been only too ready to interpret as examples of cognitively sophisticated forms of "deception" among chimpanzees (in line with the mental state attribution model) need to be reinterpreted in terms of the behavioral generalization model.

Are Our Closest Evolutionary Relatives Self-Aware?

The evidence suggesting that chimpanzees are not aware of their conspecifics as "other minds"—as conscious beings as opposed to, say, animated "skin bags"—raises the possibly heretical question: Are chimpanzees even aware of their own minds? Are they self-aware? Here, too, Povinelli argues that we need to reinterpret our usual understanding of the famous "mirror test" for self-recognition, which has been passed reliably only by humans, chimpanzees, and orangutans. Using a video monitor rather than a mirror, Povinelli has shown that whereas the vast majority of two- and three-year-old children reach up to remove a sticker from their heads when they view live images of themselves, only about a third of them do so when fed images that have been delayed by three minutes. In the delayed video condition, the children identified themselves when asked who the images were of but didn't seem to understand how these images related to them now, since their images were behaving differently from how they were behaving now. Thus, one three-year-old girl named Jennifer: "It's Jennifer ... but why is she wearing my shirt?"[19] Yet by the age of four or five, most children "confidently reached up to remove the sticker" in the delayed video condition and "no longer referred to 'him' or 'her' or their proper names when talking about their images."[20]

Povinelli suggests that when two- and three-year-old children, chimpanzees, and orangutans "recognize themselves" in a mirror, the kind of "self" they are recognizing is actually based on the recognition of a *behavioral equivalence* between their own kinesthetically experienced bodily movements and the image they see rather than on the deeper recognition of (the outer bodily form of) an inner self that has an enduring identity. In other words, they recognize only a kind of moment-by-moment *kinesthetically* (i.e. muscle sense) based sense of "self," not a temporally extended *psychologically* based sense of "self"—an autobiographical sense of "self." This means that when the visual feedback to a two- or three-year-old child is delayed, the recognition of a behavioral equivalence between their own movements and the image breaks down and they fail the delayed self-recognition test. When they are a little older, however, behavioral equivalence between the visual feedback and their own movements no longer matters: they possess an at least implicit psychologically based conception of themselves. This sense of themselves as possessing an enduring psychophysical identity enables them to connect *their* past states with *their* present state, and, in the case of this experiment, remove the sticker they have just seen on *their* three-minute-old images without a second thought.

Povinelli views this work as suggesting that children come to think of themselves as having a connected past and future at around the age of four and notes that "this finding fits nicely with the view of Katherine Nelson of the City University of New York and others who believe that genuine autobiographical memory appears to emerge in children between 3.5 and 4.5 years old."[21] (Note that I will draw directly on Katherine Nelson's significant work in the next chapter.) In contrast, Povinelli suggests that chimpanzees never transcend the recognition-of-a-behavioral-equivalence level of mirror recognition. Consistent with their mindblindness in respect of others, Povinelli suggests that chimpanzees are also mind blind in respect of themselves—that they lack the sense of an inner psychological self and, thus, not surprisingly, any form of autobiographical memory. Chimpanzees might have good memories in other respects of course, such as for social relationships and the location of things, but they would not experience these memories as belonging to *them*; these memories would just be "there," informing what they do but hardly embedded in any sort of ongoing autobiographical "life-story" that could be privately rehearsed—let alone shared with others.

Before leaving this important point regarding which beings are psychologically self-aware—and when—it is worth adding that there is independent evidence from the study of autism for exactly the kind of distinction that Povinelli draws between the recognition of behavioral equivalence on the one hand and psychological self-recognition on the other hand. The developmental psychopathologist Peter Hobson argues as follows:

When it comes to the children's self-awareness, it is interesting that young children with autism do remove a mark from their faces when they perceive this in a mirror. It looks as if this should be evidence for self-awareness, but it seems to be a kind of body-awareness rather than personal self-consciousness. For what children with autism do not show are the signs of coyness so typical of non-autistic children. In everyday life, too, they are often startlingly unaware or unconcerned about their appearance or actions, so that they might be unabashed at being seen naked. Therefore, even though they perceive their own body in the mirror, and act towards that body as altered by a mark, they may not conceive of themselves as selves in the minds of others. In this sense, many children with autism are not self-conscious.[22]

Povinelli suggests that much the same applies in respect of chimpanzees: the celebrated "mirror test" is not the test for psychological self-awareness that it has been taken to be. Our closest evolutionary relatives are not only mind blind in respect of their conspecifics, but, very likely, also in respect of themselves. (This does not mean that chimpanzees are not conscious, but rather that they are not self-conscious.) If this is the case, then it explains why chimpanzees don't make mental state attributions to others: after all, if you are not aware of the fact that you are aware, then there would seem to be no chance that you will be aware of the fact that others are also aware. (To be aware that others are aware, but not that you yourself are aware, would be bizarre beyond belief.) On the other hand, if you are aware of your own awareness, then why wouldn't you make mental state attributions in respect of others who appear to be very much like you? The fact that the evidence suggests that chimpanzees don't make these kinds of attributions would appear to be far more consistent with the hypothesis that they are not self-aware than with the hypothesis that they are.

Are Our Closest Evolutionary Relatives Implicit Mindsharers?

I suggested earlier that if you were a highly social but nonlinguistic being, and you were a mindreader, then you would presumably be highly motivated, and it would also make sense in terms of your own basic understanding of others, to attempt to communicate with your fellow beings in whatever nonlinguistic ways you could. You might therefore direct their attention to items of interest by pointing, by taking them to an item of interest or bringing the item to them, by deliberately showing them how to do things, and so on. This would amount to an *implicit* form of mindsharing since all of these activities involve nonlinguistic ways of recruiting the attention of others and then training your otherwise separate foci of attention on the same thing. Each of these behaviors is, in other words, a nonlinguistic way of deliberately seeking to *share attention* and, thus, an implicit form of mindsharing. However, if chimpanzees are not implicit mindreaders, then we would not expect to find that they engage in the kind of shared attention behaviors that characterize implicit mindsharing. After all, if you do not implicitly understand others as having mental states that you can affect and in some sense connect with, then it will not occur to you to try to recruit their attention in the first place since it will not occur to you that they have an inner attentive capacity *to* recruit. Putting the matter lightly, we could say that while philosophers worry about "the problem of other minds" (i.e., How can we really be sure that other minds exist? Couldn't everyone else be a zombie?), it never occurs to chimpanzees that there might be any other minds *to* worry about.

Field observations confirm this line of thinking (even though these observations again run against the intuitive assumptions that many people hold, or would like to hold, regarding chimpanzees). According to Michael Tomasello, one of our most respected experts on both human and nonhuman primate cognition:

In their natural habitats, nonhuman primates:
- do not point or gesture to outside objects for others;
- do not hold objects up to show them to others;
- do not try to bring others to locations so that they can observe things there;
- do not actively offer objects to other individuals by holding them out;
- do not intentionally teach other individuals new behaviors.[23]

In common with other leading primate researchers like Povinelli, Tomasello believes that chimpanzees do not do these things because they have no comprehension that their conspecifics *have* any form of awareness; thus, what's to share? As Tomasello puts it:

The most plausible hypothesis [to explain the evidence on lack of shared attention] is thus that nonhuman primates understand conspecifics as animate beings capable of spontaneous self-movement—indeed, this is the basis for their social understanding in general and their understanding of third-party social relationships in particular—but do not understand others as intentional agents in the process of pursuing goals or mental agents in the process of thinking about the world.[24]

These findings regarding the lack of implicit mindsharing activities between chimpanzees therefore reinforce the conclusion that chimpanzees understand each other in behavioral terms rather than mentalistic terms, that they understand each other in terms of "outer" doings rather than "inner" thoughts and motivations.

Although chimpanzees attend *individually* to the behavior of objects and other chimpanzees, the point being made here is that they do not engage in *shared attention* (also referred to as *joint attention*); they interact *dyadically*—or one-to-one—with objects and other chimpanzees, but they do not deliberately share attention with each other in regard to these objects or third parties. Human babies are initially like this, but (to quote Tomasello) "around nine to twelve months of age a new set of behaviors begins to emerge that are not dyadic, like these early behaviors, but are *triadic* in the sense that they involve a coordination of their interactions with objects and people, resulting in a referential triangle of child, adult, and the object or event to which they share attention" (my emphasis).[25] Tomasello refers to this emergence of shared attention as "the nine-month revolution."[26] Significantly, Tomasello continues that:

[A]mong these early deictic gestures [such as pointing or holding up an object to show it to someone] are both *imperatives*, [i.e.,] attempts to get the adult to do something with respect to an object or event, and *declaratives*, [i.e.,] attempts to get adults simply to attend to some object or event. *Declaratives are of special importance because they indicate especially clearly that the child does not just want some result to happen, but really desires to share attention with an adult* [which is clearly an implicit mindsharing behavior]. It is thus the contention of some theorists, including me, that the simple act of pointing to an object for someone else for the sole purpose of sharing attention to it is *a uniquely human communicative behavior, the lack of which is also a major diagnostic for the syndrome of childhood autism* [which, in its serious forms, effectively renders the child an iso-experient; my emphases throughout].[27]

This point is important to note because we will see when we come to the question of human attempts to teach language to chimpanzees that even when chimpanzees are *humanly enculturated* in this way, they rarely use the symbols they are taught for declarative purposes (i.e., for the purposes of sharing attention, in the sense of "Look at this"); instead, they almost always use these symbols for imperative purposes (e.g., "Give banana"). The first purpose can be unequivocally regarded as a mindsharing purpose, the second cannot.

What would your cognitive world be like then if, like chimpanzees and autistic children, you were incapable of engaging in shared, joint, or triadic forms of attention? According to Simon Baron-Cohen, a widely acknowledged expert on autism, "You would have sensations, and you would have images of people doing things and even wanting and seeing things, but you would have no way of knowing that what you and another person were seeing or thinking about was the very same thing."[28] You would, in other words, not even be capable of an implicit form of mindsharing, let alone explicit, linguistically mediated mindsharing; you would be an island of awareness and experience unto yourself; you would be an iso-experient.

A Bit of Controversy on the Implicit Mindreading Front; All Quiet on the Implicit Mindsharing Front

As already reflected in my discussion, the two research groups that have published most widely on chimpanzee cognition and, in particular, the areas that I have referred to as implicit mindreading and implicit mindsharing, are led by Daniel Povinelli at the University of Louisiana at Lafayette, in the United States, and Michael Tomasello at the Max Planck Institute for Evolutionary Anthropology in Leipzig, Germany. Now, it was the case until quite recently that these groups were essentially in agreement that careful study suggested that there was no strong evidence for the claim that chimpanzees—our closest evolutionary relatives—possessed implicit mindreading skills. Not only is this exactly the conclusion that Povinelli's studies point to, but it was also the position reached by Tomasello and his colleague Josep Call in their encyclopedic 1997 review of all that was at that stage scientifically known in regard to primate cognition, and it remained the view of Tomasello in his significant 1999 book *The Cultural Origins of Human Cognition*.[29] However, Tomasello and his colleagues have since claimed to have found evidence that chimpanzees do display some implicit mindreading skills in experimental situations involving competition for food, specifically, situations in which a subdominant animal has to compete against a dominant animal for food, and in which the subdominant animal can see whether or not the dominant animal has seen the food being hidden.[30]

However, Povinelli and Vonk have countered with a potentially fatal objection to these experiments.[31] They argue that implicit mindreading skills are not separate from but are always built on top of, and so are always additional to, predictions of behavior that are based solely

on behavioral generalizations derived from trial-and-error behavioral observation. An example of a behavioral generalization understanding of a
competitive food situation would be an implicit understanding that ran
along the lines: "If a dominant conspecific is oriented toward the food
and I go for it, then I will probably get thumped; if he is not oriented toward the food and I go for it, then I probably won't get thumped." This
is a thoroughly useful behavioral generalization that can be derived
solely from repeated experiences of getting thumped in this type of situation. An example of a mental state attribution understanding of a competitive food situation would be an implicit understanding that involved
additional information along the following (italicized) lines: "If a dominant conspecific is oriented toward the food, then *he has probably seen
the food and therefore knows where it is; therefore*, if I go for it, I will
probably get thumped; however, if he is not oriented toward the food,
then *he has probably not seen the food and therefore doesn't know
where it is; therefore*, if I go for it, I probably won't get thumped." The
second understanding is based on the same behavioral information as the
first—namely, the bodily orientation of the dominant animal—it is just
that more is *read into* the second situation; the second situation represents an exercise in both "bodyreading" *and* mindreading.

Povinelli and Vonk argue that if experimental situations are broadly
modeled on situations with which the chimpanzees would have had
considerable prior experience, such as competing for food against a
dominant animal (as in the Leipzig group's experiments), then the chimpanzees would have had ample opportunity to fine-tune some quite
sophisticated behavioral generalizations regarding how they should proceed in these situations. And this, in turn, means that these kinds of
experiments are, in principle, unable to tell us whether the chimpanzees
are in fact acting on the basis of behavioral generalizations or *also* on the
basis of mental state attributions. In Povinelli and Vonk's own (completely italicized) words: "*the research paradigms that have been heralded
as providing evidence that they [i.e., chimpanzees] do reason about such
mental states, do not, in principle, have the ability to provide evidence
that uniquely supports that hypothesis.*"[32]

Whereas Povinelli and Vonk argue that the data reported by the
Leipzig group can be interpreted as supporting either the mental state attribution model or the behavioral generalization model of chimpanzee

understanding, they equally argue that their own data, which clearly suggest that chimpanzees fail to discriminate in their begging gestures between an experimenter who can see them and one who cannot, is consistent with the behavioral generalization model rather than the mental state attribution model. In other words, they argue that this is one of those situations in which "negative evidence," collected under carefully controlled conditions, actually tells us more than "positive evidence": specifically, *finding evidence* of differences between the ways in which chimpanzees react in regard to oriented and nonoriented conspecifics in a familiar, competitive food situation does not enable us to discriminate between the two models of chimpanzee understanding, whereas *failing to find evidence* of differences in situations where you would expect them on the basis of the mental state attribution model but not the behavioral generalization model does argue for the latter model. Furthermore, Povinelli, Vonk, and others have since reported some preliminary results using a different kind of experimental procedure that they believe offers a still more sensitive test of the two models of chimpanzee understanding and, again, their preliminary data reinforce the behavioral generalization model rather than the mental state attribution model of chimpanzee cognition.[33]

I believe that the burden of the experimental evidence, together with Povinelli and Vonk's powerful argument against the Leipzig group's interpretation of their competitive food experiments, favors Povinelli's view that chimpanzees lack implicit mindreading abilities. But whatever way this disagreement in regard to the implicit mindreading abilities of chimpanzees is finally resolved, it remains the case that both Povinelli's group and Tomasello's group are in agreement that chimpanzees lack what I have referred to as *implicit mindsharing* abilities. Thus, even in the context of claiming (contra Povinelli) that chimpanzees "can understand some psychological states in others," Tomasello himself agrees that "what seems to be missing still is the shared dimension of all this ... [chimpanzees] seem not to understand communicative or cooperative intentions, and so they do not attempt to direct the attention of conspecifics by pointing, showing, offering, or any other intentional communicative signal."[34] Tomasello also notes that, even in the experiments that his group has interpreted as suggesting that chimpanzees do understand something about what their conspecifics *perceive,* there is no evidence for the more deeply social, shared dimension of the process as we observe it in human children. For example, there is no evidence that in the Hare *et al.* studies [i.e., the studies at issue in my discussion above] the subordinate knew that the dominant was having first-person experiences like her own only from a different perspective from across the cage—which would suggest an understanding of self-other equivalence and perspective ... *In all, there is basically no evidence in any sphere of ape activity that they can deal effectively with anything that is socially shared (self-other equivalence), perspectival, or normative* [e.g., as in pretend play in which beings jointly pretend that one thing is "really" another, e.g., that a pencil is "really" a toothbrush; normal children engage in this from late infancy, whereas chimpanzees never engage in this activity; my emphasis].[35]

We can conclude that notwithstanding the current controversy over whether or not chimpanzees possess limited implicit mindreading abilities, the work of our leading research groups in this area clearly suggests that our closest evolutionary relatives are not implicit mindsharers.

The Implications of This Work for Our Understanding of Other Nonhuman Beings

The fact that chimpanzees are highly social animals suggests that they would be highly motivated to engage in mindsharing activities with each other if they could, and the fact that they have relatively large, complex brains suggests that they ought to stand a better chance of realizing this goal than other beings with smaller, less complex brains. Thus, the wider significance of the findings that I have discussed here is that if chimpanzees are not implicit mindsharers (and, assuming Povinelli is right, not even implicit mindreaders), then presumably other animals are not either.

Only dolphins stand outside this generalization because only dolphins are also highly social mammals with even larger, more complex brains than chimpanzees. For example, whereas the encephalization quotient of humans is 7.44, it is 5.31 for dolphins, 2.49 for chimpanzees, 1.87 for elephants, 1.76 for whales, 1.17 for dogs, 1.0 for cats, and progressively less for horses, sheep, mice, rats, and rabbits.[36] (Encephalization quotients refer to "the amount of brain over and above that expected to be concerned with purely bodily functions, compared with an average mammalian value.")[37] Thus, as the leading dolphin researcher Louis Herman says: "measures of relative brain size place the bottlenosed dolphin, and two or three other closely related delphinid species, second only to humans and well above the great apes."[38] Even so, I deeply regret that I will necessarily have to set dolphins to one side in regard to the arguments that I develop in this book precisely because, as Herman himself states at the conclusion of his own authoritative review of the evidence in regard to the visual, sensory integration, memory and concept learning, imitation, and language-learning abilities of dolphins, "Topics such as theory of mind [i.e., mindreading], social awareness, imitation, productive language, interanimal communication, and much more, are relatively unstudied and await only the investigator and the opportunity."[39]

All I can presently add to these comments is to note that the evolutionary psychologist Robin Dunbar has reported some more recent evidence that suggests that dolphins lack mindreading abilities. Specifically, Dunbar reports that whereas some initial work in this area suggested that dolphins could pass "false belief" tests (which are specifically designed to probe for the presence of mindreading, or theory of mind, abilities), a more rigorously designed experimental procedure, which ruled out inadvertent cuing effects by the experimenters as well as "bet-hedging" answers by the dolphins themselves (in which the dolphins behaved in sufficiently ambiguous ways as to lead the original experimenters to give their answers "the benefit of the doubt" when they should not have), found that "the dolphins quite comprehensively failed to pass" this test.[40] The implication is that, like chimpanzees (assuming Povinelli is right), dolphins also lack mindreading abilities. But until we know a lot more about these intelligent large-brained animals, we are simply not in a position to reach any particularly authoritative conclusions in regard to their mindreading and mindsharing abilities. So, as I have said, for lack of more authoritative information, I will necessarily have to set dolphins aside in regard to all the conclusions that I reach herein. Moreover, I won't keep mentioning this caveat; rather, I will simply take this caveat as understood from this point on (beginning with the next paragraph) in any generalizations that I make about nonhuman beings.

The upshot of these considerations is that if we accept the reasons given above for thinking that other animals in general are not implicit mindsharers, then it follows that, on this planet at least, only normal humans are implicit mindsharers. Moreover, if Povinelli is right, then it also follows that only normal humans are implicit mindsharers *or* implicit mindreaders.

Can Our Closest Evolutionary Relatives Become Explicit (i.e., Language-Using) Mindsharers?

We can see from the preceding sections that attempts to teach chimpanzees a language—such as a sign language or a language based on lexigrams (i.e., a figure or symbol that represents a word)—must effectively represent, at the very least, experiments in what Tomasello refers to as the "socialization of attention," something that simply does not happen in the wild.[41] As Tomasello says:

[A]pes in their natural habitats do not have anyone who points for them, shows them things, teaches them, or in general expresses intentions toward their attention (or other intentional states). In a human-like cultural environment, in contrast, they are constantly interacting with humans who show them things, point to things, encourage (even reinforce) imitation, and teach them special skills—all of which involve a referential triangle between human, ape, and some third entity. Perhaps it is this socialization into the referential triangle—of a type that most human children receive—that accounts for the special cognitive achievements of these special apes.[42]

Even so, the genuinely *linguistic* abilities that emerge from this socialization of attention have been a matter of much dispute.[43] Two questions lie at the heart of this debate. The first is concerned with whether symbols are really being used *as* symbols, which is to say *referentially* (i.e., as signs that *stand for* something) rather than *instrumentally* (i.e., as a kind of tool that simply enables the ape to get what it wants). We need to bear the general point in mind here that we can train many animals to do things that make it appear, to *our* thoroughly "linguisticized" minds, as if they "understand" what a "word" *refers to* when in fact they have simply come to associate a certain kind of sound, hand movement, or visual shape with a reward. The second question at the heart of the non-human primate language-learning debate is concerned with the extent to which these humanly enculturated apes can truly be said to grasp the generative principles of grammar, that is, the syntactical rules that define the ways in which symbols may and may not be combined in order to be meaningful.

Following considerable, and now widely accepted, criticisms of the limitations of earlier work on language learning in nonhuman primates, it is now generally accepted that the strongest evidence for positive claims in regard to language learning in nonhuman primates lies with the language skills of a bonobo named Kanzi, raised and studied by Sue Savage-Rumbaugh and her colleagues. In contrast to earlier studies in this area, Kanzi was not taught language directly through behavioral reinforcement techniques but rather acquired a degree of understanding simply by being with his stepmother, Matata, while researchers were attempting to teach Matata in this way—with a conspicuous lack of success. The relative level of Kanzi's achievements therefore strongly suggests that the best way to maximize any intelligent being's chances of acquiring some degree of language skills is for them to be raised in a language-rich environment from birth, just as children normally are, since this coincides with the period during which the actual "wiring up" of the "wetware" of their developing brains is at its most responsive with respect to environmental stimuli, including language. But even trading on this advantage, it turns out that the linguistic abilities of "Exhibit A" for nonhuman primate language acquisition—Kanzi—trail off at around the level at which children's abilities take off. Specifically, Savage-Rumbaugh's evidence suggests that, with respect to certain limited kinds of linguistic formulations at least, Kanzi's speech comprehension at eight years of age was comparable to that of a two-and-a-half-year-old child, while his language production skills were limited to those of a one to one-and-a-half-year-old child.[44] Savage-Rumbaugh has subsequently replicated these findings with two other apes, so this level of linguistic performance would appear to be about the best that can be expected from humanly encultured apes.[45]

Savage-Rumbaugh naturally stresses Kanzi's comprehension skills over those of his decidedly limited expressive skills. However, in the present context, we need to note the following: it is one thing to take information in, which is all that iso-experients do, but quite another to share it, which is what mindsharers do (including when they try to teach language to beings that *are* essentially iso-experients). The upshot is that if your expressive linguistic skills remain at the level of a one to one-and-a-half-year-old child (and even this only after your attention has been "socialized" through human enculturation), then your explicit mind-sharing abilities will be quite limited—even if you chose to put your expressive linguistic skills to mindsharing purposes. I add this last rider because, as we will see, Kanzi's limited expressive linguistic skills are in any case almost all devoted to inner-demand-driven, or imperative, statements rather than genuinely mindsharing, or declarative, statements.

Even relatively sympathetic critics of Savage-Rumbaugh's work, like the cognitive scientist Peter Gärdenfors, have noted that Savage-Rumbaugh "has a tendency to over-interpret Kanzi's linguistic achievements" and that some of the ways in which a two-and-a-half-year-old child's linguistic abilities would outstrip Kanzi's are "hidden between the lines in Savage-Rumbaugh's writings."[46] Less sympathetic critics, on the other hand, like the linguist and cognitive scientist Stephen Pinker, argue, for example, that "[Kanzi] is said to use three-symbol sentences—but they are really fixed formulas with no internal structure and are not even three symbols long," and conclude that the evidence in fact suggests that "Kanzi's language abilities, if one is being charitable, are above those of his common cousins [i.e., ordinary chimpanzees] by a just-noticeable difference, but no more."[47] However, rather than wade in and add yet another voice to the evaluation of the claims and counter-claims in this controversial area, I want to make a somewhat different point—one that focuses on evaluating the mindsharing abilities of these enculturated apes rather than the question of their linguistic abilities as such. My point is this: even if we accept the claims that have been made about Kanzi's linguistic abilities at face value, the fact remains that to the limited extent that nonhuman primates can be said to acquire any genuinely linguistic skills, they neither respond to this knowledge as mind-sharers do nor use this knowledge as mindsharers do. Instead, they behave essentially like iso-experients, but iso-experients that have nevertheless had some limited language skills grafted onto them. (Recall that this situation is not unknown to us even in the human case since some autistic people roughly fit this description.)

The evidence for the claim that I am making here can be considered by first noting what happens when you add language to the minds of implicit mindsharing humans, that is, prelinguistic children who already have an innate predisposition to regard others as intentional agents like themselves. Specifically, we find that:

(i) Language develops explosively.

(ii) Language is experienced as liberating.

(iii) Language is highly fertile: mindsharers beget mindsharers.

(iv) Language is pressed into the service of recruiting and sharing attention.

(v) Language is pressed into the service of putting our inner world "out there" by telling others what we think, feel, and desire.

In contrast, *none* of these things happens when language is added to the minds of nonhuman beings that are essentially iso-experients. Let us briefly consider each of these claims.

(i) **Language develops explosively** As the cognitive science and neuroscience writer John McCrone notes, chimpanzees fail to show "the explosive growth in vocabulary that happens in children [or, as we have also seen, late language learners] once the principle of naming things has been grasped."[48] Peter Gärdenfors similarly notes in regard to Kanzi that

A human child actively seeks knowledge by asking innumerable questions. Among these are plenty of questions about what things are called. As far as I understand [from Savage-Rumbaugh's writings], Kanzi never asks such questions. He has not grasped the naming game.[49]

The kind of explosive hunger for words that typifies mindsharers' introduction to language and appears to betoken an expansion of their inner world never materializes in the case of nonhuman primates. It would be seriously newsworthy if it did.

(ii) **Language is experienced as liberating** Closely related to the first point, language is experienced as liberating by mindsharers. Those of us who learned language in the normal way did so too early to be able to remember this liberation in its initial form, but we can reflect now on the fact that there is an intimate relationship between our own ability to express ourselves and our own sense of freedom, at both the personal and political levels. Conversely, we can reflect on how tragic we think it is when a person is robbed of their ability to express themselves, by whatever means. As for those who come to language late, we have seen in the previous chapter that these people experience a liberating "breakthrough moment," followed by an immediate hunger for names. Shortly

after this, they may break down and weep, just as Helen Keller and Ildefonso did, as they realize all that they have missed out on for so long. In
contrast, enculturated chimpanzees convey no such sense of having a
"breakthrough moment" followed by a hunger for new words and behavioral signs of despair for what has gone before; nothing that would
suggest the exhilarated sense that late language learners experience of
having been freed from solitary confinement in a private mental prison;
nothing that would suggest a crossing over from being an iso-experient
to being a mindsharer.

(iii) Language is highly fertile: Mindsharers beget mindsharers   For
mindsharers, language is highly fertile, or, to use another metaphor,
highly contagious. If a baby (potential) mindsharer is deprived of contact
with any other language "impregnators" or "carriers" during its normal
development, then, as we have already seen in the cases of feral and prelingually deaf children, the baby will not develop language skills on its
own and so will not grow up to become an explicit, or language-using,
mindsharer (i.e., not unless it is rescued from its nonexplicit mindsharing
state by explicit mindsharers, although even then it may be too late for it
to be able to cross over into the explicit mindsharing realm). If, on the
other hand, a baby (potential) mindsharer is able to interact in normal
ways with even just one other language "impregnator" or "carrier" during its normal development, then it will develop language and so grow
up to become an explicit mindsharer who can, in turn, beget new language users as he or she comes into contact with the developing minds
of other baby (potential) mindsharers (most likely their own children).
This means that explicit mindsharers give rise, as it were, to (linguistically) highly fertile offspring since these offspring will beget new mindsharers simply by coming into verbal contact with baby (potential)
mindsharers. Language, then, is highly fertile in that sense.

Further evidence for the fertility—or highly contagious nature—of
language in normal mindsharers comes from some striking work by the
linguist Derek Bickerton, who has studied how a *pidgin* language (i.e.,
the kind of essentially grammarless, concocted verbal constructions that
emerge when speakers of unrelated languages come into contact) can
become transformed into a fully grammatical language in its own right,
which is then referred to as a *creole* language.[50] Bickerton showed that if

children grow up in the context of learning a pidgin language, then they can collectively converge on ways of building grammatical structure into the largely absent structure of that pidgin language and thereby transform it into a thoroughly grammatical creole in a single generation! Thus, a wholly new language can emerge in the space of two generations: the first generation must acquire the pidgin "protolanguage" and then pass it on to a second generation that uses this protolanguage as the raw material from which it develops the emergent, genuinely grammatical creole language. Language, then, is highly fertile or highly contagious stuff—giving even a little of this stuff (such as an essentially grammarless pidgin) to genuine mindsharers can end up producing effects out of all proportion to the initial stimulus (such as a creole language, with its own grammatical rules).

In complete contrast to these kinds of lessons regarding the fecundity of language in the case of genuine mindsharers, we find that when explicit mindsharers "impregnate" the hitherto iso-experiential minds of chimpanzees with language, the resulting hybrid offspring are linguistically infertile. That is to say, even if we accepted the strongest claims that have been made to date regarding the linguistic abilities of humanly enculturated apes, there is no good evidence that these hybrid minds are themselves able to successfully "impregnate" others of their own kind—and, thus, give rise to new language users. For genuine mindsharers, a little linguistic input (such as an essentially grammarless pidgin) can easily ratchet up in the second generation (to a grammatical creole), whereas, for beings that are not genuine mindsharers, a lot of grammatical linguistic input goes nowhere in the second generation (i.e., there is no ratchet effect).

(iv) Language is pressed into the service of putting our inner world "out there" by telling others what we think, feel, and desire   The psychologist Merlin Donald notes that even when raised in a language-rich environment, as Kanzi was, nonhuman primates, in distinct contrast to young children, seem to lack any form of inner awareness that would *motivate* them to describe their own mental states:

Kanzi has never tried to describe his own experiences or feelings, using symbols. He cannot construct the kinds of memories that we call autobiographical, even though he has been given a set of symbols that could in theory enable him to do this. Human children use language in this way very early in their development, even before they can form grammatical sentences, but Kanzi has never tried this kind of self-description, despite his considerable symbolic and grammatical skills. He does not say "I think" or "I feel" or "I want." This suggests that his self-awareness is not like that of most humans. He seems to have no natural state that would motivate him to construct such self-referential expressions.[51]

If Kanzi lacks awareness of the fact *that* he is aware, and so lacks an enduring, inner, psychological sense of self (which is consistent with Povinelli's interpretation of mirror recognition experiments in chimpanzees), then why *would* he use his language skills for mindsharing purposes in regard to his inner mental states? As Donald notes, the lesson here seems to be that "Language per se has no magical power to transform the awareness of an individual beyond its innate capacity. In itself language cannot bestow self-awareness, although it undoubtedly has a major impact on self-awareness, given a basic capacity for it."[52]

(v) Language is pressed into the service of recruiting and sharing attention Not only does Kanzi not refer to his own inner states, but he doesn't refer in a declarative way to much at all. Rather, 96 percent of the "words" he acquires are used for imperative purposes (an example of which would be: "Give banana") rather than declarative purposes (an example of which would be: "Look at this").[53] In contrast, children begin engaging in declarative pointing from well before they can speak (recall Tomasello's outline of the "nine-month revolution") and carry this mindsharing mode of communication into their use of language from the very beginning.[54]

The fact that Kanzi's use of language is limited in this way should not surprise us since, as we now know, the evidence from chimpanzees that have not been humanly enculturated suggests that they are not naturally predisposed to any form of mindsharing. Thus, Tomasello points out that although chimpanzees "actually communicate in more flexible and interesting ways with gestures rather than with vocalizations," it is nevertheless the case that in their natural state they "still do not use their gestures referentially."[55] Tomasello argues that

This is clear because (1) they almost invariably use them [gestures] in dyadic contexts—either to attract the attention of others to the self or to request some behavior of another toward the self (e.g. play, grooming, sex)—not triadically, to attract the attention of others to some outside entity; and (2) they use them exclusively for imperative purposes to request actions from others, not for declarative purposes to direct the attention of others to something simply for the sake of sharing interest in it or commenting on it.[56]

It seems, then, that what goes for apes in the wild also goes, very largely, for humanly enculturated apes, even after they have been socialized into referential triangles, and even when they have acquired a small degree of language. Grafting language on to beings that are not essentially mindsharers does not magically turn them into mindsharers. In accord with this, you will recall that, earlier in the chapter, I defined explicit (i.e., language-using) mindsharers as *beings that have acquired language in the presence of developmentally normal implicit mindreading and implicit mindsharing (i.e., shared attention) skills.*

What Is It Like to Be an Intelligent Human Who Is Not an Explicit Mindsharer? Wild (or Feral) Children and Prelingually Deaf and Deaf-Blind Children

The previous discussion suggests that no amount of exposure to language or language training can turn a being that lacks implicit mindsharing skills into an explicit mindsharer. This suggests that nonhuman iso-experients will never learn language to the point at which they might be both able and intrinsically motivated to tell us what it was like to have been an iso-experient. The best avenue we have for approaching this question—or something like it—is therefore to consider those cases of human beings who, for one reason or another, have been isolated from language until a relatively late stage of their development. Once these humans have been introduced to some form of language, we can then try to find out from them directly, or at least try to infer from what they are able to say, what it was like to have been deprived in this way, what it was like, in other words, *not* to have been an explicit mindsharer.

(It would be simpler, and more expressive, here to say "what it was like, in other words, to have been an iso-experient." However, this formulation is not appropriate in the case of humans since, unlike nonhumans, even language-deprived humans possess innate implicit mindsharing capacities. But then neither is it appropriate to refer to all language-deprived humans as implicit mindsharers because some of these language-deprived humans have been so badly mistreated that they have not been able to express their innate implicit mindsharing capacities and so *are* functionally equivalent to iso-experients. Thus, in the human case, it is actually simplest to use the negative formulation "what it was like not to have been an explicit mindsharer" rather than the positive formulations "what it was like to have been an iso-experient" or "what it was like to have been an implicit mindsharer" since the negative formulation includes both of the latter possibilities. All that said, Helen Keller's personal testimony, which we will come to, suggests that the difference between being an iso-experient and being a completely language-deprived human is perhaps a very fine line; that is, it may be that humans' innate implicit mindsharing abilities do not actually amount to much if they do not serve, primarily, to carry a person into the world of language.)

As we saw in the previous chapter, the rare documented cases we have of human linguistic isolation fall into two general categories: (i) people who have been physically deprived of human company, such as "wild," or "feral," children and children "raised" in solitary confinement (by "parents" whose depravity beggars description); and (ii) those who have been, at least in part, physiologically deprived of the means for language acquisition, such as deaf and deaf-blind children who, for one reason or another, have not been introduced to one of the various forms of sign language. I will consider the cognitive worlds of these two categories of people in turn. (Note, however, that I will focus only on wild, or feral, children with respect to examples of children who have been physically deprived of human company. This is because these children have at least been able to adapt to some form of social behavior, even if it is not human, whereas the poor wretches who have survived in solitary confinement are damaged in ways that go well beyond any "simple" lack of language.)

Wild, or Feral, Children

John McCrone provides a compelling overview of these often overlooked cases and concludes that a composite picture of the better documented cases shows that, upon discovery, these children:

(i) cannot speak (even though they can hear), and all have extreme difficulty learning to speak after capture (all of which puts paid to the older belief that full-blown linguistic expression is an innate power of humans rather than one that is acquired through immersion—especially early immersion—in a linguistically mediated mindsharing context);

(ii) do not walk upright or do not routinely do so (thus, even our upright walking posture is not wholly innate);

(iii) are unresponsive to humans (in particular, the human voice seems to have no special significance for them);

(iv) have an unfocused sexual response (they show arousal at puberty, but they don't know how to direct it); and

(v) most importantly, in this context:

They seemed somehow to *lack memory and self-awareness*. As the detailed accounts of Bonnaterre [the professor of natural history who was the first to examine the much-documented and discussed nineteenth-century case of Victor, "the wild boy of Aveyron"], Itard [the doctor from Paris's Deaf-Mute Institute who subsequently devoted five years to instructing Victor], and Singh [the missionary who captured the "wolf-girls" Amala and Kamala, discovered living with wolves in India in 1920 at about the ages of three and five, and who tried subsequently to socially rehabilitate the girls in his orphanage in Northern India] make clear, the thoughts of Victor and the wolf-girls *were limited to the world of the here and now.* They could make simple associations and learn to recognize familiar people and situations. But they seemed *unable to reflect on the past or the future*, or to have any insight into their own plight [my emphases].[57]

McCrone notes that commentators at the time often tried to dismiss these kinds of findings in terms of the alleged feeblemindedness of the children concerned—notwithstanding the fact that they had survived in the absence of other humans. (And how many of us would be able to do that?) These commentators preferred to believe that memory, self-awareness, and reason were all "natural" to humans, so the fact that "the dumb, blank animality of [these] children did not fit in with this preconceived picture" meant that it was easier to play down the evidence than question their own assumptions.[58] However, in the context of the evidence that we will come to regarding deaf and deaf-blind late language learners, it seems far more reasonable to accept these findings as supporting the claim that it is language that allows us, among other things, to break free of the mental confines of the here and now. And this applies not only in the sense of developing a fully fledged, temporally structured memory system, but even in the more limited sense of being able to escape from the hold of particular percepts—like the image of *this* tree—to that of more general concepts. Thus, the clinical neurologist Oliver Sacks notes that "when Itard, Victor's teacher, taught him the word 'book', this was first taken to refer to a *particular* book, and the same failure occurred with other words, all of which he understood to name some particular thing, not a category of things."[59] Combined with the evidence from late language learning in deaf people, Sacks concludes that it is "language, internalized by the child, that allows it to move from sensation into 'sense', to ascend [and note here the metaphor of rising above or *transcending*] from a perceptual into a conceptual world."[60]

The Prelingually Deaf and Deaf-Blind

Prelingually deaf children are capable of acquiring as richly textured a system of sign language as hearing people are able to acquire through speech. These children are therefore emphatically not without language. But what about those prelingually deaf children who are cut off from visually accessed forms of sign language either because they are not introduced to it in the normal course of their development or because they are blind as well as deaf? These children in some ways constitute a better source of evidence for what it is like not to be an explicit mindsharer than the cases of wild, or feral, children. This is because these prelingually deaf children have at least grown up in the presence of other humans and so, unlike any wild child, have had continuous access to, and thus have been able to model their own behavior on, normal modes of human behavior—with the exception of linguistic practices of course. Even so, the accounts we have of the inner experience of prelingually deaf children (and, in some cases, adults) show a considerable correspondence with the accounts we have of the cognitive worlds of feral children.

For example, Oliver Sacks provides an account of an apparently intelligent eleven-year-old boy, Joseph, who had not been diagnosed as deaf until his fourth year, had not been taught any form of language, and had not been exposed to sign language until his entry to the school in which Sacks met him. At his new school, Joseph was "just beginning to pick up a little Sign, beginning to have some communication with others," which "manifestly gave him great joy."[61] Although Joseph seemed to Sacks to show clear behavioral indications of inquisitiveness and even a kind of uncomprehending yearning and desire to reach out to others (implicit mindsharing?), Sacks tellingly observes that

It was not only language that was missing: there was not, it was evident, a clear sense of the past, of "a day ago" as distinct from "a year ago." There was a strange lack of historical sense, the feeling of *a life that lacked autobiographical and historical dimension*, the feeling of *a life that only existed in the moment, in the present* ... Joseph saw, distinguished, categorized, used; he had no problems with *perceptual* categorization or generalization, but he could not, it seemed, go much beyond this, hold abstract ideas in mind, reflect, play, plan. He seemed completely literal—unable to judge images or hypotheses or possibilities, unable to enter an imaginative or figurative realm. And yet, one still felt, he was of normal intelligence, despite these manifest limitations of intellectual functioning. It was not that he lacked a mind, but that he was not *using his mind fully* [first two emphases mine].[62]

Sacks provides a range of other examples that speak to this same theme, a theme that we saw above in regard to the inner life of feral children. In sum, it appears that the inner worlds of those prelingually deaf people who have remained cut off from immersion in linguistically mediated culture (in their case, sign language), or who come to such immersion too late, developmentally speaking, for it to have its normal neurological effect (i.e., in terms of how the developing brain wires itself up), are limited to the here and now, to the concrete, literal world before them; the worlds of imagination, metaphor, and possibility lie beyond them. This speaks directly to one of the central points I made in the previous chapter: language (acquired in a developmentally normal context) enables its users to cognitively transcend the here-and-now perceptual immediacy of the biophysical realm; without language, there is no such transcendence.

In the case of the deaf-blind, the situation is even more difficult. Helen Keller (1880–1968) is, of course, the most famous example of a deaf-blind person who, through her teacher Annie Sullivan, was able to overcome the significant odds against her in order to achieve (in her case, exceptional) linguistic competence. As I noted in the previous chapter, Keller provides us with the single most articulate account in existence of what it *was* like to have been a nonlinguistic but emotionally supported child raised in normal human company, which means that we cannot dismiss her prelinguistic view of the world as a function of emotional deprivation or lack of human company. And, as I also noted, it is likely that we may have this account only owing to the rare combination of Keller's own inherent intelligence and drive to express herself and the peculiar nature of her illness, which robbed her of her sight and hearing at nineteen months—early enough for her subsequently to have no conscious understanding of symbols, but late enough (given her exposure to language up to the time of the illness) to have laid down or stimulated some neural foundations that could later be reinvigorated and built on by her teacher and thus enable Keller to cross the linguistic Rubicon so successfully. We may, in other words, never obtain a better first-person account of what it was like to have been an intelligent nonlinguistic being.

Although Keller is best known for her widely available 1902 autobiography *The Story of My Life*, she provides her most penetrating account of what it was like to have been a nonlinguistic being in an essay in her 1908 book entitled *The World I Live In*—a book which had, alas, been out of print for decades prior to its recent republication by New York Review Books in 2003. I take this essay, tellingly entitled "Before the Soul Dawn," to offer the most insightful first-person description we have of what it is like to be an intelligent human who is not an explicit mindsharer. The penetrating, finely nuanced insights in this description alone are worth a row of cognitive science textbooks on this question. So listen up, this is what she says:

Before my teacher came to me [when Keller was nearly seven], *I did not know that I am. I lived in a world that was a no-world.* I cannot hope to describe adequately that unconscious, yet conscious time of nothingness. I did not know that I knew aught [i.e., "anything at all; anything whatever"], or that I lived or acted or desired. I had neither will nor intellect. I was carried along to objects and acts by a certain blind natural impetus. I had a mind which caused me to feel anger, satisfaction, desire. *These two facts led those about me to suppose that I willed and thought.* I can remember all this, not because I knew that it was so, but because I have tactual memory [i.e., memory "relating to the tactile sense or the organs of touch"]. It enables me to remember that I never contracted my forehead in the act of thinking. I never viewed anything beforehand or chose it. I also recall tactually the fact that never in a start of the body or a heart-beat did I feel that I loved or cared for anything. *My inner life, then, was a blank without past, present, or future,* without hope or anticipation, without wonder or joy or faith. . . .

Since I had no power of thought, I did not compare one mental state with another. So I was not conscious of any change or process going on in my brain when my teacher began to instruct me. I merely felt keen delight in obtaining more easily what I wanted by means of the finger motions she taught me [i.e., she simply used these finger motions instrumentally rather than referentially, as symbols]. I thought only of objects [which suggests that she did not have any awareness of other *minds* and thus had no implicit *mindreading* abilities—something she seems to confirm at the end of this passage], and only objects I wanted [i.e., she "thought" only in terms of the self-directed imperatives characteristic of iso-experients, not the shared-attention-directed declaratives characteristic of mindsharers].... *When I learned the meaning of "I" and "me" and found that I was something, I began to think. Then consciousness first existed for me....* Thought made me conscious of love, joy, and all the emotions ... and the blind impetus, which had before driven me hither and thither at the dictates of my sensations vanished forever.... I came *later* to look for an image of my emotions and sensations in others. I had to *learn the outward signs of inward feelings* ... before I could trace them back to the intangible soul of another [i.e., before she became a mindreader; my emphases throughout].[63]

This truly is a "mind-blowing" statement about the inner world of a patently intelligent human who was not an explicit mindsharer: "*I did not know that I am.... I lived in a world that was a no-world ... that unconscious, yet conscious time of nothingness.... I did not compare one mental state with another.... My inner life, then, was a blank without past, present, or future.*" In another book entitled *Teacher* (Keller always referred to Annie Sullivan as "Teacher"), Keller refers to herself prior to gaining language as "Phantom" and only afterward as "Helen"![64] And in a letter of 1901, Keller refers to herself and others like her as having had a "death-in-life existence."[65] It is as if she did not really exist before she had language—at least not in the only sense that really matters to any of us as individuals. Sure, she "existed" when viewed from a purely external, third-person point of view—in the same sense that, say, a rock "exists"—but she did not exist from *within*, from her own, internal, first-person point of view. In the absence of language, it appears that she had no consciousness of self and, it would seem, no way of performing higher-order mental operations *on* her own mental states as opposed simply to being subject *to* whatever mental states happened to be operative at the time ("I did not compare one mental state with another"). Thinking of Keller, quite impersonally, as an "informational system," we could borrow a distinction employed by Andy Clark and Annette Karmiloff-Smith and say that, prelingually, she had various kinds of "knowledge *in* the system," but none of this was available as "knowledge *to* the system."[66]

Having directly experienced "that unconscious, yet conscious time of nothingness," Keller found that when she reached the other side of the linguistic Rubicon she could "not hope to describe adequately" what the side she had left behind was like.[67] In her letter of 1901, she says: "Words are powerless to describe the desolation of that prison-house, or the joy of the soul that is delivered out of its captivity."[68] How, then, are those of us who acquired language so easily as infants to imagine—seriously imagine—what it would be like to be "us" without language? In what meaningful sense would we even be "us"?

It gets worse. As deaf-blind people go, Keller was, believe it not, one of the lucky ones. The fact that she lost both her hearing and sight as a result of an illness when she was nineteen months old meant that her developing brain had already had, let's say, infinitely more exposure to sight and sound, including speech, than those who are born deaf-blind. McCrone paints a horrific portrait of those born into this "pitiful state":

Unlike the active Helen Keller, such a child may spend years slumped in one spot; an inert vegetable, unable to feed itself or meet its most basic needs. A child born deaf/blind does not even seem to be able to use its remaining senses of touch and taste. At best, it will rock quietly on its haunches or, occasionally, burst into a frenzied screaming fit. Without eyes and ears, the deaf/blind child seems to have no conception that the outside world exists, let alone an inner code with which to order that conception.[69]

McCrone describes the prognosis for these people in these terms: if such a child is forced "to build up an internal image of the outside world" through touch—by someone's placing a spoon of food in the child's mouth, then on its lips, its chin, in its hands, and so on—then, over "months and even years of painstaking training," such a child can be "transformed from a senseless, gurgling and sprawling heap into a dimly aware and house-trained inmate of an institution."[70]

The overall conclusion to be drawn from the evidence that I have considered in this chapter is that there is a world of cognitive difference between beings who have acquired language in the presence of developmentally normal implicit mindreading and implicit mindsharing (i.e., shared attention) skills and beings that have not. In particular, there is a world of cognitive difference between fully fledged explicit mindsharers and iso-experients, since the latter lack not only explicit mindsharing abilities but also implicit mindsharing abilities and (assuming Povinelli is right) even implicit mindreading abilities.

I will pursue these differences even further in the next chapter in order, ultimately, to draw out their ethical implications. Doing this will enable me to build on the theory of responsive cohesion's differentiated model of our obligations in respect of other people (presented in chapter 5) in order to present the theory of responsive cohesion's differentiated model of our obligations in respect of all beings. When this is done, I can then move on to putting the various aspects of the entire theory together in a summary form (chapter 9), applying the theory to the eighteen problems I outlined in chapter 2 that confront any attempt to construct a General Ethics (chapter 10), and, finally, offering some concluding thoughts (chapter 11).

8

Time Blindness, Autobiographical Death, and Our Obligations in Respect of All Beings

The evidence I considered in the previous chapter suggests that there are profound differences between the cognitive worlds of mindsharers and iso-experients. We can summarize these differences by saying that mindsharers live in profoundly richer cognitive worlds than iso-experients. We have also seen that it is the feature of language acquired in the normal way—that is, underpinned by the implicit mindreading and implicit mindsharing abilities that characterize normal human development—that marks the essential boundary between mindsharers and iso-experients. This means that it is essentially language acquired in the normal way that enables most humans to be mindsharers and therefore to live in profoundly richer cognitive worlds than iso-experients.

None of this is to deny that iso-experients are not sentient, aware, or conscious in a basic, nonreflective way. It is *like something* to be an iso-experient; iso-experients are so-named because they are, after all, iso-*experients*. We can therefore readily agree with the philosopher of mind Paul Churchland that "Consciousness ... is primarily a *biological* phenomenon rather than a social one"; that "The social institution of language has nothing to do with the genesis of consciousness"; and that "we share [the phenomenon of consciousness] with much of the animal kingdom."[1] However, we must also agree with Churchland that the profoundly social (i.e., mindsharing) phenomenon of language "has led to a profound transformation in the *contents* of human consciousness, and ... that transformational process is far from over."[2]

Language and the Richness of Cognitive Worlds

Churchland neatly summarizes the cognitive riches that are available to language users in terms of two ways "in which language makes a profound difference in the contents and quality of human cognition."[3] The first concerns the *historical* or *cumulative* riches that language preserves; the second concerns the fact that "Putting historical stretches aside, language makes it possible, at any time, for human cognition to be *collective*."[4] In regard to the rewards that are bestowed by language use through the historical accumulation of knowledge, Churchland observes that language provides us, at least to some degree, with

the cumulative experience of an entire culture, an experience that reaches thousands of years into the past.... Language thus constitutes a form of extrasomatic memory, a medium of information storage that exists outside any individual's brain and which survives any individual's death. With the appearance of language, the process of learning about the world is no longer limited by what can be acquired in three score and ten years. Hard-won information can be passed effectively from generation to generation, undergoing appropriate modification all the while as each generation makes its own contribution to our unfolding collective consciousness. With the introduction of written language and the permanent records it makes possible, the process is further magnified.[5]

In regard to the rewards that are bestowed by language use through the power of collective cognition, Churchland observes that, even if we set historical considerations to one side, linguistically mediated collective cognition

allows a group of humans to address and solve cognitive problems that would prove insoluble to any individual operating alone. Finding solutions need no longer be limited by one person's memory, one person's imagination, one person's intelligence, or one person's perspective. Language allows us to transcend our individual cognitive weaknesses and to conjoin our individual strengths.[6]

The fact that "Language allows us to transcend our individual cognitive weaknesses and to conjoin our individual strengths" means precisely that language users are mindsharers rather than iso-experients that remain locked in upon their own (nonlinguistic) experience of the world. As we saw in chapter 6, the primate researcher and developmental psychologist Michael Tomasello refers to the historically cumulative and collectively intensified processes of linguistically mediated social learning as "the ratchet effect."[7] The psychologist Merlin Donald explains just how different this "ratchet effect" form of enculturation is from that of the nonlinguistic forms of learning that characterize even the most sophisticated iso-experients:

> Animal cognition rarely escapes the boundaries of its own embodiment, and whatever there is of animal culture, it plays a small role in forming the individual mind. Even highly sophisticated animals, such as apes, have no choice but to approach the world solipsistically because they cannot share ideas and thoughts in any detail [i.e., they are iso-experients, not mindsharers]. Each ape learns only what it learns for itself. Every generation starts afresh because the old die with their wisdom sealed forever in their brains. An older ape cannot tell the younger, "There is an orchard beyond that ridge," or "Avoid that tree; I once got very sick while eating its fruit." If the young one wants to learn that fact, it must do so either by observing others get sick or by getting sick itself. There are no shortcuts for an isolated mind. As a result of this isolation, the rate of cultural knowledge accumulation is very slow, and there is much less cultural variation between troupes of apes than there is between groups of humans.[8]

There is no comparison between the richness of the cognitive worlds that are afforded by the (linguistically enabled) generational accumulation of knowledge and the lack of such accumulation. Indeed, it is literally impossible for culturally immersed language users to imagine what it must be like to be without language and the accumulation of knowledge that it enables. We simply cannot think outside the language box—even if we think in terms of images, we are still language users who are thinking in terms of images. The closest we can get to the minds of intelligent, nonlinguistic iso-experients is to consider, as I have done in the previous chapter, careful experimental (as opposed to anecdotal) research into the workings of the minds of our closest evolutionary relatives and careful clinical research into the minds of those humans who have not had access to language.

Neither should we kid ourselves here that perhaps nonlinguistic animals live in richer sensory-perceptual worlds than language users do—as if there were some kind of evolutionary based compensation at work to "make up" for their iso-experiential state. The fact is that human brains are characterized, among other things, by highly developed *association areas*, which integrate sensory input from different sensory domains to give us a richly integrated, "cross-modal" perception of the world (i.e., a form of perception that relates and combines information from different sensory modalities). As the cognitive scientist Peter Gärdenfors argues, the available evidence suggests that:

The development of progressively larger association areas in the frontal lobe and other parts of the brain during the course of human evolution has resulted in our having a greater ability to go between the senses than have other species of animals. This probably makes it easier for us to discover different kinds of connections between phenomena in the world.[9]

This means that humans live in sensory-perceptual worlds that are, on the whole, richer than those of other animals. If we combine this conclusion with the points I have just discussed in regard to the tremendous cognitive riches that are bestowed by language use through the historical accumulation of knowledge and the power of collective cognition, then, as I stated at the beginning of this chapter, we can see that mindsharers live in profoundly richer cognitive worlds than iso-experients. Yet, even here, we need to realize that mindsharers live in cognitive worlds that are richer than those of iso-experients in ways that go well beyond these points. This is because considerations regarding the historical accumulation of knowledge, the power of collective cognition, and the richness of mindsharers' sensory-perceptual worlds still do not prepare us for the shock that even highly intelligent, highly social animals like chimpanzees do not experience each other in the most essential way in which we experience each other and probably don't experience themselves in the most essential way in which we experience ourselves. What I mean by this is that, as we saw in the previous chapter, the burden of the evidence suggests that chimpanzees do not show an awareness of the existence of other minds—they are neither implicit mindreaders nor because of that it seems, implicit mindsharers—and it is not at all clear that they are even self-aware, that is, aware of the fact *that* they are aware.

In regard to the evidence suggesting that our closest evolutionary relatives are not aware of the existence of other minds, I am accepting here (i) both Povinelli's present and Tomasello's earlier views regarding chimpanzees' lack of implicit mindreading abilities; (ii) Povinelli and Vonk's argument against the interpretation that Tomasello and his colleagues have placed on their more recent, competitive food-situation experiments, which have led Tomasello and his colleagues to change their earlier view; and (iii) Povinelli and his colleagues' most recent evidence, which again reinforces the view that chimpanzees' lack implicit mindreading abilities. Moreover, even if future evidence forced Povinelli and his colleagues to change their own presently well-supported view, it remains the case that both groups of leading researchers in this area are in agreement that chimpanzees are not implicit mindsharers.

It certainly seems to me that the most plausible explanation for why chimpanzees are not implicit mindsharers is that they are not implicit mindreaders (as Povinelli and his colleagues claim and as the earlier Tomasello claimed); after all, if chimpanzees do not have an implicit awareness that their conspecifics have inner mental states in the first place, then it would obviously never occur to them to attempt to engage in any forms of implicit mindsharing in the second place. Conversely, if I were an intelligent, highly social animal like a chimpanzee, and I was at least implicitly aware that both I and my conspecifics had inner mental states, then I reckon it would be in my and their interests to do all we could to try to connect with each others' minds by pointing, showing each other things, engaging in intentional forms of instruction, and so on. Who knows, we might even end up inventing a language of some kind.

In conjunction with the evidence suggesting that our closest evolutionary relatives are not aware of the existence of other minds, it is also arguable that they are not self-conscious. We can point to several sources of evidence and argument that suggest that chimpanzees may not be self-conscious. First, we can recall both Povinelli's reinterpretation of the "mirror test" with chimpanzees (based on his work with delayed visual feedback in children) and Hobson's interpretation of "the mirror test" with autistic children (see the section in chapter 7 entitled "Are Our Closest Evolutionary Relatives Self-Aware?"). Both Povinelli and Hobson suggest that their respective subjects showed a form of body awareness but did not possess self-awareness.

Second, it seems more plausible to suggest that self-awareness and awareness of other minds (i.e., mindreading abilities) arise together than to suggest that one can exist without the other. Consider this from both sides: How could you possibly be in a position to attribute mental states to others—even implicitly—if you were not at least implicitly aware *of* mental states in yourself? What, exactly, would you be attributing to others? Conversely, if you were at least implicitly aware *of* mental states in yourself, then how could you fail to attribute some kinds of mental states to others—at least implicitly—if they seemed to be like you in other respects? If it is indeed more plausible to suggest that self-awareness and other-awareness (i.e., mindreading abilities) arise together than to suggest that one can exist without the other, then the evidence that suggests that chimpanzees fail to attribute mental states to others can itself be taken as indirect evidence for the conclusion that they are not self-aware.

Third, it seems that even "normal" (i.e., nonautistic) nonlinguistic humans lack self-awareness, at least in any form that we would recognize. It is of course remarkably difficult to get any firsthand information about this subject in the case of "normal" nonlinguistic humans: so very few humans successfully cross over the linguistic Rubicon at a late enough stage in their development to have anything interesting to tell us in regard to "what it was like" before they crossed over, and, of those who do, even fewer actually *tell* us. Thus, for example, Susan Schaller reports trying repeatedly to get Ildefonso to answer her question "What did you think before language?" only to be told by him every time "what had happened to him and why he remained uneducated" as opposed to what it was actually *like* to be him prior to language.[10] Schaller puts this down primarily to Ildefonso being ashamed of his prelinguistic state, but, whatever the reason, she never got an answer. However, as we have seen, Helen Keller answers this question directly. She says that "Before my teacher came to me, I did not know that I am. I lived in a world that was a no-world;" it was an "unconscious, yet conscious time of nothingness;" "My inner life, then, was a blank without past, present, or future."[11] How else could you say that you were not self-aware? Keller says that she only became conscious (by which I take it she means self-aware—aware of the fact *that* she was conscious) after "I learned the meaning of 'I' and 'me' and found that I was something."[12] The clear implication here is that if this lack of self-awareness applies even in the case of "normal" nonlinguistic humans, then surely it must apply in the case of normal, likewise nonlinguistic chimpanzees, with brains only about one-third the size of ours.

It seems, then, that the more we contemplate the relative richness of the cognitive worlds of mindsharers and iso-experients, the deeper the differences run. Not only does the neurological evidence regarding the development of association areas—not to mention neural complexity overall—suggest that mindsharers have richer sensory-perceptual worlds on the whole than iso-experients, and not only is it the case that language bestows historically cumulative and collectively intensified cognitive riches upon mindsharers that are simply unavailable to iso-experients, but it also seems that mindsharers are aware of both their own awareness and the awareness of others whereas iso-experients are not.

Unobservables: Out of Sight, Out of Mind

And yet, there is more: it seems that the differences between mindsharers and iso-experients run deeper still, for there is evidence to suggest that iso-experients might be unable to reason about not only the inherently unobservable mental states of *others*, but even *any* inherently unobservable features of the world. Consider, for example, causal relationships. It is one thing to note that *observable event B* regularly follows *observable event A*, but quite another to impute a *nonobservable* or *"hidden"* causal *relationship* of some kind between A and B. To impute a causal relationship is to gain an understanding that can be transferred to other situations in which the same kind of causal relationship applies, even if the observable features of the initiating and consequential events *look* different to those I have just referred to as A and B.

Again, Povinelli and his team have led our understanding here. In *Folk Physics for Apes*, Povinelli documents a detailed series of experiments aimed at testing chimpanzees' understanding of the ways in which objects interact. The overall conclusion is that *"chimpanzees do not represent abstract causal variables as explanations for why objects interact in the ways that they do"* (Povinelli's emphasis).[13] I will not review these experiments here because they are not central to my main purpose. However, it is important to note that when Povinelli's experimental investigations into the "folk physics" of chimpanzees (i.e., chimpanzees' basic understanding of how physical things interact) are taken together with his experimental investigations into the "folk psychology" of chimpanzees (i.e., chimpanzees' basic understanding of each other and each other's behaviors), they point to a common conclusion:

Unlike humans, the chimpanzee's reasoning about both physical objects and social beings appears restricted to concepts, ideas, and procedures that are linked to the world of tangible things. In both the social and the physical case, the chimpanzee learns about the observable properties of these entities, and the kinds of behaviors that these entities typically exhibit. The chimpanzee even takes the impressive leap of generalizing to new instances. But in neither case does the chimpanzee appear to generate additional concepts, related to perceptually non-obvious phenomena, concepts which could provide a unified account of why such regularities exist in the first place.[14]

Speaking more personally about these kinds of findings, Povinelli writes:

> I used to believe that any differences between humans and chimpanzees would have to be trivial. But the results of over two hundred studies that we have con-ducted during the past fifteen years have slowly changed my mind. Combined with findings from other laboratories, this evidence has forced me to seriously confront the possibility that chimpanzees do not reason about inherently un-observable phenomena.[15]

All of this is consistent with what I have argued earlier regarding the way in which language allows us to cognitively transcend the biophysical world. If we can only cognitively transcend the perceptually immediate and, thus, *observable* biophysical world through language, then it fol-lows that it is simply not possible to represent and reason about inher-ently unobservable phenomena—such as psychological intentions and physical causes—without language. And, if this is the case, then we should not be surprised by Povinelli's findings—or, if we are, we should accept, as Povinelli and Vonk argue, that this says more about the ways in which our own (linguistically structured) minds work than it does about the minds of highly intelligent, highly social, but nevertheless non-linguistic animals like chimpanzees.[16] If nonlinguistic beings cannot rea-son about any inherently unobservable phenomena—from the mental states of others to causal relationships—then it would appear that the minds of linguistically enabled mindsharers are richer than those of iso-experients in ways in which we might never have initially imagined. And even in saying this, we need to understand that this covers far more than the depths of experience that I have mentioned here (i.e., far more than just the questions of awareness of other minds and causal relationships). Consider, for example, the inherently unobservable phenomenon of *time*, which is what I will now do.

Time Blindness

If nonlinguistic iso-experients are unable to represent and reason about inherently unobservable phenomena in general, if their world is restricted to the world of tangible things and the regularities that occur in regard to the behaviors of those observable things (including the physical bodies of their conspecifics and the physical objects in their natural environments), then we can see even more clearly why it is that they are unable to transcend their experiential immersion in the biophysical realm. Moreover, the biophysical realm in which they are experientially immersed is never the biophysical realm that existed "last Thursday" or "last autumn," but only the biophysical realm that exists here and now. This might include here-and-now experiences of hunger that *elicit* the remembered knowledge of where food can be found and setting off in the appropriate direction. But it does not include a conscious reviewing of one's past history or any conception of one's longer-term future, including one's longer-term dreams, schemes, plans, or projects. We are now in a position to see why.

If nonlinguistic iso-experients are unable to represent and reason about inherently unobservable phenomena in general, then it follows that they are unable to represent and reason about *time*. This is because time cannot be perceived, only conceived of, so if a nonlinguistic being has no means of representing inherently unobservable phenomena, it has no systematic means of representing, let alone structuring its experience in terms of, a temporal dimension.

In her important book *Language in Cognitive Development*, the distinguished developmental psychologist Katherine Nelson, puts the point this way:

To recapitulate, the child alone cannot *discover* time, because (unlike concrete objects) it is not an entity that exists to be discovered. Rather, conceptions of process and change have led different societies to *conceptualize* time in different ways, *and those ways are conveyed to children through language forms* [my emphases].[17]

Of course, we cannot interview iso-experients to try to gain some relatively direct kind of understanding of how they understand—or fail to understand—the temporal dimension of their own experience, but we can certainly look at the impressions that have been gained in regard to this question by those who have tried to look carefully at nonlinguistic humans. When we do this, we see that the overall impressions that these observers have gained of these people include a strong sense that they are blind to the temporal—especially the autobiographical—dimension of their experience. This impression ran all through the work that I reviewed in the last chapter in regard to both feral children and the prelingually deaf. For example, John McCrone's composite picture of feral children suggested that

they seemed somehow to lack *memory* and self-awareness ... [their thoughts were] limited to the world of the *here and now* ... They could make simple associations and learn to recognize familiar people and situations. But they seemed unable to reflect on the *past or the future*, or to have any insight into their own plight [my emphases].[18]

The same seems to apply in the case of the prelingually deaf. Oliver Sacks's clinically honed impression of Joseph, his more or less paradigmatic example of a prelingually deaf but otherwise apparently intelligent child, was that (and here I will emphasize Sacks's focus on temporally oriented deficits throughout):

It was not only language that was missing: *there was not, it was evident, a clear sense of the past, of "a day ago" as distinct from "a year ago."* [Just stop and consider this lack as you read this: no clear sense of the past, no way of telling a day ago from a year ago. This is a profound cognitive deficit, one that is unimaginable to normal language users.] There was a strange *lack of historical sense*, the feeling of *a life that lacked autobiographical and historical dimension*, the feeling of *a life that only existed in the moment, in the present* ... Joseph saw, distinguished, categorized, used; he had no problems with perceptual categorization or generalization, but he could not, it seemed, go much beyond this, hold abstract ideas in mind, reflect, play, *plan* [my emphases].[19]

Whereas Sacks says that "It was not only language that was missing," and then proceeds to highlight his strong impression that Joseph lacked a temporal dimension to his experience, the evidence and arguments that I have been reviewing here suggest that, in another sense, it *was* "only language that was missing," for to be without language is to lack the tool that is necessary in order to temporally structure one's experience.

Consistent with this claim, Schaller found in teaching sign language to her otherwise intelligent twenty-seven-year-old Mexican student Ildefonso that "he had no concept of time as we learn it"; that for a long time he "could not understand any lesson on time"; and that nothing remained more difficult throughout the course of teaching him than trying to get him to understand temporal concepts.[20] Temporal concepts in general were for a long time beyond him. In reviewing other contemporary cases of late language learners, Schaller found the same problem and notes in regard to one case that "The most difficult task, *as usual*, was schedules and time. *The student's only time was the present*" (my emphases).[21] Even so, Ildefonso painfully and gradually gained a sense of time following his eventual breakthrough into the cognitive world of sign language. Revisiting Ildefonso after having lost touch altogether for over seven years, Schaller explains in one passage how, in a Vietnamese restaurant, Ildefonso signs, and emphasizes, the word *never* to her—which is to say, not at any *time*—in regard to the fact that his brother has "never tasted food like this—never." Schaller's reaction?: "The sentence delighted me, because I had once given up trying to teach Ildefonso what *never* meant and how to use it. It had seemed an impossible concept."[22]

Helen Keller's rare "inside story" report on what it was like to have been a nonlinguistic human reinforces the general point that I am making here. She tell us that her inner life lacked any kind of temporal structure: "My inner life, then, was a blank without past, present, or future, without hope or anticipation...."[23]

These considerations lead to the following conclusion: to live in a linguistically structured cognitive world is to live in a temporally structured cognitive world; not to live in a linguistically structured cognitive world is to live in a cognitive world that lacks any kind of temporal structure. Or more simply: to live in language is to live in time; to be without language is to be *time blind*.

If this conclusion applies even in the case of nonlinguistic humans, who may or may not still be capable of implicit forms of mindsharing, then it certainly applies in the case of nonhuman iso-experients, which are not capable even of implicit forms of mindsharing. Moreover, the evidence we have in regard to humans who are introduced to language late in their development suggests that the distinction between a nonlinguistic human and a nonhuman iso-experient might be a very fine line in crucial respects. This is because it seems that both nonlinguistic humans and nonhuman iso-experients lack self-awareness and a temporally structured dimension to their experience. As we will see further below, to lack these crucial features of experience is to live in cognitive worlds that are so different from the cognitive worlds of fully fledged, explicit mindsharers that it makes sense to see nonlinguistic humans as being much more like iso-experients, pure and simple, than they are like explicit mindsharers. (As I noted in the previous chapter, it seems that humans' innate implicit mindsharing abilities do not actually amount to much if they do not serve, primarily, to carry a person into the world of language.)

In view of these considerations—and because it is precisely the features of self-awareness and temporally structured experience that I will be pursuing in what follows—I will, for convenience, generally talk from now on in terms of a contrast between mindsharers, by which I mean fully fledged, explicit mindsharers, and iso-experients. This is simpler than continually contrasting mindsharers with nonhuman iso-experients *and* nonlinguistic humans, who may or may not be capable of implicit mindsharing and therefore not be like iso-experients in all respects. The point here is that nonlinguistic humans are exactly like iso-experients in respect of the question that I will be pursuing in what follows, namely, what follows from the fact that iso-experients and non-linguistic humans both lack self-awareness and a temporally structured dimension to their experience.

Autobiographical Blindness

The evidence suggesting that iso-experients lack both self-consciousness and a temporally structured dimension to their experience points strongly to the conclusion that iso-experients lack the cognitive resources that are necessary for any kind of *self-narrative*, which is also to say, any kind of *autobiographical awareness*. I say that the evidence points "strongly" to this conclusion because to lack *either* of these cognitive resources is to lack the resources that are necessary to conceive of oneself in autobiographically structured terms. This is because, in order to do this, it is necessary to be able to conceive both *of* one's self—that is, to be self-conscious—*and* of that self—that "inner being"—as persisting through time (the course of a lifetime in fact).

We should not really be surprised by this. Katherine Nelson's work on, and review of work on, the development of autobiographical mem-ory in children shows that (i) it develops well after the development of language and (ii) it is dependent upon language for its development. Let us consider these points in turn. In regard to its timing, Nelson notes that the evidence suggests that "autobiographical memory—enduring chronologically sequenced memory for significant events from one's own life—has its onset only during the later preschool years, $3\frac{1}{2}$ to 4 years on average."[24] (A quick survey around the dinner table with your family or friends will confirm this.) According to Nelson's work and review of the evidence, children who are younger than three and one-half to four years do have some memory of *events*, which is often referred to as *episodic memory*, but these memories tend not to survive for long, and those that do tend to be "fragmentary and not accessible to deliberate recall."[25] (Following the work of Endel Tulving, *episodic memory* is typically contrasted with *semantic memory*, which just involves recalling a piece of information, like a phone number or, in the case of some nonhumans, where you buried some food, without any detailed recollection of the circumstances in which this knowledge was gained.)[26] In contrast to these early examples of episodic memory, "temporally dated memory," which "is properly considered autobiographical," does not emerge until three and one-half to four years.[27]

It is worth recalling here that Povinelli links his own work regarding the age at which young children recognize delayed visual images of themselves as *them* to Nelson's work on the onset of autobiographical memory (see my discussion of this point in the previous chapter). That is, Povinelli draws a connection between the age at which children begin to develop an at least implicit psychologically based conception of themselves (i.e., the age at which they begin to become self-conscious) and the age at which they begin to develop an autobiographically structured memory. And, of course, by this age, children have also been immersed in, and are becoming increasingly proficient at participating in, linguistic cultures in which discourse is *framed in terms of* temporal concepts: not only do we have specific words that refer to past, present, and future, but the language we use is itself framed in terms of past, present, and future tenses. To utter a sentence is to use a verb; to use a verb is to employ a tense; to employ a tense is to express a temporal relation between what is being reported in a sentence and the time that the sentence is uttered.

In regard to the point that autobiographical memory is dependent upon language for its development, Nelson argues that the research shows that "the social influences expressed through *discourse* about past and present experiences in early childhood transform *episodic memory* into *autobiographical memory*" and that these "narrative models and influences in early childhood," which "help to transform the episodic memory system into a long-lasting *autobiographical memory* for significant events in one's own life," enable one to construct "a self-history," which is "determinant to a large extent of one's self-concept" (my emphases).[28]

According to Nelson, language development is necessary to the development of any autobiographical sense of self. In the conclusion of her book, she sums up the matter like this:

> [U]ntil the various uses of language make it possible to imagine a past and future self, and to imagine that other people have different pasts and futures, as well as different presents, one cannot speak of a fully determined self *distinct from ongoing experience* ... Language uniquely enables contemplating a self that is different from present experience, and imagining a self that will grow older as well as a self that was once a little baby [my emphasis].[29]

Moreover, Nelson points out that even "To understand the perspective of now one must have a sense of an enduring self existing through time [i.e., an autobiographical self]."[30] Thus, even when observers note that nonlinguistic humans seem to live lives that exist only in the moment, in the present, or that their only time is the present (to paraphrase both Sacks and Schaller above), they do not mean—they cannot mean—that these nonlinguistic humans themselves have any sense of *now*, of *the present moment*, in the way in which language users do. Rather, they are simply time blind.

Taken all in all, then, the considerations that I have outlined here suggest that language is fundamental to the development of the temporal, historical, or narrative structuring of experience. We do not innately or automatically structure our experience in this way in the absence of language. This temporal structuring of experience is, in turn, fundamental to the autobiographical structuring of our experience. And this autobiographical structuring of experience is, in turn, crucial to our own conception of ourselves, of *who we are*. Now, if it is necessary to be able to conceive both *of* one's self—that is, to be self-conscious—*and* of that self—that "inner being"—as persisting through time in order to have an autobiographical sense of self, and if it is necessary to be a language user (i.e., a mindsharer) in order to have a sense of self as persisting through time, then it follows that nonlinguistic beings are necessarily incapable of structuring their experience in autobiographical terms. To be without language is to be time blind, and to be time blind is to be autobiographically blind—and more besides, as I will discuss next.

Awareness of Death and Understanding of Death

If a fundamental feature of *who you are* is that you are a self-conscious being that exists for a certain duration, and that others are like you in this respect, then you will have an understanding of death that is obviously inaccessible to beings that lack either self-consciousness or a temporally structured dimension to their experience. Indeed, gaining a conception of death—of what is lost when a being dies—would seem to be considerably more difficult than gaining a conception of oneself or of time, not least because a conception of death presupposes both of these prior conceptions. These considerations therefore suggest that conceiving properly of death is an extremely sophisticated cognitive achievement, which seems to be restricted to language users, or mindsharers. The sophistication of this cognitive achievement is underlined by research in developmental psychology demonstrating that, even for humans, a proper understanding of basic facts about what it means to be dead—such as the fact that something is not "dead" simply because it is an inanimate object (like a rock)—does not occur until after the age of ten. As the comparative psychologist Marc Hauser summarizes this research:

Children under the age of ten tend to believe that dead is simply the opposite of living, that is, not living. In this sense, inanimate objects are dead, and so are animate objects that have their eyes closed and fail to move. As the developmental psychologist Susan Carey has pointed out, some time after the age of ten, children undergo a conceptual transformation that provides them with a new way of thinking about life and death. This conceptual transformation teaches them that only animate things can die, that upon dying, the brain no longer works, that if they die the same things will happen to them, that killing is bad, and that they have the potential to end another's life as well as take their own. In this sense, a psychologically interesting representation of death depends on self-awareness [not to mention temporal awareness] and a richly structured set of beliefs about the meaning of life.[31]

My claim that both self-awareness and temporal awareness are necessary in order to have a proper awareness, let alone understanding, of death is consistent with the views of other commentators on the kinds of beliefs you need to have, if only implicitly, to understand what it means to die;

to understand that death is the end of the existence of a cognitive world. For example, Peter Gärdenfors considers that "An awareness of death presumes not only that you are aware that you have a consciousness [i.e., are self-aware], but also that you realize that this consciousness will end at some point in time."[32] (And you then need to be able to transfer this understanding to another in order to understand what it means for them to die.) Marc Hauser similarly considers that "understanding death reveals a deep sense of time, a sense of what the past has been like and what the future holds" and, as he makes clear in the quotation above, self-awareness as well.[33]

To lack autobiographical awareness—to lack either self-consciousness or temporal awareness—is, then, to lack the cognitive resources that are necessary to have an awareness of death, let alone any proper understanding of death, which itself represents an extremely sophisticated cognitive achievement even in humans.

What Is Lost When a Mindsharer or an Iso-Experient Dies?

These considerations have obvious consequences for our understanding of how mindsharers and iso-experients understand—or fail to understand—death. Let us consider this from first-, second-, and third-person perspectives, although it will be most convenient to do this in reverse order. From an external, third-person, objective, "God's-eye-view" perspective, mindsharers can see that much, much more is lost when a mindsharer dies than when an iso-experient dies precisely because of the vastly richer cognitive worlds that typify mindsharers as opposed to iso-experients. In contrast, iso-experients cannot see this: because iso-experients are not aware of other minds, they are incapable of having any idea of the difference between the richness of the cognitive worlds that are lost in these two cases.

It also seems to be the case that what we might call *negative concepts*—concepts regarding the notions of absence, lack of, "not," and so on—seem to be beyond the reach of nonlinguistic beings, even in the face of intensive training. It seems that negative concepts can only, and only then rather painfully, be grasped by them if they are able to cross over into the mindsharing world of language and so become mindsharers themselves. Consider Schaller's reflection, which I noted above, on what seemed to be the impossibility of teaching Ildefonso the word "never." He evidently only acquired this word during the years in which Schaller lost touch with him—years that lay well and truly on the other side of him having crossed over the linguistic Rubicon and during which he was eagerly advancing his knowledge of sign language. Or consider this example: reviewing work by another research team with Ai, "the most mathematically educated of all chimpanzees," Povinelli points out that

Although [Ai's intensive] training has gradually forced her "understanding" of zero into a position further and further down the "number line," even to this day, after thousands of trials, Ai still reliably confuses 0 with 1 (and in some tasks, with 2 or 3 as well). However one wishes to interpret such findings, they are certainly not consistent with an understanding of the very essence of zero-ness.[34]

Given that the evidence suggests that iso-experients don't "get" the idea of conscious *being*—that they lack both self-consciousness and awareness of other minds—and given that, of all concepts, the ones that they seem to have "zero" chance of "getting" (in their capacity as nonlinguistic beings) are negative concepts, it seems that the idea that nonlinguistic iso-experients can have any hope of "getting" the "Big *not*"—that is, the idea of *not being*—is entirely fanciful.

The same general conclusion applies—with a vengeance—from a second-person perspective, that is, from the point of view of those beings that know the being that has died. This is because mindsharers who know each other understand each other not just in general, third-person terms as the possessors of "the kinds of rich cognitive worlds that typify normal mindsharers," but rather as individual, unique, and, thus, irreplaceable cognitive worlds. When someone you know well dies, you possess direct second-person knowledge of the cognitive world that has been lost—forever. In contrast, iso-experients have no idea of either the general or the particular nature of the cognitive world that has been lost. The fact that iso-experients are blind to the existence of unobservable mental states in general means that they simply do not have the cognitive resources to understand, even implicitly, that the death of one of their conspecifics is the death of another mind. They therefore lack the cognitive resources to appreciate the more precise nature of the loss that has occurred when the death involves a conspecific with which they have routinely interacted.

This is a radical conclusion in terms of the anecdotes that abound and are fed to us in nature documentaries on television in regard to the ways in which many animals respond to the death of their conspecifics. However, it follows directly from what we have learned about the lack of even implicit mindreading abilities, let alone implicit mindsharing abilities, in our nearest evolutionary relatives, and is also in line with more considered analyses of death awareness in animals (as we will see below). Because we are irrepressible mentalizers, we find it virtually impossible not to interpret the behavior of other animals toward each other in terms of them making mental state attributions in regard to their conspecifics as opposed to them operating on the basis of behavioral generalizations. The same applies to death awareness in animals. Our interpretations say more about *our* habitual mentalizing ways of thinking than they do about what is actually going on in the minds of the animals concerned. Thus, the comparative psychologist Marc Hauser takes the view that:

I do not question the observations of animals responding to dead group members. What I question is their interpretation. Given the lack of evidence for self-awareness as well as the capacity to attribute mental states to others, my own hunch is that no animal will be found to have a system of beliefs about death. Animals will care for those who fail to respond like normal living individuals, and may even show signs of depression when a mate or relative has died ... [However] *Feeling a loss and understanding what it means to die are two different things* [my emphasis].[35]

Indeed, even the question of the extent to which iso-experients do "feel a loss" in the face of (a lack of understanding of) death—or at least "feel a loss" in anything like the kind of sense that we would normally understand by this expression—seems dubious to some careful observers. For example, Peter Gärdenfors observes that

When a young chimpanzee dies the mother can carry it around for some days before she abandons the body. She seems to be perplexed rather than mourning. I have witnessed the same phenomenon in a troupe of Chacma baboons at Cape Good Hope. A female was carrying her dead infant by the tail in her mouth, seemingly relaxed. When she stopped to eat, she left the corpse on the ground, but when she moved on, she picked it up by the tail again.[36]

It may be, then, that our attribution of "feeling a loss" to iso-experients—and what *we* understand by that—again says much more about the ways in which (our) mindsharers' minds work than the ways in which iso-experients' minds work.

Finally, we come to the first-person perspective, the perspective of the being that dies. If it requires both self-awareness and a linguistically conceptualized awareness of time to understand the fact that you will die, then we clearly have no reason to believe that iso-experients understand that they will die; no reason to believe that they have any understanding that their consciousness will one day cease to be—forever. It follows from this that we have no reason to believe that the termination of their conscious experience at some point in the future should be a source of concern to iso-experients. This is because they lack the cognitive requirements for having a life-story (or self-narrative or autobiography) that is constituted by a past, present, and future, which, being unrealized, necessarily consists of plans, hopes, and dreams toward which they presently orient themselves.

When an iso-experient dies it means that its here-and-now oriented awareness ceases at *this* moment rather than some later moment. However, considered from the iso-experient's internal experience of the world, its death does not mean that it is thereby "cut off" from its "future" because in the absence of both self-awareness and temporal awareness—in the absence, in other words, of any autobiographical awareness—it is not aware now (or at any other time) that it has a "future" from which it could be "cut off." Rather, its here-and-now oriented awareness simply ceases at *this* moment rather than some later moment. Mindsharers, on the other hand, are acutely aware of their futures, routinely orient their present in terms of it, and make sense of many of their present and past endeavors in terms of what their future-oriented plans, hopes, and dreams are or were. (Indeed, if you think about what you did today, even why you are reading this, it is likely that you will only be able to make proper sense of these activities in terms of your temporally structured experience of the world and, ultimately, in terms of your own life-story or autobiography.) The death of a mindsharer, especially the premature death of a mindsharer, therefore does represent a "cutting-off" from an imagined or desired future, with the consequence that this autobiographical severing—whether in reality or contemplation—can be deeply challenging to our ability to "make sense" of life. A premature death, especially, can lead some to reflect on the absurdity of life, others to look to some hypothetical transcendent realm in order to try to make sense of events that "don't seem to make any sense" in the imperfect quotidian world, and yet others to a reawakening of their deepest values and long-term goals.

Killing Iso-Experients and Killing Mindsharers

If we move from the fact of death to the act of killing, then these considerations clearly suggest that there is a world of difference between the killing of an iso-experient and the killing of a mindsharer. In particular, this difference highlights the distinction between the two kinds of harm that I referred to in chapter 5 in the context of my discussion of the theory of responsive cohesion's approach to interhuman ethics. I distinguished in that chapter between the harms of causing *unnecessary pain and suffering* (or *affective harm*) and causing *unwanted autobiographical death* (or *autobiographical harm* in the deep sense of harm to a person's autobiographical capacities). We saw that these two forms of harm are dissociable—it is perfectly possible to cause one without causing the other—and that they need to be understood *as* forms of harm in different terms. In particular, we saw that the kind of death that is at issue in understanding death as a form of *harm* is not biological death as such but rather autobiographical death. If we mistakenly think that the only kind of nonaffective harm we can cause is painless biological death (which, of course, guarantees autobiographical death), then we are left with no basis on which to object to (i) painlessly sedating someone into a permanent coma (while otherwise keeping them alive until they die of "natural causes"); (ii) painlessly stripping them of self-consciousness (with a self-consciousness-zapping device, which leaves basic, non-self-conscious forms of awareness intact); or (iii) painlessly stripping them of any form of "temporalized" awareness (with a temporal-awareness zapper). After all, none of these actions causes pain and suffering or biological death. Yet to do any of these things is to kill the *person*, even if they do not cause the biological death of that person's body. To destroy someone's self-conscious awareness or temporally structured awareness, let alone both, means that they lose any sense of their own identity; that they no longer exist from their own first-person point of view; that they "die to themselves." Whereas there was "someone at home" before any of these interventions, there is "no one at home" after them, whatever projections we might continue to place on their behavior.

These considerations also allow us to see that painless biological death is not some additional harm that exists further down the temporal track than painless autobiographical death. Once a person has died to themselves—undergone autobiographical death—then "they" cannot be harmed by biological death, because "they" no longer exist. The only real reason to continue to keep a "person" alive who is already autobiographically dead is if those mindsharers who have in interest in the case might wish to do so, either because they directly desire it or because they wish to respect the person's previously expressed wishes to this effect. But many people these days understand that there is nothing to be gained by expressing such wishes, for once they are autobiographically dead, biological death cannot harm them in any additional way. The only kind of painless death to fear, therefore, is painless autobiographical death, not painless biological death as such. By the same token, the only kind of painless killing that it makes sense to object to is painless autobiographical killing, not painless biological killing as such.

Now the distinction between causing unnecessary pain and suffering (or affective harm) and causing unwanted autobiographical death (or autobiographical harm) was not central to my development of the theory of responsive cohesion's differentiated model of our obligations in respect of other people in chapter 5 because it is clear that mindsharers can be harmed in either of these ways. (This is why I was able to collapse the distinction between these two forms of harm, which were both included in table 5.1, in order to draw the simplified differentiated obligation matrix shown in table 5.2.) However, this distinction is central in regard to iso-experients because they can be harmed in one way but not the other. Putting the matter bluntly, iso-experients can clearly be harmed in terms of being caused unnecessary pain and suffering (they are, after all, *experients*, that is, sentient), but they cannot be harmed in terms of being painlessly killed. This is because, as we have now seen, considered from their own internal perspective, iso-experients do not have a conception of themselves, let alone a temporally structured conception of themselves; that is, they do not have an autobiographical conception of themselves. This means that they simply do not have the cognitive capacity to contemplate either their own death—their own *not being*—or to regard it as cutting them off from a desirable "future." The upshot is that the painless killing of an iso-experient represents the end of its (more or less) moment-to-moment experience, but it does not rob it of any envisioned "future" for "itself" because it has neither a concept of itself—a self-concept—nor a concept of the future.

In distinct contrast, the painless killing of a mindsharer thwarts, in that very moment, all the future-oriented plans, hopes, and dreams to which the mindsharer lays claim, whether implicitly or explicitly. The painless killing of a mindsharer therefore *does* rob that being of an envisioned future for itself—even if that is just the conscious pursuit of a presently open-ended life narrative. Moreover, if the death of a mindsharer is premature, then it can, in a very real sense, rob the mindsharer of the *meaning* of their past and present, since so much of what they have done and are doing (e.g., going to university to pursue a certain career, attempting to complete a certain kind of project, working hard to "retire in the sun") was and is oriented toward the realization of particular goals. That is why the premature death of a mindsharer can rightly be regarded as tragic (i.e., as justly described as "mournful or pitiable"), but it is also why mindsharers who feel that they have essentially completed their "journey" can "die at peace with themselves" and be regarded as having done so by others: they have completed what they themselves, and those who know them well, consider to be the end of their own "life story." We can also reflect here on the fact that if a mindsharer knows that they have just a few months to live, then they are likely to radically reorganize their present priorities precisely because their present priorities are always framed in terms of a future orientation. In contrast, iso-experients lack the cognitive capacity to have any possibility of understanding that their conscious experience will *not be* in a few months and so will carry on doing exactly the same things as before insofar as they are able.

The Theory of Responsive Cohesion's Differentiated Model of Our Obligations in Respect of All Beings

With these considerations in mind, we are now in a position to revisit the theory of responsive cohesion's differentiated model of our obligations in respect of other people and expand it to include our obligations in respect of all beings. We saw in chapter 5 that this model represented the most responsively cohesive way of combining the primary salient features of the interhuman ethics problem situation, namely, the multiple perspective factor, the onerousness factor, and the beneficiaries' desires factor. The most responsively cohesive outcome of the interplay between these factors was summarized in table 5.1 and, more simply, in table 5.2. These tables were arrayed in terms of basic forms of harming and helping down the left-hand column (i.e., the harm–help spectrum of causing unnecessary pain and suffering, causing unwanted autobiographical death, offering saving help, offering ongoing supportive help, and offering bonus help) and classes of people along the top row (i.e., super-significant others, significant others, and others-in-general).

However, the theory of responsive cohesion's differentiated model of our obligations in respect of other people was advanced (in chapter 5) before I introduced the theory of responsive cohesion's theory of contexts (in chapter 6), and this theory of contexts introduced us to a profoundly important distinction between two kinds of beings: mindsharers and iso-experients. Pursuing the differences between these two kinds of beings, we have now seen that whereas any *being* (i.e., any entity that it would be *like* something to be) can be harmed in the sense of being caused unnecessary pain and suffering, only explicit mindsharers can be harmed in the sense of being caused unwanted autobiographical death, because only explicit mindsharers can live autobiographically structured lives. This means that whereas the injunction to avoid causing both kinds of harm applies in the case of mindsharers, only the injunction to avoid causing unnecessary pain and suffering can apply in the case of iso-experients.

The upshot of these considerations is that we are now in a position to expand the theory of responsive cohesion's differentiated model of our obligations in respect of other people to include *all* beings. However, in order to do this, we need to do more than simply expand the super-significant others, significant others, and others-in-general schema to include a category for iso-experients. This is because, once we properly admit all beings into our considerations, *we can no longer simply assume that the supersignificant others, significant others, and others-in-general schema refers only to other humans.* Rather, it is part of our common experience—and a highly salient feature of the vastly expanded moral problem situation that we are now addressing—that nonhuman companion animals can easily figure in any of these categories for any particular moral agent. This means that we now have to understand each moral agent's categorization of supersignificant others, significant others, and others-in-general as potentially including iso-experients as well as other mindsharers. We are, in other words, no longer cashing out the term *others* to mean supersignificant *humans*, significant *humans*, and other-*humans*-in-general but rather to mean supersignificant *beings*, significant *beings*, and other-*beings*-in-general.

The picture therefore becomes a little more complex than that shown in the matrix for the differentiated model of our obligations in respect of other people (see table 5.1). This can be explained as follows. First, if a moral agent regards an iso-experient—such as a companion animal—as a supersignificant or significant other being, then the epistemological and motivational asymmetries that the moral agent will experience in regard to that iso-experient will be analogous to, and perhaps even of a similar order to, those in regard to supersignificant or significant humans. As any devoted owner of a companion animal will attest, the beings that we personally classify as representing supersignificant others and significant others can come in all sorts of shapes and sizes. Thus, as the old adage attests, for some people, a dog really can be their "best friend"—or certainly one of them. The word "friend" is telling here, for it is one of the first words we reach for when describing those significant others to whom we feel personally close.

These considerations mean that the distinction between mindsharers and iso-experients effectively drops out of consideration in regard to the categories of supersignificant and significant others for a combination of two reasons. First, any given moral agent can include particular mindsharers and particular iso-experients in either of these categories. Second, the positive obligations that we have in regard to supersignificant and significant others—which extend to offering ongoing supportive help and offering saving help in the case of supersignificant others and offering saving help in the case of significant others—supersede the negative injunction of merely not harming by a wide margin. The upshot is that questions regarding the differential ways in which mindsharers and iso-experients can be harmed effectively become irrelevant and so drop out of consideration in this context. (See also my later discussion on the protection that all moral agents are obliged to extend to those iso-experients that have been specifically and individually *incorporated* by other mindsharers into the mindsharing realm, even if those iso-experients do not constitute supersignificant or significant others to us personally.)

However, the distinction between mindsharers and iso-experients assumes a special significance when we come to consider the category of others-in-general. This can be explained as follows. We saw in chapter 5 that, *even in the interhuman situation*, the only reasonable expectation or, more formally, obligation that moral agents are required to answer to in regard to this category is that of not harming others (i.e., moral agents are *not* obliged to offer saving help, ongoing supportive help, or bonus help to others-in-general). Now, in the interhuman situation, not harming others means not causing them unnecessary pain and suffering and not causing their unwanted autobiographical death. However, in the case of iso-experients, it turns out that it is entirely possible to cause them unnecessary pain and suffering, but that *it is not possible to cause their autobiographical death*. This is because, for the reasons that I have now explained, they are not "autobiographically alive" in the first place; they are not autobiographical beings because they do not possess a self-conscious temporally structured form of awareness. They simply cannot be autobiographically harmed, because they do not possess any autobiographical capacities. And because what is objectionable about painless killing is, as we have seen, the fact that it causes autobiographical death rather than the fact that it causes biological death as such, it follows that causing the painless biological death of an iso-experient is not objectionable in itself precisely because it does not and cannot also cause the autobiographical death of an iso-experient.

The upshot of these considerations is that we clearly need to distinguish between affective harm and autobiographical harm when we come to the question of our obligations in respect of other-beings-in-general since it turns out that mindsharers can be harmed both affectively and autobiographically, whereas iso-experients can be harmed only affectively. This means that, in terms of reworking the matrix shown in table 5.1 so as to be applicable to all sentient beings, we need (i) to preserve the distinction between the two basic kinds of harm in the left-hand column (i.e., we cannot collapse these two kinds of harm into a single category of harming as I was able to do in table 5.2), and (ii) to distinguish between *two* kinds of others-in-general along the top row, namely, others-in-general who are mindsharers and others-in-general that are iso-experients. (Note that the words "who" in regard to mindsharers and "that" in regard to iso-experients are used advisedly here. This is because mindsharers are sentient beings *who* are self-aware of an ongoing auto-biographical identity. They therefore constitute psychological selves in the full sense of that term, and I use the word "who" in referring to them in recognition of this fact. In contrast, iso-experients are sentient beings *that* are not aware of any sort of ongoing autobiographical identity. They therefore do not constitute psychological *selves* in any recognizable sense of that term. I therefore use the word "that" in referring to them in recognition of this fact. To be sure, iso-experients are not objects, but neither are they *selves*; rather, they are sentient beings, but sentient beings that lack both self-awareness and temporal awareness, sentient beings that lack an autobiographical dimension to their lives. They "are" but they don't know that they "are.")

These points regarding how we should approach the expanded question of our obligations in respect of *all* beings can be summarized as follows. On the one hand, the distinction between mindsharers and iso-experients drops out of consideration in regard to the categories of supersignificant and significant others. This is because, like mindsharers themselves, iso-experients can belong to either category, and the positive obligations that attach to these categories supersede the merely negative injunction of not harming by such a wide margin that questions regarding the differential ways in which mindsharers and iso-experients can be harmed effectively become irrelevant in this context. On the other hand, the distinction between mindsharers and iso-experients assumes a special importance in regard to the category of others-in-general, since our only obligations in regard to this category involve those of not harming, and it turns out that mindsharers and iso-experients can be harmed in different ways. Specifically, mindsharers can be harmed both affectively and autobiographically, whereas iso-experients can only be harmed affectively. The upshot is that our obligations not to harm—which are the only kinds of obligations we have in respect of others-in-general—are considerably more extensive in respect of other-mindsharers-in-general than they are in respect of other-iso-experients-in-general.

A further important salient feature must immediately be added to this picture, although it is one that arises naturally from the points I have already made. This is the point that just as we ourselves *incorporate* iso-experients, such as our own companion animals, into the mindsharing realm by regarding them as beings that are supersignificant or significant to us, by giving them personal names, by interacting with them verbally and in leisure and play on a daily basis, by training their behaviors in various ways, by providing for their needs from food to shelter to medical treatment, and so on, so other-mindsharers-in-general do the same in regard to their companion animals. Thus, there are a vast number of iso-experients that have been incorporated into the mindsharing realm. I therefore refer to all these iso-experients as *incorporated iso-experients*. But make no mistake here, the fact that these iso-experients have been incorporated into the mindsharing realm does not thereby magically transform them into mindsharers; they remain iso-experients. However, their "incorporated" (into the mindsharing realm) status does mean that they have been largely detached from the ecological webs that would have characterized their natural biophysical habitats; instead, they have been thoroughly incorporated (albeit unilaterally) into the webs of meaning that characterize the mindsharing realm.

Now the vast majority of incorporated iso-experients will just belong to the category of others-in-general to us, since they will simply be the companion animals of people who are themselves others-in-general to us. What, then, would be wrong with painlessly killing an incorporated iso-experient if it is just an other-being-in-general to you (e.g., the companion animal of someone who is just an other-person-in-general to you)? After all, I have argued that it is permissible to cause the painless death of an iso-experient (since we cannot cause it autobiographical harm, which is the only objectionable form of death), but that it is not permissible to cause it unnecessary pain and suffering. The answer is obvious enough: just as we do not want others to kill those iso-experients that are supersignificant or significant to us (i.e., our own companion animals), so other-mindsharers-in-general feel the same way about the iso-experients that they have incorporated into their mindsharing realms. Although we would not cause any autobiographical harm or, if killed painlessly, even any affective harm to incorporated iso-experients in killing them, we would cause much harm to those mindsharers who regard these iso-experients as supersignificant or significant others. Not only would we cause the owners of these companion animals grief and sorrow in the present, but we might even harm them to such an extent that this event forms a grief-filled marker in the story of their own lives from that point on. This can apply to people even when their companion animals die from thoroughly natural causes. For example, my wife cannot talk about two very special cats she had some years ago without her eyes filling with tears *now*—the memory of their loss remains intensely painful. This is not, I think, an uncommon experience.

The way in which we can best be responsive to these concerns in our everyday lives is therefore to distinguish between *incorporated* and *unincorporated iso-experients* and to accept that we have different obligations in respect of them. *Incorporated iso-experients* are those iso-experients that have been *specifically and individually incorporated (by someone) into the mindsharing realm,* even if they do not constitute supersignificant or significant others to us personally. These will include, most commonly, the companion animals of other people, but they will also include other kinds of animals, such as the humanly enculturated chimpanzees that have been the subjects of the research that I have discussed in these pages. *Unincorporated iso-experients* are those that have not been so incorporated—effectively, all other animals. Having made this distinction, we can see that the best way to be responsive to the concerns raised in this part of the discussion is to accept that incorporated iso-experients-in-general should be treated as occupying the same moral status as mindsharers-in-general since a harm to, or the death of, an incorporated iso-experient is simultaneously a harm to a mindsharer(s).

I think that this distinction between incorporated iso-experients-in-general (such as the companion animals of other people) and unincorporated iso-experients-in-general (such as wild animals and general livestock) and this way of responding to the issues that arise in regard to the distinction is almost universally understood at an implicit level and very widely acted upon in practice. It explains why a great many thoughtful people simultaneously consider (i) that it is wrong to cause unnecessary pain and suffering to any being, but (ii) that it is permissible to kill unincorporated iso-experients in (relatively) painless ways, and (iii) that, notwithstanding (ii), it is wrong to kill the family's cat or dog or anyone else's companion animals without good reason (such as relieving irresolvable pain and suffering if the animal has a terminal disease, or in self-defense). Simple-minded arguments to the effect that it is as wrong in principle to kill a wild boar (a common practice in, say, Italy to this day) as it is to kill the family's companion animal fail to come to grips with all that we have learned about the limited cognitive worlds of iso-experients as well as the reasons that I have just outlined for making and being responsive to the distinction between incorporated and unincorporated iso-experients. In contrast to a simplistic one-size-fits-all approach, the theory of responsive cohesion's differentiated model of our obligations in respect of all beings provides us with a sensibly graded set of obligations in respect of different categories of beings.

In sum, then, the theory of responsive cohesion's differentiated model of our obligations in respect of all beings builds on the theory's earlier model of our obligations in respect of other people (as shown in table 5.1) by recognizing several further salient features of the expanded moral problem situation. Specifically, these include preserving the distinction between two basic kinds of harm (affective harm and autobiographical harm), distinguishing between two kinds of beings (mindsharers and iso-experients), and, finally, distinguishing between two kinds of iso-experients-in-general (incorporated iso-experients and unincorporated iso-experients). The complete model is summarized in table 8.1.

General Notes to Table 8.1: Information on the Categories of Beings Listed across the Top of the Table

Table 8.1 condenses the full development of the theory of responsive cohesion's differentiated model of our obligations in respect of all beings. Although the information on the categories of beings listed across the top of the table has been largely covered in the text in both chapter 5 and this chapter, I will nevertheless summarize—and even, where necessary, add to—this information here in a fairly formal way so that it is available in the same place as table 8.1 and to act as an immediately locatable aid in interpreting this table. If this formal summary starts to get a bit tedious, then you can "cut to the chase" and simply read the summary paragraph at the end of this section—or, if you like, read that summary paragraph first and then come back and read what lies between.

The categorization of others in terms of their "significance" ordinarily refers to (i) the moral agent's psychological closeness to these others and/

Table 8.1
The Theory of Responsive Cohesion's Differentiated Model of Our Obligations in Respect of All Beings
This matrix addresses our obligations in respect of other sentient beings. The cells are responses to the question: *Are you obliged to respect injunctions 1–5 in regard to the categories of beings listed across the top of the table?* (See "General Notes to Table 8.1" for information on the categories of beings.)

Beings / Obligations	A: Super-signif-icant others	B: Signif-icant Others	Others-in-General C: Mind-sharers and incor-porated iso-experients	D: Unincor-porated iso-experients
1. Don't cause unneces-sary pain and suffering	✓	✓	✓	✓
2. Don't cause unwanted autobiographical death[A,B]	✓	✓	✓	✗ (N/A)
3. Offer saving help	✓	✓	✗	✗
4. Offer ongoing support-ive help	✓	✗	✗	✗
5. Offer bonus help	✗	✗	✗	✗

Note A: The full injunction at obligation 2 here should read: Don't cause unwanted autobiographical death *or kill without good reason* (such as to relieve a being's irresolvable pain and suffering) *in the case of incorporated iso-experients-in-general*. This (italicized) expansion is necessary because iso-experients cannot be autobiographically killed, yet, as we have seen, the incorpo-rated (into the mindsharing realm) status of some iso-experients means that we nevertheless treat them *as if* the injunction not to cause autobiographical death extends to them.
Note B: Another obviously salient feature of the problem situation that would lead us to qualify this second obligation arises in those relatively rare situations in which one causes the unwanted autobiographical death of another, but does so in genuine self-defense. Many ethical theorists seem to proceed as if self-defense needs no defense; they seem simply to assume the validity of this principle rather than argue for it—even though its validity might actually be acutely prob-lematic for, say, (act) utilitarians, who, in committing themselves to serving the greater good, are logically obliged to accept that self-defense is *not* justified if allowing someone to kill you would in fact serve the greater good overall! We will see in the next chapter that, in contrast to those ethical approaches that sim-ply assume the validity of the principle of self-defense, the theory of responsive cohesion offers an explicit justification for this principle—one that flows directly from the theory's multiple perspective account of moral agency.

or (ii) the degree of specifically personal responsibility that the moral agent has taken on in regard to these others (e.g., through becoming a parent or the owner of a companion animal). Thus, the categorization of others in terms of their "significance" ordinarily refers to their significance from the moral agent's own point-of-view. (The matrix thereby reflects the *agent-relative* orientation of the theory of responsive cohesion's multiple perspective account of moral agency.) However, extraordinary circumstances can arise in which, for whatever reason, a moral agent perversely denies their own degree of psychological closeness to, or personal responsibility for, another being and so tries to engage in some rapid "significance-shifting" in order to escape the full weight of their associated obligations. In these perverse cases, the notion of "significance" and the obligations that attach thereto should obviously be viewed in terms of what can reasonably (as opposed to perversely) be said to be the case in regard to the moral agent's degree of psychological closeness to, or personal responsibility for, another being. Thus, the ranking of significance is always agent-relative; it is just that this ranking is cashed out in terms of being relative to honest and truthful moral agents not to perverse moral agents. It is important to note that this means that perverse moral agents can and should be held to account on the basis of the obligations that would attach to them if they were honest and truthful moral agents.

With this understanding in mind, we can elaborate on categories A–D as follows:

Category A: Supersignificant others   This includes the fuzzy and frequently overlapping subcategories of (i) (psychological) *intimates*, such as your partner, and (ii) *dependents*, such as your own children and companion animals (these subcategories are fuzzy and frequently overlap because their members can in some cases and senses belong to either or both subcategories at any given time).

Category B: Significant others   This includes your close friends (i.e., it does not necessarily include people like, say, your teacher or boss, unless you are also personally close to them; if you are not, then, psychologically speaking, these people still belong to the general category of others-in-general for you, even though you need to interact with them for a part of your life). This category can also include specific other animals that you have become personally close or attached to (such as a companion animal of one of your friends; perhaps one that you look after yourself from time to time).

Category C: Others-in-general who belong to or, importantly, that have been incorporated into the mindsharing realm   This category includes:

(i) Beings who are themselves mindsharers (i.e., other language users) or are on their way to becoming mindsharers (like newborn humans) but who are nevertheless just others-in-general to you (i.e., people you don't know or are not especially close to).

(ii) Beings that are iso-experients rather than mindsharers but that have nevertheless been specifically and individually "woven into" the day-to-day fabric of the mindsharing realm by people who are others-in-general to you. This happens when these other mindsharers assign specific, individual iso-experients a psychologically significant place or meaning within the context of their own day-to-day lives (e.g., the companion animals of others-in-general, other kinds of humanly enculturated nonhuman animals, or, in some cases, the profoundly retarded nonlinguistic children of others-in-general). We can refer to these beings as *incorporated iso-experients* since they are iso-experients that have been deeply incorporated into the day-to-day fabric of the mindsharing realm by particular mindsharers.

Just as we personally incorporate iso-experients (typically in the form of companion animals) into the day-to-day fabric of our own lives and expect some (limited) degree of general respect for them from other-mindsharers-in-general, so other-mindsharers-in-general do the same and expect the same from us. The sensible way in which to be responsive to these corresponding expectations and get them to stick—to be cohesive with each other—is to accept (i) that incorporated iso-experients are members of the mindsharing *realm* (i.e., not that they are mindsharers themselves, but that they are deeply incorporated into the general life-realm of mindsharers) and (ii) that we should treat all members of the mindsharing-*realm*-in-general *as if* they were *mindsharers*-in-general (i.e., to accept that we have an obligation not to cause them unnecessary pain and suffering and not to kill them without good reason; however, that is all: we do not also have a positive obligation to offer them saving, ongoing supportive, or bonus forms of help). The practical difference that this makes to those iso-experients that have been specifically and individually incorporated into the mindsharing realm as opposed to those that have not is that we accept that we are obliged not to cause unnecessary pain and suffering and not to kill incorporated iso-experients except in special circumstances (such as to relieve them from irresolvable pain and suffering, or in our own self-defense), but that we are only obliged not to cause unnecessary pain and suffering to unincorporated iso-experients.

Category D: Others-in-general that belong only to the biophysical realm (i.e., beings that are not mindsharers themselves and that have not been incorporated into the mindsharing realm). For the reasons just outlined under category C, these beings can also be referred to as *unincorporated iso-experients*. This includes all iso-experients that do not fall under any of the previous categories. Category D therefore covers the vast bulk of sentient beings, including wild animals and general livestock.

Summing all this up as simply as possible, then, category A typically includes your partner, children, and household companion animals; category B, your close friends; category C, other-people-in-general, their companion animals, and other humanly enculturated iso-experients; and category D, all other sentient animals.

Killing Unincorporated Iso-Experients for Food (and Other Purposes)

In my discussion to this point, I have contrasted the harm of causing unnecessary pain and suffering with the harm of causing painless unwanted autobiographical death. It has been important for expository and theoretical purposes to separate out these two forms of harm in order to highlight the central issues that are at stake in regard to each of them. In practice, however, these forms of harm are usually entangled to various degrees because the killing of a sentient being—whether a mindsharer or an iso-experient—typically does not take the form of, say, painless sedation until death but rather also involves varying degrees of pain and suffering. Thus, although it has been important to separate out these two forms of harm for expository and theoretical purposes, there inevitably comes a point—especially in ethical discussion—when one has to step down from the theoretical, separating-issues-out level of discussion and "mix it" with the messy, entangled-issues nature of the lived world. With this in mind, it is important to remind ourselves at this point—as I did in presenting the theory of responsive cohesion's differentiated model of our obligations in respect of other people in chapter 5—that the obligations that I have been discussing above should be taken to represent *prima facie obligations* of the "other things being equal" variety, and that it is of the nature of the theory of responsive cohesion that these general obligations allow for reasonable exceptions and variations based on further salient features that enter into more particular situations.

What, then, should we do in regard to the specific problem situation of using nonhuman animals for food (and, by extension to other specific problem situations, for other purposes as well)? The theory of responsive cohesion's differentiated model of our obligations in respect of all beings tells us that it is permissible to kill unincorporated iso-experients (see row 2). This is because the injunction not to cause autobiographical death, which, as I have explained, is the only objectionable form of death, does not extend to the killing of unincorporated iso-experients because they are not autobiographical beings. However, this model also tells us that the injunction not to cause unnecessary pain and suffering does extend to all beings. And since we are very likely to cause some pain and suffering in (biologically) killing unincorporated iso-experients, perhaps we should not kill them for *this* reason, even if they are not autobiographical beings. However, to take this view is to remain locked into the theoretical, separating-issues-out level of discussion and to fail to "mix it" with the messy, entangled-issues nature of the lived world. This is because the immediate salient features that enter into the lived world of human predation upon unincorporated iso-experients are twofold. First, humans are themselves the outcomes of evolutionary and ecological processes such that they are adapted to eating a certain amount of meat and other animal products in their diet (I will say more about this when I discuss the predation problem—problem 8—in chapter 10) and are, in general, desirous of doing so.[37] Second, it is a blunt and inescapable fact of ecological life that the kind of death that iso-experients typically experience in nature is rarely painless, to put it mildly. As Mark Sagoff argues, animals typically die violently in nature through predation, starvation, disease, parasitism, and cold; most do not live to maturity and very few die of old age; and many might "reasonably prefer to be raised on a farm, where the chances of survival for a year or more would be good, and to escape the wild, where they are negligible."[38]

These considerations suggest that the relevant, messy, lived-world comparison to bear in mind in regard to the question of the killing of unincorporated iso-experients is the degree of pain and suffering that they are likely to experience by dying or being killed in the context of nonhuman nature as opposed to being killed by mindsharers. Given this, the theory of responsive cohesion's approach to the question of human predation—understood as humans killing unincorporated iso-experients for food—is that it is permissible to kill unincorporated iso-experients in ways that are, at a minimum, no more painful than they would be likely to experience in nonhuman nature and, preferably, in ways that are considerably less painful than they would be likely to experience in nonhuman nature. Thus, the injunction not to cause unnecessary pain and suffering in engaging in the permissible practice of killing unincorporated iso-experients for food should realistically be understood as enjoining us to kill these beings, if we kill them, in ways that are *relatively* painless (i.e., relative to the kinds of deaths that would await them in the absence of being killed by humans, but, preferably, in ways that are in fact much less painful than that). This has implications for both the conditions in which animals are kept for food as well as the kinds of deaths that they are entitled to meet at our hands. (I will also say more about these matters when I discuss the predation problem—problem 8—in chapter 10.) Moreover, we can extend similar kinds of considerations to other problem situations, such as animal experimentation, where, again, the emphasis must be on the moment-to-moment quality of life of the animals concerned, including the swiftness of their deaths if they are to be killed but not the fact of their deaths as such.

None of this, however, should be taken to imply that it is permissible to kill unincorporated iso-experients relatively painlessly "just for the hell of it." The reason for this should be obvious: we have arrived at the theory of responsive cohesion's differentiated model of our obligations in respect of all beings, and thus the claim that it is permissible to kill unincorporated iso-experients relatively painlessly, by way of having first established (and then further developed) the basic claim that responsive cohesion is the foundational value. And because all life forms—and many other things besides—exemplify the foundational value of responsive cohesion, it follows that any form of life (or, for that matter, any form of responsive cohesion generally), considered in isolation, is valuable on that account and so, prima facie, should be preserved. It is therefore wrong to destroy life forms—and other responsively cohesive things —"just for the hell of it," even if, where relevant, this is done relatively painlessly.

However, the situation changes when we consider each form of life in terms of its wider context, which the theory of responsive cohesion is always pushing us to do. Specifically, the theory tells us that although all examples of responsive cohesion (including iso-experients) are valuable when considered "in their own right" (i.e., in isolation), it is nevertheless the case that considerations regarding contextual responsive cohesion are ultimately more important than considerations regarding internal responsive cohesion. This means that, as a general principle, examples of responsive cohesion may be modified or destroyed if they detract from or if their modification or destruction will contribute to wider, or contextual, forms of responsive cohesion. And since the theory of responsive cohesion does not prohibit the relatively painless killing of unincorporated iso-experients in this context, it follows that mindsharers are permitted to kill unincorporated iso-experients relatively painlessly on the basis of considerations regarding contextual responsive cohesion. Thus, it is permissible to kill unincorporated iso-experients if they detract from contextual responsive cohesion (e.g., see my discussion of problem 10: the *indigenous/introduced problem* in chapter 10) or if doing so answers to the needs of others to maintain "body and soul" (e.g., by answering to their needs for food, clothing, shelter, general health, social interaction, systems of meaning, and so on) since maintaining the internal responsive cohesion of others, who, in their turn, interact with yet others, clearly contributes to the maintenance of wider cycles or contexts of responsive cohesion, such as food webs, social webs, and webs of meaning. In contrast, it is precisely the needless or meaningless destruction of life forms—or any other forms of responsive cohesion—that we object to when someone destroys such things or beings "just for the hell of it." In terms of the theory of responsive cohesion, what we are objecting to in these circumstances is the fact that we are witnessing the destruction of a form of responsive cohesion when that destruction does not contribute in any way to wider, or contextual, forms of responsive cohesion.

It should be clear from this discussion that the theory of responsive cohesion's differentiated model of our obligations in respect of all beings is built on top of its more general basic claims regarding, first, the foundational value of responsive cohesion and, second, the relative priority accorded to contextual responsive cohesion over internal responsive cohesion. Thus, the theory's differentiated model of our obligations in respect of all beings places some additional constraints on the working out of the more general theory of contexts. These constraints kick in at the point at which we start discussing not just any old forms of responsive cohesion but rather those forms of responsive cohesion that possess an interior, experiential dimension, namely, iso-experients and mindsharers. This means that the theory tells us the following, respectively, in regard to our treatment of unincorporated iso-experients. (I will discuss the case of mindsharers and their incorporated iso-experients below.) First, it tells us that unincorporated iso-experients are valuable when considered "in their own right" (i.e., in isolation) because they exemplify the foundational value of responsive cohesion. Second, it tells us that we may modify or destroy examples of internal responsive cohesion when doing so contributes to wider, or contextual, forms of responsive cohesion because considerations regarding contextual responsive cohesion are ultimately more important than considerations regarding internal responsive cohesion. On the face of it, this suggests that it is permissible to modify or destroy those forms of internal responsive cohesion that we class as unincorporated iso-experients to the extent that doing so contributes to wider, or contextual, forms of responsive cohesion. But third, when we come to the more particular constraints that kick in with regard to our obligations in respect of unincorporated iso-experients, the theory's differentiated model of our obligations in respect of all beings confirms that it is indeed permissible to modify or destroy (i.e., kill) iso-experients but adds the constraint that, if we do this, then we are obliged to do so in ways that are relatively painless (i.e., relative to the kinds of deaths that would await them in the absence of being killed by humans, but, preferably, in ways that are in fact much less painful than that).

It is important to point out, however, that the same kind of argument does not apply in the case of mindsharers (or, by implication, in the case of incorporated iso-experients, since mindsharers can control and be held accountable for the behavior of these iso-experients). Consider: the theory tells us the following, respectively, in regard to our treatment of mindsharers. First, it tells us that mindsharers are valuable when considered "in their own right" because they exemplify the foundational value of responsive cohesion (although see my discussion of problem 1: the *"Why are humans valuable?" problem* in chapter 10 for a much

fuller answer). Second, it tells us that we may modify or destroy examples of internal responsive cohesion to the extent that doing so contributes to contextual forms of responsive cohesion because considerations
regarding contextual responsive cohesion are ultimately more important
than considerations regarding internal responsive cohesion. On the face
of it, this suggests that it is permissible to modify or destroy those forms
of internal responsive cohesion that we class as mindsharers to the extent
that doing so contributes to wider, or contextual, forms of responsive cohesion. But third, when we come to the more particular constraints that
kick in with regard to our obligations in respect of mindsharers, the theory's differentiated model of our obligations in respect of all beings tells
us that, prima facie, it is not permissible to cause the unwanted autobiographical death of mindsharers against their will.

The upshot of this combination of considerations is that we can reach
something of a standoff in the theory between the claims of preserving contextual responsive cohesion—especially biophysical responsive
cohesion—and the claim that it is not permissible to cause the unwanted
autobiographical death of mindsharers. Yet there is an obvious way to
be responsive to both of these kinds of claims, namely, to accept (i) that
the claims of mindsharers to continue their autobiographically structured
existences are strong enough to warrant the injunction that it is not
permissible to cause their unwanted autobiographical deaths (or, by extension, the biological deaths of those iso-experients that they have specifically incorporated into the mindsharing realm), while also accepting
(ii) that the claims of preserving contextual responsive cohesion—and especially biophysical responsive cohesion—are strong enough to warrant
all kinds of legislative and associated enforcement measures in order
to modify the activities of mindsharers (and thus the incorporated iso-
experients for which they are responsible) in appropriate ways.

This solution makes sense not only in terms of acknowledging
the strengths of both claims within the theory itself, but also in terms of
the possible solutions that are *available* in the case of mindsharers in
contrast to iso-experients. Consider: if mindsharers detract from contextual responsive cohesion—biophysical, social, or compound material—
through their activities, then they can be reasoned with, persuaded, or
simply told to obey laws, and punished if they do not. We can gain the

compliance of mindsharers in these ways precisely because they *are* mindsharers. In contrast, if unincorporated iso-experients detract from contextual responsive cohesion through their activities, then they cannot be reasoned with, persuaded, or simply told to obey laws. If they could be, then they would be mindsharers. Thus, on this one dimension of consideration alone, we can see that the contextually destructive behaviors of mindsharers (and the incorporated iso-experients for which they are responsible) are, in principle, open to modification in ways in which the contextually destructive behaviors of unincorporated iso-experients are not. This means that, even if we set considerations regarding the relative value of iso-experients and mindsharers to one side, it is simply the case that we can, in principle, gain the compliance of mindsharers (and the incorporated iso-experients for which they are responsible) with the claims of contextual responsive cohesion in ways that we cannot in the case of unincorporated iso-experients. (I will pursue the general issue of killing unincorporated iso-experients when they detract from biophysical responsive cohesion while legislating to control the behaviors of mindsharers—and, by implication, their incorporated iso-experients—when they do so in my extended discussion of problem 10: the *indigenous/introduced problem* in chapter 10.)

The Animal Welfare Approach Revisited

Where, then, does my overall argument in this chapter leave the most influential arguments for animal welfare, specifically, Peter Singer's animal liberation approach and Tom Regan's animal rights approach?

Singer is the author of *Animal Liberation*, which is, by a wide margin, the most influential tract against the use of animals for food (and various other purposes) that has ever been written. Singer's argument proceeds in this book, and in various other books and papers, from a quotation to be found in Jeremy Bentham's *An Introduction to the Principles of Morals and Legislation*, first published in 1789. This quotation is the one in which Bentham makes the point that the relevant question to ask in deciding whether or not a being is deserving of moral consideration is not whether or not it can reason or talk but rather whether or not it can suffer. The concluding words of this quotation are precisely: "the question is not, Can they *reason*? nor, Can they *talk*? but, Can they *suffer*?"[39] This quotation occupies pride of place in the opening chapter of Singer's *Animal Liberation*—as it should, for Singer's central argument essentially just unfolds the implications of Bentham's point. Singer then proceeds to argue against many of society's usual, and admittedly abysmal, treatments of nonhuman animals and to argue, in particular, toward vegetarian conclusions (the first appendix in the first edition of *Animal Liberation*, entitled "Cooking for Liberated People," was an introduction to vegetarianism, complete with a list of vegetarian cookbooks).

The problem is, however, that Singer takes up his quotation of Bentham about halfway through the *footnote* in which it appears in Bentham's text, and it never seems to occur to most people influenced by Singer (including philosophers) to go back and check the full context of Bentham's footnoted remarks. What Bentham actually says prior to Singer's variously repeated quotation of him is, basically, that we ought to feel free to eat as many of the rest of "animal creation" as we like, so long as we do not cause more suffering to these animals in killing them (and, by implication, one assumes, in raising them, if they are not wild) than they would experience "in the inevitable course of nature":

If the being eaten were all [i.e., setting the question of suffering to one side], there is very good reason why we should be suffered [i.e., permitted] to eat such of them as we like to eat: we are the better for it, and they are never the worse. They have none of those long-protracted anticipations of future misery which we have. The death they suffer in our hands commonly is, and always may be, a speedier, and by that means a less painful one, than that which would await them in the inevitable course of nature.[40]

This means that Bentham, Singer's own classical utilitarian mentor, *is actually in closer overall agreement with what I have argued here* than he is with the general thrust of Singer's detailed extension of the latter part of Bentham's argument—or at least with the overall message that people have drawn from Singer's work in this regard. For while Bentham rightly proceeds to object vigorously to the idea that we should be in any way permitted to "torment" other animals, he clearly argues that it is nevertheless permissible to kill nonhuman animals for food if we minimize their "torment" in doing so. Indeed, he argues that nonhuman animals are generally *better off* being killed and eaten—or otherwise used—by us than they are dying or being killed in "the inevitable course of nature"!

Although the animal liberation movement is often popularly associated with a principled stance against meat eating (and for vegetarianism or even veganism), it is in fact the case that the principled objection at issue is, and has been ever since its philosophical roots in Bentham, to unnecessarily painful practices involving nonhuman animals, not to the killing of them per se, since this can be done in a relatively swift and humane way. But even if Singer accepts, on the basis of his own utilitarian roots, that he is theoretically obliged to agree with this—as he seems to do in various places, including interviews—he also has to accept that this is not the overall message that he has directed people toward or that people have drawn from his work. Instead, Singer has consistently championed the argument in the second half of Bentham's footnote regarding the moral relevance of sentience, and thus the moral argument against causing unnecessary pain and suffering, while failing to emphasize the argument in the first half of Bentham's footnote regarding the moral acceptability of killing nonhuman animals for food in relatively swift and humane ways. Thus, for example, Singer is candid enough to state in both the opening and closing chapters of *Animal Liberation* that the issue of the wrongness of killing is "more complicated" than the wrongness of causing pain and suffering but nevertheless explicitly states that he has "kept, and shall continue to keep, the question of killing *in the background*" (my emphasis) so as to focus on the issue of animal pain and suffering.[41] But why should it be kept in the background? Bentham, Singer's own mentor, put it in the foreground (in so far as a footnote can put anything in the foreground) by *first* stating that nonhuman animals are better off being killed speedily and relatively painlessly by humans than awaiting a more painful death in "the inevitable course of nature."

It is of more than passing interest to note here that Singer does quote from the first half of Bentham's footnote (i.e., the "If the being eaten were all" section that I have quoted above) in a chapter in *Animal Liberation* in which he explores the *history* of speciesism, but he does this only to accuse his own mentor of speciesism in regard to the question of the killing of animals. Specifically, Singer says in regard to the first half of this footnote (and a related passage from Arthur Schopenhauer) that "One cannot help feeling that in these passages Schopenhauer and Bentham lowered their normal standards of argument."[42] Yet the odd thing here is that Singer at no stage mentions that the very quotation from

Bentham that he is criticizing is part and parcel of the same footnote in which Bentham offers the insight that represents the fundamental point of departure for the development of Singer's animal liberation approach since this is the very footnote in which Bentham proceeds to argue that "The question is not, Can they *reason?* nor, Can they *talk?* but, Can they *suffer?*" As far as the reader is concerned, the passages from Bentham that Singer condemns as exhibiting a low standard of argument (i.e., the first half of Bentham's footnote) and extols as showing us the correct way to approach the question of our treatment of animals (i.e., the second half of Bentham's footnote) might as well come from completely different sections of Bentham's work, even though Bentham himself linked them directly together. Thus, unbeknownst to his general readers, Singer is in fact asking them to believe that Bentham suddenly jumped in the space of a few sentences from a relatively low standard of argument to the highest possible one, which is to say, to the basic idea upon which Singer initially founded his reputation. In contrast, and consistent also with the view that I have developed here, I think that Bentham was making entirely valid points throughout his footnote and that Singer should have taken him seriously throughout rather than try to dismiss him as having stooped to a lower standard of argument in the section that does not accord with his own views.

In contrast to Singer's approach, Regan's influential animal rights approach is opposed in principle to the killing of certain kinds of animals—those that are what he refers to as the "subjects-of-a-life." Regan characterizes subjects-of-a-life as, among other things, beings that possess beliefs and desires together with a sense of the past (memory) as well as a sense of the future, including the individual's *own* past and future, and, thus, "a psychophysical identity over time."[43] He argues that only subjects-of-a-life have "rights." However, unfortunately for Regan's argument, the evidence that we have considered (and which Regan has not considered, even in his most recent work) makes it clear that the only kinds of beings that possess the kinds of characteristics that he specifies as necessary to be the subjects-of-a-life and, thus, to have rights are human language users—the very opposite of his intention! Regan's argument for the rights of nonhuman animals turns out to be built on sand; it amounts to what soccer players and commentators refer to as an "own goal" (i.e., when a player accidentally scores a goal against their own side). Indeed, it is perhaps one of the more spectacular "own goals" to have been scored in recent philosophical history.

In contrast to the views of both Singer and Regan, the conclusions that I have reached here suggest that it is permissible for us to kill unincorporated iso-experients for food—and for other purposes—in relatively painless ways (i.e., relative to the kinds of deaths that would await them in the absence of being killed by humans, but, preferably, in ways that are in fact much less painful than that). When these considerations are coupled with the theory of responsive cohesion's theory of contexts, which places highest priority on the preservation of biophysical responsive cohesion, they suggest not only that it is permissible for *us* to kill unincorporated iso-experients for food but also that it is *not* permissible for us to intervene in the processes of *nonhuman predation* in any serious way (as, say, a matter of policy). This is because to intervene in the processes of nonhuman predation would be to interfere massively in central structural features of ecological forms of responsive cohesion. It would be to interfere massively, in other words, with the very fabric of biophysical forms of responsive cohesion.

To be sure, there is nothing especially tender minded about the theory of responsive cohesion's approach to the question of the killing of nonhuman animals—understood in the theory as referring to unincorporated iso-experients. But, equally, this theory does attempt to take a clear and detailed look at this question on the basis of the best evidence that we have regarding the cognitive worlds of (nonlinguistic) iso-experients and (linguistic) mindsharers. In contrast, animal liberation and animal-rights-based approaches to these questions are essentially innocent of any detailed consideration of the kinds of evidence that I have explored here. (And then, of course, there are the potentially ecologically disastrous problems that attend these individualistically focused, acontextual approaches in any case, such as those summarized in problems 8–13 in chapter 2.)

The development in this chapter of the theory of responsive cohesion's differentiated model of our obligations in respect of all beings represents, together with the theory of responsive cohesion's even more embracing theory of contexts, the culmination of the development of the central aspects of the theory of responsive cohesion. It is now time to put the various elements of this theory together in a coherent summary form and then to apply the theory to the range of problems that I introduced in chapter 2. These are the problems that, as I stated at the time, need to be adequately addressed by any attempt to develop a truly General Ethics. I will turn to these two tasks—of summary and application—in the next two chapters respectively.

IV

Summary, Applications, and Concluding Thoughts

9

Putting It All Together: The Shape of a General Ethics Worthy of the Name

Let us now put the various elements of the theory of responsive cohesion together and see what they add up to, both theoretically and practically. To do this, I will first set out the basic features of the theory of responsive cohesion in a systematic form, listing them as a series of points.

The Theory of Responsive Cohesion in Ten Points

(1) There are three basic kinds of relational qualities, which can be characterized as *fixed cohesion*, *responsive cohesion*, and *discohesion* (chapter 3).

(2) The relational quality of responsive cohesion characterizes the best examples to be found in every domain of interest (chapters 4 and 5)—and even the very possibility of valuing (see my discussion regarding the responsively cohesive organization of the brain in chapter 4).

The particular range of reasons given for judging one thing better than another may vary from domain to domain and from case to case, but the fact that the relational quality of responsive cohesion underpins the objects of these judgments remains invariant. Thus, the relational quality of responsive cohesion is a deep feature, often perhaps not even explicitly recognized, of the objects of informed evaluative judgments. Putting the matter bluntly, we can say that responsive cohesion trumps both fixed cohesion and discohesion in informed evaluative judgments.

(3) The evaluative evidence from across the widest range of domains of interest, together with the fact that we cannot reduce something as basic, deep, and abstract as a relational quality to anything else, points to the conclusion that the relational quality of responsive cohesion is the *foundational* value, the value upon which all our other informed

judgments of value are ultimately based, whether we realize it or not (chapter 4).

(4) If we move from the discussion of values in general (formally referred to as "axiology") to the discussion of ethics specifically, it follows from the above points that we ought to live by the value of responsive cohesion.

Why does this follow? Ethics is concerned at the most general level with not just any old values (like a personal preference for acoustic music over electric music, or blue over green) but rather those values that we are rationally obliged to respect. That is, ethics (as distinct from axiology in general) is specifically concerned with the values that we should *live by* and how we should live by them. The argument that we should live by the value of responsive cohesion can be put in this simple syllogistic form:

Premise 1: If there is a foundational value, then we ought to live by it (to the extent that we reasonably can).

Premise 2: There is a foundational value, and it takes the form of the relational quality of responsive cohesion.

Conclusion: Therefore, we ought to live by the value of responsive cohesion (to the extent that we reasonably can).

I discussed both the self-evident reasonableness of premise 1 and the unreasonableness of its denial in the opening few pages of chapter 3 (see the section entitled "The Idea of the Foundational Value," in which I noted, among other things that the best answer to the inescapable question "What value(s) should we live by?" is surely "The most fundamental value(s) we can discover" rather than "The second (or third or forty-second) most fundamental value(s) we can discover"). I then argued for premise 2 directly throughout chapter 4 and indirectly throughout chapter 5, in the sense that chapter 5 demonstrated the superiority of the responsive cohesion approach relative to other approaches in the important domain of interhuman ethics. When we put these two premises together, the conclusion follows that we should live by the value of responsive cohesion to the extent that we reasonable can. I will say more about *how* we ought to live by this value as this chapter progresses and in the next chapter.

(5) An important distinction can be made between the degree of *internal* responsive cohesion that any item of interest has and its degree of *contextual* responsive cohesion (chapter 6).

(6) Although all forms of responsive cohesion are valuable, if conflicts arise between internal and contextual forms of responsive cohesion, as they often do, then considerations regarding the preservation and regeneration of contextual responsive cohesion are ultimately more important than considerations regarding the preservation and regeneration of internal responsive cohesion. We saw that this follows directly from the idea that responsive cohesion is the foundational value. If we deny this priority rule—if we operate on the reverse principle (or even on something like a 50:50 basis) and so routinely get the appropriate direction of fit the wrong way around—then we will find ourselves routinely deconstructing "large chunks" of responsive cohesion (i.e., contexts' worth of responsive cohesion) to fit in with "small chunks" of responsive cohesion (i.e., newly arrived items that happen to be internally responsively cohesive). This amounts to a state of permanent revolution on the largest contextual scales since newly arrived items—or "small chunks" of responsive cohesion—will routinely initiate the whole process of dismantling and attempting to reconstruct the relevant context all over again. This would leave us permanently condemned to a state that is functionally equivalent to discohesion. Thus, the foundational value of responsive cohesion itself tells us that considerations concerning internal responsive cohesion should defer more to those concerning contextual responsive cohesion than vice versa since this is clearly the best way to preserve and further enhance the foundational value. (These points were all argued in chapter 6.)

(7) Bringing the perspective of the theory of responsive cohesion to bear on the question of what-constitutes-the-context-of-what suggests (a) that the most appropriate way of "carving nature at its joints" issues in three major realms, which we can refer to as the *biophysical realm*, the *mindsharing realm*, and the *compound material realm* (or *human-constructed realm*); and (b) that the biophysical realm constitutes the overarching (indeed, the formative and sustaining) context of the mindsharing realm, and the mindsharing realm constitutes the overarching (indeed, the formative and sustaining) context of the compound material realm. These ideas can be referred to as the theory of responsive cohesion's *theory of contexts* (chapter 6).

(8) Not only is contextual responsive cohesion ultimately more important than internal responsive cohesion (which is point 6 above), but some forms of contextual responsive cohesion are, in turn, ultimately more

important than others. This follows directly from points 6 and 7 above since some contexts constitute the context of other contexts; thus, examples of responsive cohesion in subsidiary contexts should defer more to examples of responsive cohesion in their overarching contexts than vice versa. What this means in terms of the theory of responsive cohesion's theory of contexts is that, although all forms of contextual responsive cohesion are important, the contextual responsive cohesion of the biophysical realm is ultimately more important than the contextual responsive cohesion of the mindsharing realm, which, in turn, is ultimately more important than the contextual responsive cohesion of the compound material contextual realm. Thus, when there are tensions between these different forms of contextual responsive cohesion, as indeed there often are, considerations regarding the contextual responsive cohesion of the compound material realm should defer more to considerations regarding the contextual responsive cohesion of the mindsharing realm than vice versa, and considerations regarding the contextual responsive cohesion of the mindsharing realm should defer more to considerations regarding the contextual responsive cohesion of the biophysical realm than vice versa (chapter 6).

(9) Turning now to the theory of responsive cohesion's approach to the question of our obligations in respect of other people—in preparation, of course, for the theory's even more encompassing approach to the question of our obligations in respect of all beings—we can say that, prima facie, we have (i) an obligation not to harm any others (bearing in mind here that harm to other mindsharers can take the form of either unnecessary pain and suffering or unwanted autobiographical death); (ii) an obligation to offer saving help only to supersignificant and significant others; (iii) an obligation to offer ongoing supportive help only to supersignificant others; and (iv) no obligation to offer bonus help to anyone. Conversely, we can say that within the mindsharing realm, it is, prima facie, (i) not morally permissible to harm any others; (ii) morally permissible not to offer saving help or ongoing supportive help to others-in-general; (iii) morally permissible not to offer ongoing supportive help to anyone other than supersignificant others; and (iv) morally permissible not to offer bonus help to anyone. To require more than this is to ignore or gloss over the interplay between the multiple perspective factor, the onerousness factor, and the beneficiaries' desires factor, which, as we

saw in chapter 5, collectively constitute the central salient features of the interhuman ethics problem situation.

Of course, it's good if we choose to offer saving help, ongoing supportive help, or bonus help to others above and beyond the limits of these obligations. But we don't need a theory to tell us this: it's simply good from the point of view of the person who benefits, and they can tell us this themselves. However, what we really do need a good explanation for, what we do need a theory to help us see, is where the *reasonable expectations*—or, more formally, the *obligations*—that can be placed upon us begin and end. Another way to put this is to say that we need a theory to help us see where moral agents (including ourselves) are *to blame* if they fail to honor certain guiding principles in their actions, and, of equal importance, where they are *not to blame* if they fail to honor these guiding principles, precisely because the theory provides an explanatory account of where and why the application of these principles "runs out."

The theory of responsive cohesion's differentiated model of our obligations in respect of other people does exactly this. If we go beyond the obligations outlined in this model in ways that help others, then well and good; we've done something good from the point of view of the person who benefits. But from the perspective of the theory of responsive cohesion, these are actions that go above and beyond what can be reasonably expected of us—or, again more formally, above and beyond our obligations in respect of others. This means that these actions constitute what are traditionally referred to (employing one of the uglier terms in the philosophical arsenal) as *supererogatory* actions, although I prefer to use the simpler, more straightforward term *supramoral* to describe these actions (the prefix "supra-" meaning "over," "above," "beyond," or "greater than"). The fact that the theory of responsive cohesion allows for supramoral actions is a distinctly *good thing*: any decent ethical theory ought to allow for such actions. In contrast, an ethical theory that requires us constantly to go beyond the expectations that we believe it is reasonable to place upon our behavior is an ethical theory that has been designed more for some nonexistent ideal world populated by saints than for a busy, messy world populated by flesh-and-blood moral agents who are constantly being bombarded by various kinds of demands upon their time and energy in trying to live their own lives.

The theory of responsive cohesion's differentiated model of our obligations in respect of other people provides us with a nuanced interhuman ethics that reflects and reinforces our strong, pretheoretical intuitions that we do in fact have differing kinds and levels of *obligations* to other people, even though these others might be equally *entitled* to similar kinds of treatment *considered from a purely third-person point of view*. Unlike the dominant forms of modern ethics, the theory of responsive cohesion's *multiple perspective account of moral agency* provides a cogent analysis and explanation of what we might refer to as the *entitlement-obligation gap*. By this I mean that the theory accounts for and explains the fact that equal entitlement as judged from a detached, external, agent-neutral, God's-eye-view perspective does not mean that each and every variously situated, multiple-perspective-laden, individual moral agent has anything like an equal personal obligation to deliver on these entitlements to each and every holder of these God's-eye-view "entitlements." This represents a vigorous challenge to the most dominant forms of modern ethics, which have perhaps tried to ape science by attempting to judge moral matters purely from an objective, detached, third-person perspective. Their apparent fascination with the third-person perspective has rendered these forms of ethics blind to the realities of the first- and second-person perspectives that are also held by those to whom moral obligations are actually addressed, that is, individual, multiple-perspective-laden moral agents. This has led these forms of ethics to conflate the distinction between impartially judged entitlements—that is, entitlements as judged from a purely third-person, agent-neutral, or God's-eye-view perspective—and the moral obligations that it is reasonable to require of individual, multiple-perspective-laden moral agents.

(10) The theory of responsive cohesion proceeds from the argument that the relational quality of responsive cohesion is the foundational value to develop not only a differentiated model of our obligations in respect of other people but also a *theory of contexts* (as noted in point 7, above). This theory of contexts introduces, among other things, a significant distinction between two general kinds of beings: *mindsharers* and *iso-experients*. (I pursued the distinction between these two kinds of beings in increasing detail throughout chapters 6, 7, and 8.) The distinction between these two kinds of beings is ethically significant because it

turns out that these beings can be harmed in differential ways. Specifically, whereas we can cause both affective harm and autobiographical harm to mindsharers (by causing them either unnecessary pain and suffering or unwanted autobiographical death respectively), we can only cause affective harm to iso-experients (although I only developed this point explicitly in chapter 8, this development was heavily dependent on all that we had learned about iso-experients in chapters 6 and 7). Combining this understanding with the theory of responsive cohesion's differentiated model of our obligations in respect of other people, we can expand this model to arrive at a set of differentiated obligations in respect of *all* beings—not just people. This is summarized in the theory of responsive cohesion's *differentiated model of our obligations in respect of all beings.*

The theory of responsive cohesion's differentiated model of our obligations in respect of all beings (chapter 8) tells us that, prima facie, we have (i) an obligation not to cause unnecessary pain and suffering to any other beings; (ii) an obligation not to cause the unwanted autobiographical death of mindsharers and not to kill incorporated iso-experients without good reason (such as to relieve irresolvable pain and suffering, or in self-defense); (iii) an obligation to offer saving help only to supersignificant and significant others (which may include incorporated iso-experients as well as mindsharers); (iv) an obligation to offer ongoing supportive help only to supersignificant others (which, again, may include incorporated iso-experients as well as mindsharers); and (v) no obligation to offer bonus help to any beings. Conversely, the theory of responsive cohesion's differentiated model of our obligations in respect of all beings, tells us that, prima facie, it is (i) not morally permissible to cause unnecessary pain and suffering to any other beings, whether mindsharers or iso-experients; (ii) not morally permissible to cause the unwanted autobiographical death of mindsharers or to kill incorporated iso-experients without good reason, but, importantly, it is morally permissible to kill unincorporated iso-experients in relatively painless ways (when doing so contributes to wider, or contextual, forms of responsive cohesion); (iii) morally permissible not to offer saving help or ongoing supportive help to others-in-general (a category that includes both iso-experients-in-general, whether incorporated or not, and mindsharers-in-general); (iv) morally permissible not to offer ongoing supportive help to any beings other than supersignificant others (which may include certain incorporated iso-experients as well as certain mindsharers); and (v) morally permissible not to offer bonus help to any beings.

As I noted toward the end of chapter 8, the theory of responsive cohesion's differentiated model of our obligations in respect of all beings is built on top of its more general basic claims regarding, first, the foundational value of responsive cohesion and, second, the relative priority accorded to contextual responsive cohesion over internal responsive cohesion. This means that the theory's differentiated model of our obligations in respect of all beings places some additional constraints on the working out of the more general theory of contexts. These constraints kick in at the point at which we start discussing not just any old forms of responsive cohesion but rather those forms of responsive cohesion that possess an interior, experiential dimension, namely, iso-experients and mindsharers.

Conclusion: Employing the theory of responsive cohesion's account of our obligations in respect of all beings (i.e., point 10) in the context of the theory of responsive cohesion's theory of contexts (see especially point 8) provides us with a complete account of our obligations. This account is directly (as opposed to merely indirectly) applicable to any evaluative situation. This, in turn, means that the theory of responsive cohesion is as comprehensive as any ethics *can* be. It is, in short, a General Ethics.

The Theory of Responsive Cohesion in a Nutshell

For the sake of brevity, convenience, and as an aid to memory, we can summarize even the above summary, shorn of any supporting commentary, as follows:

1. There are three basic kinds of relational qualities: *fixed cohesion, responsive cohesion,* and *discohesion.*
2. The relational quality of responsive cohesion is best.
3. The relational quality of responsive cohesion is the most basic value there is; it is the *foundational* value.
4. We ought, therefore, to live by the foundational value of responsive cohesion.

5. It is important to make a distinction between *internal* responsive cohesion and *contextual* responsive cohesion.

6. Although all forms of responsive cohesion are valuable, if conflicts arise between internal and contextual forms of responsive cohesion, as they often do, then considerations regarding the preservation and regeneration of contextual responsive cohesion are ultimately more important than considerations regarding the preservation and regeneration of internal responsive cohesion.

7. It is important to distinguish between three major realms or contexts: the *biophysical realm*, the *mindsharing realm*, and the *compound material realm* (or *humanly constructed realm*). Each realm constitutes the overarching context of the subsequent realm(s).

8. Although all forms of responsive cohesion are valuable, if conflicts arise between biophysical, mindsharing, and compound material forms of responsive cohesion, as they often do, then considerations regarding the preservation and regeneration of responsive cohesion in the biophysical realm are ultimately more important than those regarding the preservation and generation of responsive cohesion in the mindsharing realm, and these, in turn, are ultimately more important than considerations regarding the preservation and generation of responsive cohesion in the compound material realm (from 6 and 7).

9. As far as interhuman ethics goes, the kinds of prima facie obligations we have to others vary as follows. We have an obligation not to harm any others, an obligation to offer saving help only to supersignificant and significant others, an obligation to offer ongoing supportive help only to supersignificant others, and no obligation to offer bonus help to anyone.

10. As far as ethics in respect of *all* other beings goes, the kinds of prima facie obligations we have to other beings vary as follows. We have an obligation: (i) not to cause unnecessary pain and suffering to any other beings; (ii) not to cause the unwanted autobiographical death of mindsharers and not to kill incorporated iso-experients without good reason; (iii) to offer saving help only to supersignificant and significant others (which may include incorporated iso-experients as well as mindsharers); (iv) to offer ongoing supportive help only to supersignificant others (which, again, may include incorporated iso-experients as well as mindsharers); and (v) no obligation to offer bonus help to any other beings. The fully developed implications of these points importantly include the point that it is morally permissible to kill unincorporated iso-experients in relatively painless ways when doing so contributes to wider, or contextual, forms of responsive cohesion.

Conclusion: Employing the theory of responsive cohesion's account of our obligations in respect of all beings (i.e., point 10) in the context of the theory of responsive cohesion's theory of contexts (see especially point 8) provides us with an ethics that is as comprehensive as any ethics *can* be. It therefore constitutes a truly General Ethics.

The Basic Credo of the Theory of Responsive Cohesion and Its "Primacy of Self-Defense" Implications

These ten points collectively inform the way in which we should interpret—or unpack the implications of—what we might in turn refer to as the basic credo (or principle, or maxim, or rule) of the theory of responsive cohesion. This credo can be stated as follows:

In being responsive to your own goals and desires—that is, in living *your* life—do what you reasonably can to *preserve* examples of the relational quality of responsive cohesion where you find them, *regenerate or create* examples of it in and through your chosen undertakings, *reflect and reinforce* it in your judgments and ways of proceeding, and so on.

It is important to note that this formulation does not attempt to suggest—in God's-eye-view, agent-neutral fashion—that moral agents should drop their own personal concerns and enlist in a full-time crusade to *maximize* responsive cohesion in the world in general. Rather, this formulation is informed by the theory of responsive cohesion's multiple perspective account of moral agency (and so represents a realistic ideal as opposed to a fanciful one) in that it recognizes the epistemological and motivational asymmetries that are constitutive of every moral agent. This formulation therefore tells moral agents what kinds of choices they should make *in the process* of being responsive to their own goals and desires, that is, *in the process* of living their own lives; hence, the credo's opening phrase: "In being responsive to your own goals and desires—that is, in living *your* life …" This credo captures, if you like, the *stance* that we ought to take in regard to the ten points that I have outlined above.

Among other things, this realistic credo accepts the primacy of self-defense in ethical matters because it guides us in the direction that we ought to take *in* pursuing our own goals and desires, and these goals and desires typically include remaining alive and relatively safe as a fundamental basis from which to pursue our more particular goals and desires. This means that any objections to the theory of responsive cohesion that are based solely on a detached, external, agent-neutral, God's-eye-view conception of the importance of responsive cohesion in the universe betray a fundamental misunderstanding of the theory. Here is an example: "The universe is a marvelously responsively cohesive structure. So what are we supposed to do if a comet is hurtling toward us, threatening to destroy much of, if not the entire, planet? Isn't this just the marvelously responsively cohesive patterns of the universe playing themselves out? Shouldn't we just accept this and allow it to happen?" Well, not if your basic credo is the agent-relative one of the theory of responsive cohesion, since, to repeat, this credo guides us in the direction we ought to take *in* pursuing our own goals and desires— goals and desires that typically include remaining alive and relatively safe as a fundamental basis from which to pursue our more particular goals and desires. The response of the theory of responsive cohesion to this scenario is therefore: "Bring on the comet zappers!"

Still, why all this fuss about the primacy of self-defense? Surely every ethical theory worth its salt just accepts this, doesn't it? Why go to the trouble of justifying it in terms of the theory of responsive cohesion? Well, virtually all serious ethical theorists *say* that they accept the primacy of self-defense in ethical matters—that is, they accept that genuine self-defense can override other prima facie obligations, such as "Do not kill other people"—but it is not at all clear that they are always theoretically *entitled* to say this. For example, as I have previously noted, utilitarians adopt a third-person, agent-neutral, or God's-eye-view perspective; the moral agent's own desires are supposed to be viewed from a detached, external point of view such that they assume no more significance in the moral agent's own moral deliberations than anyone else's desires. It therefore follows that utilitarians are actually theoretically committed to saying that you are not entitled to defend yourself—that you ought, in effect, to roll over and die—if your being killed would serve the greater good in terms of happiness or preference satisfaction. Now how does this strike you? It seems to me that most thoughtful people would agree that it is indeed very good of the person who makes this kind of sacrifice (since it's obviously good for the people for whose sake it is done), but that no ethical theory worth its salt has any right to demand this of us. The reason why utilitarianism in particular is not entitled to demand this of us is because it reaches this conclusion on the basis of a rationally indefensible mono-perspective account of our obligations (i.e., an account that is based purely on the third-person perspective and that ignores the inescapable first- and second-person perspectives—and, thus, the epistemological and motivational asymmetries—that are constitutive of every moral agent).

We can see, then, that although most ethical theorists *say* that self-defense trumps other moral obligations, they are not always theoretically *entitled* to say this. Still other ethical theorists seem to feel that they are entitled to say this on the (negative) grounds that their own ethical theory does not actually preclude them from saying it. For these theorists it seems that the primacy of self-defense is such a widely shared, pretheoretical commitment that it doesn't need to be explicitly justified *by* their own theory; they simply allow it to "get home free" without subjecting it to any real critical scrutiny. In contrast to these approaches, the theory of responsive cohesion explicitly justifies the primacy of self-defense. The fact that this theory recognizes the epistemological and motivational asymmetries that are constitutive of every moral agent means that its basic credo is expressed in agent-relative fashion so as to guide us in the direction we ought to take *in* pursuing our own goals and desires; goals and desires that typically include remaining alive and relatively safe as a fundamental basis from which to pursue our more particular goals and desires.

These considerations enable us to understand exactly which "overarching context" constitutes the largest overarching context that is relevant for all practical purposes. As we have already seen, the theory of responsive cohesion assigns the highest priority to the preservation and regeneration of the responsive cohesion of the biophysical realm. This is because the biophysical realm represents the overarching context of the other two main realms—the mindsharing and compound material realms—and the theory assigns a higher priority to the preservation and (re-)generation of contextual forms of responsive cohesion than internal (or subcontextual) forms of responsive cohesion. But just how large should we consider the biophysical realm that we are prioritizing in this way to be? Is it the ecosystem or biome that we happen to live in; is it the whole planetary ecosphere; is it the universe itself? The answer has just been given. If we accept the primacy of self-defense in ethical matters (which is a straightforward consequence of the theory of responsive cohesion's acceptance of the inescapable epistemological and motivational asymmetries that are constitutive of every moral agent), then the largest context that should be prioritized is the largest context that can be prioritized consistent with the moral agent's ability to live—and continue to live—their own life as a moral agent. This means that, for all earthly purposes, *the largest context that should be prioritized is the earth itself—the whole planetary ecosphere.* We should therefore oppose its destruction not only from without (thus, "Bring on the comet zappers!" when required) but also, and more to the point in our present historical context, from within.

That said, however, I want to guard vigorously against the possibility that anyone might perversely portray all that I have said here as suggesting that "we should not interfere with nature at all" (as if the satisfaction of our own needs were not a salient feature of the problem situation) or that "we should go back to the stone age." I suggest, in the first instance, that any such "interpreters" reread the theory of responsive cohesion's agent-relative basic credo and my comments between that statement and this. The theory of responsive cohesion seeks to guide us in our choices from "where we're at." Even if the changes that accrue from this guidance are small and incremental, any student of evolution, complex systems, mathematics, or economics will tell you that incremental changes that build on each other in an iterative fashion can, in sometimes surprisingly short order, lead to rather bigger overall changes than anyone might have originally envisaged.

With this final thought firmly in mind, let us now turn to considering how this theory can be applied to the range of problems that I introduced in chapter 2. As I stated at the time, these are the problems that need to be adequately addressed by any attempt to develop a truly General Ethics.

10

Applying the Theory of Responsive Cohesion

Now that the central elements of the theory of responsive cohesion have all been put together, and put together in increasingly condensed form, I want to show that this theory represents a successful approach—perhaps as successful an approach as we can reasonably hope for—to a General Ethics that is truly worthy of that name. In order to do this, I want to come full circle and outline the theory of responsive cohesion's response to each of the central problems related to the other main ethical approaches that I outlined in chapter 2. I will not, of course, argue for the theory of responsive cohesion all over again in regard to each problem but rather will simply outline the theory's main lines of response in regard to each problem, based on everything we have learned about the theory herein. Further elaboration would certainly be possible in each case—indeed, one could devote a book to each of these problems, whereas this is a single chapter—however the main lines of response given here ought to be enough to indicate the orientation that such elaboration would take.

The next thing to note is that I will not address the central problems that I outlined in chapter 2 in the order in which I outlined them there, but rather, and appropriately enough in this context, in the order that makes most sense considered from the perspective of the theory of responsive cohesion. The problems that I outlined in chapter 2 were presented in an order that began with our traditional concerns with interhuman ethics and then moved steadily away from those concerns to address further problems raised by animal welfare approaches, life-based approaches, and ecosystem integrity approaches to ethics. However, looking at these problems from the perspective of the theory of responsive cohesion, it is clear that the appropriate order in which to address them is to work in a contextually based way from the outside in; to consider, in other words, those problems that apply to the biophysical realm, then those that apply to the mindsharing realm, and then those that apply to the compound material realm. This way, we can conveniently situate later answers within the context of what has gone before, which is appropriate because, as we have seen, the views we develop in regard to subcontexts should be understood in the context of, and, where appropriate, should defer to, the views we develop in regard to overarching contexts. Although this way of proceeding means that I will be addressing the problems I outlined in chapter 2 in a very different order to the one in which they were presented in that chapter, I will still number these problems exactly as I did in chapter 2 for ease of reference, as readers might well wish to reacquaint themselves with the nature of these problems as we go through the theory of responsive cohesion's responses to them here.

Here we go then. How well does the theory of responsive cohesion do in addressing the eighteen problems I outlined in chapter 2?

Responses to Problems Relating to the Biophysical Realm

Problem 15: The "Why Is Ecosystem Integrity Valuable?" Problem

The theory of responsive cohesive assigns greatest value to the overall responsive cohesion of the largest context, which, for all practical, earthly purposes, means the whole planetary ecosphere (as we have just seen at the conclusion of the previous chapter). I will therefore refer to this ecospherical level of biophysical consideration as the *base context*, for the obvious reason that this is, for all earthly purposes, the basic context that we need to proceed from in considering questions of responsive cohesion.

The ecosphere—our base context—is a self-organizing system that is, in effect, the outcome of billions of years of "research and development" into what "fits" with what. Speaking in highly metaphorical terms, we can say that the multifarious components of the planetary ecosphere have no option but to bump, grind, and jostle against each other in various ways. In doing this they either wear each other in or wear each other out; that is, they either shape each other in mutually accommodating ways, such that they "figure out" ways of "getting along" in a "long-term relationship" of some kind or they knock each other out of existence altogether. Things that can't find a way of "fitting in" with the rest of the system sooner or later get eliminated (and it is this sense of "fitness" that is intended when Darwin's theory is glossed as "the survival of the fittest"; that is, "the survival of the fittest" does not necessarily refer to the survival of those that are physically the biggest or the strongest but rather those that can find a way of "fitting in" with the rest of the world around them—at least until they themselves are able to reproduce). There is no intentional agency at work that causes the elimination of those "bits" that don't "fit"—it is just what happens to things when they can't be accommodated to, or manage to accommodate themselves to, the rest of a self-organizing system. Even so, the outcome of these entirely natural (as opposed to intentional, or artificial) forms of "selection" can be forms of existence that are so exquisitely fitted to each other that it is difficult to imagine that they were not intentionally designed to fit together. But appearances, in this case at least, are deceptive—and all the more so for those who do not have a general grasp of evolutionary processes or, more generally, the kinds of order that self-organizing systems can spontaneously generate. Rather than representing an exquisite example of design, or intentional organization, the ecosphere represents an exquisite example of self-organization. Moreover, the fact that the ecosphere is constituted by elements that have evolved together in a trial-and-error, wear-each-other-in-or-wear-each-other-out way over long periods means that, like any self-organizing system, it constitutes an exquisite example of the relational quality of responsive cohesion: each element has "found" a way of "answering" to the others that constitute its environment, and, thus, of contributing to the responsive cohesion of the overall system. The overwhelmingly important thing about the ecosphere, however, is that it exemplifies the relational quality of responsive cohesion in our base context.

This, then, explains how the theory of responsive cohesion addresses the *"Why is ecosystem integrity valuable?" problem*: established, nondegraded (or well-preserved) ecosystems and, especially, a nondegraded ecosphere are accorded the highest value in the theory of responsive cohesion's scheme of things because these systems exemplify the foundational value of responsive cohesion in what is ultimately the most important (because the most overarching) context, namely, the biophysical realm.

It is important to note that the answer given here represents a radical departure from other attempts to answer the "Why is ecosystem integrity valuable?" question. First, this answer does not address the question simply in terms of the instrumental value of these systems for our own survival. These answers can be added on to the present one, but the answer given here is an "in principle" answer; it addresses the value of these systems in their own right.

Second, this answer does not address the question in terms of trying to show (i) that these systems are literally alive and, in respect of that fact (apparently), (ii) that they literally have interests, needs, or a good of their own (which, it is then argued, ought to be respected). This is a good thing because, even setting arguments over (i) aside, you will recall that I argued in chapter 2 that (ii) represents an entirely flawed line of argument when it comes to answering the "Why is life valuable?" question. Specifically, I argued in regard to (ii) that nonsentient living things cannot literally be said to have interests, needs, or a good of their own, which can somehow be harmed or benefited from some genuinely internal point of reference because they do not *have* any kind of internal perspective. By definition, it is not *like* anything to be a nonsentient living thing. Nonsentient living things just unfold as they do; they thrive or otherwise without any internal sense of having interests, needs, or a good of their own that can be either "satisfied" or "frustrated." We make these kinds of attributions from without ("That plant 'needs' water"), but they lack any internal correlative when considered from the "perspective" of the nonsentient living thing that is the object of our attributions because it does not actually have a perspective. (I also argued in chapter 2 that this way of approaching the *"Why is life valuable?" problem* issues in a nonilluminating circular argument.)

Third, although the theory of responsive cohesion rejects the flawed "ecosystems are alive, therefore have interests, needs, or a good of their own, and so should be respected on that account" line of argument, it nevertheless advances an objectively based reason for valuing these systems rather than retreating into the kind of subjectivist approach that settles simply for advocating a shift in our inner, moral sentiments. The theory of responsive cohesion's answer is an objectivist one because it anchors its claims about value in independently existing features of the world, specifically, the relational quality of responsive cohesion. It then provides an elaborated supporting argument as to why we should accept the conclusion that this relational quality exemplifies the foundational value and why instances of it should be respected on that account. That said, like all "matters of fact," our judgment as to what does and does not exemplify the relational quality of responsive cohesion obviously turns on our interpretation of certain features of the external world. However, the point in this context is that the adequacy of our interpretation is directly answerable *to* those independently existing features of the world of which it is an interpretation. Something does not exemplify the relational quality of responsive cohesion just because we say it does: some things clearly do possess this relational quality, some things clearly don't, and some both do and don't in various ways and to various degrees, which we can hope to explore in an informed way.

All this means that the theory of responsive cohesion's answer to the "Why is ecosystem integrity valuable?" question stands in stark contrast to the kind of subjectivist approach that suggests that we should shift our inner, moral sentiments such that we come to regard ecosystem integrity *as if* it is valuable in its own right. This is a good thing, too, since, as I suggested in chapter 2, the problem with retreating into a subjectivist approach to the "Why is ecosystem integrity valuable?" question is that it does not adequately address the theoretically difficult issue that is at stake, namely: "*Why* should we shift our sentiments in such a way as to regard ecosystem integrity *as if* it is valuable in its own right?" If we should do this simply because it is in our interests to do so, then we are back with an old-fashioned instrumental approach to ecosystems, which needs no fancy supporting argument. If, on the other hand, we should do so because of some rationally compelling reason that explains why eco-systems are valuable forms of existence in their own right (such as the reason provided by the theory of responsive cohesion), then this sub-jectivist approach just represents a staging-post on the way to a more satisfactory objectivist approach. Either way, a purely subjectivist approach to this problem is unstable: if it is to do any effective work in this context, then, as I suggested in chapter 2, it must either collapse into a watered-down instrumental approach or "toughen up" and strive for an objectively anchored foundation.

Finally, the theory of responsive cohesion's answer to the "Why is ecosystem integrity valuable?" question does not simply gesture in the direction of suggesting that (to paraphrase Gary Varner) "the mere existence of ecosystem integrity—of longstanding, self-sustaining, complex webs of relationships between individual living things and between them and their physical environments—adds *something* to the goodness of the world." We saw in chapter 2 that Varner at one point employs precisely this kind of "argument" in regard to his own favored life-based approach, but that he fails to tell us what the "something" that is added to the goodness of the world is. In contrast, the theory of responsive cohesion identifies what that "something" is. Specifically, consideration of the best examples of their kind from across the broadest range of domains of interest drives us to the conclusion that the relational quality of responsive cohesion is the foundational value, and that nondegraded ecosystems and, ultimately, a nondegraded ecosphere exemplify this foundational value in the *base context* (i.e., the ecosphere), which is the most overarching (and therefore the most important) context within which we live our lives. *That* is why nondegraded ecosystems and a nondegraded ecosphere are valuable in their own right, and *that* is why we should seek to preserve and, where appropriate, regenerate these systems.

The upshot of these considerations is, as I have said, that the theory of responsive cohesion's answer to the "Why is ecosystem integrity valuable?" question represents a radical departure from previous attempts to answer this question. However, once we have grasped the essence of this answer, it is relatively easy to see how the answers should fall out to all the other ecosystem-related problems that were raised in chapter 2.

Problem 16: The Subtraction and Addition of Ecologically Benign Species Problem

The theory of responsive cohesion is opposed to both the arbitrary subtraction and addition of ecologically benign species since, setting considerations of ecosystem sustainability aside (which is the point of referring to these species as ecologically benign), doing either of these things still lessens the ecosystem's degree of responsive cohesion overall. Artificial subtraction of species does this because it suddenly destroys some of the mutually shaping, responsively cohesive relationships that have existed in that place; artificial addition of species does this because it suddenly imposes the establishment of new entities—and thus new forms of ecological relationship—that bear no historical connection to the place in which they now exist. This second point highlights the fact that the relational quality of responsive cohesion can clearly be evaluated in both space (and, obviously, space alone when considering static systems) and time (when considering dynamical systems). It makes perfect sense not only to consider the degree of responsive cohesion that, say, a (static) painting has, but also the degree of responsive cohesion that, say, a (spatially distributed) ecosystem has over time. New features that can be explained in terms of the responsively cohesive operations of the system (i.e., emergent features) and that either add to its overall degree of responsive cohesion or at least don't subtract from it obviously possess a kind of responsive cohesion in terms of the dynamical history of the system. In contrast, this temporally based form of responsive cohesion is obviously lacking in those features that are just arbitrarily added to the system—such as the example in which ecologically benign species are arbitrarily added to an ecosystem.

Problem 17: "The (Catastrophic) Way Evolution Works" Problem

In embracing the value of responsive cohesion in the biophysical realm, the theory of responsive cohesion is not remotely committed to any version of the view that we should "Let cosmic collisions (with the earth, our base context) take their course (because that is the way evolution works)." Instead, it is explicitly opposed to this view. The reasons for this were explained in the last chapter when I discussed the theory of responsive cohesion's basic credo and its explicit endorsement of the primacy of self-defense. It was clear from this discussion that we should take the whole planetary ecosphere as our base context in making decisions about the preservation and (re)generation of responsive cohesion.

Problem 14: The "Why Is Life Valuable?" Problem

Living things are valuable because, as I noted when introducing the idea of responsive cohesion in chapter 2, they constitute paradigmatic examples of the relational quality of responsive cohesion, which is the foundational value. As with the theory of responsive cohesion's response to the "Why is ecosystem integrity valuable?" question, this response to the "Why is life valuable?" question likewise represents a radical departure from previous attempts to address it. This is because, as we have already seen in considering the standard objectivist response to the "Why is ecosystem integrity valuable?" question (which transforms the question into a species of the "Why is life valuable?" question), the answer given by the theory of responsive cohesion does not address the "Why is life valuable?" question in terms of trying to show that living things literally have interests, needs, or a good of their own that ought to be respected, but rather in terms of the value of the relational quality that is exemplified by the organizational form of living things. This is an ideal level at which to address the "Why is life valuable?" question because the *defining* feature of those things that we deem either to be literally living things or to have a metaphorically "living" quality about them, as opposed to those things that we deem to be literally or metaphorically "dead," lies in their organizational form. And this very direct level of response to the "Why is life valuable?" question mercifully has nothing to do with the conceptually overstretched and therefore entirely controversial—indeed, I would say fanciful—attribution of "interests," "needs," or "a good of their own" to nonsentient living things in their own right.

Problem 7: The "Why Are Sentient Beings Valuable?" Problem

Sentient *beings* are even more valuable than "merely" (i.e., nonsentient) living *things* (such as plants) because they represent even more compelling examples of responsive cohesion than do "merely" living things. Not only do sentient beings represent more compelling examples of responsive cohesion in terms of their observable physical structure (e.g., there are massive differences between the kinds and sophistication of responsively coordinated organization in plants as opposed to sentient animals), but these beings also introduce a qualitatively new form of responsive cohesion into the world relative to "merely" living things. Specifically, sentient beings exemplify neural forms of responsive cohesion that underpin various forms and degrees of awareness of the world. These forms of awareness allow sentient beings to be more responsive to the world across a wider range of situations than is the case with respect to "merely" living things and so to be able to keep better track of—and, in this sense, cohere with, "stick with," or "cling to"—the changing world around them in more active and diverse ways (recall here that "cohere" derives from a Latin root meaning "to cling," "adhere," or "stick"). Sentience therefore introduces a qualitatively new form of responsive cohesion into the world. The increased degree of inner sensitivity (or inner responsiveness) to changes in the world that sentience bestows allows its possessors to respond more appropriately than they otherwise might to changes in their environment, and so (by better fitting into or cohering with their environment), to maximize their chances of surviving and reproducing their relatively sophisticated forms of responsively cohesive structure and, with it, their own qualitative forms of inner sensitivity to the world.

These considerations mean that although all living things and beings are valuable, sentient beings are more valuable than "merely" living things because they exemplify more compelling forms of responsive cohesion both structurally and in terms of sentiency (by definition, "merely" living things do not exemplify any form of responsive cohesion in terms of sentiency). Thus, considered in the abstract, which, in this case, is to say considered *in isolation* (or considered *noncontextually*), a sentient being is more valuable than a nonsentient living thing. So far, so good: this view accords with an extremely widespread judgment about the relative value of sentient beings and "merely" living things. Even if we might find it difficult to articulate the reasons for this judgment, we generally consider it to be an ultimately extremely well-founded judgment rather than merely reflecting a widespread "being-ist" prejudice. This judgment explains, for example, why many people think that there are at least sensible questions to be asked about killing sentient beings for food—whichever way one ultimately goes on this issue— but that (shorn of contextual issues like rarity and so on) there are no sensible questions to be asked about "killing" plants for food. (Just try finding *any* convincing argument to the effect that a nonsentient living thing considered in isolation—such as a cabbage—is more valuable than a sentient being considered in isolation—such as a zebra. You think you've got one? How many informed judges do you think you will convince?)

However, adjudicating on the relative value of living things and beings when considered *in isolation* does not get us very far because *nothing exists in isolation.* Yet here's the problem that comes with this realization: we are often not particularly good at considering matters in context (or in sufficiently broad contexts), so we really need some theoretical help, such as that offered by the theory of responsive cohesion, in order to sort out questions of value in real-world contexts. Now, if there is one thing that the theory of responsive cohesion teaches us in this regard, it is that judgments regarding the value of things based on their degree of internal responsive cohesion (which amounts to saying their degree of responsive cohesion when considered in isolation) must ultimately defer to judgments regarding their degree of contextual responsive cohesion. Once we realize this, we can see that the fact that the theory of responsive cohesion assigns different values to different kinds of living things and beings when considered in isolation—and, equally, similar value to similar kinds of living things and beings when considered in isolation— does not mean that we yet know how to act on the basis of the theory when it comes to contextually saturated real-world issues concerning living things and beings. The problems that follow in this section all deal with the theory of responsive cohesion's approach to precisely these kinds of contextually saturated real-world issues.

General Comments on Problems 9–13: The Wild/Domesticated Problem, the Indigenous/Introduced Problem, the Local Diversity/ Monoculture Problem, the Species (or Global Biodiversity) Problem, and the Ecosystem Integrity/Preservation in Botanical Gardens and Zoos and Farms Problem

All the issues collectively referred to here represent problems for the life-based and animal welfare approaches for the same reason: these approaches are focused entirely upon the value of *individual* living things or beings and so are theoretically "blind" to contextual issues. The best that the advocates of these approaches can do if forced to consider them—and "forced" seems to be the operative word here since they typically ignore these issues or attempt to dismiss them with facile responses—is to consider them in an unsatisfactory second-order or derivative way. For example, we should preserve ecosystem integrity not because there is anything valuable about ecosystems considered in their own right but rather because preserving ecosystem integrity is good for those kinds of *individual* entities that *are* valuable in their own right, namely, individual sentient beings or, more controversially, individual living things in general. Thus, the influential animal liberationist Peter Singer argues that when it comes to "the case for the preservation of wilderness ... we should *confine* ourselves to arguments based on the interests of sentient creatures, present and future, human and non-human" (my emphasis).[1]

The individualistic focus of the life-based and animal welfare approaches means that they are simply unable to "see" the extraindividual, contextually based distinctions that run through the list of problems given above. Thus, from the perspective of these approaches, a domestic, introduced, monoculturally representative, globally plentiful, or botanical garden, zoo, or farm-enclosed plant or animal is just as valuable in its own right (which is also to say, considered independent of context) as a wild, indigenous, biodiversity-indicative, globally endangered, or ecosystemically situated plant or animal (assuming, of course, an "other things being equal" clause where appropriate for the purposes of the relevant comparison, e.g., in regard to relative levels of sentience and experiential satisfaction and so on). And that is that: no contextually related considerations are explicitly built into the theoretical frameworks of the individualistically focused life-based and animal welfare approaches.

In contrast, the theory of responsive cohesion is not only able to "see" but actively "looks for" the kinds of distinctions that run through the list of problems given above. This is because the theory is, as we have seen, a context-saturated one: the idea of responsive cohesion generates an obvious distinction between internal and contextual forms of responsive cohesion; further consideration of this distinction led us to see that contextual forms of responsive cohesion are ultimately more important than internal forms of responsive cohesion; these considerations in turn led to the need to generate a full-blown theory of contexts; and the theory of responsive cohesion is then properly applied within the framework offered by this theory of contexts (as with the eighteen problems being considered here). Thus, as we have already seen, the theory of responsive cohesion ultimately assigns higher priority to preserving the responsive cohesion of the whole planetary ecosphere—our base context—and the subsidiary ecosystemic contexts that constitute it than it does to those subcontextual forms of responsive cohesion that are exemplified by individual living things and beings. What this means with respect to the problems listed above can be outlined as follows.

Problem 9: The Wild/Domesticated Problem

First, the theory of responsive cohesion is especially concerned about the preservation of (indigenous) wild living things and beings since they are crucial to the preservation of the overall responsive cohesion of our base context. That said, the theory also recognizes that the domestication of living things and beings exemplifies other forms of responsive cohesion—from humans' own biophysically based needs for food to the multifarious sociocultural arrangements surrounding the cultivation, preparation, and sharing of food in the mindsharing realm, to the incorporation of companion animals into the mindsharing realm (and we have already seen that the theory of responsive cohesion assigns a higher level of obligations to moral agents in respect of incorporated iso-experients, such as companion animals, than unincorporated iso-experients). However, the crucial thing from the perspective of the context-saturated theory of responsive cohesion is that the domestication of living things and beings should not actively detract from the responsive cohesion of our biophysical base context. Ecologically informed judgments will be critical in deciding where to draw the line here, but one obvious form of feedback that tells us if we have gone too far is this: if indigenous species become threatened as a result of domestication practices, then that is a sure sign that these practices are actively detracting from the responsive cohesion of our biophysical base context.

These considerations mean that the theory of responsive cohesion favors a judicious balance of wild and domesticated living things and beings, where the fine-sounding but often vague phrase "judicious balance" is cashed out in terms of deference to the preservation of the overall responsive cohesion of our biophysical base context. It remains to say that there is plenty of evidence to suggest that, in numerous ways and in numerous places, we have already passed the point at which the domestication of living things and beings actively detracts from the responsive cohesion of our biophysical base context. This therefore increases the theory of responsive cohesion's presumption in favor of the preservation of the wild side of the wild/domesticated distinction.

Problem 10: The Indigenous/Introduced Problem

The theory of responsive cohesion obviously offers a strong presumption in favor of the preservation of indigenous species and against the preservation (or further introduction) of introduced species. Reasons for this have already been outlined in my discussion (above) of problem 16: the *subtraction and addition of ecologically benign species problem.* However, these reasons can be powerfully reinforced in this context for this reason: whereas my discussion of problem 16 was concerned with what is wrong in principle with artificially adding new species to an ecosystem—and so set considerations of ecosystem sustainability aside by simply assuming, for the sake of the argument, that it is possible to add ecologically benign species to an ecosystem—it turns out that, practically speaking, we simply cannot assume that any introduced species are ecologically benign. Rather, we need to regard more or less every introduced species—although especially those that have an established record of being invasive—as a potential threat to the temporal and spatial forms of responsive cohesion that characterize the ecosystems into which they are introduced. As the Worldwatch researcher Chris Bright points out in his important study of "bio-invasions in a borderless world":

[A] very rough rule of thumb, sometimes called the "tens rule," is that 10 percent of exotics introduced into an area will succeed in establishing breeding populations, and 10 percent of those will go on to launch a major invasion ... Since the global economy is continually showering exotics over the Earth's surface, there is little consolation in the fact that 90 percent of these impacts are "duds" and only 1 percent of them really detonate. The bombardment is continual, and so are the detonations.... [Moreover, we] don't know *which* organisms will become successful invaders. No common characteristic has been detected ... We don't know *where* invasions will occur ... We don't know *when* an invasion will occur ... We don't know *what* any invasion will do. Because invasive exotics can do a great deal more than simply displace native species, they have a considerable capacity for surprise ... Bioinvasion may be the least predictable of all the major forms of environmental disruption ... It may also be the hardest to fix.[2]

Yet if we value planetary biodiversity in any way at all, then we ought to make concerted efforts—and many environmental agencies around the world are now doing just that (often over the objections of animal welfare advocates!)—to try and fix these problems and prevent them from occurring in the future. Why? Because *introduced species now represent the second leading cause of the loss of global biodiversity. New Scientist* cites a groundbreaking report from two U.S. environmental agencies (The Nature Conservancy and the Environmental Defense Fund) based on a "painstakingly compiled list of some 6,500 species in North America that are under threat of extinction, along with the reasons why each species is in trouble."[3] The researchers found that

alien species were the second most common reason for the problem [i.e., threat of extinction], affecting 49 per cent of the species. Only habitat alteration, which affected 85 per cent, was a bigger threat. Experts believe this ranking will hold good elsewhere in the world as well, though there are as yet no good studies outside the US.[4]

Bright rightly reflects that "Bioinvasion is now a profound and global challenge to our economic system, to our technical conservation skills, and to our ethics—our ability to recognize a 'right to existence' in other living things."[5] The theory of responsive cohesion offers an approach that completely endorses the preservation of the responsively cohesive dynamics that characterize the relationships between species and the places in which they are indigenous. And it patently stands opposed both to stopping these dynamical relationships from continuing to unfold (i.e., the "deep-freezing" or fixed cohesion approach to ecological management) and to allowing a free-for-all with respect to the introduction of species (i.e., the "anything goes" or discohesive approach to ecological management).

At this point in our planetary proceedings, it would seem to me that any ethic that fails to come to grips with a problem as global and significant as the preservation of planetary biodiversity—which, as we have now seen, means any ethic that fails, among other things, to offer the strongest form of presumption in favor of indigenous over introduced species—should immediately be assigned to the past. Yet the relatively new, post-human-centered, but still individualistically focused life-based and animal welfare approaches to ethics entirely fail to get any kind of direct theoretical grip on this contextually saturated problem. Instead, there are now examples around the world of supporters of animal welfare approaches actively objecting to programs that involve the extirpation of introduced (nonhuman) sentient species (i.e., iso-experients). After all, an introduced animal can be just as sentient or just as much the subject-of-a-life and therefore just as capable of suffering or just as valuable in its own right as an indigenous animal. Alas, like the influential interhuman approaches to ethics that preceded them, the animal welfare and life-based approaches to ethics focus on certain ethically significant aspects of the problem situations they address yet end up doing (possibly unintended) damage by failing to see these problem situations in a sufficiently broad context. And this, to repeat, is because they are simply theoretically unequipped to "see" those salient features of the problem situation that only come into view when one has an ethical framework that can also accommodate broader contextual considerations.

A further consideration that must be added here is this: some people are quick to attempt to downgrade the kind of argument offered here by suggesting that it has repugnant conclusions when applied to humans. That is, they think that these conclusions can be mapped in a quick and dirty way onto the human situation to suggest that (at least some) humans should be "sent back to where they came from"—or some such vague notion—or in other ways eliminated from "places where they don't belong." However, this is a very quick and very dirty "argumentative" tactic that glosses over fundamental differences between two quite different levels of discussion to such an extent that it represents a significant misapplication of the arguments outlined in this section. Let us consider some of the main differences between these two levels of discussion.

First, the discussion here has been concerned with the introduction of *different species* (such as the introduction of species like cats and foxes into Australia, where they wreak havoc upon the indigenous wildlife), not with the introduction of new members of the *same species* (as when people migrate to another country). These are fundamentally different orders of difference. The fact that the first kind of difference concerns *interspecies* differences, whereas the second concerns *intraspecies* differences means that the first concerns substantial biophysically based differences, whereas the second does not since all human beings belong to a single species. To run these kinds of differences together—as many do—is to confuse issues from the outset. It is to run issues that are properly discussed at the level of the biophysical realm (in this case, biophysically based species differences) into differences that are properly discussed at the level of the mindsharing realm (such as cultural and ideological differences). Failure to disentangle the important differences between these two realms of discussion (which I will do in my third point here) is a form of sloppy thinking that leads to error and confusion rather than any penetrating insights.

Second, even if we completely miss the above point (as many seem to), it is not remotely clear that we can meaningfully talk about "indigenous" and "introduced" *humans* in anything like the same way that we can talk about indigenous and introduced *nonhuman species*. This is because the *point* of the distinction between indigenous and introduced nonhuman species is to say that "introduced species" were introduced to new regions (whether directly or indirectly) *by another species, namely, human beings.* If these species were genuinely *self-introduced* rather than *human-introduced* (whether directly or indirectly), then we would not be discussing the present issue in the way we have been here. This is because we would see their (self-)introduction as, by and large, natural parts of the spontaneous self-organization processes of the ecosphere. To go around extirpating species that are self-introduced would amount to a form of "deep freezing" ecological systems as they presently exist, which, as we have seen, is a practice that the theory of responsive cohesion opposes. But if the point of the distinction between indigenous and introduced nonhuman species is to say that introduced species were introduced to new regions *by another species, namely, human beings,* then it is incoherent to apply the indigenous/introduced distinction to humans in anything like the same way that we apply it to nonhuman species because humans have not been introduced to new regions *by another species.* Rather, human diffusion over the globe has been a process of self-introduction and has thus been "natural" in the same way that we tend to regard it as natural when other species introduce themselves to new regions. Applying the indigenous/introduced distinction to humans in the same way that it is normally applied to nonhuman species therefore betrays a deep conceptual confusion.

But however we understand the indigenous/introduced distinction, the real worry regarding introduced species focuses on the preservation of biophysical responsive cohesion. The theory of responsive cohesion stands opposed not only to "deep freezing" ecological systems, which allows no introductions, not even self-introductions, but also to allowing a free-for-all approach to introductions, which leads to ecological discohesion. Since humans have effectively been specializing in the latter approach, both deliberately and otherwise, through their own activities, it follows that the theory of responsive cohesion is especially concerned in the present era with the problems caused by human-introduced as opposed to self-introduced species.

Third, the discussion here has been concerned with the introduction of nonindigenous species entirely within the *biophysical* realm (i.e., with the introduction of unincorporated iso-experients), not with the introduction of nonindigenous species that are also members of the *mindsharing* realm (which includes not only mindsharers but also the incorporated iso-experients for which they are responsible). If the first point regarding "between species" versus "within species" differences weren't significant enough, the implications of this point, when suitably expanded, are huge. They include the following:

(i) We can reason with mindsharers and ask them, or legally compel them, to modify their behavior (or even leave an area) if there are good reasons for doing so, whereas we cannot do this with "merely" living things nor with iso-experients (if we could, they would be mindsharers).

(ii) The theory of responsive cohesion's differentiated model of our obligations in respect of all beings shows that whereas we are ordinarily obliged not to kill mindsharers (or, more precisely, not to cause the unwanted autobiographical death of mindsharers), we are only obliged not to cause unnecessary pain and suffering to unincorporated iso-experients.

From the perspective of the theory of responsive cohesion, these considerations mean that:

(i) since we can reason with mindsharers and, if necessary, use mindsharing institutions—such as the legal system—to persuade or compel them to modify their own actions (or even leave an area) for the sake of preserving ecosystemic forms of responsive cohesion; and

(ii) since the theory of responsive cohesion gives the highest priority to the preservation of the overall responsive cohesion of biophysical contexts and, ultimately, of our planetary biophysical context, or base context; and

(iii) since we should not ordinarily kill mindsharers;

it follows that:

(iv) we should therefore reason with mindsharers and, if necessary, use mindsharing institutions—such as the legal system—to persuade or compel them to modify their own actions (or even leave an area) where that is necessary for the sake of preserving ecosystemic forms of responsive cohesion. Moreover, this conclusion can also be extended to include the incorporated iso-experients for which mindsharers are responsible.

Equally, the theory of responsive cohesion endorses the view that:

(i) since we cannot reason with "merely" living things nor with iso-experients and since we cannot use mindsharing institutions—such as the legal system—directly to persuade or compel them to modify their own actions (or even leave an area) for the sake of preserving eco-systemic forms of responsive cohesion; and

(ii) since introduced unincorporated iso-experients at best detract from and at worst actively destroy the overall responsive cohesion of the bio-physical contexts into which they are introduced; and

(iii) since the theory of responsive cohesion gives the highest priority to the preservation of the overall responsive cohesion of biophysical contexts and, ultimately, of our planetary biophysical context, or base context; and

(iv) since we are not obliged not to kill unincorporated iso-experients; that is, since it is permissible to kill unincorporated iso-experients (i.e., destroy their own internal responsive cohesion) for the sake of preserving contextual responsive cohesion, providing we seek to minimize the pain and suffering we cause in doing so;

it follows that:

(v) we should therefore support the removal of nonindigenous unincorporated iso-experients where it is practicably possible—especially those that have an established record of being invasive—and accept that since we cannot directly persuade or compel them to modify their own actions (or even leave an area) for the sake of preserving ecosystemic forms of responsive cohesion, this will often mean that they will have to be killed for the sake of preserving the overall responsive cohesion of biophysical contexts.

The proviso here, as noted in (iv), is that if we kill unincorporated iso-experients for the sake of preserving the overall responsive cohesion of biophysical contexts, then we should seek to do so in relatively painless ways. However, as I also noted in chapter 8 in regard to the question of killing unincorporated iso-experients for food (and other purposes), the relevant, messy, lived world comparison to bear in mind in regard to the question of the killing of unincorporated iso-experients is the degree of pain and suffering that they are likely to experience by dying or being killed in the context of nonhuman nature as opposed to being killed by mindsharers. Thus, the notion of relatively painless killing needs to be understood in this context in the sense of "relative to the kinds of deaths that would await these unincorporated iso-experients in the absence of being killed by humans (although, preferably, in ways that are in fact much less painful than that)." This is important to bear in mind because there are obviously genuine, practical limits to how much it is possible to limit the pain and suffering that is caused in killing unincorporated iso-experients for the sake of preserving the overall responsive cohesion of biophysical contexts.

The theory of responsive cohesion does not shirk from its own implications here. In arguing that

(i) we should give the highest priority to the preservation of the overall responsive cohesion of the biophysical context that is under consideration; and

(ii) that we should employ the least painful means available to uphold this priority in regard to the killing of nonindigenous unincorporated iso-experients;

the theory accepts that

(iii) at the limit (and hopefully in rare cases), it is permissible to cause as much pain as would be experienced in the course of other forms of (obviously unmedicated) natural death—which, needless to say, are neither pleasant nor pretty—for the sake of preserving the overall responsive cohesion of biophysical contexts.

Since every plant and animal lives somewhere, it is only by preserving the biodiversity that characterizes local regions (i.e., local biophysical responsive cohesion) that we will preserve the overall biodiversity of the whole planetary ecosphere, and thus the overall responsive cohesion of our base context. This is, in practice, the trade-off that wildlife management agencies across the world are tending to make, but, as I have noted, they are often doing so over the strong objections of individualistically focused animal welfare advocates.

Problem 11: The Local Diversity/Monoculture Problem

The theory of responsive cohesion's response to this problem is obvious: as just stated, it favors the preservation of the temporal and spatial forms of responsive cohesion that characterize the relationships between species that are indigenous to an ecosystem or biome. This means that the theory favors the preservation of *characteristic biodiversity* as opposed to both uncharacteristic monoculture (which exemplifies the relational quality of fixed cohesion) and uncharacteristic biodiversity (which exemplifies the relational quality of discohesion). However, to the extent that humans find it convenient or necessary in being responsive to their own goals and desires (recall here the formulation of the theory of responsive cohesion's credo) to cultivate or breed monocultures for food and other purposes, then, as per my comments regarding the nature of the "judicious balance" that is permissible with respect to the wild/domesticated problem, the crucial thing is that these practices should at least not proceed beyond the point at which they actively detract from the overall biophysical responsive cohesion of their local or regional contexts. This means that, at most, they should not proceed beyond the point at which they begin to threaten the continued existence of indigenous species. If they lead to the loss of indigenous species, then that should be taken as a sign that these practices have been pushed too far; that it is time to back up and back off, or to "reduce pressure" as I have heard fisheries' experts say, over and over, in the context of discussing threatened fisheries.

Problem 12: The Species (or Global Biodiversity) Problem

Individualistically focused life-based and animal welfare approaches to ethics cannot value species per se (i.e., considered as "entities" in their own right) because there is no sense in which species can be said to be alive, sentient, or the subjects-of-a-life (only the individual members of species can possess these characteristics), and these are the only features to which these approaches assign value. In contrast, the theory of responsive cohesion values species in their own right because, as populations of mutually responsive living forms that perpetuate the existence of their own kind over long periods of time, each species represents an irreplaceable form of biophysical responsive cohesion when considered in its own right. (That said, it should be noted that the fact that I am discussing the question of the value of species "in their own right" here means that I am discussing their value in the abstract; that is, shorn of contextual questions. This means that I am simply proceeding on the nonproblematic basis that every species is indigenous to some place. Where a species is introduced and, especially, is invasive, however, then contextual considerations kick in that override the value of species considered "in their own right," since, as we have already seen, the theory of responsive cohesion assigns greater importance to contextual forms of responsive cohesion than internal forms of responsive cohesion.) We are therefore right to feel that the world is diminished when our activities directly or indirectly drive another species to extinction. This is because we have diminished the very forms of responsive cohesion that characterize our most important context, our base context. We have, in other words, diminished the degree of the foundational value that will be exemplified by our most important context *henceforth*. In terms of the theory of responsive cohesion, this amounts to sacrilege. It ought, therefore, to induce a kind of cosmically weighted shame—and an equal determination to do better.

Problem 13: The Ecosystem Integrity/Preservation in Botanical Gardens and Zoos and Farms Problem

Although they might not wish to say it, the advocates of individualistically focused approaches are logically compelled to say that free-ranging sentient animals that actively participate in rich networks of ecosystemic processes, including food webs, are no more valuable or deserving of moral consideration than the same number of sentient animals confined in a zoo or on a farm (assuming, once again, an "other things being equal" clause, where appropriate, for the purposes of the relevant comparison, e.g., in regard to relative levels of sentience and experiential satisfaction and so on). The same goes for plants in the wild as opposed to botanical gardens. We can have just as many "units" of life, sentience, general satisfaction, or subjects-of-a-life in either kind of situation. In contrast, the theory of responsive cohesion rejects such an equation outright for the very reason that gives the theory its name: if we dismantle rich networks of ecosystemic processes and place the living forms that we have carefully collected into botanical gardens, zoos, and farms, then we will find that we've left something important behind, namely, the relational quality of responsive cohesion that characterized these networks. We have, in other words, left behind these living forms' collective exemplification of the foundational value. Moreover, installed out-of-place in their new locations, these living forms will now largely exhibit the relational qualities of fixed cohesion and/or discohesion. The value of the world has thereby been diminished.

Problem 8: The Predation Problem

As we saw in chapter 2, the animal welfare approaches cannot adequately explain why we should, on the one hand, stop the suffering or rights' violations of other animals in terms of our predation upon them, but, on the other hand, *not* attempt to intervene to stop the suffering or rights' violations of other animals in terms of their predation upon each other. The problem here is that, from the point of view of the animal being torn apart, it doesn't necessarily make any difference whether it is a human or a nonhuman animal that is causing its suffering or violating its rights. The influential ecosystem-integrity-oriented philosopher J. Baird Callicott considers this inconsistency to be so significant as to constitute the Achilles' heel of the animal liberation and animal rights movements.[6] (If we assume that the advocates of these movements stand on two legs, as it were, and so have two heels, then I would immediately suggest that the indigenous/introduced problem constitutes their other Achilles' heel, and that this is at least as much of a problem for them as the predation problem.)

The inconsistency I have just described does not arise for the theory of responsive cohesion. Not only does the theory not object in the first place to either nonhuman predation or human predation upon nonhuman animals (understood, in this context, as referring to unincorporated iso-experients), but it provides detailed, principled grounds for *not* interfering in nonhuman predation (at least not as a matter of general policy) as well as detailed, principled grounds for *allowing* human predation upon unincorporated nonhuman sentient animals. The principled grounds for not interfering in nonhuman predation (at least as a matter of policy) consist in the argument that the processes of predation collectively constitute extremely complex food webs; that these webs constitute fundamental features of the responsive cohesion of the whole planetary ecosphere; and that the preservation and, where appropriate, regeneration of the responsive cohesion of this realm—our base context—ultimately have the highest priority when considering trade-offs against even other forms of responsive cohesion.

The principled grounds for allowing human predation upon unincorporated nonhuman sentient animals are laid out in the theory of responsive cohesion's differentiated model of our obligations in respect of all beings. This model is based upon a considerably more detailed analysis regarding what it is like to be a nonhuman sentient being than are the other leading animal welfare approaches. Even the most current versions of these approaches have entirely failed to explore the sources of evidence that I have explored here in regard to what it is like to be a sentient nonhuman animal—which, as we have now seen, turns out to mean what it is like to be a non-explicit-mindsharing, non-implicit-mindsharing, and (very likely) even nonmindreading *iso-experient*. Pursuing the ethical implications of this argument, we saw that whereas mindsharers and nonmindsharers alike can be affectively harmed, only mindsharers can be autobiographically harmed because only mindsharers are able to live autobiographically structured lives. The upshot of this is that, even when we extend the injunction not to harm "others" to other beings in general (i.e., to all sentient beings), this injunction can only mean that we should not affectively harm iso-experients since they cannot be harmed autobiographically. The fact that they cannot be harmed autobiographically means that we are not obliged not to kill iso-experients—that is, that it is permissible to kill iso-experients—as long as we minimize the affective harm (i.e., pain and suffering) we cause when we do so (and assuming, of course, that we are referring to unincorporated iso-experients). Moreover, it is realistic to speak here of *minimizing* the affective harm we cause rather than *avoiding* causing affective harm altogether since these animals would in all likelihood experience pain and suffering in the process of dying or being killed in any other way. Indeed, if humans minimize the pain and suffering they cause in killing other animals, then, in well-controlled situations, it is overwhelmingly likely that the animal will experience less affective harm in being killed by humans than in dying or being killed in any other way.

This conclusion, arrived at through the framework of thinking offered by the theory of responsive cohesion, means that it is morally acceptable to eat the meat of unincorporated nonhuman animals, but that moral agents should also seek to minimize the harm they cause in doing so. This speaks to the need to kill unincorporated nonhuman animals as swiftly and painlessly as possible and not to harm them if we keep them before we kill them; in other words, to keep them in decent conditions— conditions that are suitable to their own behavioral adaptations. This latter point clearly implies that we should seek deep changes in many modern (market-driven, factory-like) farming practices—changes that can and should be pursued from our own choices as consumers (e.g., we should buy meat that comes from free-range animals) to politically driven and legally enforced changes in agricultural policies—but it does not constitute an objection to meat eating in principle.

I think that the general conclusion reached here is one that many thoughtful people hold. They can see the point of the animal welfare ethicists' essentially simple arguments for vegetarianism, yet they feel that there is something missing in these arguments—that there is "more to the story" than these arguments suggest—even if they can't quite articulate what it is. The theory of responsive cohesion is, therefore, among other things, an attempt to articulate what the rest of that story is, and why it is not only a more complete story but also a more defensible one than the story that the animal welfare ethicists have told us.

These considerations clearly shift the moral question of meat eating from that of killing unincorporated nonhuman animals per se to that of the conditions these animals live in before they are killed. If failing to provide these animals with living conditions that minimize affective harm is the "only way to meet demand," then that ought to serve as a warning that there is a lack of responsive cohesion between present human population levels and/or levels of meat consumption and our obligations in respect of unincorporated iso-experients. In other words, from the perspective of the theory of responsive cohesion, plentiful supplies of cheap meat is too high a price to pay, ethically speaking, for keeping unincorporated nonhuman animals in obnoxious conditions; meat eating is morally acceptable in itself, but we need to cause less harm than we generally do to the animals that are destined for our consumption. Surely the best way of saying grace before a meal consists not so much in whether we *say* it or not but in whether we have contributed in some way (if only through our own purchasing power) to the animals whose meat we are consuming having been treated with at least some degree of goodwill and favor during their lives, however long or short (my dictionary lists the third meaning of "grace" as "goodwill or favor").

Finally, there is, in any case, another reason why many of us should reduce our consumption of meat, namely, many of us consume unhealthily high levels of meat. Again, the theory of responsive cohesion points the way here. We are responsive to the biophysical basis of our own existence every time we attend to our biophysical needs, including eating.

But what is the best way to be responsive to this aspect of our existence (in the service of our own biophysical cohesion overall of course) when we eat? The answer is exceedingly obvious: by following an eating pattern that resembles that of our evolutionary ancestors—forget the word "diet" here; our ancestors weren't "dieting," they just had a particular pattern of eating that enabled them to get by. This is the eating pattern to which the human body became adapted, which is another way of saying the eating pattern that is most responsive to—that most answers to—our desire to maintain our bodily cohesion such that we are more likely to hold together in better shape for longer. Once we understand this, we don't actually need a doctor to tell us that most of us now eat far too much sugar, fat, and salt. Instead, we can just imagine the general kinds of (unprocessed) foods that would have been eaten by our evolutionary ancestors, which, of course, did include limited amounts of meat, including fish. However, we may need a doctor to tell us that a non-evolutionary eating pattern—one that is high in sugar, fat, and salt—is responsible for many of the "diseases of civilization," like diabetes, clogged arteries and heart disease, and high blood pressure (which is driven up by high salt—for which you can largely read "processed food"—intake and which can dramatically increase the risk of strokes). Indeed, doctors around the world tell patients this, on a personal basis at least, every hour of every day. (And alcohol and tobacco? Well, you only get one guess as to the theory of responsive cohesion's approach to questions regarding the overconsumption of alcohol and the deliberate and habitual ingestion of smoke into one's own lungs, both of which constitute major health problems.) None of this means playing Tarzan and Jane and trying to "ape" exactly what our evolutionary ancestors ate. However, it does mean taking note of the kinds and amounts of food that their bodies were adapted to and eating in ways that are consistent with that in a modern context, which is to say consistent with human health.

Responses to Problems Relating to the Mindsharing Realm

Problem 1: The "Why Are Humans Valuable?" Problem
Human life (in the normal case) is especially valuable because humans are mindsharers, and mindsharers live in astonishingly rich, linguistically

mediated, autobiographically structured cognitive worlds. (Here we can refer to all the differences between mindsharers and iso-experients that I detailed through chapters 6–8.) Human beings possess all the structural and qualitative forms of responsive cohesion that iso-experiential sentient beings possess (see my earlier discussion of problem 7: the *"Why are sentient animals valuable?" problem*) and much more besides. They manifest inner, experiential worlds that can clearly be specified in any number of significant dimensions—temporal and spatial, psychological and social, affective, cognitive, and volitional—to be qualitatively far broader, deeper, and more richly textured than the nonlinguistically mediated, nonautobiographically structured, non-explicit-mindsharing, non-implicit-mindsharing, and (very likely) even nonmindreading cognitive worlds of iso-experiential sentient beings. Moreover, human beings are constituted as explicit mindsharers *through* the linguistically mediated mindsharing of others. As participants in these mindsharing networks, they bring forth and thus exemplify qualitatively new (mindsharing) forms of responsive cohesion in the world. Specifically, whereas iso-experients live within *biophysical and behavioral webs* (which, at best, are only implicitly comprehended), mindsharers live also within *explicitly formulated webs of meaning*, which, in their best forms, constitute compelling examples of responsive cohesion in their own right. (I say "in their best forms" here because structures of meaning—or the lack thereof—can also exemplify the relational qualities of fixed cohesion and discohesion.) Indeed, it is only through participation in these webs of meaning that mindsharers become mindsharers; thus, mindsharers can only be properly understood *as* mindsharers within the context of the webs of meaning within which they participate.

In sum, then, mindsharers live in astonishingly rich cognitive worlds, which, at their best, exemplify qualitatively new forms of responsive cohesion both internally—from the way we put our own knowledge about the world together to the way in which we structure our own life-story—and contextually—through the creation of webs of meaning that are constituted by the mindsharing activities of mindsharers-in-general, and which, by definition, are forever closed to iso-experients.

It follows from these considerations that to kill a mindsharer is a Big Deal since to do this is to destroy an astonishingly rich cognitive world—

one that, crucially, is autobiographically structured. Moreover, killing a mindsharer without good reason, even painlessly, represents not only an autobiographical harm to them but also one of the most serious possible forms of affective harm to those who are close to them. This is because the surviving mindsharers comprehend what is lost when another mindsharer dies (in ways that are simply closed to iso-experients) and so can experience this loss acutely when they are personally close to the person who has died. The obligation not to harm others therefore extends to both affective harm and autobiographical harm in the case of mindsharers, which is to say humans (in the normal case). This means that we should not kill a human being without very good reasons, such as self-defense or the reasons that apply in the special circumstances discussed in the next two problems.

Problem 2: The Abortion Problem

Although a human embryo or (from the end of the second month) a fetus generally has the capacity to become a mindsharer, it is not itself a mindsharer, or anything like one, for it is not even an iso-experient in the early stages of gestation. Many potential parents in general and pregnant women in particular therefore consider that they are entitled to ask whether or not they wish to take on the obligations that would be entailed *if* they allowed the embryo or fetus to develop into an iso-experient and, later, a mindsharer. The theory of responsive cohesion fully supports not only the right of potential parents in general and pregnant women in particular to ask this question and to act in accordance with their answer to it but also the importance of them asking it, for at least two broad reasons. The first can be easily stated, but the second is more complex.

The first reason proceeds from considerations relating to the larger biophysical realm. Specifically, it is clear that the environmental pressures that people are exerting upon the planet are now working against the preservation of responsive cohesion in our base context. The response of the theory of responsive cohesion to this fact is therefore to say that in living their own lives and thus in making their own decisions regarding whether or not to proceed with a pregnancy, potential mothers and parents in general should have regard to this fact, which is basically to say that, in the present historical context, they should not proceed with a pregnancy (assuming they have an option) unless that child is genuinely wanted.

The second reason proceeds from more detailed considerations regarding what is involved in incorporating an iso-experient into the mindsharing realm. In exploring this reason, we will see that the theory of responsive cohesion overwhelmingly endorses the legitimacy of the potential mother, and ultimately the potential mother alone (i.e., notwithstanding any contrary wishes from partners, potential grandparents, and so on), to make her own decision regarding whether or not to allow a pregnancy to proceed. Let us now see why this is the case.

The theory of responsive cohesion's differentiated model of our obligations in respect of all beings makes it clear that it is permissible to kill unincorporated iso-experients, providing one avoids causing unnecessary pain and suffering in doing so. This means that the theory allows the relatively painless killing of an embryo or fetus *if it is deemed to be an unincorporated iso-experient.* Now, an iso-experient only becomes an incorporated iso-experient if it is incorporated into the mindsharing realm by a mindsharer. The relevant question to ask here of course is who can decide about this incorporation in the case of an embryo or fetus? The answer lies in the biology of pregnancy. Consider: anyone who finds a stray cat or dog on the street can decide to look after it and make it their companion animal and thereby an incorporated iso-experient. They can then reasonably expect others to regard it as an incorporated iso-experient, which is to say that they can reasonably expect others-in-general to treat the incorporated iso-experient *as if* it were a mindsharer-in-general. This means that they can reasonably expect others-in-general not to cause it unnecessary pain and suffering or to kill it without good reason. But *someone* has to decide to look after the animal in the first place in order to set this incorporation process in motion. Conversely, if no one is prepared to look after the stray cat or dog, then it remains an unincorporated iso-experient, which, from the perspective of responsive cohesion, means that it is permissible—not obligatory, merely permissible—to kill it in a relatively painless way. And, indeed, this is in fact the practice that modern societies generally sanction in the case of stray domestic animals that cannot be found—that is, incorporated into—a "good home."

In contrast, an embryo or fetus growing in a woman's womb is not like an independently existing stray cat or dog that *anyone* can decide to "look after" and thereby incorporate into the mindsharing realm. An embryo or fetus is a physical part of a woman's body until such time as it has been born. This means that, in general, no one besides the pregnant woman *can* look after it during this time, which means that no one else *can* directly incorporate it into the mindsharing realm during this time. Even if the embryo or fetus could be transplanted into another woman who does wish to incorporate it into the mindsharing realm—or perhaps even transferred to an artificial womb that would "look after it" until birth, at which time a mindsharer would then look after it and thereby directly incorporate it into the mindsharing realm—the theory of responsive cohesion makes it clear that this cannot be done without the pregnant woman's permission since to forcibly take the embryo or fetus from her would be an assault upon *her*, and, as such, a monumental form of affective harm.

The question of consent is paramount here. There is no comparison between the harm done to a woman (i.e., a female *mindsharer*) in forcibly removing a fetus from her and the harm done to a fetus (i.e., an *iso-experient, if that*) in terminating its life at the pregnant woman's request. To forcibly remove a fetus from an existing mindsharer, which is to say someone whose inner world is already constituted by autobiographically structured webs of meaning, is to cause that mindsharer psychological pain and suffering, potentially for the rest of her life, of a kind that few of us could truly bear to contemplate in any detail—even if the removal of the fetus itself is performed painlessly at the time. In contrast, to terminate the life of a fetus at a pregnant woman's genuine request is to cause the potentially painless death of an unincorporated iso-experient, which the theory of responsive cohesion permits. The fact is that we have massively different kinds of obligations to mindsharers, who lead richly textured autobiographically structured lives, and iso-experients that have the potential to become mindsharers but are not yet and have never been anything like mindsharers. If one allows a potential mindsharer to *become* a mindsharer, *then* new kinds of obligations kick in.

These considerations add up to this: the fact that *someone* has to directly incorporate an iso-experient into the mindsharing realm (such as the person who found the stray cat or dog) before others can legitimately be called upon to respect this decision, and the fact that only the pregnant woman *can* directly incorporate her own embryo or fetus into the mindsharing realm or give the relevant consent for someone else to be able to do this since only she can "look after it" during this period or sanction its removal for transplantation to another womb, together mean that only she is directly in a position to decide whether or not to incorporate or allow the incorporation of the embryo or fetus into the mindsharing realm. Some women will fervently wish to do this, but some will just as fervently wish not to do this. In the latter case, the embryo or fetus remains an unincorporated iso-experient, which, from the perspective of the theory of responsive cohesion means that it is permissible to terminate that pregnancy. The fact that some others (e.g. potential grandparents, "right-to-life" advocates, or even, in some cases, the potential father) might feel that they want to incorporate the embryo or fetus into the mindsharing realm and so override the wishes of the woman who does not wish to do this is ultimately neither here nor there during the course of the pregnancy itself. This is because these others are not in a position during the course of the pregnancy itself to either directly look after the embryo or fetus and thereby directly incorporate it into the mindsharing realm, or sanction its forcible removal from the woman in order to allow its transplantation since to do so would be to sanction an assault upon a mindsharer.

All this speaks to the legitimacy of a pregnant woman exercising her own discretion with respect to whether or not to proceed with a pregnancy. But where does the exercise of this discretion begin and end in the context of human life? The theory of responsive cohesion enables us to see that we are *normally* right to draw the line at the socially significant event of birth in these admittedly complex matters (I will say something about the qualification indicated by my use of the word "normally" here in the paragraph that follows). Prior to its physical entry into the social world of humans, a fetus clearly belongs entirely to the biophysical realm, even if it has developed to the point of becoming an iso-experient. However, from virtually the moment of its entry into the world, a human baby is plunged into an intensely social, mindsharing world. The parents begin to interact with the newborn in ways that are vastly more complex, both behaviorally and communicatively, than were *possible* prior to birth, *and many other mindsharers begin to do so as well*. The upshot is that the newborn infant is rapidly *incorporated* into the mindsharing realm by all around it and is rightly regarded (even if not in the following terms) as an incorporated iso-experient that is on its way to assuming its own fully fledged explicit mindsharing status. This means that the element of choice that the potential mother (or, if acting in concert, the potential parents) had in respect of continuing with the pregnancy is now closed off. The newborn baby is now as much a (human) *social fact* as it was previously a *private fact* in the lives of the potential mother and/or parents. It is thereby now deemed to be incorporated into the mindsharing realm by mindsharing society in general, whether, to put it bluntly, the mother or parents like it or not. (That said, in many modern societies at least, mindsharers in any case simply assume that the mother and/or parents already regard the baby as incorporated into the mindsharing realm, since they assume that the fact that the baby has been carried to term *means* that the mother and/or parents have already incorporated the baby into the mindsharing realm.) And this is why, as complex as these matters are, the theory of responsive cohesion endorses the widely shared view (certainly widely shared in practice) that the termination of an unwanted pregnancy (which is to say, an *unincorporated* iso-experient) is permissible, whereas the killing of a newborn baby (which is to say, an *incorporated* iso-experient and mindsharer-in-the-making) is normally regarded as murder.

The primary exception to the above—and the reason for my use of the word "normally" in the above paragraph—occurs when a baby is born so prematurely or in such a profoundly neurologically damaged state that it cannot yet be regarded as anything like a mindsharer-in-the-making or will perhaps never be able to develop into anything like a normal mindsharer. In these circumstances, the baby can only reasonably be regarded as an iso-experient whose mindsharer-in-the-making status is still in doubt or is already largely or completely closed off to it. Moreover, such a baby will normally be the subject of such intensive medical care that, unlike a normal baby, it will not have physically entered any part of the social world beyond the immediate hospital environment in which it has been born. In these extremely difficult circumstances, I think that it is most consistent with the theory of responsive cohesion to suggest that the choice as to whether to regard the newborn as an *incorporated* iso-experient (regardless of the fact that it is not and may never be a mindsharer) or whether to regard it as an *unincorporated* iso-experient and, thus, to accept the permissibility of it being allowed or caused to die in a relatively painless way now lies in an area to be found between the views of the mother alone and mindsharing society in general. The choice is no longer up to the mother alone because she is no longer—and never again will be—the only person who can look after the baby and thereby directly incorporate it into the mindsharing realm. However, neither is this choice completely closed off to the mother by virtue of mindsharing society in general having deemed the baby to be an incorporated iso-experient and mindsharer-in-the-making. This is because the baby at this stage still occupies a twilight, hospital-based world that lies between that of incubation in its mother's womb and the beginnings of anything like normal contact with mindsharing society in general. In these situations, mindsharing society in general does not yet have, and may never have, any contact with the baby, let alone any direct claim upon the baby as a mindsharer-in-the-making.

In view of these considerations, it seems most responsive to the twilight situation that I have described to say that the choice as to whether or not to regard the baby as an incorporated or unincorporated iso-experient and, thus, to accept the permissibility of it being allowed or caused to die in a relatively painless way lies with the *parents*—generally in considerable consultation with those hospital staff who may be the baby's immediate caregivers. I say "with the parents" here rather than "with the mother" because the fact that the baby has physically entered the world, even if only tenuously and briefly, means that it can be cared for and thus directly incorporated into the mindsharing realm by the father as well as the mother and/or that its form of treatment or artificial incubation can be consented to by the father as one of its legal guardians as well as the mother. But medical personnel also have an important role to play here since they will often be the immediate caregivers of a baby in this situation. Ideally, the parents and their medical advisors will reach a responsively cohesive decision in these situations—and the theory of responsive cohesion supports their legitimacy in doing this without reference to the wider mindsharing society, which does not yet have, and may never have, any direct claim upon the baby as a mindsharer-in-the-making. Sometimes, of course, agreement will not be reached, and a court case may ensue in order to reach a final decision. For example, the parents might want to keep a baby alive while medical specialists might believe that continued life support and resuscitation would only prolong a wretched quality of life for the baby. In these unhappy cases, the theory of responsive cohesion will side with the most informed view regarding the best interests of the baby on the grounds that we have an obligation not to cause (and, by extension, not to cause the prolongation of) unnecessary pain and suffering to any iso-experient or mindsharer.

Problem 3: The Euthanasia Problem

The theory of responsive cohesion's differentiated model of our obligations in respect of other mindsharers tells us that we have obligations both not to cause unnecessary pain and suffering (or, by extension, not to contribute to the prolongation of unnecessary pain and suffering) and not to cause unwanted autobiographical death. The implication of these considerations is that it is permissible to (painlessly) cause both *genuinely wanted autobiographical death* and, in those cases where autobiographical death (whether wanted or unwanted) has already occurred, *biological death*. However, the idea that it is permissible to (painlessly) cause genuinely wanted autobiographical death clearly needs to be qualified by the following caveat: precisely because people live autobiographically structured lives, which, as we all know from experience, can embrace extreme lows as well as extreme highs, it is only permissible to accede to causing wanted autobiographical death in those situations in which there are no legitimate grounds for believing that the person would ever change their mind if they were effectively forced to continue living. This typically means that it will only be permissible to cause wanted autobiographical death in the context of an underlying and worsening organic disease process whose prognosis provides us with strong grounds for believing that this request would not be reversed by the person if they were effectively forced to continue living. This in turn means that it will generally be medical specialists—and often only medical specialists—who are in a position to make an informed judgment as to whether or not this is likely to be the case in the context of any individual's prognosis.

The reason for including this caveat is obvious: the possibility that the person might later change their mind if they were effectively forced to continue living means that there is a real risk of causing autobiographical harm to the person if their request to die "now" were to be granted simply on the basis that they were presently experiencing a very bad time in their life. In contrast, a person is being provided with what effectively amounts to *autobiographical help* if their life has truly run its course in their own terms of reference, if they genuinely "want to go," *and* if their medical prognosis provides no reasonable grounds for believing that this wish would be reversed. Thus, the medically based question of a person's future quality of life—and, by implication, the chances that they would be likely to reverse their request if they were effectively forced to continue living—is a highly salient feature of the euthanasia problem situation. If we are to avoid the risk of inadvertently causing someone autobiographical harm by granting their wish to die simply on the basis that they are presently experiencing a very bad time in their life, then we clearly need to be responsive to this salient feature of the euthanasia problem situation. The obvious way in which to do this is to include the above "medically based prognosis" caveat in any considerations regarding euthanasia.

In view of these considerations, we can say that it is wrong to cause either unwanted autobiographical death, whatever the disease state of the person concerned, or wanted autobiographical death *in the absence of* the kind of disease state that I have just described. If we therefore assume for the purposes of this discussion that this disease state does exist, or else that the person is already autobiographically dead (e.g., due to the permanent loss of their consciousness), then it follows that there are three kinds of situations in which euthanasia either is permissible or might be permissible. The first occurs when a person has positively and consistently expressed a wish not to continue their life-story by continuing to endure either irresolvable pain and suffering or an irreversible comatose or persistent vegetative state (in which case their wish would, obviously enough, have been expressed prior to their entry into the comatose or persistent vegetative state). This is known as *voluntary euthanasia* for the obvious reason that the person has exercised their own autonomy, or volition, in clearly stating their wishes. If medical specialists do not grant someone's wishes under these circumstances, then, assuming the person is at least partially conscious, these specialists are effectively causing the patient to be affectively harmed by prolonging their pain and suffering (including their mental anguish) when doing so serves no autobiographical point—indeed, when doing so is marring the life-story of the author (which is also to say the patient) in that author's own terms of reference. If, on the other hand, the person who has expressed these wishes is already in an irreversible comatose or persistent vegetative state, then a failure by medical specialists to grant these wishes obviously represents a failure to honor the person's previously expressed wishes for their own body not to be left in this state. In addition, failing to honor someone's wishes in these latter circumstances means that medical staff and resources are being tied up when they could instead be used to help others who are at least capable of being helped by virtue of being at least partially conscious—even if they too are dying.

If medical specialists effectively force a person—or that person's nonconscious body—to continue their/its life-story beyond the point at which the person has positively and consistently said that they wish their life to end, then these specialists fail in their duty of care toward the *person*, which is to say the patient considered as a whole human being, as an autonomous being who is the author of their own life-story. Thus, in the above kinds of circumstances, the theory of responsive cohesion goes as far as supporting *active voluntary euthanasia* (i.e., taking active steps to cause painless death through sedation) *at a time of the patient's choosing* rather than merely *passive voluntary euthanasia* (i.e., the mere withdrawal of life support or other forms of life-saving treatment until such time as the person happens to die "of their own accord"). (Active voluntary euthanasia is at present legal in the Netherlands but currently remains illegal in most other countries.)

The second situation in which euthanasia either is permissible or might be permissible occurs when the person has not positively and consistently expressed a wish either way in regard to any form of euthanasia and is no longer in a position to express such a wish because, for example, they are in an irreversible comatose or persistent vegetative state. Euthanasia in these circumstances is known as *nonvoluntary euthanasia* because the person has simply not volunteered a wish one way or the other in regard to how their body should be treated under these circumstances. The fact that the patient has not and will not be able to express any wishes in regard to euthanasia means that other features of the problem situation become rather more salient, such as what those who know most and care most about the person believe that the person would most have wanted if they had addressed that situation, the allocation of medical resources, and so on. In these circumstances, it can often be decided that the best way of getting the various salient features of the problem situation to answer to each other—that is, the most responsively cohesive answer—is to "allow the patient to die" (e.g., by withdrawal of life-supporting treatment and posting "do not resuscitate" orders). This is referred to as *passive nonvoluntary euthanasia* because it is a "passive" form of response to the body of a person who has not volunteered a wish as to how their body should be treated under these circumstances.

It is understandable that some people might ask here "Well, why not just painlessly terminate the person's life processes in a more direct way in these circumstances?" That is, why not perform *active* nonvoluntary euthanasia in these cases—*if* it were legally permissible? However, even if it were legally permissible, it is equally understandable that medical specialists might feel that they had no warrant from the person themselves to take such an active course of action—even though their passive, withdrawal of treatment course of action amounts to the same thing—and so might prefer to "let nature take its course" by withdrawing treatment rather than hasten nature's course themselves by "playing God." These factors represent understandable, salient features of the problem situation and so, to that extent, are underwritten by the theory of responsive cohesion. However, if a person is already autobiographically dead (through having lost consciousness forever), then the theory of responsive cohesion does not actually object *in principle* to the life of that person's body being actively terminated, since the theory does not object to the causing of painless biological death in those circumstances in which autobiographical death has already occurred. (As I argued in chapter 5, if a person is already autobiographically dead, then painless biological death does not represent any further kind of harm to them.) Moreover, there may be very good reasons to take such active steps, since it is costly in all kinds of ways to maintain the life of "someone" who is no longer a "someone"—who is autobiographically dead, not a mindsharer, and very likely not even an iso-experient. Against that, however, other salient features of the problem situation include a family's understanding of what the person would have wanted, what the family itself wants, and so on. This means that taking active steps to terminate the life of "someone" who is already autobiographically dead *might* cause affective harm to these closely related mindsharers.

This last point is likely to come to the fore especially in the third kind of situation in which euthanasia might be permissible. This is the situation in which a person is in an irreversible comatose or persistent vegetative state but has previously clearly stated that they would not want to be either actively killed or "allowed to die" in these circumstances but rather would want their body to be kept alive by all possible means. To proceed with euthanasia under these circumstances would clearly be a form of *involuntary euthanasia*, which represents such a dark area in most people's thinking about these matters that they prefer not to "go there." Even so, the response of the theory of responsive cohesion in these circumstances is *not* one of outright agreement with the (already autobiographically dead) person's previously expressed wishes. Rather, the person's wishes represent a salient feature of the problem situation and one that, especially, might be of great consequence to their living relatives and friends. However, against this, we also need to weigh the following kinds of considerations: the (autobiographically dead) person's wishes might actually be experienced by their relatives and friends as a burden that they themselves feel they should not have been asked to bear; respecting these wishes ties up costly medical resources, perhaps for days or weeks, but perhaps even for years; and, as emphasized by the theory of responsive cohesion, once autobiographical death has occurred, biological death itself cannot harm the person further, whatever their previous wishes in regard to biological death itself might have been. It would therefore seem that the best we can hope for in these kinds of situations is that relatives and medical specialists will reach for a responsively cohesive solution to the particular combination of salient features that are in play in each particular situation in which autobiographical death has already occurred.

The upshot of these considerations is that whereas the theory of responsive cohesion offers clear support for voluntary euthanasia—even active voluntary euthanasia—subject to the "medically based prognosis" caveat that I outlined earlier, it also offers *potential* support for nonvoluntary euthanasia and even involuntary euthanasia (again, including potentially active as well as passive forms), depending upon the particular mix of salient features in each particular situation. That said, the shades-of-gray nature of the increasingly difficult circumstances that apply in regard to nonvoluntary and involuntary forms of euthanasia respectively should prompt us to think about what our own wishes would be—if we feel we have any—in the context of possible end-of-life scenarios and to issue a "living will" that clearly states our wishes in regard to medical treatment in the event of our own autobiographical death. This kind of document represents an important *autobiographical directive* that can help both medical specialists and our loved ones attend to the ways in which we would wish and would not wish our own life-stories to end—subject to what is legally allowable.

Problem 4: The "What Are Our Obligations to Other People?" Problem
This problem has been comprehensively addressed by the theory of responsive cohesion's differentiated model of our obligations in respect of other people. This model was discussed at length in chapter 5 and was summarized in matrix form in tables 5.1 and 5.2 and verbally at point 9 in both the longer and "in a nutshell" summaries of the overall theory of responsive cohesion in the previous chapter. Specifically, the model tells us that, as far as interhuman ethics goes, the kinds of prima facie obligations we have in respect of other people vary as follows: we have an obligation not to harm any others, an obligation to offer saving help only in respect of supersignificant and significant others, an obligation to offer ongoing supportive help only in respect of supersignificant others, and no obligation to offer bonus help to any others.

We also saw in chapter 8 and specifically in table 8.1 that the theory of responsive cohesion's differentiated model of our obligations in respect of other people turns out to represent a subset of the theory's differentiated model of our obligations in respect of all beings. This larger model underpins the responses that have been given to the problems relating to nonhuman beings (or iso-experients) that were discussed in the previous section of this chapter, "Responses to Problems Relating to the Biophysical Realm" (see especially problems 7–13).

Problem 5: The "What Is the Best Structural Form of Politics?" Problem
The theory of responsive cohesion's answer is, of course, that the best structure for politics is the structure that most exemplifies the relational

quality of responsive cohesion in the domain of politics. More specifically, this means that the best structural form of politics is a democratic structure. This is because, as we saw in chapter 4, this is the form of politics in which both a government and the population it governs cohere in virtue of their mutual responsiveness to each other: governments are answerable to the people they govern in various ways (including free and fair elections, a free press, an independent judiciary, and so on) and the people they govern are answerable to the government in various ways (through the laws of the land). This structural form of politics exemplifies the relational quality of responsive cohesion in the structure of the polis itself.

Problem 6: The "What Is the Best 'Flavor' of Politics?" Problem

In view of the answer to problem 5, above, this question effectively becomes: "What is the best kind of democracy?" or "What kind of democracy should we (democratically) strive to create?" Putting the short answer somewhat rhetorically, we can say that the theory of responsive cohesion's answer is that the *kind* of democracy we should strive to create is, essentially, a *kind* democracy. What this means, and the reason for putting it this way, can be explained as follows. According to the theory of responsive cohesion, we do not, *as individual moral agents* (which has been the unremitting focus of my concerns in this book), have an obligation to offer saving help to other-people-in-general. However, when we consider the distinction between supersignificant others, significant others, and others-in-general in our capacity as *political citizens*, as opposed to private individuals who are just trying to get on with our own lives in the best ways we can, then we can see that the membership of these categories of people shifts as follows. If I consider others *from my perspective as a member of a particular polis*—that is, from my perspective as a member of a particular politically identified citizenry, and here let's take the most common modern example and say from my perspective as a member of a particular nation-state—then I can see that the distribution of who is a significant other and who is an other-in-general falls as follows. Those who live in other nation-states are, in political terms, others-in-general to me. In contrast, those who live in my nation-state are, in political terms, my significant others. These are the people whose views I have no choice but to take account of—if only through

respecting the outcomes of their collective decisions at the ballot box—
and vice versa.

Now, according to the theory of responsive cohesion, we owe saving
help to significant others but not to others-in-general. This, together with
the preceding analysis, straightforwardly suggests that we therefore owe
saving help *at the political level* to those who are our significant others *at
the political level*. What this means is that although we do not, *as private
individuals*, owe saving help to other private individuals who are others-
in-general to us, we do have an obligation to support a (democratic) form
of *politics* that will offer saving help to other members of our nation-
state since these people represent significant others *at the political level*.
This means that, according to the theory of responsive cohesion, we
should seek to pursue the kind of democracy that offers support to those
in serious need; our democratic politics should have a distinctly "social"
flavor; it should be, as I said at the beginning of this discussion, a *kind*
democracy.

I think that this kind of analysis—which represents a direct extension
of the theory of responsive cohesion to the political level—provides
us with a solid basis for understanding something that many of us feel
but find hard to articulate with clear reasons. This is the feeling—which
may arise in an acute form if we walk past a beggar on the street for
example—that we are not *directly obliged* to offer saving help to others-
in-general (although we are still free to give such help), but that we are
obliged *as political citizens* to support the kind of democratically elected
government that does offer such help through the taxes we pay—*and
ought to be prepared to pay* (which brings us directly to the next point).

We can easily extend the above analysis and say that if other members
of our nation-state in general are our significant others at the level of
political consideration, then representatives of the government are, in a
sense, our supersignificant others at the level of political consideration.
Now, according to the theory of responsive cohesion, we owe ongoing
supportive help to those who are supersignificant others. So how does
this fit in? Well, perfectly, because we do deem it appropriate to offer ongoing supportive help in respect of these supersignificant others; specifically, we pay taxes on an ongoing basis to support their programs. Of
course, we do not pay these taxes to them as individuals, and the theory
of responsive cohesion suggests precisely that we do not owe them these

payments on a personal basis since, considered on a personal basis, these people are just others-in-general to us, and we don't even owe saving help to others-in-general, let alone ongoing supportive help. However, we do owe these people the ongoing supportive help of our taxes in their capacity as representatives of a government that is pursuing the governance of our own country because it is *in that capacity* that they are supersignificant others to us. That said, we do not owe these people ongoing supportive help at the ballot box or in the media because the question of the kind or "flavor" of democratic politics that we should pursue is subsidiary to the question of its structural form. And, indeed, it is typically because people object to the kind or "flavor" of the democratic politics that is being pursued by their government that they seek to use democratic structures in order to change it.

This kind of analysis can be extended to still higher levels of political consideration. Thus, at the level of international politics, some other countries represent supersignificant and significant others to one's own country, and so on. Bringing the perspective of the theory of responsive cohesion to bear on this transnational level of politics again suggests that although you, as an individual, owe nothing directly to these other countries, there are kinds of help that your nation-state will owe to some of these other nation-states. And this kind of analysis can be pushed to a more global level as well in which we consider ourselves to be members of certain confederations of countries that in turn recognize other confederations as their equivalent of supersignificant others, significant others, and others-in-general. Suffice it to say that the general rule in pursuing this kind of analysis is basically that entities that were others-in-general at one level of political consideration move "closer" to you (i.e., come to be seen as significant or supersignificant others) as you move to higher levels of political consideration. However, the obligations that are then entailed by their now "closer," or more significant, classification are owed *at that higher level* and not at a lower level, since consideration at a lower level would render them, once again, beyond the sphere of our obligations in respect of that lower level.

These last remarks are, necessarily, quite abstract as it has never been my intention in this book to pursue the wider political implications of the theory of responsive cohesion beyond the great many that have already been explicitly or implicitly discussed in response to the eighteen problems addressed in this chapter. Instead, my primary task in this book has been to offer a General *Ethics* (or an *ethical* "Theory of Everything"), not a General *Politics* (or a *political* "Theory of Everything"). However, I do hope that others might pursue the suggestive ideas that have been outlined in this section.

That said, the main point in this section has simply been to show that the theory of responsive cohesion goes beyond endorsing democratic forms of politics in general to endorse democratic forms of politics that have a strong "social" flavor in particular. From the perspective of the theory of responsive cohesion, we could therefore say that socially oriented democracies are "sweet" while non-socially oriented democracies are "sour." Of course, one could perhaps intuit that something like this would be the view endorsed by the theory of responsive cohesion simply by asking what kind of society would best exemplify the relational quality of responsive cohesion. In which case, why not proceed simply from this basic insight and forego the more detailed level of analysis that I have outlined above? The answer is that going into the analytical possibilities offered by transposing the theory of responsive cohesion's differentiated model of our obligations to the political level (so that, appropriately reinterpreted, it becomes a differentiated model of our political obligations) enables us to see in rather more detail why, and to what extent, the theory of responsive cohesion endorses a "sweet" form of democratic politics rather than a "sour" form. Moreover, this discussion has also helped to demonstrate that, whether you proceed simply from the theory of responsive cohesion's foundational value of responsive cohesion, or from its more elaborated ideas, such as its differentiated model of obligations, you get to the same answer. This speaks to the internal consistency of the theory.

Responses to Problems Relating to the Human-Constructed Realm (or the Compound Material Realm)

Problem 18: The Human-Constructed Environment Problem or the Comprehensiveness Problem

I explained in both chapters 1 and 2 that we do not presently have an ethics that is *directly* applicable to issues regarding the human-constructed environment—or what I later referred to, more formally, in chapter 6, as the compound material realm. I also explained that any ethics that cannot directly address problems in this "third realm" is not even a candidate for a General Ethics. This means that we can think of this last, human-constructed environment problem as a test for the *comprehensiveness* of any approach that is already able to address problems in respect of the biophysical and mindsharing realms. For this reason, it is convenient to refer to this problem not only as the *human-constructed environment problem* but also as the *comprehensiveness problem*, which is what I have done in the heading for this section.

We have now seen in some detail that the theory of responsive cohesion is *directly* applicable to questions regarding the human-constructed realm. If the theory of responsive cohesion posited some kind of ultimate value such as the possession of a soul or rationality, the ability to feel, or being alive (i.e., those values that have been held to apply directly to humans, sentient beings in general, or living things in general, respectively), then the limited nature of this ultimate value would be such that the theory would not be directly applicable to the nonhuman, nonsentient, and nonliving human-constructed realm. However, as we have seen, the theory of responsive cohesion makes the case that the relational quality of responsive cohesion is the foundational value, and since everything is organized in one way or another, this means that the theory is applicable to everything—it is, indeed, an ethical "Theory of Everything." Thus, in regard to the human-constructed (or compound material) realm, the theory says, in short:

When you make material things, make them so that they exemplify both contextual and internal responsive cohesion. If tough choices have to be made between these two forms of responsive cohesion, then give priority to contextual responsive cohesion over internal responsive cohesion. And if tough choices have to be made between contextual forms of responsive cohesion themselves, then give priority to biophysical over mindsharing forms of responsive cohesion, and mindsharing over compound material forms of responsive cohesion. Or in simpler terms, give priority to contextual responsive cohesion with the natural realm over the human social realm, and the human social realm over the human-constructed realm. But on no account engage in prioritizing things in any of these ways unless you are confronted with a genuinely forced choice. The thing to aim for is responsive cohesion at all levels. To settle for less is actually to settle for a failure of design.

I argued all these points with specific reference to the built environment —which is the most "in our faces" example of the human-constructed realm—in developing the theory of responsive cohesion's theory of contexts in chapter 6. However, these points are, of course, applicable to any aspect of the human-constructed (or compound material) realm.

But even if the theory of responsive cohesion is applicable in principle to the human-constructed (or compound material) realm, we might still want to ask the following kinds of questions. First, is this aspect of the theory worth taking seriously or is it just philosophical pie-in-the-sky with no real connection to such eminently practical activities as designing and constructing material things such as buildings? And if this aspect of the theory is worth taking seriously, is it just laboring the obvious and so not saying anything new, at least relative to the dominant conventions of those practices that are primarily involved in creating the human-constructed realm? According to the Australian architects and university architecture teachers Terry Williamson, Antony Radford, and Helen Bennetts, who have picked up on a shorter, earlier version of the ideas that I am advancing here, these ideas are eminently practicable, mark a distinct change in terms of the dominant conventions of these practices, and so ought to make a considerable difference to the ways in which planners, architects, designers, and builders proceed. In the last chapter of their book *Understanding Sustainable Architecture*, Williamson, Radford, and Bennetts provide a clear, succinct outline of the concept of responsive cohesion, with examples relating it to the design process (I include this outline here simply because it can often be instructive to approach new ideas, such as those that I have been developing in this book, through the words of several authors):

Warwick Fox uses the term "responsive cohesion" to describe a state in which the various elements of a "thing" (design work, community, creature) or process (design, construction, etc.) exhibit a reciprocal interaction between elements that constitute it, and the context in which it is located. The adjective responsive refers to the way in which the elements of the thing respond to the challenges set by the other elements: responses to the claims of different stakeholders in a design process, or to the impacts of different building elements in a design work. The noun cohesion refers to the way the result holds together: mutual accommodation in a design process, or a sense of unity in a design work. Responsive cohesion contrasts with domination by one factor, pattern, or force, and equally with the absence of any cohesion, where work or process appear anarchic and uncontrolled (Fox 2000: 219). In the context of sustainable architecture, the various elements of the design will be responding to the objectives of the programme and the means for the production of a building. It also suggests that the architect will be more of a pluralist than a formal purist.[7]

Williamson, Radford, and Bennetts then proceed to argue that the contextual implications of the idea of responsive cohesion mark a distinct change in terms of the dominant conventions of architectural design and philosophy, and so ought to make a considerable difference to the ways in which planners, architects, designers, and builders proceed:

> Fox argues that upholding the principle of responsive cohesion in sustainable architecture entails responding to ecological, social and built contexts, in that order of priority (Fox 2000: 225). Similarly, architect Paul Pholeros characterizes architecture as concerned with place, people and stuff, in that order, which shows agreement about priorities between architect and philosopher.... The emphasis on order is important.... The orthodox anthropocentric position in both architecture and philosophy would have put the social context ahead of the ecological context. [The authors indicate in a chapter note at this point that "Paul Pholeros says 'he used to put people first', but now considers the environmental issues of place to be paramount (personal communication)." Although no reference is provided to any published work by Pholeros, it can be seen that the priority ordering that the theory of responsive cohesion gives to contextual responsive cohesion over internal (or subcontextual forms of) responsive cohesion explains why Pholeros was right to change his ordering.] Putting ecological [concerns] first illustrates the degree to which environmental concerns have moved to the forefront. Architecture is most obviously manifested in the third concern, the stuff or built context, including the aesthetical tectonics of space and form as well as building and landscape materials. *Indeed, conventionally architecture would put concern about stuff first, and placing this last in the order corresponds to a view of the issue* [that asks] *what can architecture mean for sustainability rather than vice versa; in other words how can the stuff of architecture be mobilized to advance our sustainability objectives for the environment and society* [my emphasis].[8]

It is worth adding here that the contextual priority ordering that emerges from the theory of responsive cohesion's theory of contexts has equally significant implications for many other aspects of our lives as well—think of the design (or lack of it) and manufacture not only of the built environment (so much of which is thoroughly dispiriting) but of almost everything we use.

Williamson, Radford, and Bennetts have drawn on the concept of responsive cohesion not only in their theoretical work (as evidenced by the book from which I have just quoted) but also in their research into the design and procedural practices of some award-winning Australian architects. For example, during the time in which I have been writing this book, Williamson and his colleagues have won an approximately A$250,000 research award (spread over three years) from the Australian Research Council for a project entitled "Building and Ethics: Understanding A Corpus of Contemporary Australian Award-Winning Houses as Responses to Ecological, Social and Built Contexts." Their project proposal utilizes the concept of responsive cohesion in the formulation of the project's working hypothesis and states that the results will be analyzed "within the responsive cohesion framework."[9]

Happily for the theory that I am advancing, then, the work that is being done by Williamson and his colleagues at the University of Adelaide allows me to make the claim that the theory of responsive cohesion is not only applicable *in principle* to the human-constructed realm but is *already being applied* by at least these architect researchers in terms of both theory and practice-related research. Taken together with the fact that the theory of responsive cohesion is also applicable to the biophysical and mindsharing realms—as evidenced by its approach to the other seventeen problems that I have addressed in this chapter—it is reasonable to conclude that the theory's direct applicability to the human-constructed realm means that it passes the comprehensiveness test for being classed as a General Ethics. Moreover, it is the only theory I know of that passes this test—and, thus, the only candidate I know of for a General Ethics—since I know of no other approach to ethics that, in addition to being *directly* applicable to the biophysical and mindsharing realms, is also *directly* applicable to the human-constructed realm.

Let us conclude.

11

Conclusion

What do we know?

A Brief Overview of the Theory of Responsive Cohesion

I have argued that our most informed evaluative judgments across the broadest range of domains of interest leads to the conclusion that the best examples in each domain exemplify a common feature, namely, the relational quality of responsive cohesion (as opposed to fixed cohesion or discohesion). Different kinds of reasons will be given in each instance as to why these examples are superior to their alternatives, but the fact remains that they all exemplify the relational quality of responsive cohesion. Moreover, when the evaluative evidence from across the widest range of domains of interest is taken together with the fact that we cannot reduce something as basic, deep, and abstract as a relational quality to some more primitive notion, then we are driven to the conclusion that the relational quality of responsive cohesion is the *foundational* value, the value upon which all our other informed judgments of value are ultimately based, whether we realize it or not.

If we accept that responsive cohesion is the foundational value and proceed to push this understanding forward, then the rest of the theory of responsive cohesion can be viewed (at least in retrospect) as falling out as a matter of course. For example, if we apply the basic method of the theory of responsive cohesion to interhuman ethics (i.e., by defining the problem situation, specifying the salient features of this problem situation, and then working toward a solution that exhibits the most responsively cohesive relationship between these salient features, i.e., the solution that can best be characterized in terms of these salient features answering to each other in the service of generating and maintaining cohesion overall), then we are more or less compelled to take into account considerations regarding (i) each moral agent's multiple epistemological and motivational perspectives (the multiple perspective factor), (ii) the level of onerousness involved in acting on behalf of potential beneficiaries (the onerousness factor), and (iii) the potential beneficiaries' levels of concern to have their desires met (the beneficiaries' desires factor). When we do this, we can see that an obvious responsively cohesive solution to the interhuman ethics problem situation effectively "falls out." Specifically, because moral agents are generally more knowledgeable about and motivated to act on behalf of those to whom they are personally closest, and because it generally becomes increasingly more onerous for any moral agent to meet the desires of potential beneficiaries as we move across the harm–help spectrum of possibilities from simply not harming to actively helping (i.e., simply not harming is generally a lot easier than actively helping), and because the concern of potential beneficiaries to have their desires met generally decreases as we move across this spectrum of possibilities (i.e., people generally want not to be harmed a lot more strongly than they want actively to be helped), then the following responsively cohesive solution effectively "suggests itself": we should "wind down" the expectation that moral agents should act on behalf of others as the beneficiaries concerned become more psychologically remote from any given moral agent *and* as we move across the not harming-actively helping range of possibilities. When we do this, we are left with the theory of responsive cohesion's *differentiated model of our obligations in respect of other people.*

In my view this model represents the most sensible and defensible approach to the interhuman ethics problem situation precisely because it bows to the acceptance of features of the problem situation that cannot be escaped. Yet this approach is radically at odds with most modern ethical thinking. Nowhere is this more obvious than in regard to the theory of responsive cohesion's explicit highlighting and acceptance of a multiple perspective account of moral agency. This is because modern ethical thinking in its dominant and (as feminists would have it) "masculine" Kantian- and utilitarian-inspired forms has emphasized the third-person perspective—and, with it, the idea of obligations that are impartially owed to all—to the virtual exclusion, if not outright rejection, of the other two (i.e., first- and second-person) perspectives while feminist approaches have emphasized the second-person perspective—and, with it, the idea of obligations that are owed primarily to those with whom we have a direct personal relationship—to the virtual exclusion, if not outright rejection, of the other two perspectives.

However, the development of the idea of responsive cohesion hardly stops with the theory of responsive cohesion's differentiated model of our obligations in respect of other people because we have yet to meet both the theory's *theory of contexts* and its *differentiated model of our obligations in respect of all beings*. In regard to the first of these, we saw that the idea of responsive cohesion naturally generates a distinction between internal responsive cohesion and contextual responsive cohesion. When we considered the relative merits of these forms of responsive cohesion it was, in turn, easy to see that contextual responsive cohesion is ultimately more important than internal responsive cohesion. This is because it is only this priority ordering that leads to the preservation or creation of responsive cohesion overall in any given situation (and, needless to say, the value of acting in this way follows directly from the fact that responsive cohesion is the foundational value). These considerations in turn led us to consider which contexts are more embracing than others, and thus ultimately more important than others, and hence to the theory of responsive cohesion's theory of contexts. The best (which is to say, the most responsively cohesive) approach that we have to the problem of what-constitutes-the-context-of-what is the rational-empirical approach (i.e., the stunning idea of critically considering the potentially publicly available evidence that bears on the problem), and this approach suggests that the biophysical realm constitutes the context of the mindsharing realm, which constitutes the context of the compound material realm.

We saw that the lives of sentient beings are completely enmeshed in the biophysical realm unless they are able to attain some degree of cognitive transcendence over that realm (our best evidence suggesting that there is no other kind of transcendence), and that they can only attain such cognitive transcendence through the combination of linguistically adequate brains and immersion in the linguistically mediated mindsharing realm. These considerations therefore led us to distinguish between iso-experients and mindsharers and to explore the differences between their cognitive worlds in some detail. This had direct implications for the question of the value of the lives of mindsharers as opposed to iso-experients and, thus, our sense of "what is lost" when either of these kinds of beings dies. Moreover, we also saw that whereas both iso-experients and mindsharers can be harmed in terms of being caused unnecessary pain and suffering, only mindsharers can be harmed in terms of being caused unwanted autobiographical death. This is because unwanted autobiographical death is the only kind of (painless) death that any being has to fear—or can properly fear; only mindsharers lead autobiographically structured lives; and thus, only mindsharers can be harmed by being caused unwanted autobiographical death. This had direct implications for the (separable) questions of causing pain and suffering on the one hand and causing death on the other hand. Specifically, we do not harm iso-experients by killing them relatively painlessly, whereas we do harm mindsharers by killing them relatively painlessly because we do them, and only them, autobiographical harm. Adding these considerations (as well as other obvious considerations regarding the status of iso-experients that are specifically and individually incorporated into the mindsharing realm by mindsharers) to the theory of responsive cohesion's differentiated model of our obligations in respect of other people enabled us to generate the theory's differentiated model of our obligations in respect of *all* beings.

When we considered this differentiated model of our obligations in respect of all beings in terms of the theory of responsive cohesion's overall theory of contexts, we saw that this model places some additional constraints on the working out of the more general theory of contexts. These constraints kick in at the point at which we start discussing not just any old forms of responsive cohesion but rather those forms of responsive cohesion that possess an interior, experiential dimension, namely, iso-experients and mindsharers. Combining the theory of responsive cohesion's general theory of contexts and its differentiated model of our obligations in respect of all beings in this way then enabled us to generate sensible and highly defensible answers to each of the eighteen significant problems that I suggested in chapter 2 would need to be adequately addressed by any form of General Ethics.

This brief concluding overview, then, is to show that the theory of responsive cohesion is all of a piece. Once we have the idea of the foundational value of responsive cohesion, it is, in a sense, straightforward to derive both the theory of responsive cohesion's theory of contexts and its differentiated model of our obligations in respect of all beings. And that, essentially, is it; that's the whole theory. What it gives us, in sum, is a General Ethics.

Concluding Notes on the Structure of Any Future Version of General Ethics

Any truly General Ethics must offer a coherent ethical framework—that is, a coherent framework in regard to the values we should live by—that can deal with issues that range from individual living things and living beings to whole ecological systems, from the natural environment to the human-constructed environment, and from our obligations in respect of other beings at the personal level to our obligations in respect of other beings at the political level. Moreover, this framework must incorporate sensible ways of sorting out priorities when there are tensions or outright conflicts between different values. As we have now seen, the theory of responsive cohesion does all these things.

The alternative to a General Ethics (which I defined in chapter 1 as constituting an *integrated* approach to the realms of "interhuman ethics + ethics of the natural environment + ethics of the human-constructed environment") is the adoption of a "pluralistic" or "pragmatic" approach that lacks any theoretically coherent (and thus nonarbitrary) way of adjudicating between conflicts of value. In contrast, the theory of responsive cohesion embraces all the salient features of any particular problem situation (and so is in this sense highly pluralistic) and recommends quite specific answers to quite specific problems (and so is in this sense highly pragmatic), yet it does all this within the context of an integrated theoretical framework that enables us to sort out which values have priority over which (e.g., the responsive cohesion of the bio-physical realm is ultimately more important than the responsive cohesion of the mindsharing realm, which, in turn, is ultimately more important than the responsive cohesion of the compound material realm; mind-sharers considered in isolation are more valuable than iso-experients considered in isolation).

The theory of responsive cohesion presently constitutes the only basis I know of for a General Ethics. Perhaps others will be developed. I can't presently see how, but then I would say that: having invested the time and energy I have in the development of the responsive cohesion approach to General Ethics, I must be the first to admit that I am no doubt blinkered by my own vision in this regard. What I would maintain, however, is that any alternative attempt to develop a General Ethics will necessarily need to adopt certain *structural* features of the present attempt, even if the *content* differs in significant respects. What I mean by this is the following.

First, any alternative attempt to develop a General Ethics will need to offer an *integrated theoretical framework* that (i) comprehends the widest possible range of ethical concerns—from individuals to wholes, from the natural world to the world of human-constructed artifacts (including the built environment), from personal obligations to political obligations; and (ii) provides sensible and defensible ways of adjudicating between the conflicts of value that will arise in the context of embracing such a vast range of concerns. Any alternative attempt to develop a General Ethics must do this in order to qualify *as* a General Ethics.

Second, any alternative General Ethics will surely still need to incorporate some kind of *theory of contexts* in order to have a prayer of sensibly adjudicating between the conflicts of value that will arise in the context of embracing such a vast range of concerns. This means that in order to represent an improvement on the theory of responsive cohesion an alternative approach to a General Ethics will need to offer a more defensible theory of contexts than the one given here.

Third, any alternative General Ethics will surely still need to incorporate some kind of *differentiated* model of our obligations in respect of other people and other beings in general. The idea that we have exactly the same level and kinds of obligations to every single person or every single being—that is, that a nondifferentiated model of our obligations in respect of other beings will do the trick—just flies in the face of the inescapable epistemological and motivational asymmetries that apply to each of us in living our lives. This realization necessitates the explicit development of a multiple perspective account of moral agency. And once we have a multiple perspective account of moral agency—let alone an appreciation of the likewise inescapable salient features of any moral problem situation that I referred to as the onerousness factor and the beneficiaries' desires factor—then we are rationally compelled to develop a differentiated model of our obligations in respect of other people and other beings in general. These considerations mean that in order to represent an improvement on the theory of responsive cohesion, an alternative approach to a General Ethics will need to offer a more defensible differentiated model of our obligations than the one presented here.

In sum, then, any alternative attempt to develop a General Ethics must in any case incorporate the following *structural* features of the theory of responsive cohesion. First, in order to qualify as a General Ethics it must offer an integrated theoretical framework that embraces the widest possible range of ethical concerns together with priority-ordering principles in order to resolve conflicts of value. Second, and in order to do this, it will need to offer a theory of contexts. Third, and likewise in order to do this, it will need to develop a differentiated model of our obligations in respect of all beings. In my view, these structural features are in all likelihood fundamental to any form of General Ethics—the first by definition, the latter two by rational necessity. If this seems sound and therefore saves time and energy by providing a structural template for other possible forms of General Ethics, then well and good.

However, in the absence of any other presently existing forms of General Ethics, I commend the theory of responsive cohesion to you not only as *a* General Ethics that is worthy of the name but as the *only* presently existing form of a General Ethics that is worthy of the name. If sufficient people and sufficient powers-that-be took the framework offered by the theory of responsive cohesion seriously, then we would live in a world that was, among other things, (i) ecologically more coherent (i.e., responsively cohesive in the biophysical realm); (ii) democratic, respectful of liberty at the individual level, and socially oriented at the political level (i.e., responsively cohesive in the mindsharing realm, but all this subject to the first, biophysical point); and (iii) in which the human-constructed features of the world were designed so as to be responsively cohesive with the biophysical realm, the needs and desires of mindsharers, and the pre-existing human-designed contexts of each feature (but, again, in that order of priority insofar as conflicts arise—and bearing in mind that good design can accommodate all three levels of concern so that serious conflicts need not arise in the first place).

A world that was more responsively cohesive along these lines would, according to the theory of responsive cohesion, be a better world. Many are trying to build this world, but we are presently very far from it, whether we are talking about the biophysical realm, the mindsharing realm, or the compound material realm. Of course, we are further from it in some respects and in some places than others, but no place is immune from these problems. Even those who are lucky enough to live in countries that are democratic, respectful of liberty at the individual level, and socially oriented at the political level are often living in environments that are ecologically ravaged and architecturally insensitive and dispiriting—if not just plain ugly and brutal—within their borders. Moreover, those living in these countries are also, through the conduct of their governments, corporations, and citizens, at least indirectly party to the export of a range of social and environmental problems that have an impact upon the biophysical, mindsharing, and compound material realms globally. I therefore hope that the argument of this book gives moral courage and helpful mind-tools to those who are reaching for a better, more responsively cohesive world in these testing times. I also hope that it is persuasive to those who, at a time when many settle for simplistic answers to complex problems (and was there ever not such a time?), are looking for some *reasoned* moral bearings in order to reflect upon the best way to live their lives in a "big picture" context and then to orient their personal actions accordingly within that context.

Notes

I provide full reference details the first time I cite a source within each chapter. This avoids the need to turn to the bibliography in order to find the complete publication details for any given reference. I abbreviate this information somewhat—but in a readily identifiable way—in subsequent references to the same source within each chapter. Thus, if you come across an abbreviated reference, you will find its full details by skimming back up through the notes for *that* chapter—often just the notes that are most immediately above. Where I refer to "classic," widely reprinted papers, I try to refer to their location in readily available, and often widely used, anthologies, rather than to their original places of publication, which may be gathering dust on university library shelves in the pages of journals that may have come out any time in the last two to three decades.

Chapter 1: Introduction: The Idea of a General Ethics

1. John Passmore, *Man's Responsibility for Nature: Ecological Problems and Western Traditions*, 2nd ed. (London: Duckworth, 1980), 15.

2. Ibid., 113.

3. For further elaboration of this point by myself and others see Warwick Fox, "Introduction: Ethics and the Built Environment," in Warwick Fox, ed., *Ethics and the Built Environment* (London and New York: Routledge, 2000), 1–12. This introduction also contains references to the few previous contributions to the ethics of the human-constructed environment.

4. "[J]ust as traditional, anthropocentrically focused forms of ethics have exhibited a major blind spot in their theorizing with respect to the non-human world, so the development of environmental ethics has thus far exhibited a major blind spot of its own [namely, the human-constructed environment]." Ibid., 2.

Chapter 2: Problems That Any General Ethics Must Be Able to Address

1. Peter Singer, "Famine, Affluence, and Morality," reprinted in Hugh LaFollette, ed., *Ethics in Practice: An Anthology*, 2nd ed. (Malden, Mass., and Oxford: Blackwell, 2002), 572–581, at 573.

2. Ibid.

3. Peter Singer, *Animal Liberation*, 2nd ed. (London: Jonathan Cape, 1990); Tom Regan, *The Case for Animal Rights* (Berkeley: University of California Press, 1983); Tom Regan, *Animal Rights, Human Wrongs: An Introduction to Moral Philosophy* (Lanham, Md.: Rowman and Littlefield, 2003).

4. Richard Ryder, *Animal Revolution: Changing Attitudes towards Speciesism* (Oxford and New York: Berg, 2000); Richard Ryder, *Painism: A Modern Morality* (London: Centaur Press, 2001).

5. Singer, *Animal Liberation*, 171.

6. Mark Sagoff, "Animal Liberation and Environmental Ethics: Bad Marriage, Quick Divorce," reprinted in Michael Zimmerman, ed., *Environmental Philosophy: From Animal Rights to Radical Ecology*, 3rd ed. (Upper Saddle River, N.J.: Prentice Hall, 2001), 87–96, at 91.

7. Ibid., 92.

8. Ibid.

9. J. Baird Callicott, "Review of Tom Regan, *The Case for Animal Rights*," *Environmental Ethics* 7 (1985): 365–372, at 371.

10. Callicott, "Review of *The Case for Animal Rights*"; Steve Sapontzis, "Predation," in Marc Bekoff, ed., *Encyclopedia of Animal Rights and Animal Welfare* (London and Chicago: Fitzroy Dearborn, 1998), 275–277.

11. Sapontzis, "Predation," 276.

12. Callicott, "Review of *The Case for Animal Rights*," 370.

13. Tyler Cowen, "Policing Nature," *Environmental Ethics* 25 (2003): 169–182, at 170.

14. Bob Holmes, "Day of the Sparrow," *New Scientist*, June 27, 1998, 32–35; Chris Bright, *Life Out of Bounds: Bioinvasion in a Borderless World* (London: Earthscan, 1999).

15. Sagoff, "Animal Liberation and Environmental Ethics," 92.

16. I note these authors in the text in chronological order of their most notable contributions to this approach. However, as noted above, I provide references here simply to currently readily available publications of the most notable contributions to this approach by these authors (or at least to readily available critical overviews of their contributions, as in the case of Schweitzer). For a general overview and critical introduction to Schweitzer's views, see Mary Anne Warren, *Moral Status: Obligations to Persons and Other Living Things* (Oxford and

New York: Oxford University Press, 2000), chap. 2; Kenneth Goodpaster, "On Being Morally Considerable," reprinted in Zimmerman, ed., *Environmental Philosophy*, 3rd ed., 56–70; Robin Attfield, "The Good of Trees," reprinted in David Schmidtz and Elizabeth Willott, eds., *Environmental Ethics: What Really Matters, What Really Works* (New York and Oxford: Oxford University Press, 2002), 58–71; Paul Taylor, *Respect for Nature: A Theory of Environmental Ethics* (Princeton, N.J.: Princeton University Press, 1986); Gary Varner, *In Nature's Interests?: Interests, Animal Rights, and Environmental Ethics* (New York and Oxford: Oxford University Press, 1998); Gary Varner, "Biocentric Individualism," in Schmidtz and Willott, eds., *Environmental Ethics*, 108–120. (Note that the Schmidtz and Willott anthology also carries reprints of Singer's "Famine, Affluence, and Morality" and Sagoff's "Animal Liberation and Environmental Ethics," so that provides another readily available form of access to these classic papers.)

17. Singer, *Animal Liberation*, 9.

18. Peter Singer, *Practical Ethics*, 2nd ed. (Cambridge: Cambridge University Press, 1993), 279.

19. Taylor, *Respect for Nature*, 63.

20. Varner, "Biocentric Individualism," 114.

21. Ibid., 113.

22. Ibid.

23. Aldo Leopold, *A Sand County Almanac* [1949] (Oxford: Oxford University Press, 1981), 224–225. The concluding "Land Ethic" essay is also reprinted in each of the anthologies referred to above by LaFollette, Schmidtz and Willott, and Zimmerman.

24. James Heffernan, "The Land Ethic: A Critical Reappraisal," *Environmental Ethics* 4 (1982): 235–247, at 237.

25. Ibid.

26. Ibid., 247.

27. J. Baird Callicott, "Do Deconstructive Ecology and Sociobiology Undermine Leopold's Land Ethic?," *Environmental Ethics* 18 (1996): 353–372, at 372.

28. Leopold, *A Sand County Almanac*, 225, 203, and 225 respectively.

29. J. Baird Callicott, ed., *Companion to "A Sand County Almanac": Interpretive and Critical Essays* (Madison, Wisc.: University of Wisconsin Press, 1987); J. Baird Callicott, *In Defense of the Land Ethic: Essays in Environmental Philosophy* (Albany, N.Y.: State University of New York Press, 1989); J. Baird Callicott, *Beyond the Land Ethic: More Essays in Environmental Philosophy* (Albany, N.Y.: State University of New York Press, 1999).

30. David Hume, *A Treatise of Human Nature* [1739–1740], ed. L. A. Selby-Bigge, 2nd ed. rev. P. H. Nidditch (Oxford: Oxford University Press, 1978), 575 and 618.

31. Ibid., 415.

32. Robert Arrington, *Western Ethics: An Historical Introduction* (Malden, Mass., and Oxford: Blackwell, 1998), 234.

33. Leopold, *A Sand County Almanac*, 223.

34. David Hume, *A Treatise of Human Nature*, 468.

35. Aldo Leopold, "Some Fundamentals of Conservation in the Southwest," *Environmental Ethics* 1 (1979): 131–141; Heffernan, "The Land Ethic: A Critical Reappraisal."

36. Callicott, "Do Deconstructive Ecology and Sociobiology," 372.

Chapter 3: Introducing the Idea of Responsive Cohesion

1. See the entries on "fundamental forces" and "grand unified theories" (GUTs) in John Gribbin, *Companion to the Cosmos* (London: Phoenix, 1997), 182–185 and 209–213 respectively.

2. Jeremy Campbell, *The Improbable Machine* (New York: Touchstone, 1989), 145 and 143.

3. Note that, unless otherwise specified, all references to dictionary definitions in this book are to the marvelous *Collins English Dictionary: Complete and Unabridged*, 6th ed. (Glasgow: HarperCollins, 2003). I will simply take this as understood in all further implied or explicit references to definitions herein.

4. Christopher Alexander, *The Timeless Way of Building* (New York: Oxford University Press, 1979), 41. See also Christopher Alexander's monumental four-volume classic-in-the-making *The Nature of Order: An Essay on the Art of Building and the Nature of the Universe* (Berkeley: The Center for Environmental Structure, 2002–2004).

5. Tor Norretranders, *The User Illusion: Cutting Consciousness Down to Size* (London and New York: Allen Lane, 1998), 70.

Chapter 4: The Best Approach to Everything

1. John Rawls, *A Theory of Justice*, rev. ed. (Oxford and New York: Oxford University Press, 1999; originally published 1971).

2. Aldo Leopold, *A Sand County Almanac* (Oxford: Oxford University Press, 1981), 216.

3. Christopher Norberg-Schulz, *Genius Loci: Towards a Phenomenology of Architecture* (New York: Rizzoli International Publications, 1980), 190.

4. Christopher Alexander, *The Timeless Way of Building* (New York: Oxford University Press, 1979).

5. Gerald Edelman and Giulio Tononi, *Consciousness: How Matter Becomes Imagination* (London and New York: Penguin Books, 2001), 36.

6. Ibid., 44.

7. Ibid., 44–45.

8. John McCrone, *Going Inside: A Tour Round a Single Moment of Consciousness* (London: Faber and Faber, 1999), 9.

9. Note that although all complex adaptive systems (CASs) exhibit the relational quality of responsive cohesion, the fact that something exhibits this relational quality does not necessarily mean that it is a CAS. Responsive cohesion is therefore a broader category than that defined by CASs, or, to put it another way, CASs represent a special subset of the class of things that can be characterized as exhibiting the relational quality of responsive cohesion. See the section on complexity theory in the appendix to chapter 4.

Appendix to Chapter 4: A Note on the Concepts of *Responsive Cohesion, Reflective Equilibrium, Organic Unity, Complex Systems,* and So On

1. John Rawls, *A Theory of Justice*, rev. ed. (Oxford and New York: Oxford University Press, 1999; originally published 1971).

2. Simon Blackburn, *The Oxford Dictionary of Philosophy* (Oxford and New York: Oxford University Press, 1994), 323.

3. Robert Nozick, *Philosophical Explanations* (Cambridge, Mass.: The Belknap Press of Harvard University Press, 1981).

4. Robert Nozick, *Anarchy, State, and Utopia* (New York: Basic Books, 1974).

5. See Simon Hailwood, *Exploring Nozick: Beyond Anarchy, State, and Utopia* (Aldershot: Avebury 1996); A. R. Lacey, *Robert Nozick* (Chesham, Buckinghamshire: Acumen, 2001).

6. Simon Hailwood, *Exploring Nozick*.

7. Robert Nozick, *Invariances: The Structure of the Objective World* (Cambridge, Mass.: The Belknap Press of Harvard University Press, 2001).

8. See, for example, Stuart Kauffman, *At Home in the Universe: The Search for Laws of Self-Organization and Complexity* (London: Viking, 1995).

Chapter 5: The Best Approach to Conventional, Interhuman Ethics

1. Hugh LaFollette, ed., *Ethics in Practice: An Anthology*, 1st ed. (Malden, Mass., and Oxford: Blackwell, 1997), 3 and 1 respectively.

2. See chap. 3, n. 3, herein.

3. For a critical elaboration, see Mary Anne Warren, *Moral Status: Obligations to Persons and Other Living Things* (Oxford and New York: Oxford University Press, 2000), chap. 5.

Chapter 6: The Theory of Responsive Cohesion's Theory of Contexts

1. Christopher Day, *Places of the Soul: Architecture and Environmental Design as a Healing Art* (London: Thorsons, 1995), 18. See also Christopher Day, "Ethical Building in the Everyday Environment: A Multilayer Approach to Building and Place Design," in Warwick Fox, ed., *Ethics and the Built Environment* (London and New York: Routledge, 2000), 127–138.

2. John Searle, *Mind, Language, and Society: Doing Philosophy in the Real World* (London: Weidenfeld and Nicolson, 1999), 100–103. (Searle himself takes this useful "direction of fit" terminology from his own early mentor J. L. Austin.)

3. Merlin Donald uses this marvelous term, which I believe is original with him, exactly twice as far as I have noticed (and his index reports) in his important book *A Mind So Rare: The Evolution of Human Consciousness* (New York and London: W. W. Norton, 2001). However, I want to highlight this wonderfully rich, evocative, and yet precisely descriptive term here and, if possible, bring it to much wider notice.

4. John Searle uses this bathtub example in stressing the importance of the distinction between features of the world that are *intrinsic* and those that are *observer relative*. See John Searle, *The Rediscovery of the Mind* (Cambridge, Mass.: The MIT Press, 1994), xii–xiii.

5. Thomas Nagel's famous paper "What Is It Like to Be a Bat?", originally published in the *Philosophical Review* (1974), is now reprinted in just about every general anthology in philosophy of mind. See, for example, Ned Block, Owen Flanagan, and Guven Guzeldere, eds., *The Nature of Consciousness: Philosophical Debates* (Cambridge, Mass.: The MIT Press, 1997), 519–527; David Rosenthal, ed., *The Nature of Mind* (New York and Oxford: Oxford University Press, 1991), 422–428.

6. Searle, *Rediscovery of the Mind*, 1.

7. Terrence Deacon, "Biological Aspects of Language," in Steve Jones, Robert Martin, and David Pilbeam, eds., *The Cambridge Encyclopedia of Human Evolution* (Cambridge: Cambridge University Press, 1994), 128–133; Peter Gärdenfors, *How Homo Became Sapiens: On the Evolution of Thinking* (Oxford: Oxford University Press, 2003), see chap. 6, "The Dawn of Language." The classification of signs as *indexes*, *icons*, and *symbols* derives from the work of the significant American philosopher and founding father of philosophical pragmatism, Charles Sanders Peirce (1839–1914).

8. For an accessible introduction to the complexities of Noam Chomsky's hugely influential ideas in linguistics, see Steven Pinker, *The Language Instinct: The New Science of Language and Mind* (London: Penguin Books, 1995).

9. Derek Bickerton, *Language and Species* (Chicago and London: The University of Chicago Press, 1992), 122.

10. Pinker, *The Language Instinct*, 33.

11. Piero Scaruffi, *Thinking about Thought: A Primer on the New Science of Mind* (New York: Writers Club Press, 2003), 380.

12. William Calvin, *How Brains Think: Evolving Intelligence, Then and Now* (London: Weidenfeld and Nicolson, 1997), 66.

13. Ludwig Wittgenstein, *Philosophical Investigations*, ed. G. E. M. Anscombe and R. Rhees (Oxford: Blackwell, 1953), see sections 243 ff. For an accessible form of the argument as I discuss it, see K. T. Maslin, *An Introduction to the Philosophy of Mind* (Cambridge: Polity, 2001), chap. 8, esp. 8.6.

14. For accounts of these and other cases, see especially John McCrone, *The Myth of Irrationality: The Science of the Mind from Plato to Star Trek* (New York: Carroll and Graf, 1993), chaps. 5 and 6 ("Wolf Children" and "Deaf and Dumb"); Michael Newton, *Savage Girls and Wild Boys: A History of Feral Children* (London: Faber and Faber, 2003); Oliver Sacks, *Seeing Voices: A Journey into the World of the Deaf* (London: Picador, 1991). For more on two particularly famous cases, see Russ Rymer, *Genie: A Scientific Tragedy* (New York: HarperPerennial, 1994); Roger Shattuck, *The Forbidden Experiment: The Story of the Wild Boy of Aveyron* (New York: Kodansha International, 1994).

15. Sacks, *Seeing Voices*; Susan Schaller, *A Man Without Words* (London: Ebury Press, 1992).

16. Helen Keller, *The Story of My Life* (New York: Signet Classic, New American Library, 2002; first published 1902); Helen Keller, *The World I Live In* (New York: New York Review Books, 2003; first published 1908). See also Merlin Donald's perceptive discussion of Keller's case in *A Mind So Rare*, chap. 6.

17. Oliver Sacks, "Forward," in Schaller, *A Man Without Words*, 13.

18. All quotations from Keller in this section are taken from *The Story of My Life*, 17–18.

19. Schaller, *A Man Without Words*, 44.

20. Ibid., 45.

21. Sacks, *Seeing Voices*.

22. Ibid., 54.

23. Keller, *The Story of My Life*, 212.

24. Sacks, *Seeing Voices*, 62.

25. Donald, *A Mind So Rare*, 251.

26. James Wertsch, "Vygotsky, Lev Semenovich," in Robert Wilson and Frank Keil, eds., *The MIT Encyclopedia of the Cognitive Sciences* (Cambridge, Mass.: The MIT Press, 1999), 878–879.

27. Donald, *A Mind So Rare*, 249.

28. The useful term *affordance* was coined by J. J. Gibson and is central to his ecological approach to psychology. For Gibson, "The affordances of the environment are what it offers animals, what it provides or furnishes, for good or ill." See Eleanor Gibson, Karen Adolph, and Marion Eppler, "Affordances" in

Wilson and Keil, eds., *The MIT Encyclopedia of the Cognitive Sciences*, 4–6; the quote just given from Gibson is at p. 4.

29. Michael Tomasello and Hannes Rakoczy, "What Makes Human Cognition Unique?: From Individual to Shared to Collective Intentionality," *Mind and Language* 18 (2003): 121–147, at 129.

30. Ibid. See also Michael Tomasello's authoritative and extremely important book, *The Cultural Origins of Human Cognition* (Cambridge, Mass.: Harvard University Press, 2000), esp. chap. 2.

31. Tomasello, *The Cultural Origins of Human Cognition*, see chap. 2.

32. Ibid., 40 and 202.

Chapter 7: Exploring the Cognitive Worlds of Mindsharers and Iso-Experients

1. Simon Baron-Cohen, *Mindblindness: An Essay on Autism and Theory of Mind* (Cambridge, Mass.: The MIT Press, 1997); Daniel Dennett, *The Intentional Stance* (Cambridge, Mass.: The MIT Press, 1987); Uta Frith and Christopher Frith, "Development and Neurophysiology of Mentalizing," *Philosophical Transactions of the Royal Society London*, Series B, 358 (2003): 459–473, (http://www.icn.ucl.ac.uk/dev_group/documents/Frith&FrithPTrans03.pdf); Peter Mitchell, *Introduction to Theory of Mind: Children, Autism, and Apes* (London: Arnold, 2003); Shaun Nichols and Stephen Stich, *Mindreading: An Integrated Account of Pretence, Self-Awareness, and Understanding Other Minds* (Oxford: Clarendon Press, 2003).

2. Uta Frith, "Autism," in Robert Wilson and Frank Keil, eds., *The MIT Encyclopedia of the Cognitive Sciences* (Cambridge, Mass.: The MIT Press, 1999), 58–60.

3. Baron-Cohen, *Mindblindness*; Uta Frith, "Autism"; Neil Smith, *Language, Bananas, and Bonobos: Linguistic Problems, Puzzles, and Polemics* (Oxford: Blackwell, 2002), see chaps. 3 and 4 for details of work with "Christopher," an autistic *linguistic* savant.

4. Michael Tomasello, *The Cultural Origins of Human Cognition* (Cambridge, Mass.: Harvard University Press, 2000), 133.

5. Peter Hobson, *The Cradle of Thought* (London: Macmillan, 2002), 90.

6. Madhusree Mukerjee, "A Transparent Enigma," *Scientific American* 290 (June 2004): 24–25. See also the section on "Theory of Mind, Language Acquisition, and Autism" on the Autism Spectrum Disorders website run from the University of Oregon, http://gladstone.uoregon.edu/~klam/index.html/.

7. Hobson, *The Cradle of Thought*, see 89–92; Smith, *Language, Bananas, and Bonobos*, see chaps. 3 and 4.

8. Daniel Povinelli, "Can Animals Empathize?" *Scientific American Presents: Exploring Intelligence* 9 (winter 1998): 67, 72–75.

9. Ibid., 72.

10. Ibid.

11. Ibid.

12. Ibid., 73.

13. Ibid.

14. Ibid.

15. Daniel Povinelli, *Folk Physics for Apes: The Chimpanzee's Theory of How the World Works*, reprint ed. (Oxford: Oxford University Press, 2003), 72.

16. Daniel Povinelli and Jennifer Vonk, "Chimpanzee Minds: Suspiciously Human?" *Trends in Cognitive Sciences* 7 (2003): 157–160.

17. Jonathan Marks, *What It Means to Be 98% Chimpanzee: Apes, People, and Their Genes* (Berkeley: University of California Press, 2003), 29.

18. Povinelli and Vonk, "Chimpanzee Minds: Suspiciously Human?," 157.

19. Povinelli, "Can Animals Empathize?," 74.

20. Ibid.

21. Ibid.

22. Hobson, *The Cradle of Thought*, 89.

23. Tomasello, *The Cultural Origins of Human Cognition*, 21. (On the final point regarding intentional teaching, recall my reference to Tomasello's work in the previous chapter on the difference between *emulation learning* and genuinely *imitative learning*.)

24. Ibid.

25. Ibid., 62.

26. Ibid., 61.

27. Ibid., 62–63.

28. Baron-Cohen, *Mindblindness*, 44.

29. Michael Tomasello and Josep Call, *Primate Cognition* (New York and Oxford: Oxford University Press, 1997); Tomasello, *The Cultural Origins of Human Cognition*.

30. Michael Tomasello, Josep Call, and Brian Hare, "Chimpanzees Understand Psychological States—The Question Is Which Ones and to What Extent," *Trends in Cognitive Sciences* 7 (2003): 153–156; Michael Tomasello, Josep Call, and Brian Hare, "Chimpanzees Versus Humans: It's Not that Simple," *Trends in Cognitive Sciences* 7 (2003): 239–240.

31. Daniel Povinelli and Jennifer Vonk, "We Don't Need a Microscope to Explore the Chimpanzee's Mind," *Mind and Language* 19 (2004): 1–28.

32. Ibid., 2.

33. Jennifer Vonk, James Reaux, Conni Castille, and Daniel Povinelli, "What Human-Enculturated Apes Know about Seeing: Preliminary Results" (paper

presented to the 11th Annual International Conference on Comparative Cognition, Melbourne Beach, Fla., March 24–27, 2004).

34. Michael Tomasello and Hannes Rakoczy, "What Makes Human Cognition Unique?: From Individual to Shared to Collective Intentionality," *Mind and Language* 18 (2003): 121–147, 141.

35. Ibid., 142.

36. Euan Macphail, *Brain and Intelligence in Vertebrates* (Oxford: Clarendon Press, 1982), cited in the Boyd Group papers on The Use of Non-Human Primates in Research and Testing: "Paper 2: Empirical Evidence on the Moral Status of Non-Human Primates," 2002, p. 22, published online by the British Psychological Society on behalf of the Boyd Group: http://www.boyd-group .demon.co.uk/Paper2.pdf/.

The Boyd Group, named after its chairman Kenneth Boyd, professor of medical ethics at Edinburgh University Medical School and research director of the Institute of Medical Ethics, is a UK-based "forum for open exchange of views on issues of concern related to the use of animals in science" and includes "veterinarians, scientists using animals (from industry and academia), members of animal welfare organizations, anti-vivisectionists, members of government and charitable bodies funding or directly engaged in research, philosophers, and others."

37. British Psychological Society on behalf of the Boyd Group, "Paper 2: Empirical Evidence on the Moral Status of Non-Human Primates," 22.

38. Louis Herman, "Exploring the Cognitive World of the Bottlenosed Dolphin," in Marc Bekoff, Colin Allen, and Gordon Burghardt, eds., *The Cognitive Animal: Empirical and Theoretical Perspectives on Animal Cognition* (Cambridge, Mass.: The MIT Press, 2002), 275–283, at 275.

39. Ibid., 281.

40. Robin Dunbar, *The Human Story: A New History of Mankind's Evolution* (London: Faber and Faber, 2004), 58.

41. Tomasello, *The Cultural Origins of Human Cognition*, 35.

42. Ibid.

43. Marc Hauser, *Wild Minds: What Animals Really Think* (London: Penguin Books, 2001), see chap. 8; Steven Pinker, *The Language Instinct: The New Science of Language and Mind* (London: Penguin Books, 1995), see chap. 11; Joel Wallman, *Aping Language* (Cambridge: Cambridge University Press, 1992).

44. Duane Rumbaugh and Sue Savage-Rumbaugh, "Primate Cognition," in Wilson and Keil, eds., *The MIT Encyclopedia of the Cognitive Sciences*, 669–671; P. Greenfield and Sue Savage-Rumbaugh, "Comparing Communicative Competence in Child and Chimp: The Pragmatics," *Journal of Child Language* 20 (1993): 1–26.

45. Rumbaugh and Savage-Rumbaugh, "Primate Cognition."

46. Peter Gärdenfors, *How Homo Became Sapiens: On the Evolution of Thinking* (Oxford: Oxford University Press, 2003), 153–154.

47. Pinker, *The Language Instinct*, 341.

48. John McCrone, *The Myth of Irrationality: The Science of the Mind from Plato to Star Trek* (New York: Carroll and Graf, 1993), 131.

49. Gärdenfors, *How Homo Became Sapiens*, 154.

50. Derek Bickerton, *Language and Species* (Chicago and London: The University of Chicago Press, 1992), see chap. 7, "From Protolanguage to Language." This aspect of Bickerton's work is also discussed in Pinker's *The Language Instinct* and Gärdenfors' *How Homo Became Sapiens*.

51. Merlin Donald, *A Mind So Rare: The Evolution of Human Consciousness* (New York and London: W. W. Norton, 2001), 121.

52. Ibid.

53. P. Greenfield and Sue Savage-Rumbaugh, "Grammatical Combination in *Pan paniscus*: Processes of Learning and Invention in the Evolution and Development of Language," in S. Parker and K. Gibson, eds., *"Language" and Intelligence in Monkeys and Apes* (Cambridge: Cambridge University Press, 1990), 540–578.

54. Tomasello, *The Cultural Origins of Human Cognition*, see chap. 3, "Joint Attention and Cultural Learning."

55. Michael Tomasello, "On the Different Origins of Symbols and Grammar," in Morten Christiansen and Simon Kirby, eds., *Language Evolution* (Oxford: Oxford University Press, 2003), 94–110, at 99–100.

56. Ibid., 100.

57. McCrone, *The Myth of Irrationality*, 104.

58. Ibid., 98.

59. Oliver Sacks, *Seeing Voices: A Journey into the World of the Deaf* (London: Picador, 1991), 49.

60. Ibid., 63.

61. Ibid., 39.

62. Ibid., 39–40.

63. Helen Keller, *The World I Live In* (New York: New York Review Books, 2003; first published 1908), 72, 74, and 76.

64. Donald, *A Mind So Rare*, 249.

65. Helen Keller, *The Story of My Life* (New York: Signet Classic, New American Library, 2002; first published 1902), 212.

66. Andy Clark and Annette Karmiloff-Smith, "The Cognizer's Innards: A Psychological and Philosophical Perspective on the Development of Thought," *Mind and Language* 8 (1993): 488–519.

67. Keller, *The World I Live In*, 72.

68. Keller, *The Story of My Life*, 212.

69. McCrone, *The Myth of Irrationality*, 122.

70. Ibid., 123–124.

Chapter 8: Time Blindness, Autobiographical Death, and Our Obligations in Respect of All Beings

1. Paul Churchland, *The Engine of Reason, the Seat of the Soul: A Philosophical Journey into the Brain* (Cambridge, Mass.: The MIT Press, 1996), 269 and 271.

2. Ibid., 271.

3. Ibid., 270.

4. Ibid.

5. Ibid., 269–270.

6. Ibid., 270.

7. Michael Tomasello, *The Cultural Origins of Human Cognition* (Cambridge, Mass.: Harvard University Press, 2000), 5, and at various points throughout.

8. Merlin Donald, *A Mind So Rare: The Evolution of Human Consciousness* (New York and London: W. W. Norton, 2001), 150.

9. Peter Gärdenfors, *How Homo Became Sapiens: On the Evolution of Thinking* (Oxford: Oxford University Press, 2003), 41.

10. Susan Schaller, *A Man Without Words* (London: Ebury Press, 1992), 170–171.

11. Helen Keller, *The World I Live In* (New York: New York Review Books, 2003; first published 1908), 72.

12. Ibid., 74.

13. Daniel Povinelli, *Folk Physics for Apes: The Chimpanzee's Theory of How the World Works*, reprint ed. (Oxford: Oxford University Press, 2003), 77.

14. Ibid., 338–339.

15. Daniel Povinelli, "Behind the Ape's Appearance: Escaping Anthropocentrism in the Study of Other Minds," *Dædalus: Journal of the American Academy of Arts and Sciences*, winter 2004, 29–41, at 35.

16. Daniel Povinelli and Jennifer Vonk, "Chimpanzee Minds: Suspiciously Human?" *Trends in Cognitive Sciences* 7 (2003): 157–160; Daniel Povinelli and Jennifer Vonk, "We Don't Need a Microscope to Explore the Chimpanzee's Mind," *Mind and Language* 19 (2004): 1–28.

17. Katherine Nelson, *Language in Cognitive Development: The Emergence of the Mediated Mind* (Cambridge: Cambridge University Press, 1998), 288.

18. John McCrone, *The Myth of Irrationality: The Science of the Mind from Plato to Star Trek* (New York: Carroll and Graf, 1993), 104.

19. Oliver Sacks, *Seeing Voices: A Journey into the World of the Deaf* (London: Picador, 1991), 39–40.

20. Schaller, *A Man Without Words*, 116 and 194–195; see also chap. 11 and the afterword.

21. Ibid., 197.

22. Ibid., 177.

23. Keller, *The World I Live In*, 72.

24. Nelson, *Language in Cognitive Development*, 162.

25. Ibid., 159.

26. Endel Tulving, "Episodic vs. Semantic Memory," in Robert Wilson and Frank Keil, eds., *The MIT Encyclopedia of the Cognitive Sciences* (Cambridge, Mass.: The MIT Press, 1999), 278–280.

27. Nelson, *Language in Cognitive Development*, 159.

28. Ibid., 172 and 181.

29. Ibid., 344.

30. Ibid.

31. Marc Hauser, *Wild Minds: What Animals Really Think* (London: Penguin Books 2001), 279; the reference to Susan Carey's work is to her book *Conceptual Change in Childhood* (Cambridge, Mass.: The MIT Press, 1985).

32. Gärdenfors, *How Homo Became Sapiens*, 132.

33. Hauser, *Wild Minds*, 278.

34. Povinelli, "Behind the Ape's Appearance," 41.

35. Hauser, *Wild Minds*, 281 and 278.

36. Gärdenfors, *How Homo Became Sapiens*, 131–132.

37. See, for example, Craig Stanford, "The Ape's Gift: Meat-eating, Meat-sharing, and Human Evolution," in Frans de Waal, ed., *Tree of Origin: What Primate Behavior Can Tell Us about Human Social Evolution* (Cambridge, Mass.: Harvard University Press, 2002), 95–117; Richard Wrangham, "Out of the *Pan*, Into the Fire: How Our Ancestors' Evolution Depended on What They Ate," in de Waal, *Tree of Origin*, 119–143; Gary Stix, "Homo Carnivorous," *Scientific American* 290 (June 2004): 9–10.

38. Mark Sagoff, "Animal Liberation and Environmental Ethics: Bad Marriage, Quick Divorce," reprinted in Michael Zimmerman, ed., *Environmental Philosophy: From Animal Rights to Radical Ecology*, 3rd ed. (Upper Saddle River, N.J.: Prentice Hall, 2001), 87–96, at 92.

39. Jeremy Bentham, *An Introduction to the Principles of Morals and Legislation*, ed. J. H. Burns and H. L. A. Hart (London: The Athlone Press, University of London, 1970; orig. pub. 1789), 283.

40. Ibid., 282.

41. Peter Singer, *Animal Liberation*, 2nd ed. (London: Jonathan Cape, 1990), 17 and 228.

42. Ibid., 210.

43. Tom Regan, *The Case for Animal Rights* (Berkeley: University of California Press, 1983), 243.

Chapter 10: Applying the Theory of Responsive Cohesion

1. Peter Singer, *Practical Ethics*, 2nd ed. (Cambridge: Cambridge University Press, 1993), 284.

2. Chris Bright, *Life Out of Bounds: Bioinvasion in a Borderless World* (London: Earthscan, 1999), 23–28.

3. Bob Holmes, "Day of the Sparrow," *New Scientist* 27 (June 1998), 32–35, at 35.

4. Ibid.

5. Bright, *Life Out of Bounds*, 25.

6. J. Baird Callicott, "Review of Tom Regan, *The Case for Animal Rights*," *Environmental Ethics* 7 (1985): 365–372; see also J. Baird Callicott, "Animal Liberation: A Triangular Affair," *Environmental Ethics* 2 (1980): 311–338.

7. Terry Williamson, Antony Radford, and Helen Bennetts, *Understanding Sustainable Architecture* (London and New York: Spon Press, 2003), 128. The reference to Fox 2000 is to Warwick Fox, "Towards an Ethics (or at Least a Value Theory) of the Built Environment," in Warwick Fox, ed., *Ethics and the Built Environment* (London and New York: Routledge, 2000), 207–221.

8. Williamson, Radford, and Bennetts, *Understanding Sustainable Architecture*, 128 and 130.

9. Personal communication.

Bibliography

Alexander, Christopher. 1979. *The Timeless Way of Building*. New York: Oxford University Press.

Alexander, Christopher. 2002–2004. *The Nature of Order: An Essay on the Art of Building and the Nature of the Universe*. Berkeley: The Center for Environmental Structure.

Arrington, Robert. 1998. *Western Ethics: An Historical Introduction*. Malden, Mass. and Oxford: Blackwell.

Attfield, Robin. 2002. "The Good of Trees." In David Schmidtz and Elizabeth Willott, eds., *Environmental Ethics: What Really Matters, What Really Works*. New York and Oxford: Oxford University Press, 58–71.

Autism Spectrum Disorders. University of Oregon. "Theory of Mind, Language Acquisition, and Autism." Http://gladstone.uoregon.edu/~klam/index.html/.

Baron-Cohen, Simon. 1997. *Mindblindness: An Essay on Autism and Theory of Mind*. Cambridge, Mass.: The MIT Press.

Bentham, Jeremy. 1970 (1789). *An Introduction to the Principles of Morals and Legislation*, ed. J. H. Burns and H. L. A. Hart. London: The Athlone Press, University of London.

Bickerton, Derek. 1992. *Language and Species*. Chicago and London: The University of Chicago Press.

Blackburn, Simon. 1994. *The Oxford Dictionary of Philosophy*. Oxford and New York: Oxford University Press.

Boyd Group. 2002. "Paper 2: Empirical Evidence on the Moral Status of Non-Human Primates." Papers on the Use of Non-Human Primates in Research and Testing. Http://www.boyd-group.demon.co.uk/Paper2.pdf/.

Bright, Chris. 1999. *Life Out of Bounds: Bioinvasion in a Borderless World*. London: Earthscan.

Callicott, J. Baird. 1980. "Animal Liberation: A Triangular Affair." *Environmental Ethics* 2: 311–338.

Callicott, J. Baird. 1985. "Review of Tom Regan, *The Case for Animal Rights*." *Environmental Ethics* 7: 365–372.

Callicott, J. Baird, ed. 1987. *Companion to "A Sand County Almanac": Interpretive and Critical Essays*. Madison, Wisc.: University of Wisconsin Press.

Callicott, J. Baird. 1989. *In Defense of the Land Ethic: Essays in Environmental Philosophy*. Albany, N.Y.: State University of New York Press.

Callicott, J. Baird. 1996. "Do Deconstructive Ecology and Sociobiology Undermine Leopold's Land Ethic?" *Environmental Ethics* 18: 353–372.

Callicott, J. Baird. 1999. *Beyond the Land Ethic: More Essays in Environmental Philosophy*. Albany, N.Y.: State University of New York Press.

Calvin, William. 1997. *How Brains Think: Evolving Intelligence, Then and Now*. London: Weidenfeld and Nicolson.

Campbell, Jeremy. 1989. *The Improbable Machine*. New York: Touchstone.

Carey, Susan. 1985. *Conceptual Change in Childhood*. Cambridge, Mass.: The MIT Press.

Churchland, Paul. 1996. *The Engine of Reason, the Seat of the Soul: A Philosophical Journey into the Brain*. Cambridge, Mass.: The MIT Press.

Clark, Andy, and Annette Karmiloff-Smith. 1993. "The Cognizer's Innards: A Psychological and Philosophical Perspective on the Development of Thought." *Mind and Language* 8: 488–519.

Collins English Dictionary: Complete and Unabridged, 6th ed. 2003. Glasgow: HarperCollins.

Cowen, Tyler. 2003. "Policing Nature." *Environmental Ethics* 25: 169–182.

Day, Christopher. 1995. *Places of the Soul: Architecture and Environmental Design as a Healing Art*. London: Thorsons.

Day, Christopher. 2000. "Ethical Building in the Everyday Environment: A Multilayer Approach to Building and Place Design." In Warwick Fox, ed., *Ethics and the Built Environment*. London and New York: Routledge, 127–138.

Deacon, Terrence. 1994. "Biological Aspects of Language." In Steve Jones, Robert Martin, and David Pilbeam, eds., *The Cambridge Encyclopedia of Human Evolution*. Cambridge: Cambridge University Press, 128–133.

Dennett, Daniel. 1987. *The Intentional Stance*. Cambridge, Mass.: The MIT Press.

de Waal, Frans, ed. 2002. *Tree of Origin: What Primate Behavior Can Tell Us about Human Social Evolution*. Cambridge, Mass.: Harvard University Press.

Donald, Merlin. 2001. *A Mind So Rare: The Evolution of Human Consciousness*. New York and London: W. W. Norton.

Dunbar, Robin. 2004. *The Human Story: A New History of Mankind's Evolution*. London: Faber and Faber.

Edelman, Gerald, and Giulio Tononi. 2001. *Consciousness: How Matter Becomes Imagination*. London and New York: Penguin Books.

Fox, Warwick. 2000a. "Introduction: Ethics and the Built Environment." In Warwick Fox, ed., *Ethics and the Built Environment*. London and New York: Routledge, 1–12.

Fox, Warwick. 2000b. "Towards an Ethics (or at Least a Value Theory) of the Built Environment." In Warwick Fox, ed., *Ethics and the Built Environment.* London and New York: Routledge, 207–221.

Frith, Uta. 1999. "Autism." In Robert Wilson and Frank Keil, eds., *The MIT Encyclopedia of the Cognitive Sciences.* Cambridge, Mass.: The MIT Press, 58–60.

Frith, Uta, and Christopher Frith. 2003. "Development and Neurophysiology of Mentalizing." *Philosophical Transactions of the Royal Society London*, Series B, 358: 459–473. Http://www.icn.ucl.ac.uk/dev_group/documents/Frith&FrithP Trans03.pdf/.

Gärdenfors, Peter. 2003. *How Homo Became Sapiens: On the Evolution of Thinking.* Oxford: Oxford University Press.

Gibson, Eleanor, Karen Adolph, and Marion Eppler. 1999. "Affordances." In Robert Wilson and Frank Keil, eds., *The MIT Encyclopedia of the Cognitive Sciences.* Cambridge, Mass.: The MIT Press, 4–6.

Goodpaster, Kenneth. 2001. "On Being Morally Considerable." In Michael Zimmerman, ed., *Environmental Philosophy: From Animal Rights to Radical Ecology*, 3rd ed. Upper Saddle River, N.J.: Prentice Hall, 56–70.

Greenfield, P., and Sue Savage-Rumbaugh. 1990. "Grammatical Combination in *Pan paniscus*: Processes of Learning and Invention in the Evolution and Development of Language." In S. Parker and K. Gibson, eds., *"Language" and Intelligence in Monkeys and Apes.* Cambridge: Cambridge University Press, 540–578.

Greenfield, P., and Sue Savage-Rumbaugh. 1993. "Comparing Communicative Competence in Child and Chimp: The Pragmatics." *Journal of Child Language* 20: 1–26.

Gribbin, John. 1997. *Companion to the Cosmos.* London: Phoenix.

Hailwood, Simon. 1996. *Exploring Nozick: Beyond Anarchy, State, and Utopia.* Aldershot: Avebury.

Hauser, Marc. 2001. *Wild Minds: What Animals Really Think.* London: Penguin Books.

Heffernan, James. 1982. "The Land Ethic: A Critical Reappraisal." *Environmental Ethics* 4: 235–247.

Herman, Louis. 2002. "Exploring the Cognitive World of the Bottlenosed Dolphin." In Marc Bekoff, Colin Allen, and Gordon Burghardt, eds., *The Cognitive Animal: Empirical and Theoretical Perspectives on Animal Cognition.* Cambridge, Mass.: The MIT Press, 275–283.

Hobson, Peter. 2002. *The Cradle of Thought.* London: Macmillan.

Holmes, Bob. 1998. "Day of the Sparrow." *New Scientist*, June 27, 1998, 32–35.

Hume, David. 1978 (1739–1740). *A Treatise of Human Nature*, ed. L. A. Selby-Bigge, 2nd ed. rev. P. H. Nidditch. Oxford: Oxford University Press.

Kauffman, Stuart. 1995. *At Home in the Universe: The Search for Laws of Self-Organization and Complexity.* London: Viking.

Keller, Helen. 2002 (1902). *The Story of My Life*. New York: Signet Classic, New American Library.

Keller, Helen. 2003 (1908). *The World I Live In*. New York: New York Review Books.

Lacey, A. R. 2001. *Robert Nozick*. Chesham, Buckinghamshire: Acumen.

LaFollette, Hugh, ed. 1997. *Ethics in Practice: An Anthology*, 1st ed. Malden, Mass. and Oxford: Blackwell.

Leopold, Aldo. 1979. "Some Fundamentals of Conservation in the Southwest." *Environmental Ethics* 1: 131–141.

Leopold, Aldo. 1981 (1949). *A Sand County Almanac*. Oxford: Oxford University Press.

Macphail, Euan. 1982. *Brain and Intelligence in Vertebrates*. Oxford: Clarendon Press.

Marks, Jonathan. 2003. *What It Means to Be 98% Chimpanzee: Apes, People, and Their Genes*. Berkeley: University of California Press.

Maslin, K. T. 2001. *An Introduction to the Philosophy of Mind*. Cambridge: Polity.

McCrone, John. 1993. *The Myth of Irrationality: The Science of the Mind from Plato to Star Trek*. New York: Carroll and Graf.

McCrone, John. 1999. *Going Inside: A Tour Round a Single Moment of Consciousness*. London: Faber and Faber.

Mitchell, Peter. 2003. *Introduction to Theory of Mind: Children, Autism and Apes*. London: Arnold.

Mukerjee, Madhusree. 2004. "A Transparent Enigma," *Scientific American* 290 (June): 24–25.

Nagel, Thomas. 1991 (1974). "What Is It Like to Be a Bat?" In David Rosenthal, ed., *The Nature of Mind*. New York and Oxford: Oxford University Press, 422–428; also in Ned Block, Owen Flanagan, and Guven Guzeldere, eds., *The Nature of Consciousness: Philosophical Debates*. Cambridge, Mass.: The MIT Press, 1997, 519–527.

Nelson, Katherine. 1998. *Language in Cognitive Development: The Emergence of the Mediated Mind*. Cambridge: Cambridge University Press.

Newton, Michael. 2003. *Savage Girls and Wild Boys: A History of Feral Children*. London: Faber and Faber.

Nichols, Shaun, and Stephen Stich. 2003. *Mindreading: An Integrated Account of Pretence, Self-Awareness, and Understanding Other Minds*. Oxford: Clarendon Press.

Norberg-Schulz, Christopher. 1980. *Genius Loci: Towards a Phenomenology of Architecture*. New York: Rizzoli International Publications.

Norretranders, Tor. 1998. *The User Illusion: Cutting Consciousness Down to Size*. London and New York: Allen Lane.

Nozick, Robert. 1974. *Anarchy, State, and Utopia.* New York: Basic Books.

Nozick, Robert. 1981. *Philosophical Explanations.* Cambridge, Mass.: The Belknap Press of Harvard University Press.

Nozick, Robert. 2001. *Invariances: The Structure of the Objective World.* Cambridge, Mass.: The Belknap Press of Harvard University Press.

Passmore, John. 1980. *Man's Responsibility for Nature: Ecological Problems and Western Traditions,* 2nd ed. London: Duckworth.

Pinker, Steven. 1995. *The Language Instinct: The New Science of Language and Mind.* London: Penguin Books.

Povinelli, Daniel. 1998. "Can Animals Empathize?" *Scientific American Presents: Exploring Intelligence* 9 (winter): 67, 72–75.

Povinelli, Daniel. 2003. *Folk Physics for Apes: The Chimpanzee's Theory of How the World Works,* reprint ed. Oxford: Oxford University Press.

Povinelli, Daniel. 2004. "Behind the Ape's Appearance: Escaping Anthropocentrism in the Study of Other Minds." *Dædalus: Journal of the American Academy of Arts and Sciences* (winter): 29–41.

Povinelli, Daniel, and Jennifer Vonk. 2003. "Chimpanzee Minds: Suspiciously Human?" *Trends in Cognitive Sciences* 7: 157–160.

Povinelli, Daniel, and Jennifer Vonk. 2004. "We Don't Need a Microscope to Explore the Chimpanzee's Mind," *Mind and Language* 19: 1–28.

Rawls, John. 1999 (1971). *A Theory of Justice,* rev. ed. Oxford and New York: Oxford University Press.

Regan, Tom. 1983. *The Case for Animal Rights.* Berkeley: University of California Press.

Regan, Tom. 2003. *Animal Rights, Human Wrongs: An Introduction to Moral Philosophy.* Lanham, Md.: Rowman and Littlefield.

Rodman, John. 1977. "The Liberation of Nature?" *Inquiry* 20: 83–131.

Rumbaugh, Duane, and Sue Savage-Rumbaugh. 1999. "Primate Cognition." In Robert Wilson and Frank Keil, eds., *The MIT Encyclopedia of the Cognitive Sciences.* Cambridge, Mass.: The MIT Press, 669–671.

Ryder, Richard. 2000. *Animal Revolution: Changing Attitudes towards Speciesism.* Oxford and New York: Berg.

Ryder, Richard. 2001. *Painism: A Modern Morality.* London: Centaur Press.

Rymer, Russ. 1994. *Genie: A Scientific Tragedy.* New York: HarperPerennial.

Sacks, Oliver. 1991. *Seeing Voices: A Journey into the World of the Deaf.* London: Picador.

Sacks, Oliver. 1992. "Forward." In Susan Schaller, *A Man Without Words.* London: Ebury Press.

Sagoff, Mark. 2001. "Animal Liberation and Environmental Ethics: Bad Marriage, Quick Divorce." In Michael Zimmerman, ed., *Environmental Philosophy:*

From Animal Rights to Radical Ecology, 3rd ed. Upper Saddle River, N.J.: Prentice Hall, 87–96.

Sapontzis, Steve. 1998. "Predation." In Marc Bekoff, ed., *Encyclopedia of Animal Rights and Animal Welfare*. London and Chicago: Fitzroy Dearborn, 275–277.

Scaruffi, Piero. 2003. *Thinking about Thought: A Primer on the New Science of Mind*. New York: Writers Club Press.

Schaller, Susan. 1992. *A Man Without Words*. London: Ebury Press.

Searle, John. 1994. *The Rediscovery of the Mind*. Cambridge, Mass.: The MIT Press.

Searle, John. 1999. *Mind, Language, and Society: Doing Philosophy in the Real World*. London: Weidenfeld and Nicolson.

Shattuck, Roger. 1994. *The Forbidden Experiment: The Story of the Wild Boy of Aveyron*. New York: Kodansha International.

Singer, Peter. 1990. *Animal Liberation*, 2nd ed. London: Jonathan Cape.

Singer, Peter. 1993. *Practical Ethics*, 2nd ed. Cambridge: Cambridge University Press.

Singer, Peter. 2002. "Famine, Affluence, and Morality." In Hugh LaFollette, ed., *Ethics in Practice: An Anthology*, 2nd ed. Malden, Mass. and Oxford: Blackwell, 572–581.

Smith, Neil. 2002. *Language, Bananas, and Bonobos: Linguistic Problems, Puzzles, and Polemics*. Oxford: Blackwell.

Stanford, Craig. 2002. "The Ape's Gift: Meat-eating, Meat-sharing, and Human Evolution." In Frans de Waal, ed., *Tree of Origin: What Primate Behavior Can Tell Us about Human Social Evolution*. Cambridge, Mass.: Harvard University Press, 95–117.

Stix, Gary. 2004. "Homo Carnivorous," *Scientific American* 290 (June): 9–10.

Taylor, Paul. 1986. *Respect for Nature: A Theory of Environmental Ethics*. Princeton, N.J.: Princeton University Press.

Tomasello, Michael. 2000. *The Cultural Origins of Human Cognition*. Cambridge, Mass.: Harvard University Press.

Tomasello, Michael. 2003. "On the Different Origins of Symbols and Grammar." In Morten Christiansen and Simon Kirby, eds., *Language Evolution*. Oxford: Oxford University Press, 94–110.

Tomasello, Michael, and Josep Call. 1997. *Primate Cognition*. New York and Oxford: Oxford University Press.

Tomasello, Michael, Josep Call, and Brian Hare. 2003a. "Chimpanzees Understand Psychological States—The Question Is Which Ones and to What Extent." *Trends in Cognitive Sciences* 7: 153–156.

Tomasello, Michael, Josep Call, and Brian Hare. 2003b. "Chimpanzees Versus Humans: It's Not That Simple." *Trends in Cognitive Sciences* 7: 239–240.

Tomasello, Michael, and Hannes Rakoczy. 2003. "What Makes Human Cognition Unique?: From Individual to Shared to Collective Intentionality." *Mind and Language* 18: 121–147.

Tulving, Endel. 1999. "Episodic vs. Semantic Memory." In Robert Wilson and Frank Keil, eds., *The MIT Encyclopedia of the Cognitive Sciences*. Cambridge, Mass.: The MIT Press, 278–280.

Varner, Gary. 1998. *In Nature's Interests?: Interests, Animal Rights, and Environmental Ethics*. New York and Oxford: Oxford University Press.

Varner, Gary. 2002. "Biocentric Individualism." In David Schmidtz and Elizabeth Willott, eds., *Environmental Ethics: What Really Matters, What Really Works*. New York and Oxford: Oxford University Press, 108–120.

Vonk, Jennifer, James Reaux, Conni Castille, and Daniel Povinelli. 2004. "What Human-Enculturated Apes Know about Seeing: Preliminary Results." Paper presented to the 11th Annual International Conference on Comparative Cognition, Melbourne Beach, Fla., March 24–27, 2004.

Wallman, Joel. 1992. *Aping Language*. Cambridge: Cambridge University Press.

Warren, Mary Anne. 2000. *Moral Status: Obligations to Persons and Other Living Things*. Oxford and New York: Oxford University Press.

Wertsch, James. 1999. "Vygotsky, Lev Semenovich." In Robert Wilson and Frank Keil, eds., *The MIT Encyclopedia of the Cognitive Sciences*. Cambridge, Mass.: The MIT Press, 878–879.

Williamson, Terry, Antony Radford, and Helen Bennetts. 2003. *Understanding Sustainable Architecture*. London and New York: Spon Press.

Wittgenstein, Ludwig. 1953. *Philosophical Investigations*, ed. G. E. M. Anscombe and R. Rhees. Oxford: Blackwell.

Wrangham, Richard. 2002. "Out of the *Pan*, Into the Fire: How Our Ancestors' Evolution Depended on What They Ate." In Frans de Waal, ed., *Tree of Origin: What Primate Behavior Can Tell Us about Human Social Evolution*. Cambridge, Mass.: Harvard University Press, 119–143.

Index